FOUNDATION PRESS

TAX STORIES:

AN IN–DEPTH LOOK AT

TEN LEADING

FEDERAL INCOME TAX CASES

Edited By

PAUL L. CARON

Charles Hartsock Professor of Law
University of Cincinatti College of Law

Project sponsored in part by a grant from the American Tax Policy Institute.

New York, New York
FOUNDATION PRESS
2003

COPYRIGHT © 2003 By FOUNDATION PRESS

        395 Hudson Street
        New York, NY 10014
        Phone Toll Free 1–877–888–1330
        Fax (212) 367–6799
        fdpress.com

All rights reserved
Printed in the United States of America

ISBN 1–58778–403–3

 TEXT IS PRINTED ON 10% POST CONSUMER RECYCLED PAPER

Tax Stories: An In-Depth Look at Ten Leading Federal Income Tax Cases

Contents

FOUNDATION PRESS

TAX STORIES:

AN IN–DEPTH LOOK AT

TEN LEADING

FEDERAL INCOME TAX CASES

*

Introduction

Paul L. Caron

Tax Archaeology

[A] reported case does in some ways resemble those traces of past human activity—crop marks, post holes, the footings of walls, pipe stems, pottery shards, kitchen middens, and so forth, from which the archaeologist attempts, by excavation, scientific testing, comparison, and analysis to reconstruct and make sense of the past. Cases need to be treated as what they are, fragments of antiquity, and we need, like archaeologists, gently to free these fragments from the overburden of legal dogmatics, and try, by relating them to the evidence, which has to be sought outside the law library, to make sense of them as events in history and incidents in the evolution of the law.[1]

Tax Stories, the first in a new series of *Law Stories* books published by Foundation Press, reports the result of archaeological digs into ten seminal U.S. Supreme Court federal income tax cases by ten leading tax scholars.[2] The book explores the historical contexts of these cases and the role they continue to play in our current tax law. Each of the ten chapters sets forth the social, factual, and legal background of the case, discusses the various court proceedings and judicial opinions, and explores the immediate impact and continuing importance of the case. The companion web site contains the complete record of the case in the Supreme Court, including the lower court opinions, briefs of the parties

---

[1] A.W. Brian Simpson, *Leading Cases in the Common Law* 12 (1995). *See also* Symposium, *Legal Archaeology*, 2000 Utah L. Rev. 183.

[2] Ten is, of course, not a magic number. Indeed, other books in the *Law Stories* series will profile from 10–15 cases in other subjects. As a David Letterman fan, I initially wanted all books in the series to maintain a "top ten" format but was soon convinced that pedagogy should trump attempts to build a uniform *Law Stories* "brand."

and amici curiae, oral arguments (audiotapes and transcripts, where available),[3] and the Supreme Court's opinion.[4]

Law Stories books are in the pipeline to cover the entire first-year curriculum—*Civil Procedure Stories* (Kevin M. Clermont, Editor),[5] *Constitutional Law Stories* (Michael C. Dorf, Editor), *Contracts Stories* (Douglas G. Baird, Editor), *Criminal Law Stories* (Robert Weisberg, Editor), *Property Stories* (Gerald Korngold & Andrew P. Morriss, Editors), and *Torts Stories* (Robert L. Rabin & Stephen D. Sugarman, Editors). Other *Law Stories* books will target the second- and third-year curriculum, starting with *Tax Stories*.

At one level, tax is a curious choice with which to begin a new series of books designed to give a behind-the-scenes look at the most important cases in the field. In light of the increasingly statutory and regulatory world that tax has become, Michael Oberst argues that teachers of the basic income tax course should focus on requiring students to master the intricacies of various Internal Revenue Code (the "Code") and regulation provisions rather than "provid[ing] a wide comfort zone for the student" by "spend[ing] considerable time analyzing case law."[6] In contrast, Michael Livingston contends that "technical tax teaching," with its focus on the Code and regulations, should be reserved for tax LL.M. programs, while the J.D. tax curriculum should embrace a "skills" approach emphasizing legal process issues.[7] I believe there is more need now than ever for the basic tax course to re-focus on the pivotal issues reflected in the major cases, rather than on the "noise" of the latest tax developments that students will forget (if they ever learned them in the first place) soon after the final exam. With new tax legislation now an almost annual event, along with an increasing torrent of new cases, regulations, and rulings, the basic tax course needs to convey the underlying tax architecture to empower students to understand the tax law du jour. The major cases are the best markers to guide the journey down the tax law's currents and eddies.

---

[3] Audiotapes are available for all post–1954 oral arguments. Transcripts are available for all post–1967 oral arguments, as well as for selected oral arguments from 1935–67; there are no transcripts available for pre–1935 oral arguments. Audiotapes and/or transcripts are available for four of the cases profiled in *Tax Stories*: INDOPCO, Inc. v. Commissioner, 503 U.S. 79 (1992) (Chapter 6) (audiotapes and transcript); Schlude v. Commissioner, 372 U.S. 128 (1963) (Chapter 8) (audiotape); United States v. Davis, 370 U.S. 65 (1962) (Chapter 4) (audiotape); and Knetsch v. United States, 364 U.S. 361 (1960) (Chapter 10) (audiotape and transcript). The web site also includes 10–15 minute excerpts of the oral arguments in *INDOPCO*, *Schlude*, *Davis*, and *Knetsch* suitable for classroom use.

[4] http://www.law.uc.edu/TaxStories.

[5] *See* Kevin M. Clermont, *Teaching Civil Procedure Through Its Top Ten Cases, Plus or Minus Two*, 46 St. Louis L.J. ___ (2002).

[6] Michael A. Oberst, *Teaching Tax Law: Developing Analytical Skills*, 46 J. Legal Educ. 79, 80 (1996).

[7] Michael A. Livingston, *Reinventing Tax Scholarship: Lawyers, Economists, and the Role of the Legal Academy*, 83 Cornell L. Rev. 365, 387–88, 430–32 (1998). *See also* George K. Yin, *Simulating the Tax Legislative Process in the Classroom*, 47 J. Legal Educ. 104 (1997).

Carolyn Jones has bemoaned the failure of tax scholars to join the narrative and storytelling trend in legal scholarship.[8] Her essay "attempts to open tax scholarship to the many and varied tax stories around us."[9] She identifies case law as one of the sources of stories about what she calls "real taxes."[10] It is thus perhaps fitting that *Tax Stories* is the first entrant in the *Law Stories* series designed to further research into this aspect of storytelling and to bring the fruits of this work to our students.

In tax law, as in other subject areas, there are certain landmark cases that set the law on a path that continues to shape much of the current developments in the field. In these seminal cases, the tax law was faced with a fundamental choice, the resolution of which would influence the tax law for generations to come.[11] In *Tax Stories*, we look at ten pivotal cases in the development of the federal income tax.[12] These stories provide fresh insights into both particular doctrinal areas of tax law as well as issues of wider application across the tax law.

1. *Doctrinal Lessons*

The first four chapters of *Tax Stories* deal with the income side of the ledger. Joseph M. Dodge's opening chapter focuses on perhaps *the* central question in the nascent income tax: the nature of income subject to tax.[13] Yet the tax law struggled with this question for over forty years before the Supreme Court decided *Commissioner v. Glenshaw Glass*[14] in

---

[8] Carolyn C. Jones, *Mapping Tax Narratives*, 73 Tul. L. Rev. 653 (1998). *See also* Livingston, *supra* note 7, at 366–67 ("Traditional tax scholarship today is comfortable but tired: it is overwhelmingly normative, when much of the academy is experimenting with empirical and narrative norms; methodologically simplistic, when the broader academy has become more sophisticated in economics and other disciplines. Its emphasis on a search for apolitical neutrality would be considered naïve or outdated in other subject areas.").

[9] Jones, *supra* note 8, at 653.

[10] Other sources of stories are the Code, regulations, and tax legislative history. *Id.* at 657.

[11] As Yogi Berra would put it, the tax law came to a fork in the road and took it. *Bartlett's Familiar Quotations* 754 (Justin Kaplan ed., 16th ed. 1992).

[12] In compiling this "top ten" list, we culled from an initial list of thirty cases ten cases that (1) are included in all of the major income tax casebooks, (2) are foundational in the sense that they were pivotal in the development of the income tax and continue to shape the existing tax law, and (3) have a particularly interesting story to tell based on their facts and historical context. Indeed, this was one of the more enjoyable aspects of the project, as the eleven of us fiercely debated the make-up of the list through an e-mail discussion group. We recognize, of course, that other tax scholars and commentators might not agree on the precise make-up of our list, but we are confident that our list as a whole satisfies the criteria we established at the outset.

[13] Joseph M. Dodge, *The Story of* Glenshaw Glass: *Towards a Modern Concept of Gross Income.*

[14] 348 U.S. 426 (1955).

1955. The narrow holding in the case—that punitive damages recovered by a plaintiff in commercial litigation constitutes gross income—seems quite obvious to us today with the benefit of hindsight. Indeed, the doctrine emerging from *Glenshaw Glass*—that "windfall gains" are included in gross income—also strikes us today as the only sensible outcome. But Professor Dodge unearths the great doctrinal and theoretical uncertainty faced by the parties in *Glenshaw Glass* as they struggled to give content to the Code's use of the phrase "gross income." The Court's opinion established two enduring principles of the income tax: (1) that the Code, not language in judicial opinions, is the ultimate source of tax law;[15] and (2) that the term "gross income" in the Code is a catch-all phrase that reaches all accessions to wealth, regardless of source, and not specifically excluded elsewhere in the Code. In addition, *Glenshaw Glass* set the income tax on a modern footing, "free of the clutter and distractions inherited from the nineteenth century and early twentieth century."[16]

Marjorie E. Kornhauser uses the oldest case in this book, *Eisner v. Macomber*,[17] to tell the story in Chapter 2 of the central doctrine of realization in the tax law through the life and times of Myrtle Macomber.[18] The case riveted the nation in 1920, as the decision was reported on the front page of *The New York Times* and generated much media attention, and its reverberations were felt both on Wall Street and on Capitol Hill. The treatment of realization as a constitutional aspect of income was part and parcel of a struggle between Congress and the Supreme Court over the nature and scope of government that came to be known as the *Lochner* era. But *Macomber's* lasting influence is felt most deeply in the tax law—although it did not invent the realization concept, it embedded it so early and so deeply into the fabric of our tax system that any attempt to eliminate it now would face insurmountable political and institutional obstacles. Professor Kornhauser notes that *Macomber's* embrace of realization encouraged the development of our current hybrid income/consumption tax, and she bemoans the Court's conflicting discussion of whether accretions to capital constitute income because "a system that is neither fish nor fowl can exacerbate complexity, theoreti-

---

[15] Professor Dodge calls this "the *alpha* and *omega* of approaching a federal tax issue." Page 30.

[16] *Id.* at 51. Among the "clutter and distractions" cast off by *Glenshaw Glass* were discredited prior precedents, tying tax gain to economic gain, restrictive notions of realization (discussed more fully in Chapter 2 of *Tax Stories*), and limited views of in-kind property, in-kind consumption, and dominion and control.

[17] 252 U.S. 189 (1920).

[18] Marjorie E. Kornhauser, *The Story of* Macomber: *The Continuing Legacy of Realization.*

cal inconsistencies, and practical inequities."[19] *Macomber's* legacy also can be seen in the many deferral provisions subsequently enacted to give special relief from the realization principle, the taxation of capital gains, and the taxation of corporations as separate entities. Although *Macomber* was decided over eighty years ago, "its restless ghost still walks"[20] in many of the corridors of our existing income tax law.

Debt is an invaluable lubricant in our economy, and Deborah H. Schenk explores in Chapter 3 the all-too-common situation of a borrower who fails to repay her debt.[21] The story begins seventy years ago in the plains of Texas with Kirby Lumber Company's failure to fully repay bondholders.[22] The brevity of the Court's two-paragraph opinion—holding that cancellation of a debt creates income—belies the many exceptions and uncertainties spawned by the case. Professor Schenk explains that the misguided theories undergirding the Court's holding—that Kirby Lumber did not suffer any "shrinkage of assets" under the "freeing-of-assets" theory and did not incur a loss on "the whole transaction" under the Court's prior decision in *Bowers v. Kerbaugh–Empire*[23]—led to decades of confusion which could have been avoided had the Court correctly analyzed the transaction under a loan proceeds theory. Under Professor Schenk's approach, because loan proceeds are excluded from income upon receipt in light of the offsetting obligation to repay, the borrower necessarily enjoys an accession to wealth when she repays less than the borrowed amount, regardless of what she has done with the borrowed funds in the meantime. Although Congress subsequently codified the narrow holding in *Kirby Lumber* in treating cancellation of indebtedness as income under § 61(a)(12), Congress and ultimately the courts have grafted a number of exceptions onto this rule. Professor Schenk surveys these many exceptions and finds that they are often infected by the discredited freeing-of-assets and whole transaction theories propagated in *Kirby Lumber*. Finally, Professor Schenk concludes that "the confusion engendered by *Kirby Lumber* and its progeny came home to roost in *Zarin v. Commissioner*,[24] a wonderfully wacky case that engendered four separate opinions in the Tax Court and two

---

[19] Page 95.

[20] *Id.* at 96.

[21] Deborah H. Schenk, *The Story of* Kirby Lumber: *The Many Faces of Discharge of Indebtedness Income.*

[22] United States v. Kirby Lumber Co., 284 U.S. 1 (1931).

[23] 271 U.S. 170 (1926).

[24] 92 T.C. 1084 (1989), *rev'd*, 916 F.2d 110 (3d Cir.1990). Indeed, at an early stage the working subtitle of *Tax Stories* was *An In–Depth Look at the Ten Leading Federal Income Tax Cases from* A(rrowsmith) *to* Z(arin). Again, I was soon convinced that pedagogy should trump cute subtitles.

opinions in the Third Circuit, all based on different theories that revealed in striking terms the continued uncertainty surrounding the *Kirby Lumber* rule."[25]

Karen B. Brown tells the story in Chapter 4 of how a garden variety divorce between Alice and Thomas Davis in 1955 set the stage for the Supreme Court to finally determine the tax consequences of transfers of property incident to divorce.[26] But the Court's approach in *United States v. Davis*[27]—penalizing the transferor spouse by taxing any appreciation in the transferred property and rewarding the transferee spouse with a fair market value basis in the property—resulted in differing tax consequences for divorcing couples depending on whether they lived in common law or community property states. In addition, the Internal Revenue Service (the "Service") often found itself whipsawed if the transferor spouse misreported the transaction by not reporting the gain in the year of divorce and the transferee spouse claimed a fair market value on a sale of the property many years later when the statute of limitations frequently had run on the transferor spouse's return. Congress responded by equalizing the tax treatment of divorcing couples throughout the fifty states and by empowering the Service to effectively police compliance. Professor Brown notes that § 1041 "lets the transferor spouse off the tax hook and shifts the tax burden to the transferee spouse through a carryover basis in the transferred property."[28] Since the rate of divorce has roughly doubled since the Davis' divorce in 1955,[29] the tax consequences of transfers of property incident to divorce unfortunately have become increasingly important. The enactment § 1041 reduced, but did not eliminate, *Davis'* influence in the tax law. The impact of *Davis* continues to be felt in the many tax contexts not covered by § 1041, including transfers of property (1) having no ascertainable fair market value, (2) between non-spouses in exchange for non-marital rights (including palimony), (3) to a non-resident spouse, and (4) between former spouses but not incident to a divorce.

The next three chapters in *Tax Stories* turn to the deduction side of the equation. In Chapter 5, Joel S. Newman digs into *Welch v. Helvering*,[30] the seminal case for determining deductible "ordinary and neces-

---

[25] Page 123.

[26] Karen B. Brown, *The Story of* Davis: *Transfers of Property Pursuant to Divorce.*

[27] 370 U.S. 65 (1962).

[28] Page 154.

[29] *See* U.S. Census Bureau, *Statistical Abstract of the United States* 2001 tbl. 68 (121st ed. 2001) (1955 divorce rate of 2.3 per 1,000); U.S. Dep't of Health & Human Services, 50 *National Vital Statistics Report* 1 (June 26, 2002) (2001 divorce rate of 4.0 per 1,000).

[30] 290 U.S. 111 (1933).

sary" business expenses.[31] The nature and background both of the expense in *Welch*—a businessman's repayment of debts of his former business that had been discharged in bankruptcy—and of the Supreme Court Justice who wrote the Court's opinion—Justice Cardozo, whose father had resigned in disgrace from the New York Supreme Court amid allegations of corruption—combined to produce one of the more unfortunate opinions in the Court's tax annals. Professor Newman argues that of the three threads running though the Court's opinion—that the expenses were (1) too "personal" to be deductible, (2) too "bizarre" to be ordinary, and (3) capital and thus nondeductible—Justice Cardozo was "wrong" on the first two and "right" only on the third. Professor Newman writes that "[a]lthough it long ago should have been consigned to the judicial scrap heap, *Welch's* spirit lives on in the unfortunate doctrine stifling business innovation at the very time that the twenty-first century global economy demands more, not less, business creativity."[32] Professor Newman's chapter undoubtedly is the only piece of tax literature containing country and western ditties penned by both the Tax Court and the Service, as well as a closing tax limerick!

In Chapter 6, Joseph Bankman picks up on the capitalization v. deduction theme, as well as the role of the background of the Justice who wrote the Supreme Court's tax opinion, as he unravels the most recent case in *Tax Stories*,[33] *INDOPCO, Inc. v. Commissioner*.[34] Business expenses that produce benefits beyond the year they are incurred must be capitalized rather than deducted currently; the capitalized expenses are amortized or depreciated as the asset declines in value, and the remaining basis is deducted when the asset is sold or declared worthless. But as Professor Bankman notes, in many situations "there is no natural line of demarcation between expenses that produce lasting benefit and those that do not ... [and] it is often difficult even to estimate the proper amortization of capitalized expenses."[35] Over time, courts and the Service have agreed on the treatment of certain categories of expenses within this framework; litigation, as with the expenses incurred in the "friendly" acquisition of INDOPCO, occurs in areas outside of those categories. Although the opinion in *INDOPCO* was written by Justice Blackmun, "the most knowledgeable tax jurist ever to

---

[31] Joel S. Newman, *The Story of* Welch: *The Use (and Misuse) of the "Ordinary and Necessary" Test for Deducting Business Expenses.*

[32] Page 181.

[33] Joseph Bankman, *The Story of* INDOPCO: *What Went Wrong in the Capitalization v. Deduction Debate?.*

[34] 503 U.S. 79 (1992).

[35] Page 184.

sit on the Court,"[36] Professor Bankman argues that the decision "must be seen as a failure."[37] It is replete with confusing language and unnecessary dicta that have allowed the Service to apply *INDOPCO* in an overly aggressive manner over the past decade. But in the end, the fault may lie in the income tax itself, which requires Solomonic judgments about short- versus long-term benefits of expenses and amortization schedules that mere mortals in the courts and the Service are incapable of consistently getting right. Unless and until we embrace a consumption or cash flow tax system in which *all* business expenses are deductible regardless of the length of the benefit, the best we can hope for is for the courts and the Service "to come up with some workable rules that balance administrative ease against the distorted effects inherent in misclassifying an expenditure (as a deductible expense or capital investment) or adopting the wrong amortization schedule."[38]

George K. Yin returns to the subject of debt in Chapter 7 and tells the story of how Beulah Crane laid the foundation for the modern tax shelter.[39] In determining her gain on the sale of an apartment building, the question was whether nonrecourse indebtedness secured by the property was includable in her amount realized. Professor Yin points out that the government's victory in *Crane v. Commissioner*[40] was its most pyrrhic one in the tax field, as it permitted taxpayers to include nonrecourse debt in basis as well and thus provided high-octane leverage to the available depreciation deductions. Subsequent courts elaborated on these twin aspects of the *Crane* rule and also clarified the tax treatment of post-acquisition nonrecourse debt. In the end, the government's "tunnel-vision," in insisting that Crane report the nonrecourse debt in her amount realized on sale because she had included it in her depreciable basis,[41] opened the door for the tax shelter scourge of recent years and led to many legislative and judicial responses. To be sure, as Professor Yin notes, "although the *Crane* rule was an integral part of tax shelters, the rule, on its own, was not the cause of shelters. Other tax rules—the allowance of depreciation deductions in excess of economic depreciation, the taxation of *Tufts*[42] gain at preferential tax rates, the

---

[36] *Id.* at 184.

[37] *Id.* at 206.

[38] *Id.* at 203.

[39] George K. Yin, *The Story of* Crane: *How a Widow's Misfortune Led to Tax Shelters.*

[40] 331 U.S. 1 (1947).

[41] Professor Yin also notes that the government's litigation strategy also may have been shaped by concerns about other taxpayers avoiding gain on debt-financed property despite claiming earlier depreciation deductions, as well as by concerns about the administrative practicality of the opposite rule that would have awarded the full measure of depreciation to the mortgagee until payments were made on the nonrecourse debt.

[42] Commissioner v. Tufts, 461 U.S. 300 (1983).

failure to distinguish interest from principal payments for tax purposes, the deferral permitted by the installment sale rules, to name a few— were necessary to produce the shelters in conjunction with the *Crane* rule."[43] But "[t]he flaw of the *Crane* rule—a not insignificant one in retrospect—is that it did nothing to *restrain* tax shelter activity once the economic, tax, and other conditions in this country made it ripe for such activity. Instead, it magnified the inadequacies of the other tax rules. In order to prevent shelters, it relied upon a degree of perfection among the other rules, and a level of compliance among taxpayers, that were probably unrealistic expectations of any tax system."[44]

The final three chapters of *Tax Stories* leave the income-deduction matrix and focus on three pervasive income tax issues. In Chapter 8, Russell K. Osgood tells the story of *Schlude v. Commissioner*,[45] the third in a trilogy of cases[46] holding that tax accounting under the Code may differ from generally accepted accounting principles ("GAAP").[47] Although the case arose forty years ago, the issue is ripped from today's headlines as the tales of accounting scofflaws like Enron, Global Crossing, Tyco, and WorldCom can be traced in part to the *Schlude* trilogy's sanctioning of departures in tax accounting from GAAP. President Osgood observes that "the decoupling of tax accounting from financial accounting clearly makes sense in certain areas in light of the divergent purposes of each: in tax accounting, the pressure is to minimize taxable income (and thus tax liabilities) via decreasing income/increasing deductions; in financial accounting, the pressure is in the opposite direction to maximize book income (and thus stock prices) via increasing revenues/decreasing expenses."[48] But "[a]t the end of the *Schlude* trilogy, it is hard to find articulable standards for when a business using the accrual method of accounting may be obligated to diverge from its method in order to 'clearly reflect' income for tax purposes, except that it will occur when the Commissioner so insists."[49] The shortcomings of the common law approach sanctioned by the *Schlude* trilogy regrettably are all too apparent today.

---

[43] Page 254.

[44] *Id.*

[45] 372 U.S. 128 (1963).

[46] The other two cases are American Auto. Ass'n v. United States, 367 U.S. 687 (1961), and Automobile Club of Mich. v. Commissioner, 353 U.S. 180 (1957).

[47] Russell K. Osgood, *The Story of* Schlude: *The Origins of the Tax/Financial Accounting GA(A)P.*

[48] Page 273.

[49] *Id.* at 269–70.

One issue that has dogged the income tax since its beginning has been the identification of the appropriate taxpayer to be taxed on the receipt of income. The issue initially arose in the context of husbands purporting to shift income to their wives (who were in a lower tax bracket) because the early income tax did not allow joint returns by married couples. Patricia A. Cain unravels the Supreme Court's foray into this early debate with its *Lucas v. Earl*[50] decision.[51] Professor Cain tells the story behind the income-sharing arrangement between Guy and Ella Earl, including the important role Guy Earl played in the economic development of Northern California and the tax planning objectives of the 1901 agreement. A key part of the story is the structure of the early income tax and the disparity in treatment between spouses in common law and community property states caused by the inability to file a joint tax return. In refusing to allow Ella Earl to be taxed on one-half of Guy Earl's income, Justice Holmes penned undoubtedly the most famous horticultural metaphor in tax jurisprudence: "There is no doubt that the statute could tax salaries to those who earned them and provide that the tax could not be escaped by anticipatory assignments ... and we think that no distinction can be taken according to the motives leading to the arrangement by which the fruits are attributed to a different tree from that on which they grew."[52] The immediate result of *Earl* (and the subsequent *Poe v. Seaborn*[53] decision) was that spouses in community property states were treated more favorably with respect to earned income than spouses in common law states. Congress responded to this problem in 1948 by enacting the modern joint return. The spirit of *Earl* also lives on in the hoary fruit-and-tree metaphor, which courts to this day continue to apply to cases raising assignment-of-income issues in a wide variety of contexts. Professor Cain doubts Holmes foresaw that some would convert his metaphor into a talisman, rigidly requiring that earnings be taxed to the tree that produced them. She applauds Holmes for reaching the correct result in the case to protect the integrity of the income tax's progressive rate structure: "That principle, protection of progressivity, should guide us today as we determine whether it is appropriate to tax income to the assignor or the assignee."[54]

Daniel N. Shaviro uses *Knetsch v. United States*[55] to tell the story of how courts have struggled since the inception of the income tax to draw

---

[50] 281 U.S. 111 (1930).

[51] Patricia A. Cain, *The Story of* Earl: *How Echoes (and Metaphors) from the Past Continue to Shape the Assignment of Income Doctrine.*

[52] 281 U.S. at 114–15.

[53] 282 U.S. 101 (1930).

[54] Page 310.

[55] 364 U.S. 361 (1960).

a line between permissible tax planning and impermissible tax shelters.[56] The struggle never has been more difficult than it is today, as courts are called upon to deploy judicial doctrines hatched in a very different era to increasingly sophisticated and abstruse tax-savings strategies. As the media maw chews over the tax shelter strategies of much of corporate America, and congressional committees and the Administration contemplate their next steps in this seventy-year war, it is a particularly propitious time to revisit the tax arbitrage strategy marketed by the Sam Houston Life Insurance Company and embraced by Karl Knetsch and see what lessons we can draw from the Court's response. The particulars are straight-forward: Knetsch borrowed $4 million at 3.5% interest from the company so he could invest the proceeds, with the same company, in deferred annuity bonds paying 2.5%. Although this was a guaranteed loser economically (paying $140,000 to earn $100,000 annually), Knetsch hoped to turn "pre-tax straw into after-tax gold"[57] by deducting the $140,000[58] while deferring the inclusion of the $100,000 in income. Professor Shaviro gives us a front-row seat at the bench trial in the federal district court, which ultimately agreed with the Service that the transaction lacked any economic substance. After the Ninth Circuit agreed, the issue was joined in the Supreme Court. Professor Shaviro unpacks the parties' arguments in their briefs and during oral argument, leading ultimately to the Court's holding that "there was nothing of substance to be realized by Knetsch from this transaction beyond a tax deduction."[59] Professor Shaviro observes that "*Knetsch* is the principal Supreme Court case standing for the proposition that aggressive tax planning may not be respected for tax purposes unless it meets some minimum standard of economic substance. More specifically, while '[a]ny one may so arrange his affairs that his taxes shall be as low as possible,'[60] such arrangements may be ineffective unless they additionally serve non-tax purposes, have non-tax effects (pertaining, for example, to the risks that the taxpayer bears), and, in the business or investment setting, present some prospect of pre-tax profit."[61] Although the Supreme Court has revisited anti-tax avoidance doctrine only once since *Knetsch* in the much-reviled *Frank Lyon Co. v. United States*,[62] the time

---

[56] Daniel N. Shaviro, *The Story of* Knetsch: *Judicial Doctrines Combating Tax Avoidance.* Indeed, Professor Shaviro's chapter opens by comparing the difficulty of drawing this line to Justice Stewart's famous comment about pornography: "I know it when I see it." Page 313 (quoting Jacobellis v. Ohio, 378 U.S. 184, 197 (1964) (Stewart, J., dissenting)).

[57] Page 314.

[58] At his 80% tax rate, the deduction generated $110,000 in annual tax savings.

[59] 364 U.S. at 366.

[60] Helvering v. Gregory, 69 F.2d 809, 810 (2d Cir.1934), *aff'd*, 293 U.S. 465 (1935).

[61] Page 368.

[62] 435 U.S. 561 (1978).

may be fast-approaching when the Court feels "called on to supply further guidance."[63]

2. *Institutional Lessons*

The ten archaeological expeditions undertaken in *Tax Stories* also provide fresh insights into the structure of tax litigation. For eighty years, scholars have been critical of the Supreme Court's role as the final arbiter of tax disputes.[64] Various proposals have been made to consolidate tax appeals in a national court of tax appeals, with final resort to the Supreme Court sharply curtailed. A common criticism of these proposals is that the Court hears so few tax cases each year that it lacks the technical expertise to superintend the tax litigation structure. Indeed, the complaint is that the Court often makes a bad situation worse when it does enter a tax fray. For example, Kirk Stark notes that "[t]ax lawyers have derided the Supreme Court, complaining that the Court 'hates tax cases' and generally bungles the tax cases it does hear."[65] *Tax Stories* offers fodder for the critics, as the book is filled with robust criticism of the Court's performance in these tax cases.[66] Although *Welch*

---

[63] Page 370.

[64] For influential early articles, see Oscar Bland, *Federal Tax Appeals*, 25 Colum. L. Rev. 1013 (1925); Erwin N. Griswold, *The Need for a Court of Tax Appeals*, 57 Harv. L. Rev. 1153 (1944). A 1975 article lists twenty articles subsequent to Dean Griswold's piece. H. Todd Miller, *A Court of Tax Appeals Revisited*, 85 Yale L.J. 229, 231–32 n.14 (1975). For citations to more recent commentary, see Paul L. Caron, *Tax Myopia, or Mamas Don't Let Your Babies Grow Up To Be Tax Lawyers*, 13 Va. Tax Rev. 517, 582 n.294 (1994). *See also* Steve R. Johnson, *The Phoenix and the Perils of the Second Best: Why Heightened Appellate Deference to Tax Court Decisions is Desirable*, 77 Or. L. Rev. 235, 243–47 (1998).

[65] Kirk J. Stark, *The Unfulfilled Tax Legacy of Justice Robert H. Jackson*, 54 Tax L. Rev. 171, 173 (2001) (quoting Erwin N. Griswold, *Is the Tax Law Going to Seed? Remarks Before the Annual Meeting of the American College of Tax Counsel* (Feb. 5, 1993), in 11 Am. J. Tax Pol'y 1, 7 (1994)). *See also* Charles L.B. Lowndes, *Federal Taxation and the Supreme Court*, 1960 Sup. Ct. Rev. 222, 222 ("It is time to rescue the Supreme Court from federal taxation; it is time to rescue federal taxation from the Supreme Court."); Bernard Wolfman, *The Supreme Court in the* Lyon's *Den: A Failure of Judicial Process*, 66 Cornell L. Rev. 1075, 1099–1100 (1981) ("A Supreme Court opinion ought not become the basis for tax lawyers to make a laughingstock of the Court as they now do. . . . It is too much, if not wrong, to expect the Court to develop an enduring and sophisticated tax jurisprudence. In an environment of infinitely diverse and complex transactions governed by an arcane Code, the Court cannot devote the time necessary to become expert.").

[66] For critiques of individual Justices' performance in tax cases, see Stephen B. Cohen, *Thurgood Marshall: Tax Lawyer*, 80 Geo. L.J. 2011 (1992); Robert A. Green, *Justice Blackmun's Federal Tax Jurisprudence*, 26 Hastings Const. L.Q. 109 (1998); Darlene Addie Kennedy, *Eschewing the Superlegislative Prerogative: Tax Opinions of Justice Clarence Thomas*, 12 Regent U. L. Rev. 571 (2000); Stark, *supra* note 65; Bernard Wolfman, et al., *The Behavior of Justice Douglas in Federal Tax Cases*, 122 U. Pa. L. Rev. 235 (1973).

(Justice Cardozo)[67] and *INDOPCO* (Justice Blackmun)[68] come in for the most withering criticism, none of the opinions (and their authors) escape unscathed.[69]

Commentators also are critical of the government's performance in litigating tax cases, suggesting in recent years that the government has a "dismal" track record and is often outgunned by taxpayer's counsel.[70] On one hand, the results in the *Tax Stories* cases belie this criticism: the government prevailed in nine of the ten cases in the Supreme Court (after losing four of the cases in the trial court and three of the cases in the courts of appeals):

Prevailing Party in *Tax Stories* Cases			
Case	Trial Court	Court of Appeals	Supreme Court
Glenshaw Glass	Taxpayer	Taxpayer	IRS
Macomber	-	-	Taxpayer
Kirby Lumber	Taxpayer	-	IRS
Davis	Taxpayer	-	IRS
Welch	IRS	IRS	IRS
INDOPCO	IRS	IRS	IRS
Crane	Taxpayer	IRS	IRS
Schlude	IRS	Taxpayer	IRS
Earl	IRS	Taxpayer	IRS
Knetsch	IRS	IRS	IRS

But on the other hand, in many of the *Tax Stories* cases the government prevailed despite flaws in either litigation strategy or performance.[71] In any event, many of the government's victories were pyrrhic

---

[67] Joel Newman criticizes Justice Cardozo's "whining" (pages 163, 178) and complains that the opinion offered "scant guidance" (*id*. at 166), "needlessly confused subsequent courts (as well as tax practitioners and students)" (*id*. at 181), and "long ago should have been consigned to the judicial scrap heap" (*id*).

[68] Joseph Bankman calls Justice Blackmun "somewhat of a bumbler, tax-wise," (*id*. at 203), and his opinion "must be seen as a failure" (*id*. at 206).

[69] For example, Marjorie Kornhauser argues that Justice Pitney's opinion in *Macomber* "created confusion for years in many aspects of income tax law" (*id*. at 72). Similarly, Deborah Schenk claims that Justice Holmes' opinion in *Kirby Lumber* was "confusing and led to decades of confusion" (*id*. at 104). Karen Brown contends that the result in *Davis*, although "technically correct," "did not have a salutary effect on the development of the tax law" (*id*. at 144) and that Justice Clark's opinion instead led to "complexities and confusion" (*id*. at 150). Russell Osgood characterizes Justice White's opinion in *Schlude* as "lifeless" (*id*. at 268) and bemoans the absence of any "articulable standards" (*id*. at 269).

[70] *See, e.g.*, George Guttman, *IRS Averages: Winning Little, Losing Big*, 61 Tax Notes 155, 155 (1993).

[71] *See, e.g.*, Chapter 1, page 28 (calling taxpayer's counsel better advocates than government in *Glenshaw Glass*); Chapter 6, page 204 (criticizing government for litigating case and presenting "one-sided arguments" in *INDOPCO*). In addition, Joseph Dodge offers in Chapter 1 a list of numerous tax cases "that seem to have been lost by the

ones, resulting in far more tax revenue lost in the application of the rule announced in the given case to future cases involving other taxpayers. For example, the government won the individual tax battle in *Crane* (requiring the taxpayer to include nonrecourse indebtedness in the amount realized in computing gain on the sale of property) but lost the tax shelter war (by permitting the taxpayer to include the nonrecourse indebtedness in the depreciable basis of the property in the first place). Similarly, although the decoupling of tax from financial accounting generated additional tax revenues on the deduction at issue in *Schlude*, it opened the door to greater revenue losses in the future as tax-GAAP departures evolved into a one-way street. And many of the government's victories came wrapped in judicial opinions spawning such confusion that the government was required to expend considerable time and resources to firmly establish its beachhead.[72]

Conclusion

In the end, the doctrinal and institutional lessons from *Tax Stories* do not paint a pretty picture of our tax system. Given the problematic results in these ten cases, spanning eighty years and drawing the most talented array of lawyers and jurists that our legal system has to offer, perhaps the fault lies not in the performance of these individual participants but in our income tax itself. If "the best and the brightest" of our tax brigades consistently fall short in cases which command their very best efforts in the white-hot spotlight of a Supreme Court case, the view from the trenches of daily tax practice must be even more bleak. Instead of chastising the lawyers and judges for consistently supplying the wrong answers, we should direct our fire at the Congresses and Administrations that created a tax system that inevitably asks the wrong questions. Until fundamental reform of our income tax becomes more than a chimera, *Tax Stories* will remain without a happy ending.

---

government in the Supreme Court as the result of perfunctory or inadequate advocacy, or over-reaching." *Id*. at 29 & n. 41.

[72] *See supra* notes 66–69 and accompanying text.

1

Joseph M. Dodge

The Story of *Glenshaw Glass*: Towards a Modern Concept of Gross Income

A narrow description of the holding of the Supreme Court in *Commissioner v. Glenshaw Glass Co.*[1] is that punitive damages recovered by a plaintiff in commercial litigation are gross income. A broader statement of the holding is that "windfall gains" are included in gross income. These results seem so obvious today that one may wonder why this case had to be decided by the Supreme Court as late as 1955. Yet all of the courts below had reached the opposite result. Nevertheless, *Glenshaw Glass* did not create much of a stir in 1955. Now it is considered a watershed case ushering in the modern era in thinking about "income" issues.

Background

In the early days of the income tax there was a good deal of confusion about the nature of income. Principally, discourse about it tended to be framed by concepts borrowed from business and trust accounting, where "income" was something distinct from "capital," and "capital" was often thought to include not only "investment" but, more broadly, original endowment and even nonrecurring receipts, such as windfalls.[2] The Supreme Court opinion in *Glenshaw Glass* cleared away the fog with the following language:

---

[1] 348 U.S. 426 (1955).

[2] An excellent exposition of the conflicts among early conceptions of income is found in Marjorie E. Kornhauser, *The Origins of Capital Gains Taxation: What's Law Got To Do With It?*, 39 Sw. L.J. 869 (1985).

The sweeping scope of the controverted statute is readily apparent:

"SEC. 22. GROSS INCOME.

"(a) General Definition.—'Gross income' includes gains, profits, and income derived from salaries, wages, or compensation for personal service ... of whatever kind and in whatever form paid, or from professions, vocations, trades, businesses, commerce, or sales, or dealings in ... property; also from interest, rent, dividends, securities, or the transaction of any business carried on for gain or profit, *or gains or profits and income derived from any source whatever....*" (Emphasis added.)

This Court has frequently stated that this language was used by Congress to exert in this field "the full measure of its taxing power." Respondents contend that punitive damages, characterized as "windfalls" flowing from the culpable conduct of third parties, are not within the scope of this section. But Congress imposed no limitations as to the source of taxable receipts, nor restrictive labels as to their nature. And the Court has given a liberal construction to this broad phraseology in recognition of the intention of Congress to tax all gains except those specifically exempted....

Here we have instances of undeniable accessions to wealth, clearly realized, and over which the taxpayers have complete dominion.

Although *Glenshaw Glass* was decided in 1955, the taxable years in question were subject to § 22(a) of the 1939 Code rather than its successor, § 61(a), enacted as part of the 1954 Code. Section § 61(a) reads somewhat differently than § 22(a) of the 1939 Code, but the legislative history indicates that the differences were considered to be immaterial.

Prior Proceedings

Glenshaw Glass Co. had been involved in commercial litigation against Hartford–Empire Co. that had gone all the way to the U.S. Supreme Court. Eventually, Glenshaw Glass Co. obtained both compensatory and punitive damages by way of settlement. The settlement made an allocation of the damages to various claims. The punitive damages included 2/3 of the proceeds recovered in a federal anti-trust claim.

The Tax Court

The Tax Court opinion in *Glenshaw Glass Co. v. Commissioner*[3] devoted most of its attention to sorting out the various claims, and concluded that all of the compensatory damages were for lost profits (as opposed to being compensation for lost or destroyed assets). Thus, the compensatory damages were fully included in gross income, with no basis offset. As to the punitive damages, the Tax Court summarily stated:

> It has long been established that punitive damages do not meet the test of taxable income set forth in *Eisner v. Macomber*, 252 U.S. 189, 193 [1920], as " 'the gain derived from capital, from labor, or from both combined' provided it be understood to include profit gained through a sale or conversion of capital assets."

In *William Goldman Theaters, Inc. v. Commissioner*,[4] the Tax Court again held that the punitive damages recovered in a civil anti-trust action were excludable. The portion of the Tax Court opinion dealing with this issue was again quite brief, stating that a penalty imposed by law did not meet the "derived from capital and/or labor" test of *Eisner v. Macomber* (Chapter 2 of *Tax Stories*). The Tax Court in *Goldman Theaters* distinguished "on the facts" *General American Investors Co. v. Commissioner*,[5] decided shortly before *Goldman Theaters*, holding that a corporation's recovery of insider profits[6] under § 16(b) of the Securities Act of 1934 to be gross income.

The Tax Court decisions in both *Glenshaw Glass* and *Goldman Theaters* relied on *Highland Farms Corp. v. Commissioner*.[7] That case held that a "penalty imposed by law" did not fall within the 1920 *Macomber* definition of income. *Highland Farms*, in turn, relied on *Central Railroad Co. of New Jersey v. Commissioner*,[8] involving damages for breach of fiduciary duty. The Third Circuit in *Central Railroad* interpreted the *Macomber* definition as requiring that income be derived from the *taxpayer's* capital or services.[9] Although the *Central Railroad*

---

[3] 18 T.C. 860 (1952), *nonacq.*, 1953–1 C.B. 7.

[4] 19 T.C. 637 (1953), *nonacq.*, 1953–1 C.B. 8.

[5] 19 T.C. 581 (1952) (reviewed).

[6] "Insider profits" are gains in the corporation's own stock obtained by an officer, director, or major shareholder as the result of any purchases and sales within a six-month interval.

[7] 42 B.T.A. 1314 (1940).

[8] 79 F.2d 697 (3d Cir.1935).

[9] The opinion in the *Central R.R.* case was authored by Judge J. Warren Davis, who was later indicted for bribery and was to have been subject to impeachment proceedings. Judge Davis avoided impeachment by resigning and giving up his pension. Judge Davis had

opinion stated that the statutory language perhaps encompassed windfalls, it went on to say, "But what is not income cannot be so made by
definition," followed, ironically, by a quote of the *Macomber* definition.

   Central Railroad was decided before the government's victory in
Helvering v. Bruun,[10] which held that the *Macomber* requirement of
"severability" was not a necessary element of "realization." In *Bruun*,
the Supreme Court upheld the inclusion of the value of lessee improvements acquired in possession by the lessor upon the forfeiture of the
lease. *Bruun* undermined the very core of *Macomber* insofar as *Macomber* purported to limit "income" in the *constitutional* sense. Since the
decision in *Central Railroad* appears to have been based on the assumption that the statute, but not the Constitution, encompassed the damages in question, it would seem that *Bruun* at least cast doubt on the
continuing viability of *Central Railroad*. But the Board of Tax Appeals in
Highland Farms, which was decided seven months after *Bruun*, did not
take the hint, nor did the Tax Court 12 years later in *Glenshaw Glass*
and *Goldman Theaters*.

The Third Circuit

   The Third Circuit consolidated the *Glenshaw-Goldman* punitive
damages cases and affirmed unanimously in an opinion authored by
Chief Judge Biggs.[11] The case was heard *en banc* because the government
asked the Third Circuit to overrule its prior decision in *Central Railroad*.
Judge Biggs relied on *Highland Farms* and the *Macomber* definition,
which had been incorporated as the second sentence of Regulation
§ 29.22(a)–1. The Third Circuit did not mention Regulation § 29.21–4,
which stated in part:

>   *Meaning of net income.*—... In the computation of the tax, various
>   classes of income must be considered:
>
>   (a) Income (in the broad sense), meaning all wealth which flows
>   in to the taxpayer other than as a mere return of capital ...

   The Third Circuit noted that the *Macomber* definition claimed to
capture the meaning of "income" in "common parlance" rather than in
the musings of "lexicographers and economists." The Third Circuit
conceded both that the *Macomber* definition was crafted with reference
to the problem of distinguishing "capital" from "income," and that the
Supreme Court had appeared to depart from the definition in such cases

---

been devastated by the stock market crash of 1929 and was receiving bribes in 1935 and
1936, the period of *Central R.R. See* Root Refining Co. v. Universal Oil Prods. Co., 169 F.2d
514 (3d Cir.1948) (detailed description of various cases tainted by Judge Davis without
mentioning *Central R.R.*).

   [10] 309 U.S. 461 (1940).

   [11] 211 F.2d 928 (1954).

as *United States v. Kirby Lumber Co.*,[12] involving debt-discharge income (discussed in Chapter 3 of *Tax Stories*). In that case, Justice Holmes stated, "We see nothing to be gained by the discussion of judicial definitions." Nevertheless, the Third Circuit went on to say, "Periodicy seems to be a factor," mis-citing the work of a legal academic and former government advisor, Roswell Magill.[13] Actually, the "periodicy" idea had been pretty much abandoned, as evidenced by *Bruun* and other decisions.[14]

The Third Circuit distinguished cases such as *General American Investors*, holding a corporation's recovery of insider profits to be gross income despite being a windfall,[15] stating that such recoveries were gains derived from the *taxpayer's* capital, namely, insider information. The Third Circuit opinion conceded that the *Central Railroad* decision "cannot be deemed to be overwhelmingly persuasive" as authority and that a decision taxing punitive damages would "bring symmetry into this aspect of income taxation." However, the Third Circuit went on to say that too much water had flowed over the dam to overrule its own precedent, and that any such overruling should be undertaken by the Supreme Court.

The Supreme Court Decision

The Petition for Certiorari

The government's petition for *certiorari* argued that the lower courts were split on the issue of whether the *Macomber* definition controlled all issues relating to gross income. Specifically, the split was between the punitive damages cases and the insider-profits cases. Subsequent to the Third Circuit decision in *Glenshaw-Goldman*, the Second Circuit had affirmed the pro-government decision in *General American Investors* on the recovery of insider profits.[16] Unlike the Tax Court and Third Circuit attempts to distinguish the insider-profits situation, the

---

[12] 284 U.S. 1 (1931).

[13] In the passage in question, Roswell Magill, *Taxable Income* 428–29 (rev. ed 1945), the author states, in justifying the taxation of annuities, that "regular recurrence" is a characteristic of "most incomes." In note 78 on 428–29, he states further that "periodicy . . . is characteristic of many kinds of income."

[14] *See, e.g.,* Robertson v. United States, 343 U.S. 711 (1952) (prize for a musical composition); Merchants' Loan and Trust Co. v. Smietanka, 255 U.S. 509 (1921) ("occasional" capital gains of trustee).

[15] Park & Tilford Distillers Corp. v. United States, 107 F.Supp. 941 (Ct.Cl.1952), *cert. denied*, 345 U.S. 917 (1953); General American Investors Co. v. Commissioner, 19 T.C. 581 (1952) (reviewed), then on appeal to the Second Circuit.

[16] 211 F.2d 522 (2d Cir.1954).

Second Circuit saw no distinction and expressed disapproval of *Central Railroad* and the punitive damage cases.

The government then cited assorted Supreme Court cases in which it claimed that gross income existed that was not derived from the taxpayer's capital and labor, but only one of these, *Bruun*, was really *apropos*. As noted earlier, *Bruun* involved the acquisition by a lessor of lessee improvements upon the lessee's premature forfeiture of the lease. The improvements were not directly produced by the lessor's capital but were only indirectly derived from it in the sense that the lessor's property supported the lease and, in turn, the lessee's desire to erect the improvements. A similar point might have been (but was not) made that punitive damages would not have arisen if the taxpayer's investment in its business had not been damaged.

Respondent Glenshaw Glass Co. argued that there was no conflict among the lower courts because the cases involving recovery of insider profits were readily distinguishable, and that the *Macomber* definition had been followed without dissent since 1920, and as recently as 1949, in *Commissioner v. Culbertson*,[17] but without noting that *Culbertson* was an income-attribution case, not a gross income case. Finally, Glenshaw Glass Co. argued:

> Where a rule of tax law has been in effect for many years without any doubt ever having been cast upon its correctness and with the governing statute having been repeatedly re-enacted by Congress, there is ample precedent for holding that the harsh and oppressive consequences of a retroactive reversal should not be visited upon a taxpayer in the absence of express legislative direction.

The Supreme Court granted *certiorari* in *Glenshaw-Goldman* on October 14, 1954. In addition, the losing taxpayer in *General American Investors* petitioned for *certiorari*, the government acceded, and *certiorari* was granted in that case, which was consolidated for argument with *Glenshaw-Goldman*.[18]

The Briefs

This section will treat the briefs as clustered around three main points: (1) statutory interpretation of the phrase "gross income," (2) the

---

[17] 337 U.S. 733, 740 (1949).

[18] Bernard Wolfman, formerly Dean of the University of Pennsylvania Law School and currently Professor at Harvard Law School, was on the briefs for Goldman Theaters. Professor Wolfman related in a telephone conversation with the author on March 27, 2002 that the attorneys for General American Investors, at oral argument in the Supreme Court, where its case was heard together with *Glenshaw-Goldman*, attempted to associate themselves and their client with Glenshaw Glass and Goldman Theaters, who had prevailed in the courts below, by crowding together with the latters' attorneys at the single table assigned to taxpayers' counsel.

status of the *Macomber* definition in the courts over the years, and (3) whether the Supreme Court should defer to an alleged "established rule" concerning punitive damages.

1. *Statutory Interpretation of "Gross Income"*

The government's core argument was that the statute taxed all gains from any source except those specifically exempted. The government noted that the dictionary and "plain meaning" definition of "gain" is "increase in resources," and punitive damages easily fit that description. The government cited expressions from prior cases as to the broad and comprehensive scope of the statutory language.

Surprisingly, the government's opening brief advanced an argument not made in the courts below. The government argued that the taxation of receipts "not derived from property" fell within the plenary taxing power granted by Article I, Section 8 of the Constitution and did not rest on the Sixteenth Amendment, which states only that an "income tax" is not subject to the requirement, applicable only to "direct taxes," that the tax be apportioned among the states in proportion to population. (*Pollock v. Farmers' Loan & Trust Co.*[19] had held that a tax on income from property was unconstitutional as an unapportioned direct tax.) Thus, the statutory tax on "gains or profits and income derived from any source whatever" was not comprehensively limited by any definition of "income" relating to the Sixteenth Amendment, such as that stated in *Macomber*. "Income" is a particular type of gain that relates to (is "derived from") property, as opposed to "accruing to" capital.

The taxpayers argued that the prior cases all had presumed that the gross income statute referred to "income" as that term was used in the Sixteenth Amendment. Thus, it was error to view "income" in the statute as being a separate category apart from "gain." Tellingly, the 1954 revision of the gross income statute dropped the reference to "gains" except with respect to "dealings in property," where it has the technical meaning of "the excess of amount realized over basis" upon the sale or disposition of property. Since the legislative history stated that the 1954 version of the gross income provision is not different in substance from the 1939 Code version, Congress must have thought that "gains" as used in the taxing statute had always been a subcategory of income.

The foregoing may have been an effort by taxpayers' counsel to sow confusion among "gains" in the technical sense and "gain" in the factual sense ("economic gain"). In any event, if the government were to continue to insist that the 1939 Code taxed "gain" separately from "income," then the dropping of the phrase "gains or profits" by Con-

---

[19] 157 U.S. 429, *reh'g granted*, 158 U.S. 601 (1895).

gress in its 1954 revision could result in a pro-government decision by the Supreme Court that would be rendered immediately obsolete by the 1954 statutory revision. It is not surprising, therefore, that in its reply brief the government backed away from any implication that it was arguing that "(economic) gain" is a separate taxable category, or that "gain" encompassed "income." Now the government stated that "income" in the statute encompassed "economic gain" and had done so all along. The government contended that the debt-discharge income in *Kirby Lumber* and the forfeited lessee improvements income in *Bruun* were economic gains (if not "gains" in the technical sense). Moreover, the *Macomber* definition itself referred to "*gain* [in the singular] ... derived from capital or labor, or from both combined." (Emphasis added.)

The taxpayers conceded that Congress had the power to tax punitive damages. But, if punitive damages are not "income" under the Sixteenth Amendment, then Congress' taxing power must be broader than the Sixteenth Amendment. Indeed, it *is* broader, as the 1909 corporate income tax had been upheld as an "indirect tax," not subject to the apportionment requirement.[20] Apparently, the thrust of the taxpayers' argument was that any move by Congress beyond the Sixteenth Amendment had to take the form of a specific inclusionary rule. The general "catch-all" reference to "income" was not sufficient. Moreover, the catch-all phrase had no independent meaning except as a summary of the preceding phrases, all of which implied a source in capital and/or labor.

The problem, of course, is that what is distinctive about the catch-all phrase is that it refers to "gains or profits and income *from any source whatever*." (Emphasis added.) Historically, the purpose of "any source whatever" (which echoes "from whatever source derived" in the Sixteenth Amendment)[21] was to neutralize the *Pollock* decision, which had agreed that a tax on wage "income" was constitutional as an "indirect" tax (not subject to the apportionment requirement), but that a tax on property income was really a tax on property and therefore invalid as an unapportioned "direct" tax. In other words, the function of the Sixteenth Amendment was to remove the apportionment requirement for whatever features of an "income tax" might be characterized as a "direct" tax.

---

[20] *See* Flint v. Stone and Tracy Co., 220 U.S. 107 (1911); *see also* Knowlton v. Moore, 178 U.S. 41 (1900) (1898 inheritance tax).

[21] Section 61(a) of the 1954 (and 1986) Code reverted to the constitutional phrase "from whatever source derived," but according to the 1954 legislative history, this change in language was not meant to be a change in substance. (Conceivably, the word "derived" may be taken as an implicit reference to the realization requirement, but the current view is that Congress is free to define realization.)

The taxpayers characterized the government's position to be that source is *never* relevant and then cited two situations where everybody agreed that source is relevant: (1) cases involving a receipt that was a return of capital, and (2) cases involving compensatory damages where courts agreed that the damages had to be analyzed to determine if they were a "substitute for" lost wages or profits or for lost or destroyed assets with a basis. The government conceded these points but maintained that punitive damages fell into neither of these categories.

Actually, "source" (which, under the statute and Constitution, is irrelevant) should be understood to refer to "Where does it come from?" (as from labor, capital, or neither of the two), whereas both the "return of capital" and "substitute for" notions have to do with what the receipt "is," i.e., its "nature" or "quality."

2. *Erosion of the* Macomber *Definition*

The taxpayers argued that the courts had continued to adhere to a requirement that "income" had to derive from capital and/or labor, while the government contended that the courts had moved beyond any such limitation. Several cases were mentioned by both sides as supporting their respective positions, but most of the cited cases seem irrelevant to the question of whether income could exist without a source in capital and/or labor.[22]

The *Macomber* formulation on its face does not posit any requirement that the receipt be derived from the *taxpayer's* capital or labor, and two of the cases cited by the government involved situations where the income derived from *another person's* capital. The first is *Irwin v. Gavit*,[23] which held that trust income was not exempt under the exclusion for gifts and bequests. The government pointed out that trust

---

[22] Cases citing the *Macomber* definition that *did* involve income from capital or labor do not support either side's position on the issue of gains *not* derived from capital and/or labor. Cases of this ilk cited by the taxpayers included Commissioner v. Culbertson, 337 U.S. 733 (1949) (income from partnership); United States v. Safety Car Heating & Lighting Co., 297 U.S. 88 (1936) (damages for patent infringement); Taft v. Bowers, 278 U.S. 470 (1929) (basis rule for inter vivos gifts); and Merchants' Loan & Trust Co. v. Smietanka, 255 U.S. 509 (1921) (casual capital gains). The *Macomber* definition was itself borrowed from Stratton's Independence v. Howbert, 231 U.S. 399 (1913), involving the Corporation Tax Act of 1909 and upholding the taxation of income from capital with appropriate basis offset.

Cases of this ilk cited by the government include Robertson v. United States, 343 U.S. 711 (1952) (holding a prize for musical composition to be income, and not a gift, but such income derives from taxpayer's labor); Rutkin v. United States, 343 U.S. 130 (1952) (holding gains from extortion to be income, but such gain is from taxpayer's labor); Dobson v. Commissioner, 320 U.S. 489 (1943) (taxpayer's basis in recovery of previously-deducted amounts); and United States v. Kirby Lumber Co., 284 U.S. 1 (1931) (holding debt-discharge gain to be income, but as investment gain, since borrowed cash did not have to be repaid in full).

[23] 268 U.S. 161 (1925).

income is from capital (corpus) that is beneficially owned by a different taxpayer (the holder of the remainder interest) than the taxpayer who is the income beneficiary.[24] The second case is *Bruun*, where the taxpayer (a lessor) realized income represented by lessee-erected improvements obtained on the lessee's premature forfeiture of a lease.

The government contended that cases involving a corporation's recovery of insider profits were similar to *Irwin v. Gavit* and *Bruun* because the insider profits arose from, and were measured by, the investment of the insider, not that of the taxpayer corporation. The taxpayers in *Glenshaw-Goldman* argued that the recovery derived from the corporation's own capital, namely, inside information. But even if corporate information was an asset of the corporation, it had been used by the insider to produce gain on the insider's own investment.

Along similar lines, the government stated that punitive damages in commercial litigation could be said to derive remotely and indirectly from the taxpayer's capital (the injured business) and labor (the effort to seek damages), but that it preferred to have the *Macomber* definition consigned to oblivion.

The taxpayers argued that, even if gains obtained by a taxpayer from another party's capital and/or labor *could* be gross income, commercial punitive damages were still non-income on the ground that they did not derive from *anybody's* capital or labor but instead somehow derived from the sovereign: punitive damages are a kind of fine or penalty that the government allows a private party to keep. However, the *Macomber* reference to capital or labor is to *economic* sources, not the legal source of the entitlement. For example, the entitlement to the prize in *Robertson v. United States*[25] was completely outside the taxpayer's control, yet the prize nonetheless was includable in income.

The government then noted that the Seventh Circuit, in *Commissioner v. Obear–Nester Glass Co.*,[26] decided after *certiorari* was granted in *Glenshaw Glass* and *Goldman Theaters*, squarely rejected the *Macomber* definition and held that commercial punitive damages were gross income, stating that the fundamental principal of income taxation "is that individuals will be taxed according to their ability to pay."

Perhaps the strongest case for the taxpayers was *Gould v. Gould*,[27] which held that cash alimony was not gross income to the wife. At least on the surface, alimony is not derived from the wife's labor or capital.

---

[24] Similarly, Taft v. Bowers, 278 U.S. 470 (1929), upheld taxing a donee on gain that had accrued while the donor owned the property.

[25] 343 U.S. 711 (1952).

[26] 217 F.2d 56, 60–61 (7th Cir.1954).

[27] 245 U.S. 151 (1917).

But aside from noting that *Gould* stated the maxim that taxing statutes are to be construed against the government (which the Supreme Court subsequently ignored and finally rejected in 1938),[28] the taxpayers failed to articulate any rationale for *Gould*. Indeed, the opinion in *Gould* is pretty much devoid of analysis. *Gould*, which pre-dated *Macomber*, did not purport to base its holding on a *Macomber*-like definition of income. Instead, its rationale seems to have been simply that the catch-all phrase at the end of § 22(a) adds nothing meaningful to the latter's content, a notion that is belied by the plain language of the statute itself.

In *Gould*, the Court quoted a non-tax case that stated that alimony is a portion of the husband's estate to which the wife is equitably entitled but then added that alimony payments did not decrease the net income of the husband and did not increase the wife's income. If this was meant to suggest that the wife somehow appropriated the husband's capital, then that capital must be the "right to alimony," and from that premise it would not follow that the return on that capital, the alimony payments themselves, would be *wholly* exempt.[29] Or possibly the Court thought that *Gould* was an income *attribution* case, but no reason is stated for attributing the income to the payor husband rather than to the payee wife.[30] Another possibility is that the Court realized it could not create a deduction for the husband and simply assumed that non-deductibility to the husband precluded taxability to the payee wife. However, the Court did not state that the tax treatment of one party to a transaction determined the tax treatment to the other, and indeed, it is now clear that *no such general principle exists* (apart from scattered statutory provisions).[31]

Curiously, the government did not try to distinguish, denigrate, or downgrade *Gould*, but instead noted that Congress had the power to tax alimony to the wife. Congress exercised this power in 1942 by enacting the predecessors of §§ 71 and 215.

---

[28] White v. United States, 305 U.S. 281, 292 (1938).

[29] The analogy would be to an annuity, the taxation of which is now governed by § 72, prescribing the method(s) for recovering basis. Presumably the basis of a right to alimony would be its value at the time acquired. *See* Rev. Rul. 67–221, 1967–2 C.B. 63 (basis to wife of property acquired in divorce is equal to fair market value on receipt).

[30] Of course, the very act of treating a case as an "income attribution" case presupposes that the item in question can only be taxed to one party in the transaction. However, in the classic income-attribution cases that treat the income as being that of the transferor, inclusion by the transferee is barred by the statutory "gift" exclusion. In *Gould*, however, the alimony was not excludable by the wife as a gift.

[31] Commissioner v. Duberstein, 363 U.S. 278 (1960), flatly rejected the government's contention that a "business gift" was includable by the recipient *because* it was deductible by the transferor. Congress responded, ineffectually, to *Duberstein* by enacting § 274(b), which denies a deduction to a donor of a transfer that is excludable by the transferee solely under § 102(a).

The next case seemingly favoring the taxpayers was *United States v. Supplee–Biddle Hardware Co.*,[32] which involved the proceeds of life insurance payable to a corporation. The corporate income tax statute provided that gross income for a corporation was the same as for an individual, and the gross income statute for individuals specifically exempted life insurance proceeds payable to "individual beneficiaries." The Supreme Court simply construed the corporate income tax provision to incorporate the individual income tax exclusion. The Court declined to rule that an income tax on life insurance proceeds would be unconstitutional. The Court's opinion, however, did state:

> The benefit to be gained by death has no periodicity. It is a substitution of money value for something permanently lost either in a house, a ship, or a life. Assuming without deciding that Congress could call the proceeds of such indemnity, income, and validly tax it as such, we think that in view of the popular conception of the life insurance as resulting in a single addition of a total sum to the resources of the beneficiary, and not in a periodical return, such a purpose on its part should be express, as it certainly is not here.

Taken in context, this passage simply appears to offer a rationale for the statutory exclusion under the individual income tax, and this rationale also would apply under the corporate income tax. If so, this passage should not be viewed as a gloss on the catch-all phrase of the gross income statute. Alternatively, the quoted passage could be viewed as expressing the "replacement of capital" idea, which also was the basis for excluding compensatory damages for personal injury,[33] but in that case, it would have no relevance to the punitive damages issue. In any event, the result in *Supplee-Biddle Hardware* could not have been based on the idea that the gains were not derived from capital or labor because the insurance proceeds were receivable as a result of the taxpayer's investment in the form of insurance premiums.

The third case presenting potential problems for the government was *Edwards v. Cuba Railroad Co.*,[34] holding that a non-shareholder contribution to the capital of a corporation was not gross income to the corporation. The Court seemed to base its decision on the fact that the payments, which were subsidies from the Cuban government, were earmarked for capital expenditures by the taxpayer and were not payments for services. This decision appears to follow the then-business

---

[32] 265 U.S. 189 (1924).

[33] *See* 31 Op. Att'y Gen. 301, 308 (1918) (viewing recoveries for personal injury as being a replacement of human capital); *accord*, Hawkins v. Commissioner, 6 B.T.A. 1023 (1927), cited by Glenshaw Glass Co. in its brief.

[34] 268 U.S. 628 (1925).

accounting convention that additions (not out of earned surplus) to a corporation's earnings base were "capital" and not income. However, an unearmarked windfall cannot be viewed as any kind of contribution to capital.

3. *Should the Court Let Congress Change the Rule as to Punitive Damages?*

The government ridiculed the idea that there was a long-standing rule that punitive damages were excludable. It stated that the 1935 *Central Railroad* case (involving damages for breach of fiduciary duty) did not lay down a rule for punitive damages, and that *Central Railroad* was never followed, except by the Board of Tax Appeals in 1940 in *Highland Farms,* to which the Commissioner registered its non-acquiescence.[35]

At oral argument, the Solicitor General was asked to submit a memorandum setting forth the government's administrative practice concerning punitive damages in commercial litigation and related issues. The Solicitor General submitted a memorandum in March 1955, stating that: (1) the Commissioner's consistent position was that compensatory damages were taxable if for lost profits or for assets with no basis; (2) the Commissioner continued to assert deficiencies with respect to punitive damages in a commercial context after its non-acquiescence in *Highland Farms*; (3) the Commissioner's published policy was that a decision of the Board of Tax Appeals (later the Tax Court) would not be viewed as precedent until the Commissioner announced its acquiescence in the decision;[36] and (4) the Board of Tax Appeals, in a case holding that compensatory damages for injury to *personal* reputation did not involve gain, had reserved the question of punitive damages.[37]

In their briefs, the taxpayers attempted to articulate as a reliance interest with respect to the rule of *Highland Farms* that commercial-litigation plaintiffs would take non-taxability into account in deciding whether to settle cases.

In a Motion for Leave To File a Brief as *Amicus Curiae*, Dean Milk Company argued that antitrust policy would be deeply affected by a reversal of the *Highland Farms* "rule," and that such action should be left to Congress.

4. *Observations*

The briefs of the parties took a "scattershot" approach that was broad but not very forceful. All of the briefs cited cases that did not

---

[35] 1941–1 C.B. 16.

[36] III–2 C.B. IV (1924).

[37] *See* Hawkins v. Commissioner, 6 B.T.A. 1023 (1927).

support their position in any way, except perhaps for "boilerplate" language in the opinions. Although only a few of the cited Supreme Court cases offered anything that had much bearing on the punitive damages issue, the briefs failed to give any emphasis to these cases, nor did they attempt to articulate what these cases really stood for in a way that connected to the taxability of punitive damages. As noted earlier, the government could have made better use of *Bruun*, and taxpayers might have tried to wield *Gould* more effectively. Perhaps these points were addressed in oral argument, but there is no record of the latter.

The taxpayers never tried to construct a real argument around the *Macomber* definition, other than the fact that it had been cited a lot. Why *should* "income" be restricted to gains derived from capital or labor, i.e., from economic activity?[38] And, is there any tax reason to confine income to the fruits of the *taxpayer's* economic activity? Finally, any act of appropriating gain involves "some" economic activity on the taxpayer's part, but how much is enough? Perhaps merely stating these questions suggests the difficulty of providing a convincing and coherent answer. And so refuge is taken in the "common understanding" of income, where theory and analysis are absent. And just how is such understanding to be ascertained?

If a client's position is not strong on the merits, perhaps an attorney's best strategy is to create confusion in the minds of the judges. This can be accomplished by, among other tactics, taking quotes from cases out of context, treating negative inferences from *dicta* as "holdings," using terminology in a confusing way, over-generalizing favorable holdings, and distinguishing unfavorable holdings "on the facts." This is how the advocacy game is played, and the taxpayer's counsel played the game more effectively than the government's counsel in *Glenshaw-Goldman* and *General American Investors*.

The government's advocate in the Supreme Court is the office of the Solicitor General,[39] and in tax matters, the office is often at a disadvantage against highly specialized tax counsel, despite sometimes receiving assistance from the Tax Division of the Justice Department.[40] One could cite numerous tax cases that seem to have been lost by the government

---

[38] It is understandable that economists would define a term for use in their own discipline, but to say that income to economists is the result of economic activity is to state a tautology that is of little value outside of economics.

[39] There is usually an assistant Solicitor General who works on the handful of tax cases heard by the Supreme Court in a given term, but that person also handles other kinds of cases and cannot be assumed to be a tax specialist. The legal experience of the Solicitor General at the time of *Glenshaw Glass*, Simon Sobeloff, was mainly acquired as a U.S. attorney.

[40] The Tax Division of the Justice Department handles tax appeals but not cases in the Tax Court, which is the realm of Service counsel. Civil tax cases in the U.S. District Courts are relatively uncommon and are usually handled by U.S. attorneys.

in the Supreme Court as the result of perfunctory or inadequate advocacy, or of over-reaching, but that is another story.[41]

The Opinions

Oral argument in both *Glenshaw-Goldman* and *General American Investors* occurred on February 28, 1955,[42] and the decisions in favor of the government in both cases were handed down on March 28, 1955. In *Glenshaw-Goldman*, the vote in favor of the government was 7–1, with Chief Justice Warren writing the majority opinion and Justice Douglas dissenting without opinion. In *General American Investors*, the vote was 8–0, with the Chief Justice again authoring the opinion but with Justice Douglas this time concurring in the result, again without opinion.[43] Justice Harlan did not vote in either case because he joined the Court after oral argument.

The decisions in *Glenshaw-Goldman* and *General American Investors* (hereinafter referred to collectively as the *Glenshaw Glass* trilogy) appear to have been virtually ignored by the press.[44] Some of the major

---

[41] Here is a partial list of cases that come to mind: Commissioner v. Estate of Hubert, 520 U.S. 93, 114–21 (1997) (concurring opinion by Justice O'Connor blasted the government's regulations, rulings, and litigation strategy); Newark Morning Ledger Co. v. United States, 507 U.S. 546 (1993) (majority opinion openly criticized government's litigation strategy); Commissioner v. Tufts, 461 U.S. 300 (1983) (government won case despite faulty theory); Frank Lyon Co. v. United States, 435 U.S. 561 (1978) (allowing "business purpose" to trump lack of economic substance); M.E. Blatt Co. v. United States, 305 U.S. 267 (1938) (government's theory of the case was incoherent); Burnet v. Logan, 283 U.S. 404 (1931) (government should have insisted that transaction was an exchange, not a contingent-payment sale); Poe v. Seaborn, 282 U.S. 101 (1930) (government argued that income from community property was attributable to husband, which would have made community property couples worse off, tax-wise, relative to couples in common-law states).

[42] Those participating in the oral argument were a distinguished group. Arguing for General American Investors was Norris Darrell, head of the prominent Wall Street firm Sullivan & Cromwell and president of the American Law Institute for 15 years. In 1947, Darrell was elected to the American Law Institute Council and was head of the ALI project that laid the foundation for the Internal Revenue Code of 1954. *See* Newsday, Aug. 16, 1989, at 45, 1989 WL 3402329. Arguing the cases for the government was Solicitor General Simon Sobeloff, formerly Chief Judge of the Maryland Court of Appeals (1952–54), subsequently judge on the U.S. Court of Appeals for the 4th Circuit from1956 until his death in 1973, and Chief Judge from 1958–1964. Arguing the case for Glenshaw Glass was Max Swiren of the Chicago firm Swiren & Heineman. The Heineman was Ben Heineman, who later became CEO of the Chicago & NW R.R., and who was the taxpayer in Heineman v. Commissioner, 82 T.C. 538 (1984), which allowed deductions relating to Heineman's office at his summer estate on Lake Michigan. The lead counsel for Goldman Theaters was Samuel Levy of the Philadelphia firm now known as Wolf, Block, Schorr & Solis–Cohen LLP. *See also* note 18.

[43] The strange behavior of Justice Douglas in tax cases is the subject of Bernard Wolfman, et al., *Dissent Without Opinion: The Behavior of Justice William O. Douglas in Federal Tax Cases* 41–42 (1975).

[44] The *New York Times* of March 29, 1955, p. 18, made no mention of the decisions, and they are not mentioned in the *New York Times* index for the year 1955. The *Wall Street Journal* of March 29, 1955, at p. 4, briefly described, without comment, the

law reviews briefly noted the decisions in student-authored "Recent Developments" notes.[45] The prevailing contemporary response appears to have been, "Ho hum, now we have a new rule as to the taxability of punitive damages."

The Immediate Impact of *Glenshaw Glass*

The Supreme Court's opinion in *Glenshaw-Goldman*[46] was sweeping and gave short shrift to the taxpayers' arguments. The notion that income had to be of a type that was regular or recurring was not worth mentioning. The very short opinion in *General American Investors*[47] cited *Glenshaw-Goldman* and stated that there was no relevant basis for distinguishing recoveries for insider profits from punitive damages recoveries. In addition to the commercial punitive damages issues, the Supreme Court decisions in the *Glenshaw Glass* trilogy also held:

(1) The tax statute, not language in judicial opinions, is the ultimate source of tax law; and

(2) The catch-all phrase in the gross income statute covered all realized accessions to wealth, regardless of source, and not specifically excluded by statute.

The first of these points cannot be emphasized too strongly to the entry-level tax student. The *alpha* and *omega* of approaching a federal tax issue is the Internal Revenue Code, the ultimate source of all tax law. Unlike most other statutes, the Code does not codify or play off of any body of common law. It is a statutory creation out of whole cloth. What cases say, or even hold, is secondary to the Code language.

The second, if related, point is that the open-ended quality of the gross income statute as construed by the *Glenshaw Glass* trilogy means that economic gain is presumptively income unless covered by a statutory exclusion or other rule of law or by administrative practice. Thus, income is defined in an abstract way, rather than being constituted by an aggregate of specific statutory or regulatory examples and holdings in court cases. One cannot say that "such and such is not income because

---

Glenshaw Glass trilogy in the middle of a fairly lengthy article headlined: *"Supreme Court: Court Says State Judge Can't Bar Union Action Legal Under T–H Law."*

[45] Some recognition of the significance of *Glenshaw-Goldman* is found in Leslie Rapp, *Some Recent Developments in the Concept of Taxable Income*, 11 Tax L. Rev. 329, 358–371 (1956). *See* Note, *Recent Decisions*, 43 Cal. L. Rev. 541–46 (1955); Note, *Recent Decisions*, 54 Mich. L. Rev. 126, 151–55 (1956); Note, *The Supreme Court: 1954 Term*, 69 Harv. L. Rev. 119, 195 (1955); Note, *Taxation of Damage Recoveries from Litigation*, 40 Cornell L.Q. 345, 351–55 (1955).

[46] 348 U.S. 426 (1955).

[47] 348 U.S. 434 (1955).

no court has ever held it to be income." The *Glenshaw Glass* trilogy's approach to gross income issues is the opposite of the common law method of "extending" fact-specific holdings to new fact situations by analogy and synthesis.

But there is both more and less to the *Glenshaw Glass* trilogy. The "more" has to do with (1) the respective roles of courts, especially the Supreme Court, Congress, and the Executive, and (2) the implications of the decision for other areas of tax doctrine. The "less" is a kind of judicial restraint that avoids over-commitment to theories or definitions and avoids the unnecessary stirring up of doctrinal waters.

1. *Statutory Interpretation of "Gross Income"*

The Third Circuit's decision in *Glenshaw-Goldman* emphasized that the *Macomber* definition of income was derived from a "common understanding" of the term "income" in 1913, the year the Sixteenth Amendment was ratified and the inaugural year of the current income tax. The Supreme Court ignored this aspect of the Third Circuit's opinion, thereby implicitly rejecting both "originalist" and "common understanding" approaches to the concept of "income."[48] Basically, the Court adopted a "dynamic plain meaning" approach,[49] whereby the starting point for understanding income ("accession to wealth") is something like the literal meaning, "wealth coming in." Note that the "literal" meaning is not necessarily a dictionary meaning because a dictionary will give meanings that are based on usage in both "lay" and "specialist" communities.[50]

Any attempt to come up with a "common understanding" concept of income for tax purposes must founder because different people will come to the table with different views and expertise.[51] "Originalism" suffers from similar difficulties because there is no on-point legislative history.

---

[48] See Marjorie E. Kornhauser, *The Constitutional Meaning of Income and the Income Taxation of Gifts*, 25 Conn. L. Rev. 1, 9–10 (1992) (stating that popular and economics definitions of income were quite close in the early 20th century).

[49] See Glenshaw–Goldman, 348 U.S. at 432–33 ("We would do violence to the plain meaning of the statute . . . were we to say that the payments in question here are not gross income.").

[50] Income is defined in the current Merriam–Webster Dictionary (online version as of 4/4/2002, at http://www.m-w.com/cgi-bin/dictionary) as follows: "1: a coming in . . . ; 2: a gain or recurrent benefit usually measured in money that derives from capital or labor; *also*: the amount of such gain received in a period of time . . ." The dictionary definitions circa 1920, as reported in Kornhauser, *supra* note 48, at 9, n.30, laid more emphasis on the idea of regular or recurring but at the same time referred to the income of persons from all sources, not to particular items of income. Paradoxically, the *Macomber* "common understanding" definition, without explaining its origin, expressly disclaimed reliance on "lexicographers and economists," despite its "economic" flavor.

[51] See Magill, *supra* note 13, at 441.

Indeed, many crucial issues involving income measurement were pur-
posely left unresolved in 1913.[52] For example, nothing was said about the
status of non-recurring receipts. Crucial issues involving income measurement were left open in the early years because various more-or-less
"technical" concepts of income were then competing for dominance. At
least three distinct concepts of income were in play during the formative
years of the income tax.[53]

One view of income, publicized by the early twentieth century writer
E. R. A. Seligman,[54] made a sharp distinction between "capital" and
"income." Seligman treated original endowment and extraordinary
items as "capital," and identified income with "flow" and receipts that
were "regular and recurring."[55] Thus, "occasional" realized capital
gains, gifts and bequests received, contributions to capital, and windfalls
all would be excluded from income and treated as "capital." This view,
sometimes called the *res* theory of capital,[56] followed contemporary
dictionary definitions of income and coincided with the Third Circuit's
view in *Glenshaw-Goldman*. It happens that this concept was the curren-
cy of the realm in trust accounting and to a lesser extent in business
accounting, both of which had developed conceptions of income prior to
the enactment of a permanent income tax. Trust accounting law has
traditionally made a heavy commitment to the principle of "preservation
of capital," and business accounting is supposedly committed to restrain-
ing management from overstating "net income."

At least two features of the 1913 Act were contrary to the *res*
theory: (1) the inclusion of "gains ... from dealings in property" in
income;[57] and (2) the *express* exclusion of gifts and bequests received,

---

[52] *See* Sidney Ratner, *American Taxation: Its History as a Social Force in Democracy*
326–36 (1942).

[53] A handy summary of the three is found in Richard Goode, *The Economics Definition
of Income*, in Joseph Pechman (ed.), *Comprehensive Income Taxation* 1–30 (1977).

[54] *See* E. R. A. Seligman, *The Income Tax* 675–704 (1911).

[55] *See* Carl C. Plehn, *The Concept of Income, as Recurrent, Consumable Receipts*, 14
Am. Econ. Rev. 1, 5 (1924).

[56] In Latin, *res* means "thing." In trust law, *res* is the property subject to the trust
over time, and the latter can be readily identified as "capital" ("principal"), as opposed to
"income," namely, that which periodically comes in and is paid out currently to income
beneficiaries. Modern trust law is finally moving away from the *res* concept. *See* Revised
Uniform Principal and Income Act (1997), 7B Un. Laws Ann. 165 (2000).

[57] In traditional trust law, the concept of "realization" is irrelevant, since realized, as
well as unrealized, gains and losses are part of corpus as opposed to income. In business
accounting, at least *recurrent* gains were taken into income. The trust accounting approach
to gains was rejected in Doyle v. Mitchell Bros. Co., 247 U.S. 179 (1918), in favor of the
business accounting approach.

implying that gifts, at least plausibly, would be classed as income in the absence of such an exclusion.[58]

Whatever hold the *res* theory might have had in the 1910s began to seriously unravel in the 1920s. The Supreme Court upheld the taxation of occasional realized capital gains in *Merchants Loan and Trust Co. v. Smietanka*.[59] In the seminal case of *Taft v. Bowers*,[60] the Supreme Court explicitly recognized that "capital" should be identified with "basis" (previously-subject-to-tax dollars), not "original endowment of the taxpayer."[61] Even the *Macomber* definition of income did not preclude the taxation of extraordinary or non-recurring items, and such cases as *Bruun* (lessee improvements acquired by lessor) and *Robertson* (receipt of prize) confirmed that such items were not excludable simply because they were nonrecurring. Indeed, upon reflection it is evident that any exclusion for non-recurring receipts would be antithetical to rational and even-handed administration by the Service and the courts.[62]

But the *res* theory of capital and income left behind some residue that has persisted to the present day, having been codified in these provisions:

(1) The exclusion for non-shareholder contributions to the capital of corporations (originating in the 1925 *Cuba Railroad* case and now codified in § 118);

(2) The exclusion for income and gains accrued before 1913 (originating in *Doyle v. Mitchell Brothers*, decided in 1918,[63] and now codified in §§ 316(a)(1) and 1053);

(3) The fair-market-value basis rule for property acquired by bequest or inheritance (originating in a 1918 Treasury regulation and later codified into what is now § 1014);[64]

---

[58] *See* Rice v. Eisner, 16 F.2d 358, 360 (2d Cir.1926) (L. Hand, J.). Similarly, recoveries for personal injuries were held to be excludable on a replacement-of-capital theory, not because they were nonrecurring.

[59] 255 U.S. 509 (1921).

[60] 278 U.S. 470 (1929).

[61] This case upheld the predecessor of § 1015, the carryover basis rule for gifts. Taxpayers there argued that the pre-gift appreciation that accrued to the donor could not be taxed to the donee under an income tax.

[62] Thus, "How often is often enough?" Legislatures are far better equipped than courts to fashion arbitrary rules keyed to quantity. For the same reason, the "ordinary" requirement for deductibility of business and investment expenses was construed early on *not* to mean "regular and recurring." *See* Welch v. Helvering, 290 U.S. 111 (1933), discussed in Chapter 5 of *Tax Stories*.

[63] *See* note 57; *see* also Southern Pacific Co. v. Lowe, 247 U.S. 330 (1918) (dividends from pre–1913 earnings and profits were not income). Both cases were decided under the corporate income tax of 1909.

[64] If original endowment is "capital," then it must have a basis equal to its value when acquired. The early history of §§ 1014 and 1015 is recounted in Taft v. Bowers, 278 U.S.

(4) The replacement-of-capital theory underlying the exclusion of recoveries for personal injury (essentially codified in 1918 but later limited to recoveries for physical personal injuries in § 104(a)(2)); and,

(5) Perhaps viewing cash support received as a kind of "status entitlement," the exclusion for support, both in-kind (which derives from the Service's practice) and cash (the 1917 *Gould* case, codified by negative implication by present § 71).

A second view of "income" was the "accretion" theory, commonly known as the Haig–Simons (or Schanz–Haig–Simons) concept of income, which viewed income as the taxpayer's "net increases in wealth plus consumption" over the taxable year.[65] The increase in net wealth idea was anticipated by the holding in the 1935 *Kirby Lumber* case (discussed in Chapter 3 of *Tax Stories*) that a reduction in negative wealth (a debt) incurred in the acquisition of an asset (cash) produced an increase in net wealth and hence income. It is sometimes suggested that the Supreme Court's majority opinion in *Glenshaw-Goldman* adopted the Haig–Simons concept as the "new" definition of income, superseding the *Macomber* definition, but this is not an accurate characterization of what the Court actually said: "*Here we have* instances of undeniable accessions to wealth, clearly realized, and over which the taxpayers have complete dominion." (Emphasis added.) This passage does not purport to "define" the term "income." It only "translates" the *facts* of *Glenshaw-Goldman* into the legally relevant form of "realized economic gain of the taxpayer." Moreover, there is no evidence from the record that the Court and counsel were particularly aware of the Haig–Simons concept. In fact, the *Glenshaw-Goldman* formulation of the income concept deviates from the Haig–Simons definition by acknowledging the "realization" principle.[66] The *Glenshaw-Goldman* formulation also says nothing about the role of "consumption" in the concept of gross income.

Yet it must be acknowledged that "accession to wealth" sounds very much like "increase in net wealth," and to that extent, the statement from *Glenshaw-Goldman* is congruent with the Haig–Simons concept of income. Moreover, it is significant that the reputation of *Glenshaw-Goldman* in the tax community grew in tandem with an increasing

---

470, 471–72 (1929). Section 1015, the carryover-basis rule for gifts, was viewed as an anti-tax-avoidance measure, not as a codification of some basic principle.

[65] Georg von Schanz (1853–1931) was an early theorist whose work is heavily quoted (unfortunately in the original German) in Henry Simons, *Personal Income Taxation* (1938), probably the seminal work in modern income tax theory. Simon's work elaborates upon the basic concept advanced in Robert M. Haig, *The Concept of Income–Economic and Legal Aspects*, in *The Federal Income Tax* (Robert M. Haig ed., 1921).

[66] *See* William W. Hewett, *The Definition of Income and Its Application to Federal Taxation* 27 (1925).

awareness of the Haig–Simons concept as initially publicized through the writings in the late 1960s and early 1970s of Stanley Surrey, a Harvard Law School Professor and sometimes Treasury official.[67] Surrey was the driving force behind the concept of "tax expenditures," which to him essentially meant any pro-taxpayer provision that deviated from the Haig–Simons definition of income.[68] The tax expenditure concept in turn has spawned a vast debate that began in the 1970s and continues to the present day.[69] Tax expenditures have been required to be identified in Congressional and Executive budgets, although in these contexts the concept has been somewhat cut loose from the Haig–Simons definition.

The third concept of income was the "consumed income tax" ("CIT") idea, initially associated with Irving Fischer[70] and later with another Harvard Law School Professor, William Andrews, who referred to it as a "cash-flow consumption tax."[71] Under a CIT, investments are not taxed until converted to cash and available for consumption. What principally distinguishes an "income tax" from a CIT is that capital expenditures are not currently deductible and borrowed money is not includable because in each case the transaction manifests no change in net wealth. Under a CIT, business and investment capital expenditures are currently deductible in full (as non-consumption outlays) and cash borrowing is includable (as potential consumption).[72]

The basic structure of the Internal Revenue Code follows the income tax ideal. Nevertheless, many *ad hoc* statutory emendations of our so-

---

[67] Stanley S. Surrey (1911–1984) was a Professor at Harvard Law School from 1950 to 1984, the Assistant Secretary of the Treasury for Tax Policy from 1961–1969, and consultant to the Treasury Department from 1977 to 1981.

[68] *See, e.g.*, Stanley S. Surrey, *Pathways To Tax Reform: The Concept of Tax Expenditures* (1973).

[69] *See, e.g.*, Bruce Bartlett, *The End of Tax Expenditures as We Know Them?*, 92 Tax Notes 413 (2001); Boris Bittker, *Accounting for Tax Subsidies in the National Budget*, 22 Nat'l Tax J. 528 (1969) (along with a response by Surrey & Hellmuth and a Reply by Bittker); Mary L. Heen, *Reinventing Tax Expenditure Reform: Improving Program Oversight Under the Government Performance and Results Act*, 33 Wake Forest L. Rev. 751 (2000); Michael McIntyre, *A Solution to the Problem of Defining a Tax Expenditure*, 14 U.C. Davis L. Rev. 79 (1980); Victor Thuronyi, *Tax Expenditures: A Reassessment*, 1988 Duke L.J. 1155 (1988); Edward A. Zelinsky, *James Madison and Public Choice at Gucci Gulch: A Procedural Defense of Tax Expenditures and Tax institutions*, 102 Yale L.J. 1165 (1993).

[70] *See* Irving Fischer, *Are Savings Income?*, 9 Am. Econ. Ass'n Q. 21 (1908).

[71] *See* William Andrews, *A Consumption–Type or Cash–Flow Personal Income Tax*, 87 Harv. L. Rev. 1113 (1974) (contrasting consumed-income tax with Haig–Simons accretion income tax).

[72] Since investments are deductible in full, there are no basis accounts under a CIT. As to borrowings, under a CIT both principal and interest payments are deductible in full as non-consumption outlays.

called income tax, such as provisions deferring the recognition of gains[73] and allowing certain capital expenditures to be "expensed," are actually CIT features. The concept of "realization of gain" as it has existed under the income tax from the very beginning is the result of an early compromise between the Haig–Simons and CIT ideals.[74] In short, our so-called "income tax" is actually a kind of hybrid.

In recent years, the conflict between the Haig–Simons and CIT models has dominated tax policy discussion. There are many who favor replacing the income tax with a CIT. But that is yet another (and ongoing) story. In the present context, it is enough to note that the CIT ideal has had virtually no effect on administrative and judicial interpretation of the Code.[75] The *Glenshaw Glass* trilogy touchstone of income, "accession to wealth," is fundamentally incompatible with the CIT approach.

There exists a fourth concept of income, but it does not appear to have been very influential either in the formative period or in current debates. The notion is that individual income is a taxpayer's percentage share of the "pie" constituted by "national income." A problem with this view is agreeing on what constitutes "national income." For example, what about the value of household services or of volunteer work?

Under the "pie" theory, a punitive damages award is a kind of "transfer" of previously existing national income from one party to another, and as such, it should only be taxed once. The "economic income" definition advanced in *Macomber*, as well as the holding in *Gould* that alimony is not taxed to the wife, might be seen as being compatible with the pie theory, but the latter was never articulated as the basis of these decisions, and it was vigorously attacked by Haig–Simons proponents.[76] It is also incompatible with long-standing rules taxing gains from wagering and casualty insurance. Nor does the pie

---

[73] *See, e.g.*, §§ 453 (installment method of reporting gains), 1031 (deferral of gains and losses on certain exchanges of like-kind property), and 1033 (deferral of gain on reinvestment of involuntary-conversion proceeds).

[74] Under the Haig–Simons ideal, unrealized gains and (non-personal-use asset) losses are taken into account, whereas under a CIT ideal the proceeds of sale of an asset are not taxed to the extent re-invested in a business or investment asset. The income tax concept of realization of gain follows neither ideal; gains and losses are not reckoned until "realized," but there is no across-the-board deduction or exclusion for reinvestment. *See* Steven A. Bank, *Mergers, Taxes, and Historical Realism*, 75 Tul. L. Rev. 1 (2000); Marjorie E. Kornhauser, *Section 1031: We Don't Need Another Hero*, 60 S. Cal. L. Rev. 397 (1987).

[75] The most recent "realization" case in the Supreme Court, Cottage Savings Ass'n v. Commissioner, 499 U.S. 554, 559 (1991), held that virtually any in-kind exchange would trigger gain or loss under § 1001, even where the property received is virtually identical to the property disposed of.

[76] Henry Simons devoted an entire chapter of his book, *supra* note 65, at pp. 59–102, to attacking this and other competing theories of income.

theory offer any principle for determining *which* party should be taxed on a transferred item. Indeed, if the item is deductible by the transferor (as is usually the case with commercial punitive damages), would not inclusion by the transferee be mandated?[77] In any event, it is clear that the *Glenshaw Glass* trilogy forecloses judicial and administrative flirtation with the pie concept.[78]

On a more abstract level, the *Glenshaw Glass* trilogy consolidated a trend that began in the 1920s to develop a "non-originalist" and "plain meaning" concept of income *that is autonomous relative to any notion of "common understanding" and to other academic, legal, and professional fields and disciplines.*[79] At the same time, this plain meaning concept of income has proven itself "open" to revision based on evolving insights developed in other fields and disciplines.[80] Although the *Glenshaw Glass* trilogy did not explicitly commit to any single normative and comprehensive conception of personal income taxation,[81] in practice it has aligned the income tax more closely with the Haig–Simons concept of income than with any other concept (always excepting the realization principle and whatever statutory deviations from Haig–Simons that Congress may enact from time to time).[82]

---

[77] But the idea that the tax treatment of the transferee is dictated by that of the transferor has been rejected by the Supreme Court, *see supra* note 31, although Congress can legislate such a rule for particular situations. Under § 162(g), enacted in 1969, two-thirds of civil anti-trust damages are rendered nondeductible to a payor convicted of a criminal anti-trust violation. Fines and penalties "paid to a government" are nondeductible under § 162(f). Otherwise, punitive damages are subject to general principles as to deductibility.

[78] The economic-pie theory of income has its defenders. *See* Alvin Warren, *Would a Consumption Tax Be Fairer than an Income Tax?*, 89 Yale L.J. 1081 (1980) (defending the income tax). But the pie theory seems fundamentally incompatible with the notion of a personal individual income tax. *See* Robert E. Hall & Alvin Rabushka, *The Flat Tax* 55–60, 70–73 (2d ed. 1995) (proposing a system under which individuals would be taxed only on wages on the theory that all investment returns of individuals would be taxed elsewhere under a proposed separate business profits tax).

[79] The autonomy of tax relative to business accounting was made explicit in Helvering v. Midland Mutual Life Insurance Co., 300 U.S. 216 (1937), and later in Thor Power Tool Co. v. Commissioner, 439 U.S. 522 (1979).

[80] Examples include not only *Kirby Lumber* (see Chapter 3 of *Tax Stories*) but also the many cases based on an analysis of the substance of a transaction, including, ironically, *Macomber* itself.

[81] Thus, the Court in the *Glenshaw Glass* trilogy also declined the Seventh Circuit's invitation to embrace an "ability to pay" theory of income. *See* Commissioner v. Obear–Nester Glass Co., 217 F.2d 56, 60–61 (7th Cir.1954).

[82] *See* Richard A. Westin, *WG&L Tax Dictionary* 320 (2002) (stating that gross income "contemplates accretions to wealth after deducting costs of goods sold and basis of property transferred away . . . unless the accretion is excluded by a specific Code section or a judicial or administrative rule. § 61 and . . . *Glenshaw Glass* . . . are the bedrock authorities in this area.").

2. *Relationship of Statutory "Gross Income" to Sixteenth Amendment*
   "Income"

The Court in the *Glenshaw Glass* trilogy did not expressly endorse
the government's initial suggestion that the statutory reach of § 22(a) of
the 1939 Code was broader than the Sixteenth Amendment concept of
"income." But neither did the Court reject such a notion. Instead, it
coyly stated that the statutory language "exerted the full measure of the
taxing power" of Congress (from whatever source such power derived).
Taken literally, this statement leaves open the possibility that *statutory*
gross income *might* include items not considered to be income within the
meaning of the Sixteenth Amendment. Nevertheless, the facts of the
Glenshaw Glass trilogy allowed the Court to avoid this constitutional
issue. Thus, assuming *arguendo* that the congressional power is limited
to "income" as used in the Sixteenth Amendment, the economic gains at
issue in the *Glenshaw Glass* trilogy comfortably fit within the concept of
income.

The Court brushed aside the *Macomber* definition as follows:

> In that context—distinguishing gain from capital—the definition
> served a useful purpose. But it was not meant to provide a touch-
> stone to all future gross income questions. [Cites to *Bruun* and
> *Kirby Lumber* omitted.]

The Court was being respectful to the memory of *Macomber*, which had
largely been rendered obsolete by *Bruun*.[83] The only aspect of the
definition crucial to the *Macomber* decision itself was the phrase "gain
derived from capital" (emphasis added), implying that gain was something "separate from" capital. Since the facts of *Macomber did* involve
capital, and since there was no discussion in *Macomber* of situations *not*
involving capital or labor, the most that can be said about *Macomber* as a
matter of "case analysis" is that it left open the issue presented by the
Glenshaw Glass trilogy.

Still, the statement in *Glenshaw-Goldman* that Congress in § 22(a)
exerted "the full measure of its taxing power" has proved troublesome.
The phrase was coined in *Helvering v. Clifford*,[84] and the full statement
there was, *"The broad sweep of this language indicates the purpose of*
Congress to use the full measure of its taxing power *within those*
definable categories." (Emphasis added.) *Clifford* was an "income attribution" case that adopted a substance-over-form approach to property
ownership for income tax purposes. The *Clifford* statement was followed

---

[83] See the discussion in the text paragraph following note 9. The Court has since
strongly hinted that "realization" is not a constitutional prerequisite of income. Cottage
Savings Ass'n v. Commissioner, 499 U.S. 554, 559 (1991).

[84] 309 U.S. 331, 334 (1940).

by a cite to *Helvering v. Midland Mutual Life Insurance Co.*,[85] which found "interest" income to exist for tax purposes in a situation where interest was neither received in cash nor accrued on the taxpayer's books. Thus, the phrase originally appears to have had nothing to do with the constitutional scope or source of the taxing power but was merely a maxim of statutory construction, derived from the sweeping language of the gross income statute to construe the various phrases within it broadly. For example, "dividends" would include any kind of economic benefit transferred by a corporation to a shareholder on account of stock ownership, whether in cash or in-kind and whether or not treated as a "dividend" on the corporation's books.

The Court seems to have gradually abandoned the use of this "full measure of its taxing power" phrase.[86] The problem is that the phrase wrongly implies that *statutory* gross income under current § 61(a) is *already* as broad as the constitutional taxing power can extend, so that Congress has no power to expand the statutory reach of income beyond its present bounds. But Congress has in the past extended the scope of gross income beyond existing bounds, notably in overturning the result of *Gould* as to alimony and stretching (or overriding) "realization" in several instances (such as in taxing original issue discount as it accrues, in passing the net income of entities through to equity-holders, and taxing unrealized gains on certain investments). And there is little doubt that Congress could constitutionally repeal the existing statutory exclusions, including the exclusion for gifts and bequests received, as well as any of the judge-made exclusions (since codified) that arose in the early days of the income tax.[87]

3. *The Roles of Courts, Congress, and the Executive*

Glenshaw-Goldman has had an impact on the respective competencies of Congress, the courts (particularly the Supreme Court), and the Executive in interpreting tax statutes.[88] Unfortunately, the majority

---

[85] 300 U.S. 216, 223 (1937).

[86] A computer search of the January 1, 1955—April 1, 2002 period shows that the phrase was used by the Supreme Court only in United States v. Burke, 504 U.S. 229, 233 (1992), Commissioner v. Kowalski, 434 U.S. 77, 82–83 (1977), and James v. United States, 366 U.S. 213, 218–19 (1961). In *Burke* the phrase was neutered: "Congress intended . . . to exert the full measure of its taxing power, and to bring within the definition of income 'any accession to wealth.'" The phrase is notably absent from O'Gilvie v. United States, 519 U.S. 79 (1996), dealing with the inclusion of punitive damages with respect to personal injury recoveries.

[87] In 1996, Congress contracted the scope of § 104, rendering taxable compensatory damages arising from non-physical personal injuries, such as libel and alienation of affections, which in the early days of the income tax (*see* note 33) were held to be excludable under "no economic gain" and "replacement of capital" theories.

[88] These issues were not raised in *American General Investors*, where the lower courts had held for the government.

opinion in *Glenshaw-Goldman* tended to conflate what are, analytically, separate issues, but the conflation was understandable given that the same facts made this "complex" of issues easy to resolve on the merits.

A. The 1954 Legislative History

The majority opinion in *Glenshaw-Goldman* stated that the 1954 legislative history referring to the "reiteration" of the "all-inclusive" nature of gross income favored the government's position. However, the Court did not make any note of the fact, mentioned in the government's 1955 Supplemental Memorandum, that the House Ways and Means Committee in its 1954 revision of the Tax Code deleted a recommendation by the staff of the Joint Committee on Internal Revenue Taxation to permanently exclude punitive damages. The government said that this action was taken so that the matter could be studied further, suggesting that the 1954 Congress was neutral on the merits of the issue.

In their petition for rehearing, Glenshaw Glass Co. and Goldman Theaters made the claim, based on a communication with a member of the Joint Committee staff, that the decision faced by the Ways and Means Committee was "either to codify or change existing law," implying that "existing law" contained an exclusion for punitive damages. The staff member stated that the Ways and Means Committee deleted the provision excluding punitive damages "in order to avoid the implication that Congress thereby intended to tax such damages." The petition for rehearing was denied without opinion.[89]

The Court correctly ignored this spurious "history." The source was a staff member of the Joint Committee, not even a member of Congress. The House Ways and Means Committee, the Senate Finance Committee, and the House–Senate Conference Committee are deliberative bodies that create legislative history through actions taken and committee reports, not through what some individual member of the Committee might have thought about some issue that it failed to act upon. Here the action actually taken was a rejection of a proffered exclusion for punitive damages, and the only official reason given was that referring to "further study." The obvious implication was that Congress, if it intended anything, intended that the punitive damages issue be resolved by the courts. On its face, it seems fanciful to assert that the action of deleting an exclusion for punitive damages was Congress' way of confirming an exclusionary rule.

Some argue that even "official" legislative history, such as Committee Reports, should be given little weight in interpreting statutes, except perhaps to construe a statutory provision that is ambiguous on its face.[90]

---

[89] 348 U.S. 426, *reh'g denied*, 349 U.S. 925 (1955).

[90] A brief discussion of the pros and cons of using legislative history is found in Abner J. Mikva & Eric Lane, *An Introduction to Statutory Interpretation and the Legislative*

The catch-all phrase in the gross income statute may be described as being "general" or "open-ended," which is arguably not the same as being "ambiguous." Open-endedness suggests language that can be adapted by courts to changing circumstances (in this case, evolving concepts of income), in which case legislative history bearing on "intent" would be discounted.[91]

To one willing to grant a significant role to legislative history in interpreting an open-ended statutory phrase such as "income," the fact that the only "specific" legislative history on the punitive damages issue dated from 1954, not 1913 or 1939, raised a problem: the "history" post-dated the taxable years at issue. This observation raises a separation-of-powers concern: Congressional committees should not be allowed to become "shadow" Supreme Courts that create law in committee reports by expressing approval or disapproval of prior judicial decisions, especially decisions of lower courts. Simply put, the 1954 Congress is not the proper body to determine what the 1939 (or 1913) Congress intended by using a particular word or phrase. In fact, the Supreme Court, in a 1996 case holding punitive damages from personal injury to be taxable, explicitly rejected the notion that a later Congress could impute intent to an earlier one.[92] It is Congress' role to legislate by enacting statutes, and it is the courts' role to decide cases and controversies. The Supreme Court's function in particular is to review the decisions of lower courts, and Congress, short of legislating, should not impede that role.

Although the Supreme Court could have held the 1954 legislative history to be irrelevant, it nevertheless did cite at least the language in committee reports to the effect that § 61(a) of the 1954 Code was intended to be as broad as § 22(a) of the 1939 Code. Although this passage has to be considered *dictum*, the Court must have uttered it for a purpose, and presumably that purpose was to announce to the world that § 61(a) of the 1954 Code would be construed as broadly as the Court was now construing § 22(a) of the 1939 Code. This move foreclosed the re-litigation of settled issues.

B.   The Congressional Re–Enactment Doctrine

Since Congress did not "re-enact" (in substance) § 22(a) of the 1939 Code as it had been construed in 1940 by the Board of Tax Appeals in *Highland Farms* (holding punitive damages to be excludable) until 1954, which was subsequent to the taxable years in question, the so-called "re-enactment doctrine" actually would have been raised by the facts of the

---

Process, 27–41, 50–54 (1997). In general, the use of Committee Reports in interpreting federal tax statutes has long been accepted practice.

[91] *See* Kent Greenawalt, *Statutory Interpretation: 20 Questions* 228 (1999).

[92] *See* O'Gilvie v. United States, 519 U.S. 79, 90 (1996) ("[I]n any event, the view of a later Congress cannot control the interpretation of an earlier enacted statute.").

Glenshaw Glass trilogy only if one "counted" the 1939 codification to have ratified the holding of the *Central Railroad* case, decided in 1935 and involving damages for breach of fiduciary duty rather than punitive damages. But the taxpayers in their briefs seemed to have focused more on the long period from 1935 to 1955, emphasizing the 1940 *Highland Farms* "on point" decision rather than on the 1939 re-codification and the not-quite-on-point *Central Railroad* decision.

In any event, the re-enactment doctrine is a maxim of statutory interpretation to the effect that the re-enactment of a statute carries with it existing judicial gloss, at least in some circumstances. The circumstances to be considered include: (1) the "authority" of the judicial interpretation, (2) the "settledness" of the interpretation, (3) whether Congress had the interpretation before it, and (4) the reliance interests in the interpretation.[93] Here the Supreme Court, in summarily refusing to apply the re-enactment doctrine, only commented on factors (2) and (3), stating that the Service did not acquiesce in *Highland Farms* and that there was not the "slightest affirmative indication that Congress had the *Highland Farms* decision in front of it."[94] The Court restrained itself from noting that the Board of Tax Appeals was the lowest court on the totem pole and that the reasoning in *Highland Farms* was summary and conclusory.[95] Perhaps it was implicit that there could be little reliance on an unreasoned and unappealed decision of a trial court that the Service announced would not be followed. The Court did not comment on the reliance interest, but it is hard to see how "reliance" would apply to "windfalls."

C.   Congressional Acquiescence in *Highland Farms*

The taxpayers appeared to argue that mere congressional *acquiescence* in *Highland Farms* (and *Central Railroad*) itself produced a gloss on the statute. The concept of a "Congressional acquiescence in judicial construction" doctrine does not make much sense.[96] If the Supreme

---

[93] *See* Helvering v. Griffiths, 318 U.S. 371 (1943) (holding, in a case where all four factors were present, that Congress intended a statute dealing with stock dividends to incorporate the "rule" of *Macomber*).

[94] This statement appears to be incorrect as to the 1954 Congress because the Ways and Means Committee seems to have been quite aware of not only *Highland Farms* but also of the various cases then in the courts.

[95] Although the Board of Tax Appeals (and later the Tax Court) are low on the organizational chart of the court system, there would have been some awkwardness in pointing this out, since around the time of *Highland Farms* the Supreme Court was paying a high degree of deference to these courts as to matters of "tax accounting." *See* Dobson v. Commissioner, 320 U.S. 489 (1943). But this doctrine was overturned by Congress in 1948 in what is now § 7482(a).

[96] In Arkansas Best Corp. v. Commissioner, 485 U.S. 212, n. 5 (1988), the Court stated that "[a]lthough congressional inaction is generally a poor measure of congressional intent, we are given some pause by the fact that over 25 years have passed since [a prior Supreme

Court has construed a statute, that construction prevails without imputing any later intent of Congress to ratify it.[97] The same analysis would hold if many lower courts have construed the statute in a uniform fashion. If the lower courts are divided, non-action by Congress cannot mean anything, as it is a prime function of the Supreme Court to decide such conflicts.[98] That leaves only the situation where authority in the lower courts is "scant," and here the claim of congressional acquiescence can plausibly be made only if the scant authority has been "outstanding" for a considerable period of time. On the one hand, decisions of lower courts always can be upset by higher courts. On the other hand, a higher court might decide to allow a dubious lower court decision to stand if the court perceives that reasonable reliance interests outweigh "correctness." But even here it is hard to see what the idea of *congressional* acquiescence adds to the analysis. Congress does not legislate by declining to overturn decisions of courts. About the only exception might be where Congress actively considered and rejected an amendment to the statute aimed to overturn the result of a particular case.[99] In any event, even if there were such a doctrine as congressional acquiescence, the factors supporting the non-applicability of the re-enactment doctrine would weigh decisively here as well.

D.   Consistent Administrative Construction

The Court in the *Glenshaw Glass* trilogy was far more interested in the government's administrative practice relative to punitive damages than in the *Highland Farms* or *Central Railroad* decisions.[100] This is not surprising, as the concepts of congressional re-enactment and acquiescence possess greater vitality in relation to interpretation of statutes by administrative agencies (here the Service and the Treasury Department)

Court decision], without any sign of disfavor by Congress." The pause was only momentary, and the decision proceeded to virtually overrule the prior decision.

[97] The Supreme Court can overrule or cut back on its own prior decisions. *See* Arkansas Best Corp. v. Commissioner, 485 U.S. 212 (1988); James v. United States, 366 U.S. 213 (1961).

[98] *See* O'Gilvie v. United States, 519 U.S. 79, 89–90 (1996) (construing 1989 statutory provision including punitive damages with respect to nonphysical personal injuries as not constraining the courts from deciding on the includability of punitive damages with respect to physical personal injuries; also stating that the 1989 Congress, by non-action or implication from an enacted statute, cannot interpret an earlier-enacted statute).

[99] *Cf.* American Automobile Ass'n v. United States, 367 U.S. 687, 694–95 (1961) (Congress' repeal of a statute overturning the result of a prior Supreme Court decision lends support to the prior decision).

[100] The Court requested the memorandum referred to in the text at *supra* note 37. In effect, the government was asked to prove (*ex parte*) a "fact" not otherwise in the record. The high point of deference to administrative practice is, perhaps, United States v. Correll, 389 U.S. 299 (1967), where the Supreme Court, in sanctioning the "sleep or rest" rule long followed by the Service in disallowing certain meal and lodging expenses, explicitly invoked the notions of congressional re-enactment and acquiescence.

than by courts. After all, such agencies derive their rule-making power from Congress in the first place.[101] Congress is not invading the turf of the judiciary by approving or disapproving, expressly or by implication, administrative interpretations of statutes.[102] At the same time, in applying these doctrines, the courts become the referees between the Congress and the Executive. To the extent that courts treat congressional re-enactment or acquiescence as being implicit approval of administrative agency rulemaking, the courts ironically are allowing the Executive to stake out turf at the expense of Congress. The Executive is even "allowed" to "create" pro-taxpayer "law in action" by construing statutory provisions in favor of the taxpayer or by simply refusing to enforce the statute in certain situations.[103] But all of this is, yet again, another story.

E.   Accommodating Non–Tax Policy

The Supreme Court in the *Glenshaw Glass* trilogy simply ignored the arguments made by taxpayers and *amicus curiae* to construe the tax statute in a way that would accommodate what they perceived to be appropriate non-tax policy, in this case under the federal antitrust and securities laws. Although the taxability of the damages at issue might affect non-tax behavior, the extent of this influence would only have been speculative, and it was far from clear that non-tax policy would have been furthered or hindered.[104] The interaction of tax rules with non-tax policy is for legislatures to work out. Legislatures have more tools to use; tax rules are only one such tool.

The Continuing Importance of *Glenshaw Glass* Today

The *Glenshaw Glass* trilogy displayed appropriate judicial restraint by not unduly stirring up settled doctrinal sediment or opining on doctrinal issues that might arise in the future.

---

[101] *See* § 7805(a) (granting authority to the Treasury Department to issue "rules and regulations").

[102] Cases in which administrative practice undermined the government's position include Commissioner v. Estate of Hubert, 520 U.S. 93, 103 (1997), and Commissioner v. Brown, 380 U.S. 563 (1965).

[103] *See, e.g.,* Haverly v. United States, 513 F.2d 224 (7th Cir.1975) (noting Service's policy of generally not taxing free samples); Merians v. Commissioner, 60 T.C. 187 (1973) (reviewed) (acq.) (noting Service's pro-taxpayer stretching of § 212(3)); Rev. Proc. 2000–30, 2000–2 C.B. 13 (*de minimis* in-kind interest not reportable).

[104] Thus, allowing treble damages is undoubtedly an inducement to private law suits to enforce the antitrust laws, but the inducement is not infinite, and there is no reason for a court to assume that Congress wanted "more" rather than "less" of an incentive. *See* O'Gilvie v. United States, 519 U.S. 79, 88–89 (1996) (making similar point that congressional generosity in excluding compensatory damages with respect to personal injury does not imply that the exclusion should be extended to punitive damages).

1. *Effect on Prior Precedents*

One issue is whether the *Glenshaw Glass* trilogy implicitly overruled such prior cases won by the taxpayer as *Gould, Cuba Railroad,* and *Supplee-Biddle Hardware.* Except for a brief statement in the *General American Investors* opinion stating that recoveries of insider profits were not "contributions to capital," these cases were simply ignored, and no attempt was made to even distinguish them.

The *Glenshaw Glass* trilogy thus has stripped these cases of any precedential value relating to the scope of statutory gross income for individuals. As the actual "fact" holdings of these cases have been codified, the issue of their overruling is moot, at least until the codifications are repealed.

2. *Economic Gain v. Tax Gain*

From 1913 until well after the *Glenshaw Glass* trilogy was decided, the Service conceded that recoveries with respect to the loss of "personal" type rights and attributes did not produce gross income on the theory that the transaction as a whole did not produce economic gain, i.e., that the cash recovery was offset by an equivalent loss of value.[105] Does this doctrine remain viable? It was not directly addressed in the *Glenshaw Glass* trilogy because the taxpayers there got something for nothing. Nevertheless, the expression "accession to wealth" connotes economic gain, not gain in any specialized sense, so it is at least conceivable that the *Glenshaw Glass* trilogy does not undermine the "no economic gain" doctrine. But the no-gain doctrine may no longer be viable for two reasons.

First, to the extent that recoveries for the loss of personal attributes were viewed as exempt because they are non-recurring or not derived from capital or labor of the taxpayer, that theory has been laid to rest by the *Glenshaw Glass* trilogy.

Second, it was settled as early as 1918 that, in the case of property dispositions for consideration, the idea of "capital" in the tax sense (to be subtracted from the value of what was received) was not the value of the property given up but the "investment," i.e., basis (or if greater, 1913 value).[106] And, in the case of compensatory damages (or insurance recoveries) arising in commerce, the accepted approach has been to determine what the compensation is "for." If the compensation is for lost, stolen, or destroyed assets, the recovery is "offset" by the taxpayer's adjusted basis in the lost, stolen, or destroyed assets.[107] In other

---

[105] *See* Rev. Rul. 69–212, 1969–1 C.B. 34; Rev. Rul. 55–132, 1955–1 C.B. 21. The source of the doctrine was Sol. Op. 132, I–1 C.B. 92.

[106] *See* Doyle v. Mitchell Bros. Co., 247 U.S. 179 (1918).

[107] The most-cited case on this point is Raytheon Production Corp. v. Commissioner, 144 F.2d 110 (1st Cir.), *cert. denied,* 323 U.S. 779 (1944). If the taxpayer deducted the basis

words, in cases involving the disposition of property, the gain or loss taken into account is not "economic" gain or loss but gain or loss in the tax sense. The problem with recoveries for the loss of personal attributes is that no basis exists in them.[108] Otherwise, wages would not be income because what the wage-earner gives up *in terms of value* is equal to the wages received

Bowers v. Kerbaugh–Empire Co.[109] also might have been viewed as supporting the no-gain approach because that case held that a loss suffered with respect to borrowed cash could offset the gain with respect to reducing a liability. But *Kerbaugh-Empire* involved a loan transaction, and in any event, it is now considered to be a dead letter.[110]

It is sometimes argued that some personal injury recoveries are a "substitute" for untaxed benefits associated with carrying on a normal life. This argument, however, misconceives the "nature of the receipt" concept, which only goes so far as to determine whether the receipt is of the type to warrant a basis offset or comes within some acknowledged exclusion (broadly viewed).[111] The doctrine does not extend to viewing a cash receipt as counting for nothing.[112] The prototype of gross income is (again) wages, which are precisely derived from the conversion of personal attributes to cash.[113]

The point is only that the no-gain approach is no longer a valid basis for *the Service or a court* to exclude recoveries for the loss of personal attributes. That is not to say that a statutory exclusion for personal injury recoveries would have no rational basis, but that is for Congress to decide. The issue of whether such recoveries are encompassed by the catch-all gross income provision long has been masked by the broad constraint of § 104 (which dates from 1918) to exclude all recoveries

---

in a prior year, and the loss reduced taxable income, the adjusted basis would be zero. *See* § 1016(a); Dobson v. Commissioner, 320 U.S. 489 (1943).

[108] It might be said that personal attributes are not generally "transferable," but that only goes to the "sale or exchange" issue for capital gain purposes.

[109] 271 U.S. 170 (1926).

[110] *See* Vukasovich, Inc. v. Commissioner, 790 F.2d 1409 (9th Cir.1986); *cf.* Lynch v. Hornby, 247 U.S. 339 (1918) (Congress has the power to tax cash dividends notwithstanding possible offsetting decline in value of the stock).

[111] *See* Rev. Rul. 67–221, 1967–2 C.B. 63 (property received by wife on divorce was tax-free and obtains basis equal to value on receipt, presumably because the property was in lieu of tax-free support, gifts, and inheritance rights).

[112] In O'Gilvie v. United States, 519 U.S. 79, 86 (1996), Justice Breyer, writing for the majority, mentioned this notion as a possible rational basis for a statutory exclusion but not as justifying a judge-made exclusion.

[113] *See* United States v. Garber, 589 F.2d 843 (5th Cir.) (cash derived from sale of blood was income), *rev'd on other grounds*, 607 F.2d 92 (5th Cir.1979).

with respect to "tort-type" injuries.[114] However, § 104 was amended in the late 1990s to apply only to *compensatory* damages for *physical* personal injuries. Thus, non-excluded recoveries must now be considered to be gross income.

3. *In-Kind Property Income*

The "accession to wealth" idea commands the notion that in-kind property receipts are gross income (unless otherwise excluded). But this point had been incorporated into tax jurisprudence as early as 1918.[115] Shortly after the *Glenshaw Glass* trilogy, Treasury issued a regulation stating that income is includable in whatever form received, including property,[116] and another regulation specifically states that "treasure trove" is gross income when reduced to undisputed possession.[117]

4. *Realization of Gross Income*

The concept of "realization" is confirmed by way of dictum in the *Glenshaw Glass* trilogy, but the content of the concept is not specified. In some situations, the receipt of in-kind property raises the issue of "realization" *of gross income* (as distinguished from realization *of gain*). For example, in the treasure trove regulation, realization occurs when the item is reduced to "undisputed possession" (whatever that means). The *Macomber* concept of realization of income ("severance" from the capital) was overturned by *Bruun*. Yet there is a thread of realization-of-income jurisprudence that continues to possess vitality. The Supreme Court has held that the receipt of property rights whose value is so "contingent" on future conditions and circumstances that such value cannot reasonably be ascertained is not realized until valuation becomes reasonably possible.[118] These situations are typically dealt with by statute.[119]

---

[114] *See, e.g.*, Roemer v. Commissioner, 716 F.2d 693 (9th Cir.1983) (also noting that in the absence of § 104 such recoveries would probably be taxed). This expansive construction of § 104 was limited by the Supreme Court in Commissioner v. Schleier, 515 U.S. 323 (1995), which held that compensation for age discrimination was not "on account of" personal injury, and in O'Gilvie v. United States, 519 U.S. 79 (1996), holding that punitive damages were generically not "on account of" personal injuries.

[115] *See* Peabody v. Eisner, 247 U.S. 347 (1918) (dividend in form of stock of another corporation). The in-kind nature of stock dividends did not give the Court any pause in *Macomber*.

[116] Reg. § 1.61–1(a)(1) (1958).

[117] Reg. § 1.61–14 (1960), in effect "codifying" Rev. Rul. 53–61, 1953–1 C.B. 17.

[118] *See* Reg. § 1.61–4(a) (crop shares not realized until reduced to cash); Commissioner v. Lo Bue, 352 U.S. 859 (1956) (employee stock options not realized income to employee at time granted); M.E. Blatt Co. v. United States, 305 U.S. 267 (1938) (lessee improvements not realized income to lessor as of time of construction); *cf.* Burnet v. Logan, 283 U.S. 404 (1931) (sale for contingent consideration results in delayed realization of gain).

[119] *See* §§ 83(a) & (e)(3) (stock options) and 109 (lessee improvements). *See generally* Joseph M. Dodge, *Accessions to Wealth, Realization of Gross Income, and Dominion and*

5. *In-Kind Consumption*

The "accession to wealth" idea advanced in the *Glenshaw Glass* trilogy does not say anything about whether in-kind consumption is gross income. This omission was wise because in-kind consumption is the most problematic area within the gross income realm.

Turning first to theory, the Haig–Simons "definition" of income (net increases in wealth plus consumption) is ambiguous. Algebraically, there are two different ways of arriving at net increases in wealth plus consumption. One is to aggregate gross increases in wealth, then subtract all decreases in wealth (including consumption spending), and then add back all consumption obtained (whether purchased or obtained for free). The other way is to again start with gross increases in wealth but then subtract that amount which represents gross decreases in wealth *other than costs* of consumption.[120] Under the second approach, the idea of "consumption" is not a principle of gross income inclusion but rather a principle of the non-deductibility of consumption spending.

The Code and regulations embody this ambivalence. Generally speaking, under the Code personal consumption is taxed by disallowing deductions for consumption spending.[121] On the other hand, consumption-type employee fringe benefits are included in gross income (unless expressly excluded), and consumption-type benefits are encompassed within such terms as "dividends," "interest," "rents," and so on. Moreover, the regulations have stated that gross income generally includes "services" and such consumption items as (free) "meals" and "accommodations," at least where the services, etc., are received beyond the realms of family, friends, and government (in which cases they may be excluded as "gifts" or "support"). On the other hand, certain categories of in-kind consumption benefits are ignored, such as imputed income from self-owned consumer assets and from self-provided services,[122] the value of self-constructed assets,[123] the enjoyment of so-called "public goods" (where the use by one person does not preclude the use by others), and the value of various benefits one might obtain as a by-product of commercial activity (discussed below).

Control: Applying the "Claim of Right Doctrine" to Found Objects, Including Record–Setting Baseballs, 4 Fla. Tax Rev. 685 (2000) (distinguishing non-realization situation from situation where item received is subject to possible forfeiture condition).

[120] For the mathematically challenged: (increases in wealth - decreases in wealth) + consumption = increases in wealth - (decreases in wealth - consumption decreases in wealth).

[121] *See* §§ 162(a), 165(c), 167(a), 212(1) & (2), and 262.

[122] *See* Helvering v. Independent Life Ins. Co., 292 U.S. 371, 379 (1934) (*dictum* that imputed income is beyond the power of Congress to tax).

[123] *See* Morris v. Commissioner, 9 B.T.A. 1273 (1928) (acq.) (self-grown crops).

Some commentators claim that these "exclusions" are "only" made out of administrative necessity, but a "theory" that fits so imperfectly with "practice" leaves a lot to be desired.[124] In any event, as an empirical generalization, it appears that *includable* in-kind consumption items are those (1) that essentially can be presumed to manifest free spending choices on the part of the taxpayer, and/or (2) that, if excluded, would have the potential to seriously undermine the tax base. What these categories have in common is that they derive from commercial bargains (such as barter exchanges of services) or ongoing commercial relationships (such as between employer and employee).

6. *Dominion and Control*

Since the taxpayers in *Glenshaw-Goldman did* possess dominion and control of the money received, it cannot be claimed that the decision in that case *holds* that dominion and control is a prerequisite of having gross income. With two exceptions, it appears that the dominion-and-control concept has "made a difference" only in income attribution cases. One exception is a 1938 case in which the absence of dominion and control was perhaps a factor indicating that realization had not occurred.[125] The other exception is *Commissioner v. Indianapolis Power and Light Co.*,[126] but there the notion was invoked inappropriately. The case involved the issue of whether a cash deposit received by a utility company (and not put in escrow or trust) was a true borrowing. (An arms-length borrowing is excludable because the offsetting liability precludes an increase in wealth.) An alternative explanation of *Indianapolis Power & Light* is that the deposits were not "realized" as income until an event occurred that cancelled the taxpayer's obligation to repay the deposit. In short, the relevance (if any) and content of "dominion and control" outside of the income-attribution context is not clear, except perhaps that it overlaps with the realization-of-income notion.

---

[124] The notion that the value of consumption in-kind is "always" income derives from the Utilitarian tradition, where "utility" (satisfactions) is the "real" unit of income. But there is no more reason to "swallow whole" a philosophy-derived theory of income than there is to do so with any other "external-to-tax" theory. The history of tax theory is towards its autonomy relative to other disciplines.

[125] In *Blatt, supra* note 118, the Service claimed that a lessor had gross income at the time the lessee added improvements on the lessor's building. Obviously, the improvements were then under the dominion and control of the lessee, not the lessor. The lessor's position was somewhat equivalent to that of a contingent remainder following a term interest. But it was established shortly before the *Glenshaw Glass* trilogy that income could take the form of a present, and non-contingent, right to future cash or property. *See* United States v. Drescher, 179 F.2d 863 (2d Cir.1950). What ultimately defeated the Service in *Blatt* was that its right to future possession, and the then-value thereof, was highly contingent. The possessory and value contingencies in this type of case are resolved upon termination of the lease, and this was the situation presented in *Bruun*, where the government prevailed, see text paragraph following *supra* note 9.

[126] 493 U.S. 203 (1990).

The absence of dominion and control was cited "as a factor" favoring the taxpayer in *United States v. Gotcher*,[127] in which it was held that an expense-paid recruiting trip provided by a car manufacturer to a potential dealer was not gross income.[128] A similar strand earlier had emerged in the employee fringe benefit area, where it was called the "convenience of the employer" doctrine, but that doctrine since has been fully superseded by a comprehensive statutory scheme dealing with fringe benefits.[129] Although it is hard to pinpoint the precise rationale, a court may be willing to exclude an item that clearly is beneficial to the recipient where the provider possesses (1) a dominant purpose to benefit itself, and not the recipient, and (2) control over how the benefit is provided.[130] But why should these factors matter, if the item produces an acknowledged economic benefit to the recipient?

A prominent strain in the tax theory literature attempts to justify an exclusionary rule here on the basis of doubts about whether the recipient really "enjoyed" the benefit that was beyond her control.[131] However, this argument is not persuasive *in this context* because these benefits (as contrasted, for example, with the provision of tools and facilities to enable one to perform her job) are specifically designed to appeal to the recipient. Otherwise, the benefits would be ineffective to achieve the provider's goal. As a result, the acceptance of the benefit is, from a utility-based perspective, a sufficient basis for preferring a rule of includability to one of excludability. But it may be that the benefit should be excluded where: (1) the benefit did not in fact represent a free spending choice by the beneficiary, and (2) an exclusionary rule would not be susceptible to abuse given the absence of an ongoing relationship between the parties. Both the free-spending-choice and erosion-of-the tax base concepts hold that in-kind consumption should be taxed when it can be considered a substitute for, or an altered form of, an accession to wealth. Both of these factors (as compared to the taxpayer's utility) are "objective" and capable of application by judges. Unfortunately, judges

---

[127] 401 F.2d 118 (5th Cir.1968).

[128] On the other hand, the value of the trip provided the potential dealer's wife was included in the potential *dealer's* gross income, not the gross income of the wife.

[129] *See* Commissioner v. Kowalski, 434 U.S. 77 (1977); H. R. Rep. No. 98–432, 98th Cong., 1st Sess. 285–305 (1983).

[130] *Compare* Hornung v. Commissioner, 47 T.C. 428 (1967) (football star's rent-free use of auto provided by Ford Motor Co. for promotional purposes was income; taxpayer had unfettered use of car for personal use).

[131] *See, e.g.,* Moss v. Commissioner, 758 F.2d 211 (7th Cir.) (Posner, J.) (agonizing over deductibility of law firm lunch), *cert. denied,* 474 U.S. 979 (1985); H. Simons, *supra* note 65, at 122–24.

have often rested excludability on the provider's general "business purpose," without delving into the factors just noted.[132]

Although the proper status of in-kind consumption under the income concept may be somewhat murky as a matter of theory, the "law" has mostly been worked out by Congress, the Treasury, and the lower courts. The Supreme Court has been able to avoid having to squarely face this problem. The closest it came was in *Rudolph v. United States*,[133] which involved the issue of whether the value of an employer-paid convention in Manhattan was gross income. The Supreme Court held for inclusion on the basis of a factual finding below that the item was "compensation" and dismissed the writ of *certiorari* as having been improvidently granted. Thus, the Supreme Court has yet to decide under what circumstances a "freebie" is gross income when it is not compensation and does not fall within one of the enumerated gross income categories.

Conclusion

Although the Supreme Court decision in the case known in the tax literature as *Glenshaw Glass* did not create waves at the time it was decided, it is now recognized as a classic for setting tax jurisprudence firmly on a modern footing. "Modern" means free of the clutter and distractions inherited from the nineteenth century and the early twentieth century. In the modern era, tax jurisprudence is autonomous from other disciplines, while being cognizant of them. "Modernity" in tax means that courts give primacy to the tax statute and due deference to the Executive in its rule-making function. Finally, modernity means that there is at least an over-arching concept, if not a full-blown theory, of income, as opposed to a definition.

---

[132] *See, e.g.*, Commissioner v. Riss, 374 F.2d 161 (8th Cir.1967); Challenge Mfg. Co. v. Commissioner, 37 T.C. 650 (1962). Business purpose (along with "not as compensation") should be viewed as only a threshold issue since business purpose does not lie in contradiction to the notion of personal benefit.

[133] 370 U.S. 269 (1962).

*

2

Marjorie E. Kornhauser

The Story of *Macomber*: The Continuing Legacy of Realization

Tax cases rarely make front-page news. On March 9, 1920, however, *Eisner v. Macomber*, decided the previous day by the United States Supreme Court, not only made *The New York Times'* front page but also dominated the headlines.[1] The case remained in the news for several weeks, but courts (including the Supreme Court), Congress, and commentators discussed it for decades. Although the case briefly plunged the financial market into disarray and inflamed contemporary criticism of judicial review, its primary influence has been in the tax field. From the time of its decision to the present, the case has generated voluminous litigation and shaped major aspects of the income tax, including the taxability of stock dividends (the transaction at issue in the case), corporate taxation generally, exchanges of property, the definition of income (Chapter 1 of *Tax Stories*), and the requirement that realization generally occur before taxation is imposed. The key to *Macomber's* continuing importance lies in its explication of realization, one of the most basic elements of taxation. The context in which the realization issue was raised, and the manner in which the Court resolved it, heightened the case's impact. The constitutional slant that the *Macomber* Court gave to the realization requirement inevitably made the case a reference point for years. By the time that requirement was (apparently) downgraded to mere administrative convenience, the case had already left its indelible mark. In terms of both its short and long term effects,

---

[1] 252 U.S. 189 (1920). There were, in fact, several articles on the front page. *See infra* notes 42–44 & 48–50 and accompanying text.

Macomber undeniably deserves its status as "one of the most celebrated cases in the annals of federal income taxation."[2]

Background

Realization is one of the most stable, and powerful, elements of an almost constantly changing income tax code. By deferring the tax consequences of gains and losses beyond the time of their economic occurrence, realization causes economic distortion, creates inequity among some taxpayers, generates much of the complexity of the tax law, and provides many opportunities for taxpayers to manipulate their tax status to achieve desirable tax consequences. For example, taxpayers can take tax deductions by realizing losses but defer income by delaying realization on appreciated assets. In this manner, realization bestows a tax advantage on certain types of income, which in turn creates economic distortions and leads to much of the tax law's complexity by requiring, for example, detailed accounting or timing rules and rules about capital gains taxation.[3]

An easy way to understand the concept of realization and the *Macomber* case is to think about the current stock market. During the past few years, investors in the stock market, especially technology stocks, have seen the value of their holdings rise and fall as much—and as precipitously—as the scariest roller coaster. A share of TotalTech stock, for example, that you bought for $50 two years ago might have gone up in value to $150 last year before plummeting to a current worth today of only $20. Being an optimist (or lazy), you have done nothing with the stock in these two years except keep the stock certificate in the bank vault. Nevertheless, you may have acted very differently when the stock was worth $150 a share than now when it is worth $20, and people

---

[2] Boris I. Bittker & James S Eustice, *Federal Income Taxation of Corporations and Shareholders* 8–85 (6th ed. 1998).

[3] Many excellent articles discuss realization. *See, e.g.,* Fred B. Brown, *"Complete" Accrual Taxation*, 33 San Diego L. Rev. 1559 (1996); Noel B. Cunningham & Deborah H. Schenk, *Taxation Without Realization: A "Revolutionary" Approach to Ownership*, 47 Tax. L. Rev. 725 (1992); Mary Louise Fellows, *A Comprehensive Attack on Tax Deferral*, 88 Mich. L. Rev. 722 (1990); Daniel Halperin, *Saving the Income Tax: An Agenda for Research*, 77 Tax Notes 967, 967 (1997); Stephen B. Land, *Defeating Deferral: A Proposal for Retrospective Taxation*, 52 Tax L. Rev. 45 (1996); Henry Ordower, *Revisiting Realization: Accretion Taxation, the Constitution,* Macomber, *and Mark to Market*, 13 Va. Tax Rev. 1 (1993); David M. Schizer, *Realization as Subsidy*, 73 N.Y.U. L. Rev. 1549, 1582 (1998); Daniel Shaviro, *An Efficiency Analysis of Realization and Recognition Rules under the Federal Income Tax*, 48 Tax L. Rev. 1 (1992); David A. Weisbach, *A Partial Mark-to-Market Tax System*, 53 Tax L. Rev. 95 (1999); Patricia D. White, *Realization, Recognition, Reconciliation, Rationality and the Structure of the Federal Income Tax System*, 88 Mich. L. Rev. 2034 (1990). Professor David Shakow has estimated that his proposal to repeal realization would reduce the relevance of thirty percent of tax cases. David J. Shakow, *Taxation Without Realization: A Proposal for Accrual Taxation*, 134 U. Pa. L. Rev. 1111, 1117 (1986). *See also* Steven S. Bank, *Mergers, Taxes, and Historical Realism*, 75 Tul. L. Rev. 1 (2000).

may have behaved very differently towards you. For example, when your stock was worth $150 a share, you might have wanted to borrow money to buy an expensive house or take a cruise, and a bank might have been willing to lend it to you. When your stock is worth only $20 a share, however, you may no longer have wanted to borrow the money, or the bank may no longer have been willing to lend it to you.

Although the value of your stock, your wealth, and possibly even your behavior have fluctuated during the two year period, have you had any income or loss from your stock ownership since all you have done with the stock is continue to own it? When the stock skyrocketed to $150 a share did you have $100 of income? When it decreased in value did you sustain a loss? Economists might give you different answers than the Internal Revenue Code.

As Chapter 1 of *Tax Stories* has shown, what is income from an economic perspective is not necessarily income for tax purposes. Most economists would say in the above instance that you in fact had both income and a loss as the price fluctuated. To understand this, you must understand the difference between wealth and income. Both are measurements. Wealth, however, measures value at a frozen moment in time, while income is a flow, a measurement over a period of time, which could be as short as a month, as long as a life-time, but most often is a year. More formally, income, under the classic Haig–Simons definition, is "the algebraic sum of (1) the market value of rights exercised in consumption and (2) the change in the value of the store of property rights between the beginning and end of the period in question."[4] From an economic perspective, then, income and loss occur when the value changes between the beginning and end of the period of time. In the example, therefore, the mere accretion of value of the stock from $50 to $150 would have been $100 of income last year, and the decrease in value this year to $20 would be a loss of $130.

The Internal Revenue Code, in contrast, generally holds that you had neither income nor loss because the requirement of "realization" had not been met. Although realization is a basic concept in our income tax laws, its exact parameters are hazy. The core idea, however, is that the mere increase (or decrease) in an asset's value is not enough to impose income tax consequences. Rather, some transaction, usually a market transaction, must occur which changes the taxpayer's relationship to the asset. So, for example, although you would have $100 of

---

[4] Henry Simons, *Personal Income Taxation* 50 (1938). Assume that the time period is one year and at the beginning of the year, your net worth is $10,000 and at the end of the year it is $16,000. Additionally, you spent $4,000 on food, rent, and other consumption items. The Haig–Simons definition of income says that you had $20,000 of income in that year. This is true regardless of whether the $6,000 increase in net worth occurred because you had placed $6,000 of salary in a money market account or because stock you owned was worth $10,000 at the beginning of the year and $16,000 at the end of the year.

economic income if your stock increased in value from $50 to $150 while you owned it, you would not have taxable income because there was no change in your relationship to the stock—that is, no realization. If, however, you had sold the stock when it was worth $150, the $100 of increased value would be realized and taxable income would have coincided with economic income.

In most situations, the Code makes realization a necessary, but not sufficient, condition to taxation. Recognition must also occur before tax liability results. Recognition is merely the technical term the Code gives to the decision that the transaction is an appropriate time to tax. Generally, recognition occurs at the same time as realization. Section 1001(a), for example, states that gain or loss is realized on the disposition of property, and § 1001(c) provides for recognition, or assignment of tax consequences, unless some other section further defers the gain or loss by providing for non-recognition. Sometimes recognition is delayed for non-tax purposes such as a desire to encourage certain business transactions, but sometimes it is also delayed because Congress was unsure whether realization had occurred. Even the existence of recognition, however, does not ensure taxability because some other code section may exclude the gain or loss permanently, such as § 121 on gain from the sale of a residence.

In contrast to the non-recognition or exclusion sections that defer gain or loss beyond realization, there are a few sections that do the opposite: abandon the requirement entirely and require taxation as the gain or loss actually occurs or accrues in the economic sense. This abandonment of realization generally occurs only when an easily valued asset is involved. Section 1256, for example, uses a pure accretion method of taxation and "marks to market" certain easily valued assets, such as regulated futures contracts, at the end of the taxpayer's taxable year.[5] Tax liability is then imposed on the increase or decrease in value in the same manner as if the taxpayer had sold the asset. The original issue discount rules also create taxability as interest accrues rather than when it is actually received. On a broader scale, some basic aspects of the Code ignore realization. Depreciation, for example, can be viewed as the allowance of unrealized losses to the extent that they represent a loss of value due to the passage of time. The structure for taxing partners and certain corporate shareholders also ignores realization at the individual level (but not the entity level) by taxing the owner on gains and losses sustained by the partnership or corporation even though the gain or loss is not distributed to the individual owner.

There are conceptual, historical, and practical reasons why our tax system generally requires realization before tax liability is imposed.

---

[5] *See also* §§ 467, 475, 817A, 1296, and the original discount rules.

Conceptually, especially in the early years of the income tax, there was disagreement as to whether there was income without realization. As long as money is still invested in an asset, it is still at risk and arguably the fact and amount of income are uncertain. For example, if Microsoft stock is currently selling for $72 per share, and you bought it at $60 per share, you indeed have a $12 increase in value. However, the stock may plummet in value next month and the entire $72 disappear while you own the stock. Consequently, any increases in value while you hold the stock are, allegedly, merely *paper gains* that may disappear. The Supreme Court's early pronouncement in *Macomber* that realization was a constitutional component of income gave added weight to this concept of income and ensured that realization played a large role in the development of the tax laws.

Even if there were no conceptual or historical reasons to require realization, there are practical ones. A system that taxes pure accretions in value rather than waiting until realization occurs has two major administrative problems. First, there is the valuation problem. Although some assets are easily valued because they are frequently traded on an established stock market, other assets have a less discernible value. Some stock is so infrequently traded that it may be impossible to determine its value—and hence any amount of gain—until it has been sold at a definite price to a willing buyer. Second, there is a liquidity problem. Even if the exact amount of increased value can be definitely determined, the taxpayer who holds the appreciated stock may have no money with which to pay a tax unless he sells the asset in question.

The practical and conceptual aspects of realization, broadly construed, point towards a consumption tax. Both valuation and liquidity issues totally disappear when an asset is converted into cash and consumed. More theoretically, if the basis of realization is the uncertainty of gain actually materializing until the funds are no longer subject to risk, then realization, taken to its extreme, requires no taxation until money is withdrawn from investment and used to purchase items of consumption. The concept of realization, then, is entwined ultimately in the basic question of what should be the tax base—income or consumption. Of course, using a lifetime cycle—and assuming all income is consumed in a lifetime—realization does not change the *amount* of income or loss, just the *timing*. Assume, for example, that the tax rate is always 10%, and a person's lifetime consists of three taxable cycles in which she earns $10,000 each cycle but consumes only $5,000 in the first two cycles and $20,000 in the third (the $10,000 she earned that cycle plus the $10,000 she had saved from the previous two). Under both an income tax (which taxes the money when earned) and a consumption tax (which taxes only the money spent), the taxpayer has a total of $3,000 of tax over her lifetime. The timing of that tax, however, differs. Under an income tax, she has a tax of $1,000 each year. Under a consumption tax, her tax liability is $500 for each of the first two cycles and $2,000 for the last one.

The timing of taxes, however, can make a tremendous difference. Realizing losses, but not gains, can decrease present tax, and deferring the realization of gains gives the taxpayer the free use of the money that would go to pay taxes. Moreover, delaying the tax until the future is advantageous because a future tax is only a possible tax whereas a current tax is an actuality. Congress, for example, may abolish or decrease the tax; the taxpayer may figure out how to avoid (or evade) the tax.

As important as the monetary consequences of realization are, they are not the only significant consequences of basing a system on a realization requirement. Realization throws up barriers to achieving four of the classic goals of a tax system: economic efficiency, certainty, simplicity, and equity. For example, realization distorts economic behavior by favoring investment in assets that appreciate without realization (real estate, for example) over assets whose profit is annually realized (bonds). It diminishes certainty of a tax by creating confusion as to when realization will occur. Simplicity is also lost as the law attempts to deal with all these issues. Finally, equity is disturbed since, among other things, two taxpayers with the same amount of economic gain will be taxed differently.

Since realization plays such a central role in both the practical and conceptual aspects of the tax laws, anyone who wants to understand the tax system should study *Macomber*. Although the case did not invent the concept of realization, it was the Supreme Court's first elaboration of its meaning. Its constitutional aspects guaranteed *Macomber* a prominent role in tax legislation and litigation for years. Since those years were formative years of the income tax, the case helped shape not only the actual law but also administrative practice and the ways people think about tax. As a result, over eighty years after its decision, *Macomber* still exerts a powerful, even if subterranean, influence on the United States tax system, despite the disappearance of its constitutional constraints. Understanding *Macomber*, therefore, is a gateway to understanding much that is basic to the current system.

Prior Proceedings

Although the basic issue involved in realization is simply one of timing, that is when is the income taxable, the question was complicated in *Macomber* by the facts of the case as well as contemporary conceptions of income, theories of corporations, and legal precedent. In 1916, Mrs.

Myrtle H. Macomber was a stockholder in the Standard Oil Company of California when it declared a dividend to each stockholder in the form of one share of stock for every two shares already owned. As a consequence, the outstanding shares of the corporation's stock increased by 50%, and Standard Oil, for financial purposes, transferred money from earned surplus to capital stock.[6] Mrs. Macomber, who owned 2,200 shares prior to the stock dividend, received 1,100 additional shares as a dividend, thus increasing her total number of shares to 3,300. This increase in the number of shares she owned, however, did not change her percentage of ownership of Standard Oil since every other shareholder also increased his or her shares of stock by the same 50%. Moreover, although she had a greater number of shares of stock, the total value of her stock had not changed.

Standard Oil could have done one of three things with its earnings for the year; at the time of the case, the tax treatment of two of the possibilities was clear. If Standard Oil had done nothing but retain all the profits in corporate solution, Mrs. Macomber would not have been taxed. If Standard Oil had paid a cash dividend, Mrs. Macomber would have been taxed because each income tax statute since the passage of the Sixteenth Amendment had included cash dividends in income. Only the treatment of stock dividends was uncertain. The first tax laws under the amendment were silent on the issue, and initially the Internal Revenue Bureau interpreted this silence to mean that stock dividends were not taxable. By the end of 1915, however, it reversed itself. The 1916 Act reflected this new position, and for the first time, the law clearly stated that income included stock dividends paid from post March 1, 1913 profits (the effective date of the original income tax).[7]

In 1917, pursuant to the new law, Mrs. Macomber included in her 1916 income tax return—and paid tax on—the $19,877 of stock dividends that represented the portion (18%) of the stock dividends made out of post February 1913 earnings and profits. She paid, however, under protest. On February 14, 1918, she filed an appeal with the Commissioner of Internal Revenue, who disallowed her appeal. She then filed suit in the United States District Court for the Southern District of New York, claiming that the provision of the 1916 Act taxing stock dividends was unconstitutional.[8]

The case proceeded through the courts with great speed. Six months after the complaint was filed, the district court issued a one line

---

[6] 252 U.S. 189, 200–01 (1920).

[7] In February 1915, the Commissioner had announced stock dividends were not taxable, and then reversed the decision in December of the same year. T.D. 2163, 17 Treas. Dec. Int. Rev 114, *rev'd*, T.D. 2274, 17 Treas. Dec. Int. Rev. 279 (1915).

[8] Complaint at 12 [in the microfiche version it is on page 7].

memorandum overruling the government's demurrer to dismiss the complaint for lack of a cause of action but giving it leave to answer.[9] Rather than answering, the United States filed an assignment of error on March 7, 1919, and one week later, attorneys for Mrs. Macomber, joined by the government, filed a motion to advance to the Supreme Court, stating that the constitutional issue involved—whether stock dividends were income under the Sixteenth Amendment—"directly affect[] the administration of the revenue, are of grave importance and we conceive it to be in the public interest that this case should be advanced."[10] Oral arguments occurred a month later on April 16, 1919, with re-arguments on October 17th and 20th. On March 8, 1920, only 1½ years after Mrs. Macomber originally filed suit, the Supreme Court announced its decision.

The Supreme Court Decision

The rapid progress of the case was only one sign of its importance. The voluminous debates by tax and financial experts, including the noted tax expert Professor Edwin R. A. Seligman of Columbia, was another.[11] Mrs. Macomber's legal team was a powerhouse. The once and future Supreme Court Justice Charles Hughes[12] represented her, and George Wickersham, the former United States Attorney General under President Taft, filed an *amicus* brief on her behalf. Certainly, the constitutional question concerning the scope of the Sixteenth Amendment was an important, perhaps even dominant, reason for the amount of attention the case received. The financial aspects no doubt played a role as well. Indeed, George Wickersham filed the *amicus* brief in support of Mrs. Macomber's position because the issue "vitally" affected the interests of many of his clients, wealthy individual taxpayers as well

---

[9] The Memorandum said in full, "Demurrer overruled on the authority of Towne v. Eisner, 245 U.S. 418. Memorandum at 16 [in the microfiche version it is on page 8]; *see also* Peabody v. Eisner, 247 U.S. 347." (1918).

[10] Defendant-in-Error's Motion to Advance, No. 914318, filed March 15, 1919 at 6–7.

[11] Seligman, the noted economist and tax expert, claimed that stock dividends were not income in an article submitted with the Defendant-in-Error's Brief, *Are Stock Dividends Income?*, 9 Am. Econ. Rev. 1 (1919).

Opinion as to both what the court should and would do was divided. Interestingly, the *New York Times* had conflicting statements in its March 9 edition. A front-page article believed that "a preponderance of opinion lately that the decision would be unfavorable [meaning taxable]." *New Stock Issue May Follow Ruling*, N.Y. Times, March 9, 1920, at 1. The editorial for that day, however, said that the Court's decision was expected. Editorial, *The Stock Dividend Decision*, N.Y. Times, March 9, 1920, at 10.

[12] Hughes, a former governor of New York, had been appointed by President Taft. Confirmed in late 1910, he resigned in 1916 in order to accept the Republican nomination for president. In 1930, President Hoover appointed him Chief Justice, a position he filled until July 1, 1941 when he resigned. 2 *Who Was Who in America* 391 (1950).

as corporations.[13] Moreover, since uncertainty about the taxability of stock dividends affected the willingness of corporations to issue them, the pending case was also a significant factor in the financial markets for at least six months prior to the decision.[14] The government, for its part, worried about the loss of revenue if stock dividends were held non-taxable and about possible tax evasion.[15] The unsettled state of the law made planning difficult for both the government and taxpayers. Consequently, a decision, whether for or against Mrs. Macomber, was desirable to make certain the tax consequences of stock dividends. This last factor may have influenced the date of the Court's decision, which was announced just one week before the 1919 tax returns were due.

The Briefs

The basic issue in the case was not whether the stock dividend made Mrs. Macomber richer. The government, despite some language to the contrary in both the briefs and the opinion, basically conceded that the declaration and payment of a dividend, whether in cash or stock, does not make a shareholder any richer than she was the moment before the dividend.[16] What was relevant, it said, was whether the taxpayer was richer than she had been at the beginning of the taxable period. If Standard Oil earned $10,000 of profit while Mrs. Macomber owned 10% of the stock, she was $1,000 richer than before. The government agreed with the taxpayer that this increased wealth would not change regardless of whether the corporation paid her (and other shareholders) that $1,000 in the form of a cash dividend, a stock of another company, or its own stock. Both sides also agreed that if the corporation paid the profit to the shareholder in the form of cash that it would be taxable income to the shareholder.

The parties differed, however, in the situation before the Court in which the profit was paid in the form of a stock dividend. Two years previously, in *Towne v. Eisner*,[17] the Court had held that such a dividend was not taxable. The situation in that case, however, differed in two respects from that in *Macomber*. First, in *Towne* the dividend was paid out of profits earned before 1913 (i.e. pre-Sixteenth Amendment), where-

---

[13] *Amici* at 2. (Charles Smith filed the brief with George Wichersham).

[14] *New Stock Issues May Follow Ruling*, N.Y. Times. March 9, 1920, at 1 (case was one of "first importance").

[15] *Government Loses $100,000,000 Taxes*, N.Y. Times, March 9, 1920, at 1. The exact amount of tax loss was debated. *See, e.g., Sees Billion Tax Loss*, N.Y. Times, March 10, 1920, at 21. *See infra* notes 50–52 and accompanying text.

[16] 252 U.S. at 192; Brief for the United States at 16–17.

[17] 245 U.S. 418 (1918). Charles E. Hughes also argued for the taxpayer in *Towne v. Eisner*. Alexander M. Bickel & Benno C. Schmidt, Jr., 9 *History of the Supreme Court of the United States: The Judiciary and Responsible Government: 1910–1921* 502 (1984).

as some of the dividends in *Macomber* were paid out of post–1913 earnings. Second, the 1913 statute at issue in *Towne* did not specifically include stock dividends in income, whereas the 1916 statute in *Macomber* did. As a consequence of these two differences, the two sides differed on the application of *Towne* to the present case. Both argued the case in constitutional terms.

Attorneys for Mrs. Macomber claimed—and the district court agreed—that *Towne* controlled. As in *Towne*, Mrs. Macomber's receipt of a stock dividend was not income, her attorneys claimed, because she was no richer after the dividend than she had been before. More broadly, they argued, a stock dividend cannot be income under the Sixteenth Amendment because it is capital. Since a corporation is a separate legal entity from the shareholder, its undivided, undistributed profits may enrich the shareholder but cannot be income to the shareholder until they are distributed.[18] Consequently, a tax on a stock dividend is a direct tax upon property that must be apportioned under the constitution.[19]

The government, on the other hand, argued that *Towne* did not control for three reasons. First, the case applied only to stock dividends paid out of earnings accrued before March 1, 1913. Second, the opinion was one of statutory construction only. At most, then, it held only that the ordinary meaning of the word "dividend" does not include a stock dividend and consequently the 1913 Act, which did not speak specifically of stock dividends, did not include them as income. Third, the 1916 Act specifically taxed stock dividends. Since the 1916 Revenue Act specifically included stock dividends in income to the extent they represented earnings accrued after March 1, 1913, the government stated that congressional intent was clear. The "only question," therefore, was "whether the levying of such a tax is within the power of Congress."[20]

The government's answer was a resounding yes. Mrs. Macomber was richer in 1916 when she received the stock dividend than she was in 1913, and the stock dividend was "concrete evidence" of that gain.[21] The government further contended that a distribution—whether in cash or stock—was not even necessary for taxability because "the tax is levied on income *derived from corporate earnings*; that such income may be taxed either as the earnings accrue to the corporation or when they are

---

[18] Defendant's Supplemental Brief at 27–29. The Brief countered the government's argument that the Collector v. Hubbard, 12 Wall. 1 (1870), was authority for taxing undistributed profits as income by stating that *Hubbard* did not have to decide whether a shareholder's interest in undistributed profits were income because there was no constitutional question on that issue. *Id.* at 28.

[19] Brief for Defendant-in-Error (Mrs. Macomber) at 6, 36–41.

[20] Brief for the United States at 4.

[21] Brief for the United States at 16.

received by the stockholder.''[22] In other words, the government claimed that Congress had the power to tax undistributed corporate profits, and in fact, Congress had done so under the 1864 income tax act.[23] Congress had simply chosen not to do so in 1916. Instead, the 1916 act taxed shareholders only when the gain was "realized" or segregated from the corporation's undivided profit in some form such as the receipt of a stock dividend.[24]

Thus, the government argued broadly that separation from the corporation of some of its assets was not essential to the existence of income. It claimed Congress had the power to tax the income as it accrued, but if a realization or segregation of any kind were necessary, that realization occurs when the shareholder receives a stock dividend.[25]

The Opinion

On March 8, 1920, one week before 1919 income tax returns were due, the Supreme Court announced the decision that had been speculated about for weeks. Justice Pitney, speaking for a narrowly divided (5–4) Court, vividly characterized the Government's position as follows: "The Government claims the right to tax gains when wearing a new dress only when they were taxable in their old dress. The [taxpayer's] contention cannot succeed unless the new dress destroys the power to tax which existed before it was put on."[26] Speaking in the same constitutional terms as the parties, the Court held that Congress had no power to tax the gains in their old dress. Gains were taxable as income only when realized. In reaching this decision, the Court staked out a position (albeit sometimes a muddled one) on several important issues of the day, including the scope of the Sixteenth Amendment, the nature of a corporation, the definition of income, and the relationship between court and legislature.

Formally, the Court rested its decision on *Towne*, decided two years earlier. Despite the differences between the two cases, the Court stated that *Towne* controlled because it was based neither on the fact that it arose under the less specific 1913 statute nor on the fact that the source of the stock dividend was pre-Sixteenth Amendment profits. Rather, it

---

[22] Government's Supplemental Brief at 5, 10.

[23] *See* Brief for the United States at 8–10. *See also* Government's Supplemental Brief at 21–34.

[24] Government's Supplemental Brief at 5 and 35–38.

[25] Government's Supplemental Brief at 35–38. When a dividend is declared—whether in cash or stock—the shareholder's share of undivided profits are "converted into a concrete form for the convenient payment, transfer, or definite assignment to him of his share of the previously undivided profits."

[26] 252 U.S. at 192.

was based on the fact that "the essential nature of a stock dividend necessarily prevents its being regarded as income in any true sense."[27] Since a stock dividend was not income, the Court continued, any tax upon one is a direct tax that must be apportioned under Article I, section 2, clause 3 and Article I, section 9, clause 4 of the Constitution. The 1916 Revenue Act's treatment of a stock dividend as income did not change the result.

According to the Court, the purpose of the Sixteenth Amendment was not to extend Congress' taxing power but instead to remove the apportionment requirement with respect to income so that Congress could impose a tax on income "from whatever source derived." That limited purpose cannot be expanded by "loose construction," and Congress "cannot by any definition it may adopt conclude the matter since it cannot by legislation alter the Constitution, from which alone it derives its power to legislate and within whose limitations alone that power can be lawfully exercised."[28] In other words, Congress cannot turn capital into income merely by calling it so. The essence of income, the Court said, is that it must be realized or derived from capital. It is

> *not* a gain *accruing* to capital, not a *growth* or *increment* of value in the investment; but a gain, a profit, something of exchangeable value *proceeding from* the property, *severed from* the capital however invested or employed, and *coming in*, being "*derived*," that is, *received* or *drawn by* the recipient (the taxpayer) for his separate use, benefit and disposal; *that* is income derived from property. Nothing else answers the description.[29]

Although the Court created the *requirement* that realization must occur, it did not create the *concept* of realization. Some of the contemporary competing theories of income incorporated such a concept, and there were some indications that the tax laws implicitly accepted the realization concept, even though there was no explicit mention of it. The Revenue Act of 1918, for example, spoke of sustaining a gain or loss on the disposition of property. Similarly, the regulations of that year for the 1916 statute actually used the term "gain realized."[30] The *Macomber* decision not only removed any ambiguity about the existence of the requirement but also elaborated on it by clearly announcing that the principle was a component of income and a constitutional one at that. In holding that it was a component of income, however, the Court did not clearly adopt any of the available theories of income.

---

[27] 252 U.S. at 205.

[28] *Id*. at 206.

[29] *Id*. at 207 (emphasis in original).

[30] Revenue Act of 1918 § 202(a), 40 Stat. 1057, 1060 (1919); Treas. Reg. 33 art. 116, T.D. 2690, 20 Treas. Dec. Int. Rev. 126, 186 (1918).

The Court had two basic theories to choose from, each having its supporters.[31] The traditional theory, originating in a stable, land-based society, emphasized the recurrent nature of income. Under this theory, income was the periodic product of capital, and capital was the asset itself regardless of whether its size or value changed. Capital was like a pool or a tree. A fruit tree might grow from a tiny seed, increasing in size and value, but at all times the entire tree—whether large or small—was capital. Only the regular, periodic fruit of that tree was income. Consequently, under this *res* theory, if a person bought Greenacre for $100,000 and sold it some time later for $150,000, he had no income; like any prudent person he would reinvest all $150,000 as capital and never consume any of it. Only the rents from the capital were income, and only they were available for consumption. Even windfalls or occasional receipts, such as gifts, were not income under this theory. Since they were not a periodic flow or fruit, a rational person would treat them as capital.

The quantum theory, on the other hand, viewed capital as only a specific pecuniary amount. Under this theory, any increase in value beyond that amount was income. Consequently, the taxpayer who purchased Greenacre for $100,000 would have $50,000 of income when he sold it for $150,000. A quantum theory was more in tune with an American economy that accumulated much of its wealth through speculating on rapidly appreciating assets, including easily available land. Although a quantum theory of income considered changes of value when computing income, the theory did not specify when this consideration should occur. Many economists advocated accounting for these changes in value as they occurred. Under this point of view, a person who bought Greenacre for $100,000 this year would have income of $50,000 when it rose in value to $150,000 by the end of the year, even if he did not dispose of the land.

A few other economists, however, argued that taxation should occur only as income was consumed. This theory of income is akin to the *res* theory in that both focus on investment and consumption, but there are differences. For example, the *res* theory would never include in income the $50,000 representing the increased value of Greenacre because it was still capital, even if it was (unwisely) consumed. Under a consumption theory of tax, however, it would be taxed when it was consumed. Similarly, a *res* theory would always include the money received from rentals of Greenacre, whereas taxability under a consumption theory would not occur so long as the money was invested.

The *Macomber* Court's definition of income fell somewhere between the *res* and quantum theories, adopting elements of each. Its statement that income never included "enrichment through increase in value of

---

[31] *See* Chapter 1 of *Tax Stories*.

capital investment" was pure *res* theory. Its holding that realization or separation from capital was a necessary component of income, however, was more ambiguous. This criterion of income complemented the aspect of a *res* theory that focused on the *fruit* being separate from the *tree*. At the same time, however, it also was compatible with a quantum theory of income, albeit not a pure accretion model, since it indicated that the increased value of capital was taxable only when it was separated from the capital.

Macomber's emphasis on realization also involved the Court in another major tax issue: the proper taxation of a corporation and its shareholders. This depended on the nature of the corporate entity. In another entity context, a partnership, the tax treatment was clear. Partnerships were essentially viewed as fictional entities that were mere aggregates of the individual partners. Consequently, a partnership was not taxable in and of itself. Rather, the partners were taxed on their allocable share of partnership income even when they actually received no distribution of cash or other property. The tax law was not so clear about the taxation of corporations, which was not surprising since the law generally was less clear about the exact nature of a corporation. If it were a separate legal entity, what was the relationship between income to the corporation and income to the shareholder?

The *Macomber* Court examined the consequences of separate entity status. If a corporation were a separate entity, it reasoned, then a shareholder had no right to any particular asset until a dividend was declared and therefore couldn't be taxed on corporate income. If, on the other hand, the shareholder and the corporation were viewed as one, the corporation could be taxed as the income was incurred, but the shareholder could never be taxed "separately and additionally" to the corporation. Even if the shareholder received a cash dividend, it wouldn't be taxable because it would be just as if "one's money were to be removed from one pocket to another."[32]

The Court held that the corporation was a separate entity distinct from its shareholders. Consequently, the Court stated that until there was a realization or separation of the gain from the original investment, the taxpayer had only a profit on paper, and the corporation's gains could not be taxed to the shareholder. Until separation, the individual might never receive anything since his entire amount was still invested in the separate corporate entity and still at risk.[33]

The majority opinion also touched on a more practical side of the realization issue that also was unsettled. Specifically, a tax system

---

[32] 252 U.S. at 214.

[33] *Id.* at 211.

encounters two large administrative problems if it imposes a tax when the value of assets owned increases, but he does not receive cash. The first problem is determining the amount of the increased value. The second problem concerns a question of payment since the taxpayer may lack liquidity—owing a tax but having no cash with which to pay it. Both problems would be solved if taxation did not occur until the taxpayer received cash. Such a solution, of course, was untenable because it would be an open invitation to tax avoidance. Taxpayers would arrange their affairs so that even when they disposed of property, they would receive non-cash property in return. In the prior several years, statutes, administrative rulings, and courts had all tried different approaches to the problem by altering the point at which property exchanges would be taxable and varying the definition of cash equivalent.

The *Macomber* Court's definition of income minimized both valuation and liquidity problems. Requiring a separation of income from capital decreased the chance of valuation issues since at separation the taxpayer was more likely to have received cash. Therefore, separation also decreased the likelihood of liquidity problems for the taxpayer. In fact, the Court cited the lack of liquidity as an important factor in holding that realization was a necessary component of income. Receipt of a stock dividend could not be income, the Court said, since the shareholder might have to sell the stock in order to pay the tax. This fact "clearly" showed that a stock dividend could not be income.[34]

Four justices dissented in two separate opinions. On the largest issue, the scope of the constitutional power to tax, all read the Sixteenth Amendment more broadly than the majority. This broad reading left the Court with only a minimal role in the income tax area. Justice Holmes, who had written the opinion in *Towne* declaring stock dividends nontaxable, believed that they were taxable in *Macomber*. *Towne* did not control, he stated, because it was decided solely on statutory grounds, whereas in *Macomber* taxability was a constitutional question. From a constitutional standpoint, the definition of income was broad because the scope of the Sixteenth Amendment was broad. The amendment, he opined, ought to be interpreted:

> in a sense most obvious to the common understanding at the time of its adoption.... The known purpose of this Amendment was to get rid of nice questions as to what might be direct taxes, and I cannot doubt that most people not lawyers would suppose when they voted for it they put a question like the present to rest.[35]

---

[34] *Id.* at 213.

[35] 252 U.S. at 220 (Holmes, J., dissenting). Justice Day joined his short opinion.

Justice Brandeis also based his longer dissent, joined by Justice Clarke, on a broad interpretation of the Sixteenth Amendment, coupled with a presumption of interpretation that what Congress enacts should be constitutional.[36] A "grant of power so comprehensive as that authorizing the levy of an income tax," he argued, allowed the income tax laws to ignore the legal fiction of the corporate personality and tax increases in value without a segregation of assets (i.e., without realization).[37] The constitutionality of such a taxing scheme, he stated, was clear since it had existed under the Civil War income tax laws and was still used under present laws to tax partners on partnership profits regardless of whether they received any cash or other property.[38]

Justice Brandeis objected to realization on theoretical grounds as well as constitutional ones. The majority required realization, or separation of income from capital, in order to determine the existence of profits. The realization requirement failed to achieve this goal, Justice Brandeis stated, because even separation did not determine the existence of profits. Such determination could occur only when the business is finally liquidated, or at the least, only when the taxpayer withdrew an amount of cash that exceeded the original investment.[39] In other words, Justice Brandeis exposed the consumption theory of taxation that underlies a realization requirement.

Finally, Justice Brandeis stated that even if realization were a prerequisite for income taxation, it had occurred. Using a substance-over-form argument, he explained that a *pro rata* stock dividend, such as the one before the Court, was the economic equivalent of a cash dividend coupled with an option to purchase stock at a price low enough to ensure that all shareholders did so.[40]

The Immediate Impact of *Macomber*

Contemporary response to *Macomber* was both instantaneous and intense. Newspapers and journals gave the decision heavy coverage, and academic journals discussed the decision for years, as did both the Court and Congress.[41] Its impact extended beyond taxes into financial and political realms as well.

---

[36] 252 U.S. at 226, 231, 238 (Brandeis, J., dissenting).

[37] 252 U.S. at 231.

[38] *Id.* at 230–32.

[39] *Id.* at 230.

[40] *Id.* at 221.

[41] Charles E. Clark, Eisner v. Macomber *and Some Income Tax Problems*, 29 Yale L.J. 735 (1919–20); Fred R. Fairchild, *The Stock Dividend Decision*, 5 Bull. Nat. Tax Ass'n 208;

The financial market's immediate reaction to the *Macomber* decision
was extreme and chaotic. At first, it declined steeply, only to recover
shortly afterwards. This chaotic response stemmed from the procedure
by which Supreme Court decisions were announced. In 1920, the initial
announcement of a decision was oral. The entire opinion was read aloud
with no printed copies available until completion of the oral announcement. After only a few paragraphs of the decision had been read, news
correspondents rushed to report the news. Unfortunately, they had
misunderstood (or misheard) and incorrectly reported that stock dividends were taxable, which led to heavy selling of stocks, "especially in
the shares which, it was believed, would benefit by a decision by the
Supreme Court against taxing dividends."[42] Only toward the end of the
decision did the news services recognize their mistakes and send out
corrections. The time between the erroneous and correct announcements
was relatively short, varying from two minutes to almost an hour. It was
enough time, however, for the market to plummet. Although it ultimately recovered, the investment companies with private wires in Washington made big profits in the market in the minutes before the general
public was aware of the correct decision.[43]

William Hurst, the Treasurer of the New York News Bureau, stated,
somewhat defensively, that it was surprising that more mistakes were
not made. The decisions are generally read, he said, "in a low or
mumbling tone. It is necessary to strain your ears to catch the words,
and under the circumstances mistakes in interpreting the meaning are
not surprising."[44] He welcomed the various calls for an investigation that
were being made, but no investigation ever occurred, in part because of a
belief that the mistake was an "honest" one and in part because "news
agencies bow to no authority but their own."[45]

The error also did not immediately change the procedure by which
the Court announced its decision but probably influenced the change
that ultimately occurred after yet another serious mistake in reporting a

---

Thomas Reed Powell, *The Stock Dividend Decision and the Corporate Nonentity*, 5 Bull.
Nat. Tax Ass'n 247; *The Judicial Debate on the Taxability of Stock Dividends as Income*, 5
Bull. Nat. Tax Ass'n 201; *Stock Dividends, Direct taxes, and the Sixteenth Amendment*, 20
Colum. L. Rev. 536; A.M. Sakolski, *Accounting Features of the Stock Dividend Decision*, 5
Bull. Nat. Tax Ass'n 212; Edward H. Warren, *Taxability of Stock Dividends as Income* 33
Harv. L. Rev. 885 (1920); and editorial notes in Note and Comment, 18 Mich. L. Rev. 689
(1920); Recent Cases, 4 Minn. L. Rev. 462 (1920); Recent Cases, 68 U. Pa. L. Rev. 394
(1920); and Current Decisions, 29 Yale L.J. 812 (1920).

[42] *Stock Prices Down Under False News, Up on Tax Exemption of Stock Dividends;
Government Loses $100,000,000 Taxes*, N.Y. Times, March 9, 1920, at 1.

[43] *Id.*

[44] *Explanations Offered for the Error; News Bureau Man Want an Investigation*, N.Y.
Times, March 9, 1920, at 1.

[45] *See, e.g., Brokers to Ignore Error in Tax News*, N.Y. Times, March 10, 1920, at 21.

lengthy opinion. In 1935, after the Associated Press misreported the opinion in the *Gold Clause Cases*,[46] the bureau chief suggested to the Chief Justice of the Supreme Court that a written copy of the opinion be provided simultaneously with the oral reading of the opinion in order to avoid similar mistakes.[47] The Chief Justice was Charles Evans Hughes, who as the plaintiff's attorney in *Macomber*, knew well the damage that could occur when the press reported an opinion erroneously. Not surprisingly, the Chief Justice reacted favorably to the suggestion and the new practice was instituted.

Although the financial markets recovered quickly from the initial, incorrect *Macomber* decision, their response to the (correct) decision was more long-term. Immediately after the decision, companies that had refrained from issuing stock dividends while the decision was pending proceeded to declare them.[48] There was also speculation that the decision would increase merger activity, which had also been hindered by fear of taxation.[49]

The government, for its part, was faced with an immediate—and large—loss of revenue due to the necessity of refunding taxes paid in 1917 and 1918 on stock dividends, as well as the possible need for another source of revenue to replace millions lost from taxing future stock dividends.[50] By the day after the decision, the Commissioner of

---

[46] Perry v. United States, 294 U.S. 330 (1935) (U.S. or private bonds requiring payment in either gold coin or legal tender could be paid only in legal tender); Nortz v. United States, 294 U.S. 317 (1935) (same); Norman v. Baltimore & O.R. Co., 294 U.S. 240 (1935) (same).

[47] David L. Grey, *The Supreme Court and the News Media* 37–38 (1968). (Motivated by the Associated Press's mis-reporting of the opinion in the 1935 *Gold Clause Cases*, the AP bureau chief suggested to a receptive Hughes that once the reading of the opinion started, reporters receive a complete written copy). In 1920, the Justices gave the Clerk's office two proof copies of each opinion consisting of a master proof, which was sent to the printer, and a copy for the Clerk's office use. Newsmen and other interested people, such as the parties' counsel, could inspect this latter copy. Later, some Justices gave the Clerk more proofs, which in turn were given to newsmen or counsel on request. Gradually, more proofs were provided so that by November 1935 (9 months after the *Gold Clause Cases*), there were 21 authorized proofs that were available immediately following the announcement of the opinion. Clerk of Court, Memorandum for the Chief Justice, *Distribution of Proof Copies of Opinions of the Court* (November 22, 1935) *found in* Papers of Clerk Cropley, Collection of the Supreme Court. My thanks to Matt Hofstedt at the Office of the Curator, Supreme Court of the United States, for ferreting out all this information regarding the Court's provision of written copies.

[48] *See New Stock Issues May Follow Ruling*, N.Y. Times, March 9, 1920, at 1; *infra* note 72 and accompanying text (statement of Oldfield).

[49] *Id.*

[50] *Government Loses $100,000,000 Taxes*, N.Y. Times, March 9, 1920, at 1. The exact amount of tax loss was debated. *See, e.g., Sees Billion Tax Loss*, N.Y. Times, March 10, 1920, at 21. The decision, announced one week before 1919 returns were due, meant that no refunds for 1919 were involved. The *Wall Street Journal* claimed that the $100,000,000 amount was vastly overstated, and that the "average estimate" of the refund was only

Internal Revenue had already telegraphed tax collectors instructions explaining how taxpayers could claim what was expected to be more than $100 million in refunds.[51] Subsequently, Secretary of the Treasury David F. Houston, admitting that it was difficult to estimate the amount of revenue loss, stated that the $100 million figure was probably the maximum amount, and a more likely estimate of the loss was less than $25 million.[52]

The decision, with its emphasis on the separate nature of a corporation, also created concern about future revenue losses arising out of increased tax evasion. Representative Hull, the "author" of the income tax, stated that the decision opened the way to widespread tax evasion since anyone could now form an "artificial" entity and avoid his "fair" share of taxes by keeping the money in the entity while at the same time "avail himself to a large extent of [the stock's] benefits by mortgaging it, and even get a deduction of his interest paid, and therefore live upon its value without selling it, and of course, without ever paying [the sur-]tax."[53] This fear meshed with the belief, held by some, that the decision would result in a greater concentration of wealth.[54]

Some commentators saw the true importance of *Macomber* as resting not on the tax consequences of the decision but on its conception of the respective roles of court and legislature. In 1803, *Marbury v. Madison* had established the Supreme Court's power of judicial review, but the Court rarely used its powers to invalidate Congressional laws.[55] When it did, attacks upon the validity or wisdom of the Court's power of judicial review usually ensued. This was the case following *Macomber's* invalidation of the 1916 stock dividend provision. Even tax experts such as Thomas Reed Powell and Professor Charles E. Clark of Yale, who

---

$500,000. The Literary Digest 160, April 17, 1920 (quoting the Wall St. Journal). The Treasury estimated the cost of the decision at $105 million: $35 million for refunds for 1918 and a $70 million decrease in revenue in 1919. The Treasury expected a net loss of less than $25 million, however, because of the assumption that tax would ultimately be collected when the stock dividends were sold. Secretary of the Treasury, Annual Report 36 (1920).

51 *Must Give Details to Recover Taxes*, N.Y. Times, March 10, 1920, at 20.

52 59 Cong. Rec. 4466, 66th Cong., 2nd Sess. (March 17, 1920) (March 1920 letter from Secretary of the Treasury, David F. Houston, to Rep. Joseph W. Fordney, Chairman of the House Committee on Ways and Means).

53 *Government Loses $100,000,000 Taxes*, N.Y. Times, March 9, 1920, at 3.

54 *See, e.g.*, T. David Zuckerman, *Are Stock Dividends Income?* 28 J. Pol. Econ. 591, 599 (1920).

55 Marbury v. Madison, 1 Cranch 137 (1803). Charles E. Hughes, the attorney for Mrs. Macomber, wrote in his 1928 history of the Supreme Court that between the adoption of the Constitution and the Civil War only 2 acts were held unconstitutional (those in *Marbury* and in the *Dred Scott* case) and only 53 since the Civil War. Charles E. Hughes, *The Supreme Court of the United States* 88 (1928).

believed that the decision was correct from an economic standpoint, felt
that the decision was incorrect from a political standpoint. In a *Yale Law
Journal* article, Clark stated that the Court's bias in interpreting a
constitutional provision should be in favor of upholding the statute and
the judgement of Congress.[56] Other criticism of the Court's "abuse" of
its power was sharper. An anonymous editorial in the *New Republic*,
allegedly written by Felix Frankfurter, said "the deeper implications" of
Macomber "challenge the wisdom of leaving the ultimate law-making
power of the nation to nine men. At least they call for a consideration of
the safeguards to be imposed upon the extraordinary judicial power of
the Supreme Court."[57] Within weeks, Senator Nelson of Minnesota
proposed amending the Sixteenth Amendment to specifically include
stock dividends as income.[58] More than a year later, Senator Watson was
still complaining that the decision was "a perfectly rotten decision," and
that the Supreme Court had no right to annul a Congressional act.[59]

Some commentators, such as the eminent income tax expert E. R. A.
Seligman, believed that the *Macomber* Court's narrow interpretation of
the Sixteenth Amendment and the definition of income would result in a
"regrettable tying of the hands of the legislator and an undue curtail-
ment of legislative discretion, with the result of raising many new
problems in the place of the single problem which the courts [had]
endeavor[ed] to settle."[60] Seligman was correct. The constitutional aspect
of the decision necessitated an activist Court in the tax field that took
years to wane. It also created confusion for years in many aspects of
income tax law and immediately influenced actions by both Court and
Congress in at least several major areas—the taxation of capital gains,
the treatment of exchanges of property, and reorganizations. Some of
these issues were ultimately resolved (more or less) by the Court and
Congress, as with the Court's broad definition of income under *Glenshaw Glass*[61] and the current, complicated § 305 concerning the taxabili-

---

[56] Clark, *supra* note 41, at 737. *See also* Thomas Reed Powell, *The Judicial Debate on
the Taxability of Stock Dividends as Income*, 5 Bull. of the Nat'l Tax Ass'n, 247, 256 (1920)
("There is much to be said in favor of the political wisdom of Mr. Justice Holmes . . . even
though we are quite certain that the . . . economic argument of Mr. Justice Pitney is more
meritorious . . . ").

[57] *The Supreme Court vs. The Supreme Court*, 22 New Republic 235 (1920). *See*
Alexander Bickel, *The Judiciary of and Responsible Government, in* 9 *History of the
Supreme Court of the United States 1910–1921*, 511 (1984) (stating that Frankfurter wrote
the New Republic article).

[58] *Would Tax Dividends*, N.Y. Times, March 27, 1920, at 20.

[59] 61 Cong. Rec. 6473–74 (Oct. 19, 1921) (Sen. Watson).

[60] Edwin R.A. Seligman, *Introduction, in The Federal Income Tax IX* (Robert Haig ed.
1921).

[61] *See* Commissioner v. Glenshaw Glass Co., 348 U.S. 426 (1955), and Chapter 1 of *Tax
Stories*.

ty of stock dividends. In the process, the Court retreated from its activist role and seemingly abandoned the constitutional element of realization, but not before it left its indelible mark on the shape and theory of income tax. Even after the Court's retreat from the constitutional aspect of *Macomber*, its articulation of realization continues to influence not just the actual tax laws but how we think about tax policy.

This section further examines the immediate reactions to the case in 1920 and the following year. It focuses on the constitutional and political influence of *Macomber* before the Court whittled away the constitutional aspect. First, it sets the case in the context of the *Lochner* era and an activist Court. Second, it briefly explains how these constitutional and political concerns shaped both Court and Congressional action in several important areas of the tax law: corporate taxation, capital gains, and exchanges of property.

1. Macomber *and the* Lochner *Court*.

Macomber is best understood as part of the struggle during the *Lochner* era to define the nature and scope of government. The income tax played a critical function in this struggle because its broad base enables a government to expand its functions and, in theory if not practice, redistribute wealth. In fact, in 1895 *Pollock v. Farmers' Loan & Trust Co,* commonly called the "Income Tax Case," was the most criticized of the three cases that inaugurated the *Lochner* era.[62] The *Pollock* Court held the Income Tax Act of 1894, the first peacetime income tax, unconstitutional on the ground that it was a direct tax which had to be apportioned under the Constitution (Article I, section 2, clause 3 and section 9, clause 4). This decision reversed the Court's expansive view of congressional taxing power—a view that had previously upheld an income tax during the Civil War. It was, however, in keeping with the traditional scholarly view of the Court of this period as one actively protecting economic property rights against both an expanding regulatory state and the populist and progressive principle of wealth redistribution.[63]

---

[62] 157 U.S. 429, *reh'g granted,* 158 U.S. 601 (1895). The other two cases were the United States v. E.C. Knight Co., 156 U.S. 1 (1895) (the *Sugar Trust Case*) and In re Debs, 158 U.S. 564 (1895) (the labor, anti-injunction case decided one week after *Pollock*). For criticism of the case, see Charles Warren, *The Supreme Court in United States History: 1836–1918* 702–04 (1926 ed.), and Barry Friedman, *The History of the Countermajoritarian Difficulty, Part III: The Lesson of* Lochner, 76 N.Y.U. L. Rev. 1383, 1393 n.33 (2001) (*Pollock* "aroused the greatest fury of this early period").

[63] Lochner v. New York, 198 U.S. 45 (1905), which invalidated a New York law limiting the number of hours bakers could work as a violation of the freedom to contract, typifies this attitude and gave its name to a whole era. The *Lochner* era, however, stretches from the 1890s into at least the mid 1920s. *See, e.g.,* Friedman, *supra* note 62, at 1391. Today, some scholarly re-evaluations of the *Lochner* era argue that the Court was not merely protecting corporate interests but was legitimately following its legal precedents. For a

The two major criticisms of *Pollock* were typical of the *Lochner* era. The first criticism claimed that the Court's overruling of a Congressional act was an abuse of judicial discretion, especially since it was a 5–4 decision determined only after a rehearing. The second criticism denounced the decision's pro-business bias. Commentators and the parties themselves saw the case in *Lochnerian* terms of wealth and property rights, frequently speaking of socialism. Even the Justices viewed the case in this same light. Justice Brown, for example, said in his dissent that "the decision involves nothing less than the surrender of the taxing power to the money class" and might "prove the first step toward the submergence of the liberties of the people in a sordid despotism of wealth."[64]

After the passage of two decades and a constitutional amendment, Congress enacted another income tax in 1913. In 1916, the Court upheld its constitutionality, but it did so in a manner that left room for an active judicial role in income taxation.[65] Although the Court acknowledged that Congress had "a complete and all-embracing taxing power," it cautioned that this power was limited by the constitutional requirements of apportionment of direct taxes and uniformity of all other taxes. The Sixteenth Amendment, it clearly stated, gave no new powers to Congress but merely eliminated the requirement to apportion income taxes that were direct; all other direct taxes must still be apportioned.[66] By emphasizing the importance of defining income, the Court thus paved the way for *Macomber*.

The 1920s were generally a time of renewed criticism of an activist, pro-business Court,[67] and *Macomber* gave the critics plenty of opportunity to complain. Once again the Court interpreted the Sixteenth Amendment as granting no new powers to Congress. As a consequence, taxability hinged on whether stock dividends fell within the definition of income. By making that definition a constitutional issue, the Court—in the eyes of many, including the dissent—destroyed the purpose of the Sixteenth Amendment, which was to avoid making these fine decisions. More importantly, the decision put the Court on a collision course with Congress. By making the definition of income a constitutional issue, the Court actively inserted itself in the income tax process. Indeed, three

---

discussion of the *Lochner* era and description of traditional and revisionist views of it, see, for example, Seligman, *supra* note 61, at 1344–46; Friedman, *supra* note 62. Professor Barry Friedman argues, however, that judicial legitimacy is not sufficient to support the legitimacy of the Court and judicial review. There must also be social legitimacy, that is acceptance by the general public. Friedman, *supra* note 62, at 1387.

[64] 158 U.S. 601, 695 (1895) (Brown, J., dissenting).

[65] Brushaber v. Union Pacific Railroad, 240 U.S. 1 (1916).

[66] *Id.* at 13.

[67] *See* Friedman, *supra* note 62, at 1445–47.

months later the Court in *Evans v. Gore* once again interpreted the Sixteenth Amendment narrowly and overruled Congress by holding that Congress had no power to tax the income of federal judges.[68] The fact that *Macomber*, like *Pollock*, was yet again a 5–4 decision merely served to heighten the perception that the Court once again abused its power of judicial review. Add in the charges of pro-wealth bias, such as those by Senator Nelson of Minnesota,[69] and it is no wonder that many people thought that *Macomber* was the *"Lochner* of federal income taxation."[70]

Congress, well aware of the decision, expressed its concern—and sometimes outrage—several times during debates of the 1921 Revenue Act. Senator Watson, for example, stated that Congress had the power to annul the *Macomber* decision, but that the Supreme Court had no authority to invalidate a properly enacted act of Congress.[71] Representative Oldfield proposed re-enacting the provision taxing stock dividends because *Macomber* allowed great amounts of wealth to avoid taxation. Re-enacting the provision might be worthwhile, he claimed, since *Macomber* had been decided only by a 5–4 majority, and "the court might change."[72] In the end, however, Congress did not challenge the Court. The 1921 Revenue Act exempted stock dividends from income because, according to both the House and Senate Committee Reports, the *Macomber* decision required it.[73] The controversy, however, did not end. In 1923, for example, Representative Frear asserted that the *Macomber* Court wrongly contradicted the will of the people, as expressed by the passage of the Sixteenth Amendment, and the will of Congress, as expressed in its revenue act. He was particularly outraged because the decision hurt the common man and was made by a 5–4 majority. In order to prevent another judicial overturning of the people's will, he proposed amending the 1923 revenue bill so that no portion of the act could be held invalid if at least two justices dissented.[74]

---

[68] 253 U.S. 245 (1920). Justices Holmes and Brandeis once again dissented, stating that even if the original Constitution did not permit taxing judges' salaries, such a tax was constitutional under the Sixteenth Amendment since its purpose was to allow the taxation of income from whatever source derived. *Id.* at 267.

[69] 61 Cong. Rec. 6473 (1921) (Sen. Nelson). Others pointed out that the wealth could be taxed by means of an undistributed profits tax. *Id.* at 6474 (Sen. Jones of New Mexico).

[70] Kirk J. Stark, *The Unfulfilled Tax Legacy of Justice Robert H. Jackson*, 54 Tax L. Rev. 171, 198 & 214 (2001).

[71] 61 Cong. Rec. 6474 (1921) (Sen. Watson).

[72] *See also* 61 Cong. Rec. 5177 (1921) (Rep. Oldfield listing the companies that had declared stock dividends since the decision).

[73] H. R. Rep. No. 350–67, at 8–9; S. Rep. No. 275–67, at 9. Section 201(d) of the Revenue Act of 1921, 42 Stat. 227, provided that "A stock dividend shall not be subject to tax."

[74] 64 Cong. Rec. 1257 (1923) (Rep. Frear). One year later in the course of a long debate on whether Congress should re-enact the provision taxing stock dividends, he made the same proposal again. 65 Cong. Rec. 2797 (1924) (Rep. Frear).

The Court eventually withdrew from the active role in the tax area that *Macomber* necessitated by (apparently) whittling the constitutional aspect of realization down to an administrative concern. In this manner, it ceded to Congress broader discretion to determine what was taxable income. Before this occurred, however, *Macomber* and its constitutional constraint left its indelible imprint on the income tax system. As might be expected, the effect of the constitutional aspects of *Macomber* was felt most strongly by both the Court and the legislature in the first few years following the decision, but the decision consciously affected their actions in tax matters well into the 1930s and beyond. The effect of the decision was magnified because, as discussed later, the constitutional requirement has never been decisively revoked. Just as importantly, early decisions made in the strong light of *Macomber's* constitutional requirement set the tax laws in directions still felt today.

2. *The Corporate Tax*

One area heavily affected by *Macomber* was corporate taxation. The most immediate consequence of the decision, naturally, was the amendment of the stock dividend provision in 1921 to comply with the decision. The decision had broader implications for the taxation of corporations and shareholders, however, because it involved the question of whether a shareholder could ever be taxed directly on his share of corporate gain. The answer depended on whether the separate nature of the corporate entity must always be respected, which in turn was part of a more basic question about the nature of a corporation. This issue was still a matter of contemporary legal debate, and the *Macomber* decision reflected it. Although corporations had long been separately taxed, it was not entirely clear, from a theoretical standpoint, whether this was because they were considered separate entities or because they were a convenient method of reaching the shareholders' wealth. The majority opinion in *Macomber* seemed to stress the separate nature of a corporation, stating that the shareholder was not taxable until the corporate profits were separated from the corporation, whose separate identity must be respected. Justice Brandeis' dissent, in contrast, emphasized that Congress had the power to directly tax the shareholders even on undistributed corporate gain as it had done under the Civil War income tax statute, which the Court had previously upheld.[75] A closer reading of the majority opinion, however, shows that even it did not always demand separate taxation. Justice Pitney's opinion, for example, recognized that the corporate veil could be pierced in certain abusive situations. Moreover, it was arguable that the decision did not prevent taxing shareholders on undistributed corporate profits since the case held that what was being taxed in *Macomber* was not income.

---

[75] *Hubbard*, 12 Wall. at 1.

Commentators disagreed on the degree to which the decision required separate corporate taxation, although most agreed that ignoring the corporate entity would be permissible in order to prevent tax evasion.[76] Congress, however, either did not agree with this view or was unwilling to risk another direct confrontation with the Court. In its treatment of corporate taxation over the next few decades, it interpreted *Macomber* as requiring separate taxation of corporations. For example, in 1921, it revised the personal holding company provision because of doubts about the constitutionality of the then current law in the light of *Macomber*.[77] The prior law had imposed a tax on shareholders when their corporation retained what was deemed an improper amount of profits. The new law, still retained to this day in §§ 531 and 541, levied the tax on the corporation instead of the shareholder because of *Macomber's* emphasis on the separate existence of the corporation preventing corporate profits from being taxed to the shareholders when still retained in corporate form. Similarly, Congress viewed its ability to tax corporate undistributed profits in the 1930s, a great concern at the time, as greatly constrained by the case.[78] If *Macomber* made Congress unwilling to ignore the separate existence of the corporation even when tax evasion was involved, it surely was unwilling to consider more radical schemes to generally disregard the corporate structure so as to tax shareholders on undistributed profits in the same manner that partnerships did. In this manner, *Macomber* helped reinforce the idea of a separate tax on corporations and may have hindered the early exploration of integrating the corporate and individual taxes that otherwise might have occurred.[79]

The remainder of this Part concentrates on just two actions in 1921, one by Congress and one by the Court, that were influenced by *Macom-*

---

[76] *See, e.g.,* Arthur A. Ballantine, *Corporate Personality in* Income Taxation, 573 Harv. L. Rev. (1921); Thomas Reed Powell, *The Stock–Dividend Decision and the Corporate Nonentity,* 5 Bull. of the Nat'l Tax Ass'n 201 (1920). For a modern discussion, see Steven A. Bank, *The Shareholder–Based Origins of the Corporate Income Tax* (forthcoming); Marjorie E. Kornhauser, *Corporate Regulation and the Origins of the Corporate Income Tax,* 86 Ind. L.J. 53 (1990).

[77] H. R. Rep. No. 350–67 (discussing § 220 of the 1921 Act, 42 Stat. 227, 247, at 12–13, cited in Helvering v. Griffiths, 318 U.S. 371, 387 (1943)).

[78] On Congressional concern about *Macomber's* affect on the constitutionality of undistributed profits tax in 1936 as well as on provisions to stop tax evasion through the use of corporations, see Griffiths, 318 U.S. at 377, 387 (quoting from the Congressional Record as well as both House and Senate Hearings on the Revenue Act of 1936 such as the House Ways and Means Committee, 74th Cong. 2nd Sess. *See* 79 Cong. Rec. 193, 734 (the personal holding company tax)); Charles Stuart Lyon, *Old Statutes and New Constitution,* 44 Colum. L. Rev. 599, 609 (1944). Senator Hugo Black, for instance, stated that *Macomber* prevented the taxation of a shareholder on a corporation's undistributed profits. 80 Cong. Rec. 8813.

[79] *See e.g.,* Clark, *supra* note 41, at 743. It also may explain why, unlike other countries, the United States does not even have partial integration, although for a while there was a small dividend exclusion.

ber. Each decision still profoundly effects the tax law, although the connection between *Macomber* and the tax law may not be obvious today. The first is a judicial action, the Court's decision upholding the taxation of capital gains. The second is a legislative action, the enactment of provisions deferring the taxation of certain exchanges of property.

3. *Capital Gains Taxation*

In one sense, the *Macomber* decision narrowed the definition of income by requiring realization, but in another, it opened the door for broadening it. In 1920, there was some uncertainty as to whether capital gains were taxable income. *Macomber*, of course, had clearly stated that the mere increase in value of the stock while a taxpayer held it did not create taxable income, nor did the distribution of a stock dividend that left a shareholder's proportionate interest in the corporation unchanged. But what happened if a shareholder sold the stock for its fair market value of $150 when he had bought it for only $50? Today most people would agree that there would be $100 of income. In 1920, however, others argued, using an older concept of income as described earlier (and also in Chapter 1 of *Tax Stories*), that there still would be no income. Under this *res* theory of capital, the entire $150 was still capital because capital consisted of the thing itself (the stock in this instance) whether its value was $10, $50, or $150.

At the time of the *Macomber* decision, whether such gains were constitutionally taxable as income was far from clear. All revenue acts since 1913 stated that income included gains and profits from the sale or dealings with property, and since 1914 the Internal Revenue Bureau had interpreted this provision as applying to gains from the sale of capital assets. In 1919, the Treasury finally issued a regulation to this effect.[80] In 1920, however, four taxpayers challenged the Internal Revenue Bureau's taxation of their capital gains. Three of the suits were filed months after the *Macomber* decision, possibly emboldened by the Court's narrow interpretation of the Sixteenth Amendment and its concomitant narrow definition of income. In the lead case, *Merchants' Loan & Trust Co. v. Smietanka*,[81] the Court defined income to include capital gains, ostensibly using the same test of the "common understanding" of the term that it had used in *Macomber*. In reality, however, both the common and the expert opinions were divided on the issue of whether capital gains were income. The *New York Times*, for example, proclaimed that increases in the value of capital assets, in accordance with the *res* theory of capital, were not income but capital, and therefore, "if the

---

[80] Treas. Reg. 45, art. 21, T.D. 2831, 21 Treas. Dec. 176 (1919).

[81] 255 U.S. 509 (1921).

Sixteenth Amendment means anything at all it confirms the principle that direct taxes must be apportioned to populations."[82] This view of the amendment fit comfortably with the Court's narrow interpretation of the amendment in both *Macomber* and *Evans v. Gore*. Others believed, however, that capital gains were income, some even citing Justice Pitney's statement in *Macomber* that if and when a shareholder sold the stock dividend, he would be taxable on any (post-Sixteenth Amendment) profits that arose while he held the stock.[83]

The Supreme Court's position on whether capital gains were legally income, however, was more complicated than Pitney's statement. In prior cases involving other statutes, the Court had issued contradictory statements.[84] Even in *Macomber* itself, Justice Pitney both approved a definition including profits from the sale of property in income (as just described) and denied that income included the "enrichment through increase in value of capital investment."[85] In short, despite the *Merchants' Loan* Court's assurances to the contrary, neither common, economic, nor legal opinion as to the nature of capital gains clearly indicated that they were income. Why, then, with opinion undecided and legal precedent to support such taxation mixed at best, did the Court hold that capital gains were income? Although the answer can never be known definitively, several aspects of the *Macomber* decision the previous year pointed towards taxability.

First, the concern about judicial activism and the balance of power between court and legislature had not yet abated. Since the statutory and regulatory wording gave the appearance that Congress intended to tax capital gains, a Court decision to the contrary would again put the Court and Congress in direct conflict, inflaming opinion even more. Finding taxability would avoid that conflict. As the *Harvard Law Review* warned, shortly after the district court in *Brewster v. Wash* found capital gains taxation unconstitutional, "[t]he attitude of the majority of the court in *Eisner v. Macomber* in riding rough-shod over Congress' interpretation of the Sixteenth Amendment raised a storm of criticism; a declaration that capital increment cannot be taxed might well be fol-

---

[82] Editorial, *Taxation of Capital Gains*, N.Y. Times, Feb. 15, 1921, at 8.

[83] 252 U.S. at 212. *See, e.g.*, Warren, *supra* note 42, at 899 (lead article in the May 1920 issue stating that capital gains were income). If capital gains were income, then the estimates of revenue loss from the *Macomber* decision were overstated because eventually the gain would be taxed when realized. *See, e.g.*, Clark, *supra* note 41, at 738 ("And if, as hereinafter discussed, realized capital gains are taxable, the fears of Justice Brandeis and of Congressmen as to the great loss of revenue to the government are largely groundless.").

[84] *See, e.g.*, Lynch v. Turrish, 247 U.S. 221 (1918); United States v. Cleveland, Cincinnati, Chicago, & St. Louis Ry., 247 U.S. 195 (1918); Hays v. Gauley Mountain Coal Co., 247 U.S. 189 (1918); and Doyle v. Mitchell Bros. Co., 247 U.S. 179 (1918).

[85] 252 U.S. at 212, 214–15.

lowed by a constitutional amendment recalling the decision.''[86] Finding
taxability would avoid this situation, which had the potential to damage
the Court's reputation and power.

Second, a decision that capital gains were taxable could also signal
that the Court was more willing to withdraw from an active role in
determining what was income. This would encourage more certainty in
the tax law, always a desirable trait since uncertainty tends to drive up
the costs of transactions and otherwise generally hinder economic activity. With a less active Court, taxpayers could plan their activities with the
assurance that what Congress said was income was indeed income.
Moreover, a decision that capital gains were income promoted more
certainty than a decision to the contrary. If gains from the sale of capital
assets were not income, but those from the sale of business assets were,
then there would always be a question of whether the asset were a
capital one or not. The British experience of not taxing capital gains had
shown how extensive this problem could be.

Third, the *Macomber* decision may have influenced the Court to tax
capital gains because of a common view that *Macomber* favored the rich
by shielding them from tax even though their wealth had increased. If
the gain were taxed on the sale of the stock, then the wealthy would only
be allowed to defer their tax liability rather than permanently avoid it. If
capital gains were held non-taxable, however, then the wealthy would
perpetually avoid taxation. Charges of tax evasion by the wealthy might
re-emerge with even greater strength. Additionally, a permanent exclusion of the gain from income would significantly decrease revenues as
opposed to merely deferring them. This was particularly problematic in
1921 because the country was in a recession. Consequently, any decision
that narrowed the tax base was of great concern, especially in light of
both *Macomber*, which had at a minimum delayed revenues, and *Evans
v. Gore*, which had further decreased potential revenues by eliminating
judicial salaries from the tax base.

The *Macomber* decision thus provided the Court with several reasons to tax capital gains. Since legal precedent for the capital gains
decision was indeterminate (or at least conflicting), all the repercussions
of *Macomber* added weight to a decision favoring taxability and deferral
to the legislature in defining income. The battleground in the future
would not be Congressional power to tax but administrative (Treasury)
power to interpret.

4. *Realization, Recognition, and Deferral: Section 1031*

The *Macomber* decision influenced Congressional as well as Court
action in 1921. The case was specifically mentioned several times during

---

[86] Note, *Is Appreciation in Value of Property Income*, 34 Harv. L. Rev. 536, 538 (1921).

Congressional debates of the 1921 revenue act, for example, when discussing tax exempt bonds or undistributed profits.[87] Although *Macomber* was not mentioned by name during discussions of an area directly affected by the case, the realization of income on the disposition of property, the decision nonetheless influenced Congressional actions in this area. Congress had been struggling with this topic for several years prior to *Macomber*, but it was not until 1921 that Congress enacted or broadened several provisions that deferred the taxation of gain in numerous exchanges of property. These sections, still in existence today, include current § 1031 (like kind exchanges), § 1033 (involuntary conversions), § 351 (incorporations), and § 368 (corporate reorganizations). Certainly a variety of factors were involved in the passage of these sections, such as a desire to promote certain economic activity in the face of the 1921 recession and the taxability of capital gains, but realization was a crucial factor as the following short explanation of § 1031 illustrates.

Section 1031 defers taxability of gain or loss when a taxpayer exchanges one piece of property for a property of like kind. Traditional explanations of the section focus on three areas, all of which are central to realization: valuation, liquidity, and continuity of investment. Assume that Ima Investor owns Greenacre and that she transfers it to Trader Vic, who gives her Farmland in exchange. Does Ima have any gain or loss on this exchange since she has withdrawn no money from her investments? If she is to be taxed, how much should she be taxed since valuing the properties (and hence the gain) may be difficult since no cash changed hands? Finally, how will she pay the tax since she received no money? Although Congress had been grappling with these difficult issues for several years prior to *Macomber*, the decision's constitutional mandate for realization made the resolution of the issue more urgent and set the path for that resolution.

The Court's discussion of realization in *Macomber* seemed to indicate that in the exchange situation there might be no income to tax because there was no realization. According to *Macomber*, realization only occurred if the gain were separated from the capital. In analyzing whether separation had occurred in the stock dividend situation, the Court had concluded it had not because Mrs. Macomber had only a "paper gain" since all her investment in the corporation was still in corporate solution and still at risk. Moreover, the Court explicitly stated that the taxpayer, having received no cash in the transaction, would have a liquidity problem if she were required to pay tax. Realization was similarly problematic for a taxpayer who exchanged property. The same factors arguing against realization in *Macomber* were also present when

---

[87] 61 Cong. Rec. 6473 (1921) (Sen. Nelson); and 61 Cong. Rec. 5825, 6474, 6487 (1921).

a taxpayer exchanged property for like kind property. Such a taxpayer had a liquidity problem if taxability were imposed because she received no cash.[88] Similarly, she also had only a paper gain since her entire investment was still at risk in property that was of "like kind." Congressional debate on the proposed section showed that, one year after the *Macomber* decision, a great deal of confusion remained as to whether there was a profit—let alone a taxable profit—at this point of exchange.[89] Given *Macomber's* constitutional requirement that realization occur and the confusion over when that happens, a natural, and prudent, Congressional response would be to defer taxability until a time when it is clearer that realization exists. The like kind provision did exactly that.

Although the concept of realization is now more broadly defined than in 1921, § 1031 remains in the Code today in only slightly altered form. Although it is characterized as an exception to the recognition provision of § 1001(c) rather than as a realization issue, its roots lie in realization arguments advanced in *Macomber*. Expansively construed by the Court, the provision acts as a major tax shelter allowing taxpayers to exchange vastly appreciated property without incurring any current taxability. Imagine, for example, a taxpayer who purchased vacant land many years ago for $100,000. It is now worth $600,000, but the taxpayer no longer wants the property. If she sells the land for cash, she will have $500,000 of taxable income. If she exchanges it, however, for an office building worth $600,000, she will have no tax liability. Theoretically, of course, § 1031 preserves the gain for later taxation by giving the new property a basis based on the old exchanged property, so that when the taxpayer sells the new property the gain will be taxed.[90] The taxpayer, however, can defer the tax yet again by later exchanging the office building for yet another piece of like kind property. In fact, she can eliminate the tax entirely if she dies holding like kind property because all the untaxed gain will disappear when the basis of the property is stepped under § 1014 (unless the scheduled repeal of the estate tax and the accompanying imposition of a carryover basis regime occurs in 2010). Section 1031, enacted under the spell of *Macomber*, thus magnifies the benefit of deferral that realization provides—allowing a taxpayer to get richer and richer without paying tax.

---

[88] The initial version of § 1031 enacted in 1921 deferred gain even when the taxpayer received some cash in the exchange, but this was corrected in 1924.

[89] *See, e.g.*, 64 Cong. Rec. 2854–58, (1923) (Reps. Fordney, Green, and Hawley discussing both current § 1031, not requiring a tax until the "profit" has been obtained by receiving cash, as well as mentioning stock dividends).

[90] § 1031(d).

The Continuing Importance of *Macomber* Today

Realization's benefits stem from its power to defer tax liability until a future date, in other words, the time value of money. Assume that on January 1, 2003, a taxpayer invests $10,000 for 2 years, receives 10% interest, and pays a 30% tax on the investment. If the income is taxed annually, as earned, then the consequences are:

	1/1/03	12/31/03	12/31/04
Investment	$10,000	$10,000	$10,700
Profit/year	0	$1,000	$1,070
Taxable profit	0	$1,000	$1,070
Tax	0	$300	$321
After-tax return	0	$700	$749

The bottom line is that the taxpayer has paid a total of $621 in taxes and will have $11,449 in her hands, after taxes, at the end of the 2 years, of which $1,149 is profit.

If, however, the taxpayer will not have to pay any tax until there is realization when the asset is sold on December 31, 2004, then the consequences would be:

	1/1/03	12/31/03	12/31/04
Investment	$10,000	$10,000	$11,000
Profit/year	0	$1,000	$1,100
Taxable Profit	0	0	$2,100
Tax	0	0	$630
After-tax return	0	$1,000	$1,470

Under this realization scheme, the taxpayer ends up with $11,470 in her hands after taxes at the end of 2004. Although she pays $9 more in taxes, she still ends up with $21 more profit [$1,470–$1,449] than if she had paid taxes on the income as it accrued. This $21 represents the after tax return on the $300 of tax that she did not have to pay at the end of 2003. Instead, this $300 was available for investment at 10%, which yielded an additional $30 in earnings. These earnings created an additional $9 of tax liability, thus increasing after tax profit by $21.

This deferral of tax liability can be viewed as a one year interest free loan by the government of the $300. In 2003, taxpayer would pay $300 tax, but the government would lend it back to the taxpayer giving her $11,000 to invest in 2004. In 2004, taxpayer would pay $330 tax on the $1,100 of income and also would repay the $300 loan. In sum, the taxpayer would have paid a total tax of $630 and be left, after tax, with $11,470 of which $1,470 was profit.

If, in contrast, the government had loaned the taxpayer the $300 at 10%, she would still have had all $1,000 to invest in 2004 but would also have owed $30 of interest. In sum, the taxpayer would have paid the government $651, consisting of $621 in taxes and $30 in interest payments: 2003 tax of $300 on $1,000 and 2004 tax of $321 on $1,070 income [$1,100–$30 deductible interest] plus $30 interest.

An interest-bearing loan from the government would have left the taxpayer with the same $1,449 of after tax profits ($2,100–$651) as she would have had with a yearly accretion tax. Under the realization system, however, the taxpayer owes the government only $630 tax or $21 less than under the taxable loan analysis. This is equivalent to an interest free loan of 2003 tax since it represents the $30 of foregone interest (minus the $9 of tax on it). The time value of money, in other words, means that the realization requirement favors assets whose gain can be deferred to a later time since the deferral serves to increase the yield on those assets.

As the above example illustrates, the realization requirement makes taxation a two-step process. Under an accretion tax system, in contrast, taxation is a one-step process which depends on the resolution of a single question: Has there been a change in wealth? Taxation in a system that incorporates a realization requirement, however, cannot depend solely on whether a change in wealth has occurred because that increase will have occurred earlier. Realization requires an additional question: Is it time to assign tax consequences to the previous increase or decrease? This second step alleviates some difficulties existing in the one-step, pure accretion model such as liquidity and valuation problems, but it creates new ones.

By deferring tax consequences beyond the point in time when the income (or loss) economically occurs, realization significantly increases complexity, distorts economic behavior, alters wealth distribution, and frequently violates horizontal or vertical equity among taxpayers. Realization affects behavior in several significant ways. It encourages the over-investment in those assets whose gain is deferrable such as land, as opposed to investment in assets such as bonds, where taxability on profits cannot be deferred. The deferral provided by realization is also an incentive for people to hold on to their assets to avoid taxability even if they would otherwise sell them. Since deferral is so desirable, it encourages taxpayers to engage in complicated transactions whose sole or predominant purpose is to avoid realization. This in turn leads to complexity as Congress and the Service respond to these evasive techniques with new legislation and rulings, which in turn trigger other innovative transactions. Finally, the deferral of realization has equitable consequences. It can create horizontal inequity, for example, when two taxpayers have the same amount of economic gain, but only one has realized gain. It also can lead to a violation of vertical equity and affect wealth distribution since wealthier taxpayers have a greater ability to invest in those assets whose taxable gain can be deferred.

Since taxability depends on realization, identification of those events that qualify as realization events becomes critical to the tax system. This identification is not always easy since the economic gain has occurred earlier, and realization is merely the artificial event that is treated as terminating the economic process. Consider, for example, the XYZ corporation, which was worth $50 in 2001 when you bought 20% of its stock for $10. Assume it earned $5 in 2002 and broke even in 2003. Under an accretion income tax, you would have had $1 of income in 2002 and none in 2003 when you sold the stock for $11. *Macomber's* realization requirement, however, results in you having no income in 2002 and $1 of income in 2003 when you sold the stock for $11. Not all realization events are so clear, however. Would realization occur if you transferred your stock in exchange for different stock in the same company? What if you exchanged the stock for stock in another, but similar, corporation? Would it matter if that other stock were easily valued and/or marketable? What if you transferred the stock for a note that merely said that the transferee would pay you $11 in the future? Would your answers differ if you were a cash method taxpayer rather than an accrual taxpayer (that is you only had income when you received cash or the equivalent of cash)? Would you have realization if instead of selling the stock you merely borrowed $11 using the stock as security?

The Court began the process of determining which events constituted realization shortly after deciding the *Macomber* case in a series of cases involving the distribution of stock as stock dividends and as part of reorganizations. These cases, which inform our treatment of reorganization today, can really be understood only in the context of *Macomber*.[91] In most of the cases, the Court found realization and hence taxability. For example, in 1921 the Court decided *United States v. Phellis*,[92] in which a New Jersey corporation reincorporated in Delaware, using some of its assets to redeem the old New Jersey corporation's bonds and distributing all the new common stock, *pro rata*, to its old common stockholders. Justice Pitney, once again writing for the Court, stated that the instant case was unlike the situation in *Macomber* where the taxpayer received nothing she had not had before and therefore had not separated the income from the capital. In *Phellis*, he said, there was clearly a realization or separation of income from the original capital since the two corporations were not substantially identical. Since the taxpayer received "property rights and interests materially different

---

[91] *Accord* Daniel Q. Posin, *Taxing Corporate Rorganizations: Purging Penelope's Web*, 133 U. Pa. L. Rev. 1335, 1342 (1985).

[92] 257 U.S. 156 (1921). The New Jersey corporation was E. I. du Pont de Nemours Powder Company, and the Delaware corporation was E. I. du Pont de Nemours & Co.

from those incident to ownership of stock in the old company," the receipt of the stock was a taxable event.[93]

Phellis was the first of a very long list of cases in which the Supreme Court loosened the realization concept and more generally expanded the definition of income beyond *Macomber's* definition of income as "the gain derived from capital or labor, or from both combined."[94] The loosening and eventual abandonment of the separation requirement allowed Congress more flexibility in determining the definition of income. More importantly, by apparently abandoning the constitutional aspect of realization, the Court ceded to Congress much of the power in the tax area that it had retained for itself in *Macomber*. Before this abandonment occurred, however, *Macomber* had already helped shape the course of the income tax. Even after the alleged abandonment, the case continued to influence the law by serving as a point of reference, even if it was not mentioned directly. The cases that do specifically mention *Macomber*, however, together make up a large part of any basic income tax casebook. The long list includes *Bowers v. Kerbaugh–Empire*,[95] *Helvering v. Bruun*,[96] *Commissioner v. Glenshaw Glass*,[97] and most recently, *Cottage Savings and Loan Ass'n v Commissioner*,[98] decided in 1991.

Given the importance of the downgrading of realization from constitutional mandate to administrative convenience, it is somewhat surprising that there is no clear moment at which realization lost its constitutional status. Indeed, at least one current commentator believes that this status has never been lost.[99] Nevertheless, many commentators, following the lead of Stanley Surrey, view the 1940 case of *Helvering v. Bruun* as the critical point.[100]

In *Bruun*, the taxpayer owned land, which in 1915, he leased to a tenant for 99 years. In 1929, the tenant demolished an existing building on the land and erected a new one with a useful life less than the term of

---

[93] *Id.* at 173. Other cases further broadened the definition of realization as each opinion elaborated yet another set of facts in which the severing of gain from capital occurred. *See, e.g.,* Marr v. United States, 268 U.S. 536 (1925); and Cullinan v. Walker, 262 U.S. 134 (1923).

[94] 252 U.S. at 207.

[95] 271 U.S. 170 (1926); Burnet v. Sanford and Brooks Co., 282 U.S. 359 (1931).

[96] 309 U.S. 461 (1940).

[97] 348 U.S. 426 (1955).

[98] 499 U.S. 554 (1991).

[99] Ordower, *supra* note 3.

[100] Stanley Surrey, *The Supreme Court and the Federal Income Tax: Some Implications of the Recent Decisions*, 35 Ill. L. Rev. 779, 783 (1941) (taxing the improvement without severing it from the original property is "a complete denial" of the *Macomber* doctrine).

the lease. In 1933, the tenant defaulted, and Mr. Bruun repossessed the land, thereby gaining possession of the new building. The government and the taxpayer agreed that at the time of repossession the net fair value of the new building (gross value of the new building minus value of the demolished old building) was approximately $50,000. The question was not whether there was any gain but whether Bruun's repossession of the land caused realization (and hence income taxation) of that gain to occur.

Realization could occur at several points: in 1915, when the lease was signed; in 1929, when the new building was erected, or in 1933, when Mr. Bruun gained possession. According to the Haig–Simons accretion conception of income, under which increases in value are income when they occur, Mr. Bruun would have income in 1915 in the amount of the present value of the lease payments. Under a realization concept requiring separation of income from capital, Mr. Bruun had no income in either 1915, when he signed the lease, or in 1929, when the building was erected. Even under a broader definition of the concept than expressed in *Macomber*, neither event would trigger realization. Mr. Bruun still owned the building after the signing of the lease and the erection of the building added no value for him. Since its useful life was less than the lease term, Mr. Bruun would have nothing new at the expected time of repossession.

The taxpayer in *Bruun* argued that there was no realization in 1933 when he gained possession since the improvement could not be separated from the land. The economic gain arising upon repossession is not income under the Sixteenth Amendment, he argued, until he disposes of the asset. The Court, however, disagreed. In a brief opinion stating that gain need not be severed from the capital for there to be income under the Sixteenth Amendment, the Court stated that *Macomber* did not control because the language in that opinion regarding separation was not meant to be an all-inclusive definition. It was meant only to "clarify" the stock dividend situation by distinguishing between an ordinary dividend and a stock dividend. Although the Court confirmed "that economic gain is not always taxable as income," the Court stated that realization could occur without severing the improvement from the original capital as in the exchange of property.[101] Consequently, the Court held that the owner was taxable on the building's value (minus amortization costs) in 1933 when he came into possession of the land despite the fact that the landlord sold neither the building nor the land. Two years after the *Bruun* decision, Congress overruled it by enacting §§ 109 and 1019 so that the lessor had income only upon the disposition

---

[101] 309 U.S. at 469. Notice that the Court states that the exchange of property is a realization, but back in 1921, when § 1031 was enacted that was not so clear.

of the property.[102] Just because Congress had the power to tax, it did not have to exercise it to its full extent.

Bruun greatly broadened the meaning of realization but technically did not change its constitutional status, even though such experts as Stanley Surrey believed it did. Ten days later, however, in *Helvering v. Horst*,[103] the Court appeared to demote the concept to one of mere administrative convenience. *Horst* involved a taxpayer who gave his son the coupons on a bond he owned but retained the principal for himself. The primary question in the case was who should be taxed on the bond income, the donor father or the donee son. This is an assignment of income issue rather than a timing issue of when income should be taxed. The Court, however, justified its conclusion that the donor was taxable on the interest in terms of the realization concept. The donor was the proper person to tax, the Court stated, because even though he personally never received the income, realization occurred when he exercised his control over the income by gifting the coupons to his son and thereby separating the income from the capital. Realization, it said without further comment, was a rule "founded on administrative convenience," meant only to delay taxation until "the final event of enjoyment of the income."[104]

Although *Horst* clearly stated that realization was merely an administrative concern, it did not elaborate, offering neither precedent nor any rationale for this demotion. Many people, however, believed it was more than time to plainly overrule *Macomber*, especially many New Dealers who saw a reversal of the case as an opportunity to also "lay a wreath on the memory of Mr. Justice Brandeis," who had written a powerful

---

[102] Although *Bruun* changed the immediate tax consequences, the end result in terms of the amount of *gain* ordinarily will be the same. Assume the building is worth $100,000 when the landlord comes into possession, and he holds it for its entire useful life and rents it out for $12,000 per year. Under *Bruun*, if the landowner is taxed immediately on that amount when he comes into possession, he presumably then has $100,000 of depreciation to offset against the rental income. Under § 109, the owner is not immediately taxed but will have no depreciation to offset the rental income since his basis in the building under § 1019 is zero. The amount of *tax liability*, however, may differ under the two situations because the *Bruun* rule bunched the income, which potentially moved the taxpayer up into a higher tax bracket. Additionally, the amount of tax would depend on the character of the gain, which might be capital, instead of ordinary, if the taxpayer sold the building rather than retained it and rented it out.

[103] 311 U.S. 112 (1940).

[104] *Id.* at 116. The next question is when does the realization occur—when the gift is given or when the interest coupon comes due? The Court in *Horst* was not clear on this issue, perhaps because the coupon matured the same year as the gift. The timing, however, could be significant if coupons for several years were gifted. The Service and courts, however, have held that the realization does not occur at the time of the gift but rather occurs only when the donee actually receives the money. *See, e.g.,* Rev. Rul. 69–102, 1969–1 C.B. 32; S. M. Friedman v. Commissioner, 41 T.C. 428, 436, *aff'd*, 346 F.2d 506 (6th Cir.1965).

dissent in *Macomber*.[105] Three years after *Horst*, the Court had the ideal opportunity to do so in *Helvering v Griffiths*,[106] which involved a *pro rata* distribution of common stock to common stock shareholders, the exact situation in *Macomber*. Despite *Horst's* seemingly clear statements about mere administrative convenience, and the government's urgings, the Court refused to directly overrule *Macomber*.

The statute involved in *Griffiths*, written originally in 1936 with *Macomber's* constitutional limitations in mind, stated that a stock dividend "shall not be treated as a dividend to the extent that it does not constitute income to the shareholder within the meaning of the Sixteenth Amendment to the Constitution."[107] The government argued that the provision's legislative history and the administrative regulations under it provided the Court with the mechanism to overrule the *Macomber* decision because they indicated Congress' intent to challenge the constitutional validity of the decision. The Court recognized that "the question of the constitutional validity of *Eisner v. Macomber* is plainly one of the first magnitude."[108] Moreover, it acknowledged that both *Bruun* and *Horst* had "undermined further the original theoretical bases of the decision in *Eisner v. Macomber*."[109] The Court nevertheless declined to decide the constitutional issue on the grounds that it was not properly before the Court. After extensively examining the legislative history of the statute as well as that of the undistributed profits tax, the Court found no conclusive evidence of Congressional intent to challenge *Macomber*. Moreover, and probably more importantly to Justice Jackson who wrote the opinion, to retroactively overrule the statute would "unsettle tax administration and subject the Treasury itself to many demands in ways that we cannot anticipate and provide for" as well as create unfairness to taxpayers who had executed transactions based on what appeared to be clear law.[110]

---

[105] Stark, *supra* note 70, at 214 (quoting a March 27, 1943 letter from Roswell Magill to Robert Jackson).

[106] 318 U.S. 371 (1943). Stock dividends in two companion cases decided shortly thereafter were also held non-taxable. Helvering v. Sprouse and Strassburger v. Commissioner, 318 U.S. 604 (1943). *Sprouse* involved a pro rata distribution of nonvoting common stock to the holders of the outstanding voting and nonvoting common stock whereas *Strassburger* involved a pro rata distribution of nonvoting preferred stock on the voting common of its sole shareholder. Stark, *supra* note 70, at 217–19, discusses the cases in the context of *Griffiths*.

[107] Int. Rev. Code § 115(f) (1) (1939).

[108] 318 U.S. at 394.

[109] *Id.*

[110] *Id.* at 403. *See* Lyon, *supra* note 78, at 610–11 (stating that the majority placed stability of statutory interpretation above proper tax policy especially since the decision had been so widely relied upon).

While the majority decision focused on administrative concerns as a reason not to overrule its prior decision, Justice Douglas's dissent, joined by Justices Black and Murphy, concentrated on constitutional issues. It was time—past time—to overrule *Macomber*. Quoting Justice Brandeis' dissent in *Macomber*, Justice Douglas stated that stock dividends were taxable as income under the Sixteenth Amendment, which granted Congress the power to tax as income "everything which by reasonable understanding can fairly be regarded as income," including stock dividends.[111] Under this broad interpretation of the Sixteenth Amendment, Congress had the power to determine what was income. It legitimately exercised this power when it imposed a tax on stock dividends.

Ironically, the majority's refusal to deal directly with the constitutional aspect of *Macomber* created many of the administrative difficulties that the Court sought to avoid by not overruling the case. Its failure to explicitly consider the issue meant that the scope of realization's constitutional validity remained unresolved. This lack of resolution of the status of realization continued to worry Congress. In 1962, for example, Congress enacted provisions taxing United States shareholders on certain undistributed profits of their controlled foreign corporations, but the members of both the House Ways and Means and the Senate Finance Committees were concerned that the provision violated *Macomber's* constitutional realization requirement.[112] The constitutionality of taxing unrealized gains arose again in 1963 when President Kennedy proposed taxing unrealized gain at death. The question was still large enough that Treasury Secretary Dillon felt it necessary to submit a legal opinion on the issue. The opinion concluded that that there was "every probability" that the Supreme Court would uphold the constitutionality of taxing unrealized appreciation,[113] but others disagreed. The noted tax expert Roswell Magill, for example, believed that the Supreme Court "might very well conclude that it is unconstitutional."[114] Although there were

---

[111] 318 U.S. at 409.

[112] *See, e.g.*, S. Rep. No. 1881–87, at page 382–87 (1962) *reprinted in* 1962 USCCAN 3683–84; and H.R. Rep. 1447–87, at B–21 (both in Ordower, *supra* note 3, at 22). The court in Garlock, Inc. v. Commissioner, 489 F.2d 197, 203 n. 5 (2d Cir.1973), *cert. denied*, 417 U.S. 911 (1974), stated that "whatever may be the continuing validity of the doctrine of *Eisner v. Macomber,* it does not apply to the facts." *See also* Estate of Whitlock v. Commissioner, 59 T.C. 490, 506–10 (1972), *aff'd in part and rev'd in part*, 494 F.2d 1297 (10th Cir.), *cert. denied*, 419 U.S. 839 (1974). *Whitlock* distinguished *Macomber* on the grounds that the corporate earnings taxed in the controlled foreign corporation situation were current as opposed to accumulated ones in *Macomber* (a point noted by Powell back in 1920), and that in the CFC situation, the shareholder had the power to force distribution, which arguably implied some type of evasion situation (again a situation that both Powell and Ballantine had said *Macomber* would allow, piercing the corporate identity).

[113] *President's 1963 Tax Message: Hearings before the Committee on Ways and Means House of Representatives*, 88th Cong., 1st Sess. 595–97 (emphasis added).

[114] *Id.* at 1379 (statement of Roswell Magill). *See also id.* at 1363 (statement of Samuel J. Foosaner, on behalf of the N .J. Manufacturer's Association, that neither the opinion,

other reasons for defeating the proposal, uncertainty about its constitutionality certainly increased the odds that it would be defeated.

The Supreme Court's most recent pronouncement on realization reiterates that realization is only an administrative requirement but once again does not expressly overrule *Macomber*. In the 1991 case of *Cottage Savings Ass'n v. Commissioner*, the taxpayer, like most other savings and loan associations in the 1970s, held many long-term mortgages from which it received relatively low rates of income. Since current interest rates had increased, the value of these mortgages had decreased. Moreover, Cottage Savings was in the economically untenable position of having to pay interest to its current depositors and certificate holders at rates higher than it was earning on its mortgage loans. Disposing of the loans would ameliorate its financial situation because the taxable loss on disposition (due to the mortgages' decreased value) would enable it to take a tax deduction (and receive an income tax refund). It was reluctant to dispose of the mortgages, however, because Federal Home Loan Bank Board ("FHLBB") regulations required it to report any taxable losses. The reported losses would lower its net worth, which in turn would place it at risk of foreclosure. In response to this situation (and to avoid the political consequences of throwing so many S & Ls into bankruptcy), the FHLBB altered its regulations so that lenders could exchange loans without reporting them for regulatory purposes so long as the loans were "substantially identical". In 1980, Cottage Savings exchanged its loans for similar ones from another S & L. It did not report the loss for regulatory purposes but claimed a loss for tax purposes under § 165. The Service claimed the loss could not be recognized for tax purposes because the similarity of the exchanged loans meant that there was no realization.

Although the Court raised the issue of the constitutional status of the realization requirement, it did not discuss it. Rather, it simply stated that it "recognized" that realization was an administrative concept designed to avoid the administratively difficult task of valuing assets annually. As authority, it simply cited *Horst's* brief reference to realization being "founded on administrative convenience." Once again, the Court failed to explicitly overrule the constitutional necessity of realization established in *Macomber*. Instead, it accepted the concept as a valid administrative requirement and focused its attention on defining the scope of the regulatory rule.

The Court recognized that realization was not specifically defined in the statute but was contained in § 1001(a), which states that gain or loss is realized on the disposition of property. However, Treas. Reg.

---

nor the cases it cited, contain a "clear-cut statement" that unrealized gain could be income).

§ 1.1001–1 elaborates by providing that realization occurs when, among other things, property is exchanged for other property "differing materially either in kind or in extent." The Court accepted the regulation as a reasonable interpretation of the statute since it was first adopted in 1934 and had remained substantially unchanged through several reenactments of the statute.[115] The Court admitted, however, that determining what constituted a "material difference" was "a more complicated question".[116] In answering the question, the Court looked to the early cases, including *Macomber* itself, and focussed on a string of early reorganization cases beginning with *Phellis* that turned on this issue (although the regulation then used the phrase "essentially different"). These cases indicated that not all exchanges were realization events, although they did not unambiguously define the factors that prevented realization.

The Court indicated that the last of these reorganization cases, *Marr v. United States*, seemed to articulate the key issue in determining whether realization occurred: did the reorganization cause the taxpayer to acquire any legal rights in the new corporation that were different from those in the old corporation?[117] In *Marr*, General Motors of New Jersey reincorporated in Delaware, transferring all its assets to the new corporation. The Court held that the taxpayer realized gain when he exchanged all his shares in the old General Motors for shares in the new General Motors because the new corporation had different rights and powers under Delaware law than the old corporation had under New Jersey law. Consequently, the new stock was "essentially different" from the old stock even though the corporations had identical assets, and the shareholder had proportionate interest in both corporations.[118]

In *Cottage Savings*, the government offered an alternative to the *Marr* test, which focussed on legal entitlements. Its economic substance test considered all economically relevant facts including "the attitudes of

---

[115] 499 U.S. at 561. This is the re-enactment rule. The 1934 regulation, Treas. Reg. No. 86, Art. 111–1 (1934), is itself but a variation of the 1919 regulation holding that realization occurred when the property received was "essentially different" from the one disposed of. Treas. Reg. No. 45, Art. 1563, 21 Treas. Dec. Int. Rev. 170, 392 (1919) (under § 202(b)).

[116] 499 U.S. at 562.

[117] 268 U.S. 536 (1925).

[118] *Id.* at 541. In Weiss v. Stearn, 265 U.S. 242 (1924), decided one year previously, the Court held there was no realization in the only case involving two corporations organized in the same state. Justice McReynolds, the author of that opinion, noted in his separate Marr opinion, however, that the decision was based on receiving a different interest, not on the "relatively unimportant circumstance that the new and old corporations were organized under the laws of the same State." Loren D. Prescott, Jr., Cottage Savings Association v Commissioner: *Refining the Concept of Realization*, 60 Fordham L. Rev. 437, 452 (1991) (quoting 268 U.S. at 542).

the parties, the evaluation of the interests by the secondary mortgage market, and the views of the FHLBB."[119] The government argued that under this test there was no realization.

The Court, however, adopted the legal entitlement test articulated decades ago in the shadow of *Macomber*. It held that there was realization under a legal entitlement test because the exchanged loans had different debtors and different homes securing them. In so ruling, the majority ignored the similarity of the swapped loans' interest rates and their similar maturity lengths as well as the fact that the FHLBB considered the loans substantially identical for accounting purposes. Justice Blackmun, dissenting, commented that such an interpretation of a material difference contradicted "common sense."[120]

The Court's holding that realization occurred when formal legal entitlements changed allowed the taxpayer to deduct its loss. In the short run, the Service estimated that this loss, together with 96 similar pending cases, involved $419 million of taxes.[121] More importantly, by emphasizing legal rights as critical to realization rather than economic substance, the Court helped preserve tax shelters by allowing taxpayers to manipulate situations so that they could realize losses but not gains without changing their economic position. In 1929, Professor Rottschaefer had stated "the crucial question" was to determine "what differences justify the conclusion that interests are essentially different [the phrase then used instead of materially different]."[122] More than 60 years later, *Cottage Savings* showed that the question is still with us and is still crucial.

Conclusion

Realization has been called the "Achilles heel" of the income tax system because it creates so much uncertainty and complexity in the tax law.[123] Although it does have the advantage of decreasing both liquidity and valuation problems that arise under a pure accretion model of taxation, these advantages may be overstated and its disadvantages are numerous. Its benefits are exaggerated, according to some commenta-

---

[119] 499 U.S. at 562.

[120] 499 U.S. at 570.

[121] Ruth Marcus, *Supreme Court Backs S & Ls on Mortgage Tax Deduction*, Wash. Post, April 18, 1991, at B11.

[122] Henry Rottschaefer, *The Concept of Income in Federal Taxation*, 13 Minn. L. Rev. 637, 651 (1920) (another lead article; how tax issues have fallen!) (analyzing the stock dividend and reorganization cases in the 1920s and the significance of realization).

[123] William D. Andrews, *The Achilles Heel of Income Taxation*, in *Taxation for the 1980's* (Walker ed., 1983).

tors, because many assets, in fact, are easily valued and liquidity problems, to the extent they exist, can be ameliorated by such techniques as deferred payments with interest.[124] The disadvantages of realization, on the other hand, are monumental. Deferring the taxation of income beyond the point in time that the income (or loss) economically occurs significantly increases complexity, distorts economic behavior, alters wealth distribution, and frequently violates horizontal or vertical equity among taxpayers.

Despite these substantial negative aspects of realization, the concept is a central part of the United States' income tax system. *Macomber* did not create the concept; it existed prior to the case and for practical administrative reasons would probably have continued to develop. What *Macomber* did do, however, was significantly influence the development of the concept and related areas of the law, including embedding it more deeply in the system than might otherwise have occurred. This influence has been profound not just because of the content of the decision but also because of its timing.

Major decisions made when any new enterprise is established set a tone and structure that influence future decisions. This is as true for a new legal structure as it is for a new business. Fluidity that exists at the start becomes hardened into routines that are hard to break. As time goes by, people automatically think a certain way about conceptual problems, and a whole body of procedure (administrative and judicial in the case of law) develops that encourages continuing in such well-known patterns. Inertia sets in politically as well. Even if people are indifferent between option A and option B before one of the two options is selected, they may be unwilling to switch to option A after option B has been chosen and in force for some time. They may have altered their thoughts and actions to accommodate option B and now have a vested interest in maintaining that option for financial, psychological, or other reasons. And they are willing to spend time and money to maintain that option. The delivery of health insurance via one's employer is one example of how a decision made in the infancy of group health insurance has so shaped institutions, thinking, and practice, that change becomes nearly impossible (as the Clinton debacle on health care illustrated).

In the income tax area, *Eisner v. Macomber* is one of those early choices that shaped future development of the tax law. The content of the decision as well as the context in which it occurred heightened its

---

[124] Professor David Shakow, for example, states that data indicates that liquidity is not a big problem as believed. David Shakow, *supra* note 3, at 1167–76. Professor James Repetti, in contrast, argues that valuations for an annual accretions tax would present difficult valuation and liquidity issues as well as erode the tax base because taxpayers would have strong economic motives to minimize those values. James R. Repetti, *It's All About Valuation*, 53 Tax L. Rev. 607 (2000) (speaking of an annual wealth tax).

immediate impact. The holding that realization was a constitutional aspect of income was the most dominant aspect of the opinion, especially given the contemporary concerns about judicial review and the respective roles of the Court and Congress generally. Within that perspective, the Court's mixed view on the theory of income and the nature of a corporation took on extra meaning and affected legislative and judicial actions in the formative years of the development of the tax system. The uncertainty about both the necessity of the constitutional constraint and about the determination of when realization occurs continued for years, and to some degree still continues. In this way, *Macomber* has left its imprint on at least five important areas of taxation.

First, the case is a major reason for the continued general reliance on realization despite realization's many disadvantages. Although Congress has eliminated the requirement in certain limited areas where valuation is easy such as §§ 1256, 467, 475, 817A, 1296, and the original discount rules, broader proposals to switch to an accretion system have not met—and most likely will not meet—with success. *Macomber* plays a large role in this failure. By ingraining the principle of realization so early and so deeply into the fabric of the tax system, it reinforced political, popular, and institutional inertia against its elimination. Moreover, the Court's failure to decisively overrule the constitutional aspect of realization makes such a change even more unlikely because it creates uncertainty, however small, as to whether Congress has the power to make such a radical change.

Second, the initial constitutional necessity for realization and uncertainty about when it occurs helped establish important deferral sections that still exist today, including the large real tax shelter created by § 1031. Third, the Court's decision to uphold the taxation of capital gains was influenced by the virulent reaction to the *Macomber* case the previous year. Fourth, by stressing the separation of corporation and individual taxpayer, *Macomber* may have delayed early explorations of integrating the corporate tax with individual tax. Finally, the realization concept in general encourages, at a minimum, a hybrid income/consumption tax because it provides a rationale for the many consumption aspects of the income tax. The language of *Macomber* further encouraged this thinking for years with its conflicting discussion of whether accretions to capital were income. Although there may be policy reasons for consumption treatment such as to encourage savings, a system that is neither fish nor fowl can exacerbate complexity, theoretical inconsistencies, and practical inequities.

A serious reevaluation of the realization concept ultimately leads to the question of the proper tax base. The need for realization means that all increases in wealth will not be immediately taxed. Depending on the definition of realization, the moment of taxation can be manipulated—

either pulled closer to immediate taxation or pushed farther and farther back. Logically, once the idea that some change in the relationship with the asset is required, there is nothing to stop pushing back the point of taxation until the ultimate change in that relation: the consumption of the asset. Thus the logic of realization exerts pressure to change the basis of taxation from income to consumption. This is especially true when one of the foundational bases for the requirement enunciated in *Macomber* and still given today is that gains remaining in the investment are merely "paper gains." Whereas the other two major rationales for realization—problems of liquidity and valuation—are based on administrative convenience, this more theoretical justification at heart questions the existence of income. If there is no income so long as money is still at risk, then the proper basis of taxation would be consumption since it is only at that time that the money is no longer at risk.

Macomber is an old case. Its definition of income with its constitutional aspect has long since been weakened if not totally eviscerated. For this reason, some commentators claim it is now only an historical curiosity that should be relegated to the footnotes of a casebook. Mark Twain once said that reports of his death had been greatly exaggerated. As this chapter has shown, the same may be said of *Macomber*. Even if the case is truly dead, however, its restless ghost still walks.

3

Deborah H. Schenk

The Story of *Kirby Lumber*: The Many Faces of Discharge of Indebtedness Income

Surely *United States v. Kirby Lumber Co.*[1] is one of the shortest Supreme Court opinions ever to pack such a wallop. The Court's opinion is only two paragraphs long, and the first is largely a recitation of the facts. Despite its length (or maybe because of its length), it has spawned seven decades of controversy. The holding of the case is concise—the cancellation of a debt creates taxable income—but the reasoning is obscure and has produced many exceptions and much uncertainty.

The situation that gives rise to the *Kirby Lumber* issue can be stated very simply. Suppose *Lender* lends *Borrower* $10,000. Then some time later, because B is unable to repay the full amount of the loan, L agrees to accept $3,000 in satisfaction of the loan. *Kirby Lumber* holds that B has $7,000 of income. But what if B had taken the $10,000 and lost it all in his business or in gambling so that he did not make any money in the transaction? Or what if at the time L discharged the loan, B was insolvent or had declared bankruptcy? What if L was B's mother who lent the $10,000 to help B pay medical school tuition and on graduation day forgave the loan? What if L had lent B the $10,000 as the sales price of a used car, which turns out to be a lemon, and L accepts $3,000 as payment for the car? The resolution of these cases turns in large part on why the borrower in the simple case has $7,000 of cancellation of debt ("COD") income. The story begins with *Kirby Lumber*.

---

[1] 284 U.S. 1 (1931).

Prior Proceedings

Who is Kirby Lumber anyway?[2] Most Texans, including its tax lawyers, probably have no idea that the Kirby Drive they take to the Houston Astrodome has the same namesake as the well-known case. John Henry Kirby, a Houston pioneer, was born in 1860 near a settlement called Peachtree Village. Kirby was a lawyer, but he made his fortune in timber. During the state's first oil boom, he struck it rich by buying huge tracts of pine forest, which he sold to the Houston Oil Company. He kept the timber, however, and organized the Kirby Lumber Company to cut it down. In 1893, he started the first railroad through what is known as the Thicket in the vast forests of East Texas, and in 1896, he built his first sawmill at Silsbee. The chartering of his company on July 8, 1901, made headlines at the time as the largest lumber company in the world.

Kirby was extremely successful. At its height, between 1910 and 1920, his company had a dozen sawmills and five logging camps in operation, employing almost 17,000 workers.[3] But Kirby's wealth and fame was fleeting. He was plagued by litigation and bankrupted by the Depression. His company was transferred to pay off debts. In his later years, he traveled around the United States denouncing the New Deal.

The litigation in *Kirby Lumber Co. v. Commissioner* arose during the company's glory days. On July 16, 1923, the Kirby Lumber Company issued $12,126,800 in bonds. Later in the same year, Kirby Lumber retired bonds with a par value of $1,078,300 for $940,779. This was $137,521 less than Kirby received for the bonds. The government asserted that the $137,521 was discharge of indebtedness income.

That simple recitation, however, obscures a fact that was in controversy and that was lost to courts and commentators for four decades. It often has been assumed that Kirby Lumber issued the bonds for cash, probably because the Court stated the bonds were issued "at par." But in fact, they were issued for preferred stock and accrued dividend arrearages.

---

[2] When tax lawyers hear the name "Kirby Lumber," they immediately think of the taxation of loan discharges. But other lawyers think of something different when they hear the name. Kirby Lumber Co. has been involved in a number of well-known cases. When securities lawyers hear "Kirby Lumber," they think of Bell v. Kirby Lumber, 413 A.2d 137 (Del.1980), a case involving valuation of minority shareholder interests. Timber lawyers think of Kirby Lumber v. Temple, 83 S.W.2d 638 (Tex.1935), a case involving damages for cut timber. Even tax lawyers may be thinking of another case when "Kirby Lumber" comes to mind. Kirby Lumber Corp. v. Phinney, 412 F.2d 598 (5th Cir.1969), is a leading case determining what constitutes property primarily held for sale to customers under § 1221(a)(1).

[3] By the 1920s, most of the timber had been cut. It has since regrown and is now part of the Big Thicket National Preserve.

The complaint simply alleged that the bonds were issued at par. The Court of Claims repeated this statement, adding that the repurchase price was $137,521 less than the issuing price. The Court of Claims held that the "excess of the issuing price of the bonds over the purchase price" was gain but not income within the meaning of the Sixteenth Amendment. From this perspective, the consideration received for the bonds was irrelevant, and there was no reason for the lower court to focus on the consideration.

The government, however, interpreted this finding to mean that the bonds had been issued for cash. Its petition for *certiorari* states: "For these bonds the Lumber Company received cash at par for each bond."[4] At another point, it said the case involved "actual cash received during the year in excess of disbursements made or incurred."[5]

The opposition brief claimed that this statement was incorrect and emphasized that "Kirby Lumber Company DID NOT RECEIVE CASH for the bonds here involved." Although the bonds were issued at par, they "were exchanged for preferred stock . . . and accrued dividends."

In its reply brief, the government argued that it appropriately interpreted the finding. It asserted that there was "nothing in the record to sustain the respondent's allegation."[6] Quoting the finding of the Court of Claims, to wit, that the bonds were subsequently repurchased "at less than the issuing price," the government took the position that it was "assumed by all parties that the bonds were issued at par *for cash*. That statement was not challenged." Finally, the government argued that it did not matter in any event whether the company received cash for the bonds "since in some form the price received was the par value of the bonds issued."[7]

The taxpayer then filed a motion to remand the case to the Court of Claims for further findings. In that motion, it laid out its statement of the facts:

> The facts are that $11,526,800 in bonds plus $9776.94 in cash, were exchanged for preferred stock at the call price of $105 per $100 par value share plus accrued dividends of $126 per share, or a total of $231 for each $100 par value share of preferred stock . . . No cash was received for the bonds.[8]

---

[4] Government's Petition for *Certiorari* at 2.

[5] *Id.* at 4.

[6] Reply Brief for the United States at 2.

[7] *Id.* at 3.

[8] Petitioner's Motion to Remand to Court of Claims for Further Findings at 2. Bonds worth $600,000 are unaccounted for. What Kirby Lumber did with those bonds is not

The taxpayer urged the court to remand if it believed the consideration received for the bonds was material. The government opposed the motion, again arguing that there was no evidence before the Claims Court on which the finding urged by the taxpayer could be based and that it was immaterial whether Kirby Lumber received cash or securities since everyone agreed that the bonds were issued for par value.[9]

The Supreme Court Decision

The Supreme Court granted *certiorari*. The government again argued that the type of consideration received by Kirby Lumber was irrelevant,[10] and in its brief, the taxpayer agreed.[11] Thus, the record before the Court supported neither the government's position that the bonds had been issued for cash nor the taxpayer's position that they had been issued in exchange for stock and dividend arrearages. Both parties agreed that this distinction was irrelevant, however, and the Court apparently concurred. The Court's recitation of the facts states only that the bonds were issued at par.[12]

The Briefs

According to the government's petition for *certiorari*, the question before the Court was "whether a corporation which sells its own bonds for par, and during the same year purchases back some of the same bonds for less than par and retires them, thereby realizes a taxable gain."[13]

The government had always taken the position that the answer to that question was "yes." Article 545(c) of the Regulations, issued in 1918 (five years after the passage of the first income tax act), provided that if a corporation purchases and retires bonds issued at par for a price less than par, the excess of the issue price over the purchase price was income. This regulation had been repromulgated several times since

---

evident from the record. Only $1,078,300 of the $12,126,800 of bonds issued were repurchased in the transaction at issue in the Supreme Court.

[9] Brief for the United States in Opposition to the Motion to Remand at 2.

[10] Brief for the United States at 2.

[11] Brief for Respondent at 2.

[12] Although this controversy about the consideration received for the bonds is clearly outlined in the various motions and briefs, it apparently was lost to history for four decades. Several courts stated that the consideration received by Kirby Lumber was cash. In a 1977 article, Professor Boris Bittker laid out the probable facts. Boris I. Bittker, *Income From the Cancellation of Indebtedness: A Historical Footnote to the* Kirby Lumber Co. *Case*, 4 J. Corp. Tax'n 124 (1977). Despite the evidence, the notion persists that the holding in *Kirby Lumber* related to debt issued for cash.

[13] Government's Petition for *Certiorari* at 1.

1918 and had been in force for over twelve years at the time of the *Kirby Lumber* litigation.

So why did the lower court not follow this regulation? The answer lies in a case the Supreme Court decided five years earlier: *Bowers v. Kerbaugh–Empire Co.*[14] Before World War I, Kerbaugh–Empire borrowed money from a bank in Germany, repayable in marks. The funds were transferred to a subsidiary of Kerbaugh–Empire, which lost the money in business and deducted the losses. In 1921, Kerbaugh–Empire repaid the balance at a time when the German mark was depreciated. The difference between the amount borrowed and the amount repaid was $884,456. The Supreme Court held that Kerbaugh–Empire had no income when it repaid less than it borrowed because it had an overall loss on the transaction.

In not following the regulation, the *Kerbaugh-Empire* decision created a significant problem for the government. This issue had been pending for awhile. The Board of Tax Appeals had not followed the regulation, holding in several cases that discharge from indebtedness was not income. In its petition for *certiorari*, the government noted that a large number of cases on this issue were pending in the Internal Revenue Bureau, and the amount of taxes involved was $10 million. At least ten cases in the federal district courts also were pending, and in addition to *Kirby Lumber*, another appeal was pending in the circuit court.

The government argued that the Court need not rely on *Kerbaugh-Empire*. Kerbaugh–Empire was apparently insolvent, and the government argued that therefore the facts of *Kerbaugh-Empire* could be distinguished from those in *Kirby Lumber*. According to the government, *Kerbaugh-Empire* stood for the proposition that "when A borrows money and loses, through business reverses, the entire amount of money borrowed, any subsequent settlement with the lender whereby A is enabled to liquidate his obligation for less than its face amount, the difference between the amount paid to liquidate the obligation and the face amount of the obligation is not income."[15] Thus, if Kirby Lumber had been insolvent, *Kerbaugh-Empire* would have been good precedent. Since Kirby Lumber was not insolvent, the government asserted that it had cancellation of indebtedness income.

The lower court disagreed and held that *Kerbaugh-Empire* could not be distinguished. The financial position of the debtor was irrelevant. The Claims Court ignored the regulation and based its decision solely on the holding in *Kerbaugh-Empire* that the taxpayer had no income.[16]

---

[14] 271 U.S. 170 (1926).

[15] Brief for the United States at 15.

[16] 44 F.2d 885 (1930).

As the government admitted, there was no conflict in the lower courts.[17] Why did the Supreme Court grant *certiorari*? The Court simply refused to follow any of the lower court decisions.

The Opinion

There is only one paragraph of reasoning in the Court's opinion, and it does two things. First, the Court rejects any reliance on *Kerbaugh-Empire*, noting that the transaction in that case was a loss. Second, the Court accepted the "net worth theory" offered by the government in its brief. The government explained that when Kirby Lumber issued the bonds, it increased the company's assets in an equal amount.[18] On the retirement of the bonds, Kirby Lumber's liabilities decreased by $1,078,300, but its assets decreased by only $940,779. The income was the $137,521 increase in net worth. The Court accepted this approach, but it used language not found in the government's brief. The Court distinguished *Kerbaugh-Empire*, saying that "[a]s a result of its dealing it made available $137,521 [of] assets previously offset by the obligation of bonds now extinct."[19]

Kerbaugh-Empire was not the only Supreme Court decision that presented difficulties for the government. The Court's broad statement in *Eisner v. Macomber* that defined income as "the gain derived from capital, from labor, or from both combined"[20] seemed to preclude the government's position. A mere change in the taxpayer's net worth was not thought to be derived from either capital or labor, and some courts had held that discharge of indebtedness was not income under the *Macomber* definition. Kirby Lumber argued that the Court could not find that the discharge of indebtedness was income without overruling *Macomber*.[21]

The lower court in *Kerbaugh-Empire* accepted the respondent's *Macomber* argument. In refusing to accept the statement that a decrease in negative net worth could constitute income, it relied on the *Macomber* definition of income: "The improvement of the plaintiff's balance sheet is not income to the plaintiff. All that it had was a decrease in liability."[22] It went on to say that "[i]t seems clear that neither the Sixteenth Amendment nor the Revenue Act sought to levy an income tax upon

---

[17] Brief for the United States at 13.

[18] *Id.* at 7.

[19] 284 U.S. 1, 2 (1931).

[20] 252 U.S. 189, 207 (1920). *See* Chapter 2 of *Tax Stories*.

[21] Respondent's Brief at 5.

[22] 300 F. 938, 943 (S.D.N.Y.1924).

anything except income as it was actually received and ... there can be no such thing as a negative income; the two words being inconsistent."[23]

The *Kirby Lumber* Court, however, did not mention *Macomber* by name. It found that the taxpayer had discharge of indebtedness income without saying that the income was not "gain derived from capital, from labor, or from both combined." The closest it came to distinguishing *Macomber* was to say: "We see nothing to be gained by the discussion of judicial definitions."[24]

Another recent tax case that the Court did not mention was *Old Colony Trust Co. v. Commissioner*,[25] which in some ways was a precursor to *Kirby Lumber*. In that case, the Court found that an employee had additional taxable income when his employer agreed to pay his taxes. Where a third party discharges an obligation of the debtor, the transfer is the equivalent to a receipt of cash by the debtor from the third party, followed by a satisfaction of the debt by the debtor. The discharge of a debt by the creditor at a discount is the same as if the creditor had transferred cash to the debtor who used it to satisfy the debt. Nevertheless, the Court did not rely on or even mention *Old Colony*.[26]

The Immediate Impact of *Kirby Lumber*

It is easy to become confused about the source of the income in *Kirby Lumber*. Consider this hypothetical put forth in the taxpayer's brief in opposition to the petition for *certiorari* in the Supreme Court:

> [S]uppose the A Corporation purchased a factory for $150,000 of which it paid $50,000 with cash in its possession, and $100,000 with money obtained from B and secured by a mortgage on the factory. Before maturity B became in need of funds and accepted $90,000 in full payment of the mortgage. Under the Government's theory the A Corporation would make a taxable gain of $10,000, despite the fact that the transaction resulted in a total outlay by the A Corporation of $140,000.[27]

How, the lawyer is arguing, could the taxpayer have a $10,000 gain when it is out of pocket $140,000?[28] The government's lawyer, on the other

---

[23] *Id.* at 945.

[24] 284 U.S. at 2.

[25] 279 U.S. 716 (1929).

[26] Nor did it rely on United States v. Boston and Maine R.R., 279 U.S. 732 (1929), in which the Court held that a lessor had additional rent where the lessee agreed to pay the lessor's taxes.

[27] Respondent's Brief in Opposition to the Petition for *Certiorari* at 10.

[28] It is interesting that the taxpayer significantly changed this hypo in its final brief. The hypo became:

hand, took the position that the taxpayer has acquired a factory worth $150,000 but is only out of pocket $140,000.[29]

While the Court adopted the government's result in the above example, it did not adopt its rationale. The Court's reasoning is confusing and led to decades of confusion. It is worthwhile to try to sort out the Court's theory and then compare it to another possible explanation for why the taxpayer has income on the discharge of indebtedness on these facts.

1. *The Freeing-of-Assets Theory*

Justice Holmes' one paragraph of reasoning does not give us much to go on, especially since half of it is devoted to a description of another case (*Bowers v. Kerbaugh–Empire*). In two sentences, Holmes lays out what became the freeing-of-assets theory: "Here [in *Kirby Lumber*] there was no shrinkage of assets and the taxpayer made a clear gain. As a result of its dealings it made available $137,521 [of] assets previously offset by the obligation of bonds now extinct."

Numerous courts have interpreted that passage to mean that the income was not the cancellation but the freeing of assets from offsetting liabilities. Under this theory, a debtor recognizes income when a debt is discharged because the discharge decreases the debtor's liabilities but does not decrease the debtor's assets. The income arises from the increase in net worth. A determination of whether the taxpayer has income requires an examination of the taxpayer's balance sheet at the time the debt is discharged. The freeing-of-assets theory has been subjected to withering criticism on three grounds.

First, the increase in net worth notion does not stand up to scrutiny. Presumably, if Kirby Lumber was able to repurchase its bonds at a discount, they were not worth face value immediately before the repurchase. They were worth approximately $940,000 and that is what Kirby Lumber paid for them. Kirby Lumber's net worth remained the same; it merely swapped bonds worth $940,000 for $940,000 cash.

Suppose a corporation bought a factory for $150,000, paying $50,000 in cash and assuming a mortgage for $100,000. Before maturity the holders of the mortgage became in need of funds and accepted $90,000 in full settlement of the mortgage. Under the Government's theory the corporation realized a taxable gain of $10,000, although the true fact is that the factory cost but $140,000 and not $150,000.

The case where the seller of property reduces the debt is discussed below and is not the situation in *Kirby Lumber*. The original hypothetical shows a reluctance to accept the notion of income where the taxpayer *pays* out money and receives nothing tangible in return.

[29] The government noted in its brief that Kirby Lumber received property worth $137,521 more than it paid for it. Brief for the United States at 9.

Second, there was an increase in net worth in *Kerbaugh-Empire* as well, but the Court distinguished the case. Suppose a taxpayer has $100 of liabilities and $40 of assets. A creditor discharges a $20 loan. T's net worth before the discharge was -$60 and after is -$40. Only someone who has no understanding of negative numbers could fail to see that T's net worth has increased, or to put it another way, that there has been a decrease in T's negative net worth.

Third, the solvency or net worth of a taxpayer is not a determinant of the taxability of amounts received in other situations. For example, it is clear that the receipt of salary by an insolvent taxpayer is clearly taxable income even though the debtor remains insolvent after using the cash to reduce the debt.

2. *The Whole Transaction Theory*

In *Kerbaugh-Empire*, the Court took into account how the loan proceeds were used and determined that there was no income because the overall transaction was a loss. The Court implied that had the borrowed funds not been lost, the repayment of the loan with fewer funds than had been received when the loan was incurred would have resulted in income. To make that determination, the Court integrated the use to which the funds were put for eight years with the debt discharged.

By way of distinguishing *Kerbaugh-Empire*, Justice Holmes in *Kirby Lumber* restated the Court's position in the earlier case: "the whole transaction was a loss." The assumption is that the whole transaction refers to both the loan and the use to which the proceeds were put. In the absence of an overall profit, there could be no income. Under this approach, the tax treatment of the discharged debt depends on the profitability of the transaction in which the borrowed funds are used. For example, suppose A corporation has $1 million in assets. It issues bonds at par $100,000 and invests the proceeds in Project X, which fails, and A loses the $100,000. Suppose it is able to retire the bonds at $90,000. Overall, the investment in Project X "as a whole was a loss," and thus under this theory, there would be no income.

This approach flies in the face of a case the Court decided in the same year as (but before) *Kirby Lumber*. In *Burnet v. Sanford & Brooks Co.*,[30] the court had rejected transactional accounting in favor of annual accounting. The *Kirby* Court cited *Sanford & Brooks*, noting that Kirby Lumber had "realized within the year an accession to income." *Sanford & Brooks*, however, is inconsistent with the whole transaction approach of *Kerbaugh-Empire*, cited favorably by the *Kirby Lumber* Court, al-

---

[30] 282 U.S. 359 (1931).

though the *Sanford & Brooks* Court did not see it that way. The Court in *Sanford & Brooks* described the *Kerbaugh-Empire* holding as follows:

> In that case the taxpayer, which had lost, in business, borrowed money, which was to be repaid in German marks, and which was later repaid in depreciated currency, had neither made a profit on the transaction, nor received any money or property which could have been made subject to the tax.[31]

Taking into account the losses incurred with loan proceeds seems utterly incompatible with the annual accounting required by *Sanford & Brooks*.

The whole transaction approach also would effectively permit a taxpayer to deduct a loss that otherwise would be nondeductible. Suppose a taxpayer purchases a home computer for $2,000 on credit. Two years later when the computer is largely obsolete, he sells it back to the store for $500, and the store discharges the remaining $1,500 debt. If the whole transaction theory is followed, T would have no COD income. This is exactly the same as if he is taxed on the $1,500 of income but permitted to deduct the $1,500 loss on the personal computer. Or suppose the taxpayer borrows $20,000, invests it in his business, and loses the entire amount. Most likely, the loss would be deductible, and if he also were permitted to exclude the $20,000 when the lender discharges the debt, he effectively would have a double deduction.

The whole transaction theory is not only theoretically wrong, it is completely impractical. In order to apply it, one has to know the use to which the borrowed funds were put. This is a completely implausible approach due to the fungibility of money.[32] It is hard to understand how the theory would have applied in *Kirby Lumber*. The corporation issued its bonds in exchange for its preferred stock and dividend arrearages. How does one determine whether there was a "clear gain" on the transaction? What is the transaction? Tracing the proceeds of the bonds to the preferred stock tells us nothing. Should we instead trace the proceeds from the sale of the preferred stock? Even if the proceeds can be traced to a specific investment, as in *Kerbaugh-Empire*, it is clear that the corporation could have advanced other funds to its subsidiary and used the borrowed funds in other projects.[33]

---

[31] *Id.* at 364.

[32] Although one the Service has not abandoned. *See* Reg. § 1.163–8T.

[33] Another example of the impracticality of this approach is found in Helvering v. American Chicle Co., 291 U.S. 426 (1934). As part of the consideration for purchasing the assets of a company, the taxpayer assumed its outstanding bonds. The taxpayer later discharged the bonds at discount. Nothing in the record indicated what the taxpayer had done with the assets. With no facts to go on, the court assumed that there had been an overall profit, and *Kerbaugh-Empire* did not apply. The Court held that the case was indistinguishable from *Kirby Lumber*.

Furthermore, the Court in *Kirby Lumber* assumed that the transaction was profitable whereas the *Kerbaugh-Empire* transaction was not. But that does not follow, and trying to figure out whether the "transaction" in *Kirby Lumber* was profitable illustrates a flaw in the theory. It is unclear why Kirby Lumber was able to repurchase its bonds at a discount. Most likely interest rates rose, and therefore the value of the bonds fell. As a result, the value of the company presumably fell as well. It is hard to assert in that case that the "whole transaction" produced a gain.

So in one paragraph, the Court cited favorably the whole transaction approach *and* suggested that Kirby Lumber had income because assets were freed up. This is just as confusing as it sounds. The two ideas do not produce identical results. Take a simple example: Suppose B borrows $100,000 from L and uses it to drill an oil well. B hits a dry hole and loses the entire $100,000 investment. Although B is solvent, L discharges $40,000 of the debt. Under the whole transaction theory, B would have no income because "the transaction as a whole was a loss." Under the freeing-of-assets theory, B would have income of $40,000 because the discharge "made available ($40,000) assets previously offset" by the liability.

The conflict between the two theories apparently did not bother Justice Holmes, but they both cannot be right.

3. *A Better Approach: the Loan Proceeds Theory*

This theory starts from the premise that loan proceeds are excluded on receipt.[34] Because of the obligation to repay, the debtor has no accession to wealth even though his assets have increased, and he can do what he likes with the borrowed funds. Where the debt is repaid, the assumption on which the funds were excluded was warranted. When that obligation is extinguished without payment, there is no longer any authority for the original exclusion.[35] Where the taxpayer repays less than she borrowed, she has enjoyed an accretion to wealth. It does not

---

[34] This approach to discharge of indebtedness income is often attributed to Boris I. Bittker & Barton H. Thompson, Jr., *Income From the Discharge of Indebtedness: The Progeny of* United States v. Kirby Lumber Co., 66 Cal. L. Rev. 1159 (1978).

[35] There are other instances in the tax law where mistakes that turn out to be faulty are later corrected. For example, depreciation is based on the assumption that the property will decline in value. When the taxpayer takes depreciation on property that increases in value, he must recapture the deductions. § 1245. Similarly, the tax benefit doctrine requires a taxpayer to repay an earlier deduction when the funds that gave rise to the deduction are returned. § 111. The "transactional equity" of the loan proceeds theory is quite similar. *See* Louis A. Del Cotto, *Debt Discharge Income:* Kirby Lumber Co. *Revisited Under the "Transactional Equity" Rule of* Hillsboro, 50 Tax Notes 761 (1991). But the *Kirby Lumber* principle is broader than the tax benefit rule. It requires an inclusion of income even if the taxpayer received no tax benefit (other than deferral) from the loan proceeds because, for example, they were used for consumption.

matter what the taxpayer does with the funds—whether they are used in business (in either a losing or profitable venture) or spent on consumption. The taxpayer has received a financial benefit from the use of the borrowed funds, a financial benefit whose cost was less than the benefit. It also does not matter what assets the debtor has when the loan is discharged. Thus this theory applies equally well to an insolvent debtor.

Although neither *Kerbaugh-Empire* nor *Kirby Lumber* has ever been overruled (and in fact the holdings are still good law), the courts have backed away from both the whole transaction approach and the freeing-of-assets approach. Although the Supreme Court has taken notice of the utility of the loan proceeds approach, it has not adopted it exclusively. In *United States v. Centennial Savings Bank,* the Court stated:

> Borrowed funds are excluded from income in the first instance because the taxpayer's obligation to repay the funds offsets any increase in the taxpayer's assets; if the taxpayer is thereafter released from his obligation to repay, the taxpayer enjoys a net increase in assets equal to the forgiven portion of the debt, and the basis for the original exclusion thus evaporates.[36]

Notice that the Court essentially cites both the loan proceeds and the freeing-of-assets theories.[37]

The loan proceeds theory would not necessarily result in taxation in all cases in which a debt is discharged. Suppose a taxpayer loses a personal injury case and never makes good on the judgment. Does the "discharge" from this liability produce income? Under the loan proceeds theory, the taxpayer received no cash or property on the creation of the debt that was excluded from tax. This theory better explains the result in cases where the borrower did not receive cash at the time the obligation was undertaken and thus the overall profit or loss may be impossible to determine.[38]

The loan proceeds theory, the freeing-of-assets theory, and the whole transactions approach are inconsistent and do not necessarily produce the same result. Suppose, for example, that T promises to make a payment to X (in a situation that would not produce a deduction when the payment is made), and T is ultimately freed from that obligation. Under the freeing-of-assets theory, T would have COD income because his balance sheet is no longer encumbered by the obligation. Under the

---

[36] 499 U.S. 573, 583 (1991).

[37] Increasingly, lower courts have rejected these earlier theories. *See, e.g.,* Estate of Newman v. Commissioner, 934 F.2d 426, 432 (2d Cir.1991) (describing freeing-of-assets theory as "discredited rationale").

[38] *See, e.g.,* Commissioner v. Rail Joint Co., 61 F.2d 751 (2d Cir.1932), and United States Steel Corp. v. United States, 848 F.2d 1232 (Fed.Cir.1988), both of which are discussed below.

loan proceeds theory, however, T would have no income because he had not received any income or property at the time he incurred the obligation. Under the whole transaction approach, it would be necessary to know what T did with the proceeds of the loan.

The Continuing Importance of *Kirby Lumber* Today

Congress codified the *Kirby Lumber* rule in § 61(a)(12) when it adopted the Internal Revenue Code of 1954. Previously, the provision with respect to COD income was only in the regulations. The 1939 Code, however, added the predecessor of §§ 108 and 1017. The original version of § 108 permitted corporate taxpayers in "unsound financial condition" to exclude the amount of any income attributable to discharge of indebtedness that was evidenced by a security. In 1942, Congress eliminated the requirement that the corporation be in unsound financial condition. In the 1954 Code, the rule was rewritten to include individuals as well as corporations. In 1986, this election was eliminated except for insolvent and bankrupt taxpayers. When Congress subsequently added two other exemptions, it extended § 108 to apply to them.

Section 108 does not permanently exclude the COD income but requires a reduction in tax attributes, thus effectively deferring the income.[39] Tax attributes include net operating losses, capital losses, and the basis of the taxpayer's assets. The intent is not to exempt the income but to defer it. In very rare circumstances, a taxpayer actually has COD income but § 108 results in permanent forgiveness. For example, a taxpayer who has no tax attributes to be reduced and owns no property whose basis can be reduced exempts the COD income forever.

Under § 108, a taxpayer is required to reduce tax attributes in four cases: (1) where the taxpayer is in a bankruptcy proceeding, (2) where the taxpayer is insolvent, (3) in most cases where the COD income was incurred in a farming business (whether or not the taxpayer is insolvent), and (4) where the debt is qualified real property business indebtedness (whether or not the taxpayer is insolvent).

On its face, *Kirby Lumber* appeared to apply very broadly. With the possible exception of the fact pattern in *Kerbaugh-Empire*, which the Court distinguished, nothing in the opinion suggests that a debtor would not have COD income in all cases in which a debt was discharged in whole or in part. In order to provide relief from the harshness of the

---

[39] The idea of reducing basis to account for the reduced indebtedness dates back to 1926, at least, when the Board of Tax Appeals suggested in dictum that despite the fact that discharge of indebtedness did not create income, a taxpayer might be required to reduce the basis of any property that was acquired with the borrowed funds by the amount of debt canceled. This is not as broad as § 108, which requires the reduction of basis of all assets.

Kirby Lumber rule, over time the courts grafted on a number of exceptions. The confused reasoning in *Kirby Lumber* permitted the courts to use either the freeing-of-assets theory or the whole transaction theory to exempt certain transactions. Some of these exceptions were later codified, but others remain judicially created.

1. *Insolvency*

The opinion in *Kirby Lumber* does not reference the reason why the bonds were repurchased at discount. The decline in the value of the bonds was probably due to an increase in the interest rates in bonds of an equivalent risk. No evidence exists that Kirby Lumber was in financial distress or insolvent when it repurchased its bonds. The holding in *Kirby Lumber* was quite broad. It seemed to apply to all discharges of indebtedness.

Kirby Lumber was decided during the Depression when debt discharge and insolvency were prevalent. It quickly became clear that the courts were going to be reluctant to find taxable income in all cases. Thus, they began to create a number of judicial exceptions to *Kirby Lumber*. They first used the freeing-of-assets theory to justify excluding cancellation of indebtedness income of insolvent debtors. The courts essentially held that an insolvent taxpayer could not have cancellation of indebtedness income because the discharge of an insolvent taxpayer's debts did not free up any of his assets. He had a negative net worth before the discharge and a negative net worth after the discharge. The courts ignored the fact that a decrease in negative net worth was an increase in net worth.

The first case to take this position, a Board of Tax Appeals case decided a year after *Kirby Lumber*,[40] involved a corporate taxpayer that was in receivership. The corporation was insolvent, and its creditors canceled its debt to permit it to reorganize. Because the corporation was insolvent when the creditors discharged the debt, the corporation had no COD income. The court found that "[t]he parties contemplated no profit from the transaction, which merely relieved the taxpayer from a portion of its liabilities."[41] The court held that *Kirby Lumber* did not apply because no assets had been freed up. Other courts quickly followed suit.[42]

---

[40] E.B. Higley & Co. v. Commissioner, 25 B.T.A. 127 (1932).

[41] *Id.* at 127.

[42] *See, e.g.*, Dallas Transfer & Terminal Warehouse Co. v. Commissioner, 70 F.2d 95 (5th Cir.1934); Astoria Marine Constr. Co. v. Commissioner, 12 T.C. 798 (1949); Madison Rys. v. Commissioner, 36 B.T.A. 1106 (1937); Lakeland Grocery Co. v. Commissioner, 36 B.T.A. 289 (1937). Prior to *Kirby Lumber*, the government had also taken this position. I.T. 1564, II–1 C.B. 59 (1932).

In 1938, as part of the Chandler Act, Congress responded by amending the Bankruptcy Act of 1898 to provide a statutory insolvency exception that relieved a debtor from cancellation of indebtedness income in a bankruptcy proceeding. The Treasury Department opposed complete relief, and so Congress enacted another provision requiring the bankrupt debtor to reduce its basis in assets to the extent that debts were canceled or reduced. In 1939, Congress amended the Internal Revenue Code to conform, primarily at the urging of the railroads whose bonds were selling below par. Cancellation of indebtedness income was excluded in certain corporate reorganizations, and the debtor corporation was required to reduce basis.[43]

Legislative history indicates that when Congress revamped the insolvency rules as part of the Bankruptcy Act of 1980, it abandoned the freeing-of-assets theory in favor of the loan proceeds approach. Under this theory, because the debtor did not include the loan proceeds in income when borrowed due to the offsetting liability, a subsequent discharge of the indebtedness by the creditor clearly resulted in taxable income even if the debtor was insolvent. Congress recognized, however, that an insolvent debtor was in no position to pay taxes on the COD income when it was discharged. The rules adopted by Congress permitted the debtor to defer the tax. Under § 108(a), a debtor who is insolvent or in a bankruptcy proceeding excludes the COD income and reduces its tax attributes. This has the effect of deferring the tax until the debtor is able to pay it.

The insolvency exception applies only to the extent the taxpayer remains insolvent after the discharge. If the debtor is made solvent by the discharge, he has taxable income to the extent of the solvency. So, for example, if T has assets of $60,000 and liabilities of $80,000, and $30,000 of debt is discharged, T has $10,000 of income. This limitation appears to follow from the freeing-of-assets theory because $10,000 of T's assets were freed from the burden of the liabilities.

2. *Gifts*

The original regulation on discharge of indebtedness provided that the cancellation of a debt that was treated as a gift did not produce COD income.[44] Since the borrower could have received the loan proceeds as a nontaxable gift,[45] the cancellation of the loan should be treated as a gift as well. This, of course, requires a determination whether the lender

---

[43] The history of these provisions is detailed in James S. Eustice, *Cancellation of Indebtedness and the Federal Income Tax: A Problem of Creeping Confusion*, 14 Tax L. Rev. 226 (1959).

[44] Treas. Reg. § 45, art. 51 (1918).

[45] § 102.

intended to make a gift on the cancellation. In cases where the lender and borrower are related, it generally was safe to assume a donative intent. It was much less clear whether there could be such an intent in other circumstances.

One would have thought that in a commercial setting, the lender could not have such an intent. If he agreed to partially discharge the debt, most likely it was because that was all he could get for the debt. He forgave the rest only because he was unable to obtain it. But that assumption was thrown to the wind in *Helvering v. American Dental Co*,[46] where the Court held that a routine financial adjustment between a debtor and his creditors could be a tax-free gift to the debtor. The trial court had found that the creditors "acted for purely business reasons and did not forgive the debts for altruistic reasons or out of pure generosity." The Court ignored this finding: "The fact that the motives leading to the cancellations were those of business or even selfish, if it be true, is not significant. The forgiveness was gratuitous, a release of something to the debtor for nothing, and sufficient to make the cancellations here gifts within the statute."[47]

Thus, *American Dental* reaffirmed that a creditor could make a tax-free gift by canceling a debt, but much more important was the Court's finding that a purely commercial settlement of a debt could be a gift. But how was this case different from *Kirby Lumber*? The only difference appeared to be that Kirby Lumber purchased its notes in the open market whereas American Dental dealt directly with its creditors. This seems like an untenable distinction.

And it was. Six years later, the Court essentially reversed itself in a case that illustrated that the distinction was unworkable. The debtor purchased some of its outstanding bonds through a bondholders' committee and purchased other bonds directly through bondholders with whom he was acquainted. The Tax Court felt constrained to say that the former created COD income under *Kirby Lumber*, and the latter were tax-free gifts.[48] The Supreme Court recognized that was implausible. Although it did not overrule *American Dental*, it did say that it was not likely to occur again:

> It is conceivable, although hardly likely, that a bondholder, in the ordinary course of business and without any express release of his debtor, might have sold part of his claims on the bonds he held at the full face value of those parts and then have made a gift of the rest of his claims on those bonds to the same debtor "for nothing."

---

[46] 318 U.S. 322 (1943).

[47] *Id.* at 331.

[48] Jacobson v. Commissioner, 6 T.C. 1048 (1946).

It is that kind of extraordinary transaction that the respondent asks us, as a matter of law, to read into the simple sales which actually took place and from which he derived financial gains . . .

The situation in each transaction is a factual one. It turns upon whether the transaction is in fact a transfer of something for the best price available or is a transfer or release of only a part of a claim for cash and of the balance "for nothing."[49]

Subsequently, the Supreme Court crafted a definition of a gift for income tax purposes that in most cases would preclude a gift where debt is discharged in a commercial setting.[50]

3. *Purchase Price Adjustment*

Suppose T purchases a used truck from S for $30,000, paying $10,000 in cash and borrowing the remainder from S. S represents that the truck has 40,000 miles, but T subsequently discovers that in fact the mileage is 80,000. T and S settle by agreeing that the truck was worth only $25,000, and thus the outstanding amount on T's debt was only $15,000. If S had been honest, he would have sold the truck for $25,000 in the first place, and with a $10,000 down payment, T's debt would have been $15,000. A number of courts decided that the answer should be the same on a subsequent settlement.[51] In the example, T would reduce the purchase price by $5,000 rather than having $5,000 discharge of indebtedness income. In dictum, the Supreme Court agreed: "Where the indebtedness has represented the purchase price of property, a partial forgiveness has been treated as a readjustment of the contract rather than a gain."[52]

A significant amount of litigation ensued, however, because it was not always clear whether the seller/lender was reducing the purchase price, which simply would result in basis reduction, or was canceling the debt, which would produce COD income. Suppose, in the above example, S had simply settled by agreeing that T only owed $15,000 on the debt. Had S agreed that the truck was only worth $25,000, or had S reduced the debt simply to put the matter behind him or because he believed that

---

[49] Commissioner v. Jacobson, 336 U.S. 28, 50–52 (1949).

[50] Commissioner v. Duberstein, 363 U.S. 278 (1960). The Court determined that a gift is made out of "disinterested generosity." In a commercial setting, a creditor who cancels a debt in whole or in part is certainly not disinterested and is not acting out of generosity. If he could have collected the remainder of the debt, he would have done so. Section 102(c) now provides that an employer cannot make a nontaxable gift to an employee.

[51] *See, e.g.,* Commissioner v. Sherman, 135 F.2d 68 (6th Cir.1943); Helvering v. A. L. Killian Co., 128 F.2d 433 (8th Cir.1942); Allen v. Courts, 127 F.2d 127 (5th Cir.1942); Hirsch v. Commissioner, 115 F.2d 656 (7th Cir.1940).

[52] Helvering v. American Dental Co., 318 U.S. 322, 327–28 (1943).

T would sue or never pay the full principal? Each litigated dispute required the courts to make factual determinations.

To halt the litigation, Congress in 1980 added § 108(e)(5), codifying the purchase price exception, at least in part. This exception applies if (1) the discharged or reduced debt is debt of a purchaser of property to the seller of such property that arose from the purchase of the property, (2) the taxpayer is not insolvent or bankrupt when the discharge occurs, and (3) the reduction otherwise would be cancellation of indebtedness income. Unlike the judicial exception, § 108(e)(5) does not apply if the seller has transferred the debt to a third party or if the buyer has transferred the property to a third party.

Unlike the judicial exception, the seller/lender's motive is irrelevant. Under § 108(e)(5), the result is that there is no discharge of indebtedness income. This clearly creates a windfall where the debt is discounted because of the seller's need for cash or a change in the interest rates. Nevertheless, to avoid litigation over motive, Congress adopted a broad rule for exclusion.

4. *Contested Liability*

It is a truism that there cannot be discharge of indebtedness income if there is no loan. So the first step in any dispute is to determine if there is in fact a "true debt." For example, if a sole shareholder "loans" money to a corporation and never has any intention of seeking repayment, the cancellation of the loan will not create discharge of indebtedness income. The original transfer was not a true loan but rather a contribution to capital.

Fairly soon after *Kirby Lumber* was decided, the Board of Tax Appeals extended this logic to contested liabilities, holding that *Kirby Lumber* should not apply to the discharge of debt disputed by the debtor.[53] Suppose B challenges L's statement that B borrowed $10,000, arguing that the actual amount of the proceeds was $8,000. B ultimately wins the dispute, repaying L $8,000. Under the contested liability exception, B has no COD income because the amount of loan is deemed to be $8,000, and thus no part of it has been canceled.

Another good example of the "no loan-no COD" proposition is the inclusion in income of illegal income. The theory underlying the exclusion of loan proceeds is that the taxpayer must return the money. Where the taxpayer has no intention of honoring this obligation, there is no offsetting liability, and his net worth increases immediately. It took the Supreme Court three attempts at dealing with illegal income, however, to get it right.

---

[53] N. Sobel, Inc. v. Commissioner, 40 B.T.A. 1263 (1939); *see also* United States v. Hall, 307 F.2d 238 (10th Cir.1962).

Originally, the Court treated the embezzler or thief like a borrower since there was a legal obligation to make restitution.[54] Thus, it held there was no taxable income on the receipt of embezzled proceeds. In the next case, the taxpayer was an extortionist rather than an embezzler, who under threats of violence had extorted a large sum from his partner in a bootlegging venture. Since it seemed quite unlikely that the embezzler would repay and equally unlikely that the victim would squeal, the Court found that the extorted amount was taxable.[55] Four judges dissented because they could see no difference between extorted and embezzled funds. But they were unwilling to let all embezzlers and extortionists escape taxation. So they drew another untenable distinction. Those engaged in regular businesses, gamblers and bootleggers for example, should be taxed on the regular business profits, but the "sporadic loot of an embezzler, an extortionist, or a robber" was excluded.[56]

The line could not hold, and less than a decade later, the Court reversed itself and held that embezzled funds were taxed despite the legal obligation to make restitution.[57] The Court distinguished an embezzler from a borrower: The offsetting obligation should be ignored because the embezzler does not intend to honor it and as a practical matter controls the funds. An embezzler who is caught and argues after the fact that he intended to repay should be viewed with skepticism. There must be a valid loan at the time of receipt of the funds to justify an exclusion.

5. *Bonds Issued as Dividends*

The confusion over the facts in *Kirby Lumber* resurfaced when the courts considered situations where bonds were issued for property rather than cash. Two cases, where the application of *Kirby Lumber* was unclear, addressed bonds issued as dividends or in exchange for stock.

Shortly after *Kirby Lumber* was decided, the Second Circuit concluded that the doctrine should not apply to the discharge of bonds that had been issued as a dividend. In *Commissioner v. Rail Joint Co.*,[58] the Second Circuit held there was no discharge of indebtedness income arising from the discount on repurchased bonds where the bonds had been issued as a dividend to the corporation's shareholders. The Second Circuit distinguished *Kirby Lumber*, saying:

---

[54] Commissioner v. Wilcox, 327 U.S. 404 (1946). Dissenting in a later case, Justice Whittaker observed that an embezzler is "indebted to his victim in the full amount taken as surely as if he had left a signed promissory note at the scene of the crime." James v. United States, 366 U.S. 213, 251 (1961).

[55] Rutkin v. United States, 343 U.S. 130 (1952).

[56] *Id.* at 10–41 (Douglas, J., dissenting).

[57] James v. United States, 366 U.S. 213 (1961).

[58] 61 F.2d 751 (2d Cir.1932).

In the *Kirby* case a corporation issued its bonds at par and later in
the same year repurchased some of them at less than par ... The
taxpayer's assets were increased by the cash received for the bonds,
and when the bonds were paid off for less than the sum received, it
is clear that the taxpayer obtained a net gain in assets from the
transaction ... the consideration received for the obligation evidenced by the bond as well as the consideration paid to satisfy that
obligation must be looked to in order to determine whether gain or
loss is realized when the transaction is closed.... But that decision
is not applicable to the facts of the case at bar. In paying dividends
to shareholders, the corporation does not buy property from them.
Here the respondent never received any increment to its assets,
either at the time the bonds were delivered or at the time they were
retired.[59]

The Second Circuit's mistake in *Rail Joint* is quite ironic and
illustrates the value of examining the record carefully. As noted above,
like Rail Joint, Kirby Lumber did not receive cash for its bonds. Rather
it issued the bonds in redemption of its preferred stock. Justice Holmes'
opinion is unclear on the consideration received by Kirby Lumber, and it
is possible that the Court would have reached a different conclusion had
it believed the consideration for the bonds was not cash. On the other
hand, the Court was made aware of the facts in the respondent's
opposition brief. There are a number of possibilities. One is that the
Court believed that the bonds were not issued for cash but felt bound by
the finding, which it interpreted as a statement that Kirby Lumber had
received cash. In that case, its holding should apply only where the
borrower received cash, and therefore the Second Circuit in *Rail Joint*
did not need to follow *Kirby Lumber* as precedent. A second possibility is
that either the Court accepted the correction of the facts or felt it made
no difference since the Court was prepared to hold that *Kirby Lumber*
had income regardless of the consideration received. That would be
consistent with the whole transaction or the freeing-of-assets theories. If
that were the case, the *Rail Joint* court should have followed the *Kirby
Lumber* precedent.[60]

What if the corporation issues the debt to redeem preferred stock
that had been issued for cash and then repurchases the debt at a

---

[59] *Id.* at 751.

[60] The Second Circuit is not alone in assuming that Kirby Lumber received cash when
it issued the bonds. *See* Dallas Transfer & Terminal Warehouse Co. v. Commissioner, 70
F.2d 95 (5th Cir.1934) (Kirby Lumber's "assets having been increased by the cash received
for the bonds"); Fashion Park, Inc. v. Commissioner, 21 T.C. 600 (1954) ("'[T]he corporate
bonds involved had been issued at par and were retired at a figure below the price received.
There the issuing corporation after the retirement stood possessed of so much of the
consideration which it had received upon issuance as exceeded the price it paid to purchase
and retire the bonds.'").

discount? Those, of course, were the facts of *Kirby Lumber*, but the longstanding misinterpretation of the facts in that case meant that the application of the COD doctrine to those facts was clouded in mystery.

In *United States Steel Corp. v. United States*,[61] United States Steel ("USS") issued preferred stock in exchange for $100 per share. Later it recapitalized and exchanged debt with a face amount of $175 for each share of preferred stock, which was then worth $165 a share. USS ultimately repurchased the debt for $118 per share. Everyone agreed that the repurchase of the bonds at a discount triggered discharge of indebtedness income; the only real question was how much. USS argued that the amount was zero because it repurchased the bonds (at $118) for more than it received for the preferred stock ($100).[62] The government argued that USS had COD income of $47, the difference between the value of the stock exchanged for the bonds ($165) and the repurchase price ($118). The Tax Court had previously held on *Kirby Lumber* facts that no income existed when the debtor repurchased the debt for less than the amount it received on issuing preferred stock.[63]

The Claims Court refused to follow *Rail Joint* and *Fashion Park* because it believed that the cases were based on a misreading of *Kirby Lumber*'s facts. Since the Supreme Court had not inquired as to the amount received for the preferred stock by Kirby Lumber, the Claims Court believed that the amount received for the preferred could not be taken into account.[64] The Federal Circuit, however, held that the debtor had income only to the extent the repurchase price for the debt is less than the amount the corporation received for the stock.

This holding (as well as that in *Rail Joint*) is inconsistent with the freeing-of-assets theory. USS had a $175 liability on its books when it issued the debt, and thus $175 of assets were encumbered by the liability. When it removed the liability for $118, it freed up $57 of assets. By the time *United States Steel* reached the Federal Circuit, the theory had been largely discredited.[65] The decisions do make more sense, however, if a loan proceeds theory is followed. The amount originally received by the corporation that was not subject to tax must now be included in

---

[61] 848 F.2d 1232 (Fed.Cir.1988).

[62] As if the confusion created by *Kirby Lumber* were not enough, the taxpayer attempted to rely on *Kerbaugh-Empire*, arguing that it had invested the proceeds in a losing venture and thus had no overall gain. Despite the fact that *Kerbaugh-Empire* had never been overruled, the court did not feel obliged to follow it.

[63] Fashion Park v. Commissioner, 21 T.C. 600 (1954).

[64] 848 F.2d at 1237–1238.

[65] Interestingly, the government did not argue the freeing-of-assets theory in *United States Steel*, conceding that the amount of income recognized by USS was not $57. 848 F.2d at 1234.

income when the offsetting liability is eliminated without a decrease in assets.[66]

6. *Stock-for-Debt*

The stock-for-debt situation is the reverse of the bonds issued as dividends situation. Here, the corporation first issues the debt and then retires the debt by issuing stock. A series of cases developed the stock-for-debt exception to the *Kirby Lumber* rule in the 1940s. The first case, *Capento Securities Corp. v. Commissioner*,[67] involved a corporation that issued stock with a par value of $500,000 and a fair market value of $50,000 in order to retire outstanding bonds with a face amount of $500,000. Under the *Kirby Lumber* rule, the corporation would have recognized $450,000 of cancellation of indebtedness income. The Board of Tax Appeals created the stock-for-debt exception when it held that Capento need not recognize the gain created when it discharged its debt by issuing stock with a fair market value less than the face amount of the debt:

> [I]t is hard to see that gain was in fact realized. The corporation had a liability of $500,000 on the bonds, having presumably borrowed that amount. While it discharged that liability, it created a new stock interest which became a balance sheet liability called capital stock. This is plainly different from the discharge of indebtedness by the payment of money in a less amount than the indebtedness, as in *Kirby Lumber Co. v. United States*.... Even though the shares issued are ... worth only $50,000, the amount whereby the par value exceeds the present value is not a gain, for it is the par value which measures the capital stock liability.[68]

The court used a substitution-of-liabilities theory to supports its result. The argument is based on the assumption that the corporation has simply downgraded the debt into equity, that is a recapitalization of the corporation's capital structure. In the process of substituting the stock for the bond, "the corporation pays nothing." The substitution-of-liabilities rationale treated the stock as a type of "liability," and concluded discharging debt by issuing either stock or debt was simply a swap of one liability for another.[69]

---

[66] The relationship between *Kirby Lumber* and *United States Steel* is exhaustively analyzed in Alan Gunn, *Reconciling* United States Steel *and* Kirby Lumber, 42 Tax Notes 851 (1989); David J. Shakow, United States Steel *and* Kirby Lumber: *Another View*, 42 Tax Notes 1371 (1989); Alan Gunn, United States Steel *and the Functional Approach to Legal Problems*, 43 Tax Notes 213 (1989); David J. Shakow, *A Short Retort on* United States Steel, 43 Tax Notes 1173 (1989); Alan Gunn, *Gunn's Reply*, 43 Tax Notes 1414 (1989).

[67] 47 B.T.A. 691 (1942), *aff'd*, 140 F.2d 382 (1st Cir.1944).

[68] *Id.* at 695.

[69] *See, e.g.*, Tower Bldg. Corp. v. Commissioner, 6 T.C. 125 (1946).

The Bankruptcy Tax Act of 1980 codified the stock-for-debt exception, but Congress narrowed the rule in 1980 and 1984, essentially eliminated it in 1986, and repealed it in 1994. In its current form, § 108(e)(10) is thus not nearly as broad as the judicial exception. It also abandons the substitution-of-liabilities theory. Current law recognizes that a stock-for-debt swap is the same as if the debtor had sold the stock for cash and used the cash to discharge the debt. Section 108(e)(10) treats a debtor that discharges debt by issuing stock as if it had satisfied the debt with cash equal to the fair market value of the stock. As a result, the debtor realizes gain to the extent the principal of the debt exceeds the value of the stock. If the discharge occurs in bankruptcy or if the corporation is insolvent, however, there is no COD income, but the debtor must reduce tax attributes.

If the corporation uses other property to satisfy its debt, it will have COD income if the property is worth less than the fair market value of the debt. If property is also worth more or less than basis, it will realize gain or loss.[70]

7. *Debt-for-Debt*

In *Kirby Lumber*, the company used cash to buy back its debt, but there are other ways to reacquire the debt or to partially discharge it. One way is to swap one debt instrument for another debt instrument. If the principal amount of the new debt instrument is less than the principal amount of the new instrument, it is clear that there has been a discharge of indebtedness—the new instrument may simply be a means of recording the settlement.[71] The statute now codifies that result. Under § 108(e)(10), when new debt is issued to retire old debt, there is debt discharge income equal to the excess of the adjusted issue price of the old instrument over the issue price of the new instrument.

There also can be the economic equivalent of a debt discharge without changing the principal amount. Recall that in many instances, the reason the debt is repurchased at a discount is because interest rates have risen, and the value of the bond has fallen. Suppose L holds a debt instrument with a principal amount of $40,000 and an interest rate of 5%. L swaps that note for a new note in which B will pay only 1%. Economically, this is the same as reducing the principal amount. Thus, modifying the terms of an instrument sufficiently also should give rise to COD income. Historically, this was not thought to produce income. Under § 108(e)(10), however, there may be COD income where "the exchange qualifies as a realization event under section 1001 for the holder." Under the regulations, any significant modification of a debt

---

[70] Reg. § 1.108–1(c)(2); Kenan v. Commissioner, 114 F.2d 217 (2d Cir.1940).

[71] *See, e.g.*, Commissioner v. Coastwise Transport Corp., 71 F.2d 104 (1st Cir.1934).

instrument is considered an exchange of the original instrument for a
new instrument and may give rise to COD income to the borrower.

8. *Contribution to Capital*

Suppose a shareholder also holds corporate bonds. In order to
improve the corporation's finances, the shareholder cancels the bond.
The cancellation of the debt for less than its face amount has the same
effect as a contribution to capital. It is as if the corporation paid the debt
in full and then the shareholder transferred the proceeds back to the
corporation as a contribution to capital. The regulations have always
provided that the discharge in whole or in part of shareholder debt
would be treated as a nontaxable contribution to capital rather than as
discharge of indebtedness income.[72] Shortly after the decision in *Kirby
Lumber*, the Second Circuit agreed.[73]

Current law is slightly different. Section 108(e)(6) provides that a
corporation that receives a capital contribution of its own obligation has
COD income only to the extent the principal amount exceeds the
shareholder's adjusted basis for the debt. In most cases, the two will be
the same (the basis will be the amount loaned or the amount for which
the bond was purchased), and thus the corporation will have no income.
But there are cases where gain would be triggered because the bondhold-
er's basis has been adjusted downward.[74]

Note the inconsistent treatment between the § 108(e)(6) contribution to capital exception and the § 108(e) stock-for-debt exception.
Suppose a taxpayer is a shareholder who holds a bond with a principal
amount of $10,000 and a fair market value of $8,000. The shareholder's
basis in the bond is $10,000. If the bond is transferred to the corporation
for stock worth $8,000, the corporation has $2,000 of COD income. If the
corporation receives the bond as a contribution to capital, there is no
COD income.

9. *Discount Part of the Original Agreement*

Suppose an investor purchases a CD from a bank under an agreement that requires the bank to pay interest. If the investor withdraws
the funds early, however, he is subject to an early withdrawal penalty,
effectively reducing the amount that the bank is required to repay. Does
that create COD income? The Supreme Court said "no" in *United States*

---

[72] Treas. Reg. § 45, art. 51 (1918). A contribution to capital is not taxable. I.R.C. § 118.

[73] Commissioner v. Auto Strop Safety Razor Co., 74 F.2d 226 (2d Cir.1934).

[74] For example, if the corporation has filed a Subchapter S election, which permits the
shareholders to deduct corporate losses, the basis of the debt as well as the basis of the
stock may have been reduced by the passed-through losses. Or the shareholder may have
purchased the bond at a discount in which case the cost basis would be less than the
principal amount.

v. Centennial Savings Bank,[75] arguing that provisions in § 108 that benefited taxpayers probably were not intended by Congress to be used where the reduced amount was pursuant to the original agreement with the creditors:

> The rationale [of the § 108 deferral] is squarely implicated only when the debtor is seeking forgiveness or cancellation of a pre-existing repayment obligation. A debtor who negotiates in advance the circumstances in which he will liquidate the debt for less than its face value is in a position to anticipate his need for cash with which to pay the resulting income tax and can negotiate the terms of the anticipated liquidation accordingly.[76]

10. *Deduction*

Section 108(e)(2) provides that a debtor has no income if had he paid the debt, he would have been entitled to a deduction. Suppose B is a cash basis taxpayer who conducts a business. L performs services for the business, and B is unable to pay. L ultimately cancels B's debt in order to retain future business. B has no COD income. If B had actually paid for the services, B would have had a business deduction, so including the COD income would just produce a wash.

11. *Other Statutory Exceptions*

Congress also has adopted three other exceptions to the *Kirby Lumber* rule that are best thought of as subsidies or incentive provisions. There is nothing in the reasoning or logic of that opinion that supports these exceptions. Congress simply did not like the result when *Kirby Lumber* was applied to these groups of taxpayers.

Qualified real property business indebtedness. This exception was added at the urging of the real estate lobby during a period of falling prices. Faced with large debts that exceeded the value of the security, developers and investors confronted taxation of so-called phantom income if the debt was written down. Under § 108(a)(1)(D), a non-corporate taxpayer can elect to reduce basis instead of recognizing COD income on the reduction of a mortgage secured by real property worth less than the debt. In order to use the exception, according to § 108(c)(1), the taxpayer must have incurred or assumed the debt in connection with real property used in a business, the debt must be secured by the property, and it must have been incurred or assumed to acquire, construct, reconstruct, or substantially improve the property.

---

[75] 499 U.S. 573 (1991).

[76] *Id.* at 580.

Qualified farm indebtedness. Congress also had a good deal of sympathy for farmers who became over-extended and faced large tax bills if creditors provided debt relief. Like real property investors, the farmers argued that their only recourse was to sell the property to pay the debt. Under § 108(g), farmers can exclude COD income if: (1) the lender is actively and regularly engaged in the business of lending money, (2) the lender is not the person from whom the taxpayer bought the property encumbered by the debt, (3) the lender is not related to the taxpayer or seller, (4) the taxpayer incurred the indebtedness in the business of farming, and (5) farming was the source of at least 50% of the taxpayer's average annual gross receipts for the three years preceding the taxable year in which the discharge occurs.

Student Loans. Law students were largely responsible for this exception. A number of law schools adopted loan forgiveness programs in which all or a part of a student loan was forgiven provided the student performed certain kinds of legal work. Similar programs for doctors discharged indebtedness if the doctor worked in a rural or low-income area. Pesky tax professors pointed out to the creators of these programs that the debt forgiveness would constitute income, thereby not decreasing the gap between corporate and legal aid salaries as much as the students hoped. Congress adopted § 108(f) in response. It exempts debt discharge income if the indebtedness is a student loan and the discharge is pursuant to a provision of a loan program providing for the forgiveness, in whole or in part, in the event "the individual worked for a certain period of time in certain professions for any of a broad class of employers." The program under which the loan was given must be one that is designed to encourage its students to serve in occupations with unmet needs or in areas with unmet needs and under which the services provided by the students or former students are under the direction of a governmental unit or a § 501(c)(3) organization.

12.   *Sales to Related Parties*

The *Kirby Lumber* principle does not apply where a creditor sells a claim against a borrower to a third party for less than the debt's face amount. Because there is simply a substitution of a new creditor without a change in the amount of the debt, the borrower has not been discharged in whole or in part from the debt. Suppose B believes that L will accept a discount on the debt. If B settles the claim for a discount, she will have discharge of indebtedness income. Instead, she induces a friendly party—say Mom—to purchase the debt at a discount. If we assume that Mom will never enforce the debt for the full amount, B has enjoyed the economic equivalent of debt discharge without *Kirby Lumber* income.[77]

To forestall that possibility, § 108(e)(4) and its regulations treat an acquisition of a debt by a person related to the debtor as an acquisition by the debtor, which would trigger COD income if the debt is acquired at a discount.

13. *Acquisition and Disposition of Property Encumbered by Debt*

Kirby Lumber has had some of its most significant impact in cases where the debt was used to purchase property and the property is disposed of while the debt is still outstanding. Two well-known Supreme Court cases, *Crane v. Commissioner* and *Tufts v. Commissioner*, tackle the treatment of the original acquisition as well as a discharge of all or part of the indebtedness on a subsequent sale. These cases are discussed in Chapter 7 of *Tax Stories*.

The Chickens Come Home to Roost–*Zarin v. Commissioner*

The confusion engendered by *Kirby Lumber* and its progeny came home to roost in *Zarin v. Commissioner*, a wonderfully wacky case that engendered four separate opinions in the Tax Court and two opinions in the Third Circuit, all based on different theories that revealed in striking terms the continued uncertainty surrounding the *Kirby Lumber* rule.

The protagonist was a colorful character named David Zarin, whose four-month gambling spree in 1980 produced litigation that reads like a law school hypothetical. Zarin was a major real estate developer in Atlantic City. In the 1970s, he built a significant portion of Atlantic City's low-income housing stock and won civic awards for his contributions to the city. In 1978 and 1979, at the height of his career, Zarin started to frequent the Resorts International Casino, playing high-stakes craps on credit. Over a 12–month period, he lost about $2.5 million at the craps tables, almost his entire net worth. The New Jersey Casino Control Commission issued an order prohibiting Resorts from allowing Zarin to gamble on credit. The casino ignored the order because his huge bets attracted crowds. The casino believed that because of the excitement that he generated, other gamblers wagered more than they otherwise would. Resorts designated Zarin a "valued gaming patron" and gave him complimentary perks, such as the use of a luxury, three-room suite, free meals, entertainment, and access to a limousine.[78]

---

[77] *See* Forrester v. Commissioner, 4 T.C. 907 (1945) (wife's purchase of husband's debt did not produce income).

[78] Zarin was a high roller in other ways. In October 1979, the New Jersey Division of Gaming Enforcement filed a complaint against Resorts. Of the 809 violations of casino regulations alleged in the complaint, 100 concerned Zarin.

But Zarin's gambling addiction soon got the best of him. During the first four months of 1980, Zarin gambled 16 hours a day, seven days a week, all on credit. Usually he bet the house limit, $15,000, on each throw of the dice. By April, however, Resorts got fed up and cut off his credit. It demanded payment of his $3,435,000 gambling debt. Needless to say, Zarin did not have the money; Resorts sued.[79] Zarin, ever the gambler, countersued.[80] Eventually, the suits were settled. Resorts agreed to accept $500,000, and Zarin avoided paying the remaining $3 million of debt.[81]

Zarin must have thought his troubles were over, but it was only the end of Act I. The protagonist in Act II was the Service.[82] The government claimed that the discharged debt was taxable income and assessed taxes. With accrued interest, the total bill rose to more than $5.2 million. If Zarin could not pay Resorts' $3.5 million, he certainly could not pay the Service $5.2 million.

Zarin filed suit in the Tax Court claiming he had not benefited from the transaction and raising a variety of defenses.[83] By an 11–8 vote, the Tax Court upheld the Service position. The majority opinion found that Zarin had discharge of indebtedness income under *Kirby Lumber*. The overwhelming majority of the court's opinion, however, was devoted to Zarin's arguments as to why there was no COD income.[84]

---

[79] Resorts alleged that he and a business associate owed almost $4.7 million in gambling debts.

[80] The suit alleged that executives of Resorts conspired to make him lose at craps in a "malicious attempt" to appropriate his real-estate holdings in the Atlantic City area.

[81] Zarin, seeing the error of his ways, began attending Gamblers Anonymous, joined the board of a foundation dedicated to the prevention of compulsive gambling, and vowed never to gamble again.

[82] Zarin's troubles did not lie only with the Service. A New Jersey grand jury indicted him on 93 counts of theft by deception at Resorts as well as Caesars World Casino. Zarin was charged with defrauding Resorts of $4.1 million and Caesars of $210,000 by signing markers that bounced.

[83] Zarin, however, clearly knew how to benefit from the tax system. According to newspaper reports, Zarin's company was one of the first in New Jersey to use the low income housing credit. He combined the tax break with a low-interest loan from the Casino Reinvestment Development Authority to finance a $27 million project in Atlantic City. Although he acknowledged that he could not have pulled it off without the tax breaks, he nevertheless complained about how complicated the real estate tax shelter was. "Our tax attorneys needed their tax attorneys to explain it. It took us one year just to figure out what was going on."

[84] One of his defenses was that he was suffering from "a recognized emotional disorder that caused him to gamble compulsively." Neither the Tax Court nor the Third Circuit considered this defense, possibly because they did not know the relevance of Zarin's addiction to a determination of whether he had COD income. His addiction might be used to argue that he did not receive $3.5 million of value when he borrowed that amount to gamble since his consumption value was less. *See* Daniel Shaviro, *The Man Who Lost too*

Zarin relied in part on *United States v. Hall*,[85] a case that in turn relied on *Kerbaugh-Empire*, to hold that where a taxpayer lost money gambling, he had a substantial loss and the discharge only served to diminish the loss, not create income. The Tax Court rejected any reliance on *Kerbaugh-Empire* and instead used the loan proceeds approach to find income. The fact that the taxpayer lost the money was irrelevant so long as he received something of value in exchange for debt. Zarin received the opportunity to gamble, and according to the Tax Court, only his promise to repay prevented taxation on receipt of the loan. This nontaxation triggered the income in the year in which the loan was forgiven. Unfortunately, the Tax Court also referred to the freeing-of-assets theory: "The gain to the debtor from such discharge is the resultant freeing up of his assets that he would otherwise have been required to use to pay the debt."[86] This makes the theory of the case less than clear.

The Tax Court also rejected as irrelevant the fact that the debt was unenforceable and concluded that the disputed debt exception did not apply. This exception only could apply when the amount of the original debt is in doubt. But no one questioned how much credit Resorts had extended to Zarin. The only question was whether Resorts could enforce the debt; Zarin did not dispute that he would have owed $3.5 million had the debt been enforceable and in fact introduced evidence that he intended to pay the full amount.

Zarin also attempted to use the purchase price adjustment exception of § 108(e)(5), arguing that the chips he received when extended credit were property. Since the literal statutory language does not make the intent of the creditor relevant, the Tax Court could not base its decision on its obvious belief that Resorts had not discounted the price of gambling. Instead, the Tax Court found that gambling chips were not the kind of property to which Congress intended § 108(e)(5) to apply, and the "opportunity to gamble" would not be considered property.[87] Whether the chips were property under § 108(e)(5) is a red herring. The real issue is whether the exception should apply when the debtor has

---

Much: Zarin v. Commissioner *and the Measurement of Taxable Consumption*, 45 Tax L. Rev. 216 (1990).

[85] 307 F.2d 238 (10th Cir.1962).

[86] Zarin v. Commissioner, 92 T.C. 1084, 1089 (1989), *rev'd*, 916 F.2d 110 (3d Cir.1990).

[87] The majority asserted that the chips were not "normal commercial property," a term not found in the statute. In his dissent, Judge Ruwe argued that the majority failed to define the term, but if it "has a meaning, there is no reason why gambling chips should not be included." His dissent is a treatise on the meaning of property and § 108(e)(5). He seemed troubled by Zarin's plight, finding it "ironic [that Zarin] incurs a huge tax liability, the magnitude of which is in direct proportion to his losses." 92 T.C. at 1115–16.

received and used or consumed property worth the face amount of the debt when received.[88]

The dissenting judge who appeared most sympathetic to Zarin explicitly said that he was not relying on *Kerbaugh-Empire* but used reasoning that is nevertheless drawn from the whole transaction approach: "The concept that petitioner received his money's worth from the enjoyment of using the chips (thus equating the pleasure of gambling with increase in wealth) produces the incongruous result that the more a gambler loses, the greater his pleasure and the larger the increase in this wealth."[89] But then in an apparent concession to the now widely-supported loan proceeds theory, Judge Tannenwald argued that Zarin had not received anything tantamount to loan proceeds. And touching all the bases, Judge Tannenwald finally asserted that there could be no freeing up of assets since the debts were not enforceable.

Judge Jacobs' dissent starts from the proposition that there cannot be discharge of indebtedness income if there is no debt. Since the debt was unenforceable, he argued it was void. Relying on the first prong of the loan proceeds theory, he asserted that Zarin should have had income when he received the chips without paying for them because there was no offsetting liability. Like Judge Tannenwald, however, Judge Jacobs did not want to tax Zarin.[90] He would not have assessed a tax liability, however, because he believed that the "chip income" constituted gambling income against which gambling losses could be offset under

---

[88] A purchase price adjustment for the purchase of services or entertainment is often not a workable approach, but it could happen. Suppose a theater permits me to purchase a $50 ticket on credit. Halfway through the performance, the lead actor falls ill, and the performance comes to a halt. The theater refunds $25 to each patron and in my case decides that my debt is now $25. I should have no COD income although § 108(e)(5) would not protect me. But a purchase price adjustment is inappropriate where it is the creditworthiness of the borrower that has changed, and the borrower has fully enjoyed the entertainment or services. Other than the majority opinion in the Third Circuit, no one argued that Zarin did not enjoy $3.5 million of gambling. Certainly Resorts did not claim that one could pay less than $3.5 million. If I turned up at Resorts tomorrow and asked for $3.5 million in chips, chances are I would have to cough up $3.5 million.

[89] Zarin, 92 T.C. at 1101 (Tannenwald, J., dissenting).

[90] *Id.* at 1107 (Jacobs, J. dissenting) ("The result reached by the majority is tantamount to taxing petitioner on his losses."). It is true that Zarin now owed the government over $5 million and had no funds with which to pay the liability. It is also true that had Resorts not pulled the plug in April, 1980, his gambling debts would have escalated as well as his tax problems. Every dollar gambled (and lost) would have produced another dollar of taxable income. Tannenwald and Jacobs clearly feared the possibility that if somehow Resorts had allowed Zarin to gamble (and lose) $500 million, he would have had taxable income of $500 million. Theoretically, there was no limit. Practically, the limit is the amount of Zarin's assets. Once the gambling debt exceeded his assets, he would have been insolvent, and the excess would not have constituted COD income under the insolvency exception. In his rehearing motion, Zarin argued that he was insolvent and thus exempt. Since he did not raise the issue before its decision, the Tax Court denied the motion for reconsideration.

§ 165(d). Thus, the entire transaction was a loss. While this may be a more palatable way of taking the gambling losses into account than relying on *Kerbaugh-Empire*, it is a real stretch to say that the receipt of the chips from Resorts was a "gain from a wagering transaction."

Despite the sympathy he engendered in at least eight judges, Zarin ended Act II owing the government $5.2 million. But Zarin did not throw in the towel (nor did he pay up). As the curtain rose on Act III, Zarin fired his lawyers, hired new ones,[91] and appealed to the Third Circuit where he found a friendlier bench. The Third Circuit, in overruling the Tax Court, did not pass on the validity of *Kerbaugh-Empire*,[92] but it appeared to state with approval the proposition that "a court need not in every case be oblivious to the net effect of the entire transaction," thus resurrecting the specter of *Kerbaugh-Empire*.

The Third Circuit adopted the reasoning of Judge Jacobs' Tax Court dissent. It held that because the debt was unenforceable under state law, the amount of the indebtedness was in dispute, and thus there could no valid loan without which there could be no COD income. But the court did not go as far as Judge Jacobs, failing to consider whether the receipt of the gambling chips without an offsetting liability was the taxable event.[93]

As alternative support for its holding that there was no COD income, the Third Circuit treated Zarin's debt as a disputed or contested liability. The court believed that the amount of the debt was in dispute because it was unenforceable, and the settlement fixed the amount of the debt.[94] This argument is extremely difficult to understand. Presumably, Resorts settled for $500,000 because that is all Zarin had. Under the circuit court's logic, if Zarin had $700,000 in assets, and Resorts was able to claim that amount, the amount of the debt would have been $700,000. If he'd had a million, it would have been a million. Zarin was only able to gamble $3.5 million if he had $3.5 million in chips, and he was only able to obtain $3.5 million in chips by borrowing $3.5 million. He could not

---

[91] Before the Third Circuit appeal, Zarin fired his Tax Court lawyers, Reid & Priest, and hired Caplin & Drysdale to file for a rehearing. He lost that as well and responded by jettisoning those lawyers for lawyers at Drinker & Biddle. In a separate action, Zarin sued Reid & Priest in an $850 million malpractice action. He continued the suit even after he won in the Third Circuit.

[92] Zarin v. Commissioner, 916 F.2d 110, 116 n. 11 (3d Cir.1990) ("We do not pass on the question whether or not *Bowers* [*v. Kerbaugh–Empire*] is good law.").

[93] Despite its earlier statements about there being no debt and thus no COD income, the court dropped a footnote later in its opinion noting that its decision did not rest solely on unenforceability. Because, it stated, the decision "ultimately hinges" on the disputed debt rule, there was no need to consider whether Zarin had income on receipt of the chips. *Id.* at 116, n.12.

[94] The court supported this position by noting that if the only issue were unenforceability, it would have been an all-or-nothing proposition. Zarin would have paid or not but would not have settled.

have gambled $3.5 million if he had borrowed only $700,000.[95] If he had won $3.5 million, Resorts surely would not have accepted $700,000 as payment of the debt.[96]

A pure application of the loan proceeds theory to Zarin would have produced a different result. As the dissent in the Third Circuit noted, regardless of whether the loan was enforceable, Zarin received something of value when he undertook the obligation, which was not taxable.[97] Perhaps the court went off the track because Zarin did not receive cash. Because the casino was both the lender and the purveyor of what Zarin wanted to purchase with the loan proceeds—i.e., gambling—the casino skipped the transfer of cash and just handed Zarin the gambling chips.[98] If Zarin had borrowed the $3.5 million from his local bank before arriving at the casino and then lost it all gambling, he clearly would have had COD income if the bank discharged the debt. The loss of the loan proceeds would have been irrelevant. Under this approach, the unenforceability of the loan is irrelevant.[99]

So did Zarin have discharge of indebtedness income? Despite the intuitive appeal of his argument—the worse things got, the more income he had—several aspects of these facts lead to the unavoidable conclusion that he should have had discharge of indebtedness income.[100] First,

---

[95] One might make the case that Resorts knew it would get back all of its chips because of the house odds. Thus, it was really willing to loan the amount that Zarin would be able to pay, i.e., the amount of his assets. But this theory presumes that Resorts knew Zarin's worth and that is how it set the loan principal.

An alternative way to characterize Resorts' position is that, like Zarin, it essentially gambled. It was willing to put so much on the table for Zarin and if he won, it would get its money back but would lose the profit, as with any throw of the dice. If Zarin lost, it would earn the amount of Zarin's assets. It would reclaim the money on the table, and no matter what the amount of the loan, it would settle for the amount of his assets.

[96] In a footnote, the court says, "Had Zarin not paid the $500,000 dollar settlement, it would be likely that he would have had income from cancellation of indebtedness. The debt at that point would have been fixed, and Zarin would have been legally obligated to pay it." The clear implication is that Zarin had a choice. He could pay $500,000 and avoid tax on $3 million, which at his 70% bracket was $2.1 million, or he could pay nothing to Resorts and pay tax on $3.5 million, or $2.45 million. The court seems to be saying that if Zarin had $1 and Resorts took it, he would owe the government nothing. But if he had nothing, he would owe the government $5.2 million.

[97] 916 F.2d at 118 (Stapleton, J., dissenting). The dissenting opinion sets out a statement of the loan proceeds theory.

[98] *Id.* at 117. Query whether it should make a difference that Resorts would not have lent Zarin $3.5 million in cash.

[99] Another way to reach the same result without delving into debt discharge theory is to tax Zarin because he enjoyed consumption that he did not pay for and was not a gift from the transferor. What Zarin purchased with his loan proceeds was entertainment (the right to gamble).

[100] Readers should be aware that this is a minority view. The vast majority of commentators think that Zarin did not have COD income. *See* Marvin A. Chirelstein,

suppose Zarin had won and had repaid the entire debt to Resorts. The only reason he would have done so was because he was obligated to satisfy the debt. In that case, no one would have argued that there was no debt because it was unenforceable. It's either a debt or it's not, and enforceability does not seem to have much to do with it. Or suppose Zarin had not been able to settle and had repaid the entire $3.5 million. Is there any plausible argument that he would have had a deduction? Of course not, but exempting the income is the same as giving him a deduction for the full amount of his repayment. Or suppose Resorts had let him gamble $7 million but still settled for $500,000. Would Zarin have enjoyed the same amount of consumption as he did when he gambled and lost $3.5 million? Or suppose that Resorts had not bothered to make him sign markers and had simply permitted him to gamble at no cost—if he wins, he returns the chips and keeps the profit, and if he loses, he loses it but need not return it. How much consumption would Zarin enjoy? Clearly if he won, all would say that he had $3.5 million in income. Is the answer different if he loses? Does he still not enjoy $3.5 million of consumption? If so, that is the value he received in exchange for his obligation, and $3 million is therefore the amount of the discharge of indebtedness income when he satisfies his debt for $500,000.

Conclusion

The discharge of indebtedness story that began seven decades ago in the plains of Texas with Kirby Lumber continues to unfold today in the casinos of New Jersey with David Zarin. Like all of the tax stories in this book, Kirby Lumber's tale holds important lessons for beginning tax students and experienced tax lawyers alike. A deeper understanding of the underpinnings of the discharge of indebtedness doctrine helps prepare both groups to face the myriad ways in which the issue can arise in the twenty-first century economy. Perhaps never before has such a short opinion by the Supreme Court had such an impact on the development of the tax law.

Federal Income Taxation 56 (8th ed. 2002); Joseph M. Dodge, Zarin v. Commissioner: Musings About Debt Cancellations and "Consumption" in an Income Tax Base, 45 Tax L. Rev. 677 (1990); Alan Gunn, Another Look at the Zarin Case, 50 Tax Notes 893 (1991); Calvin H. Johnson, Zarin and the Tax Benefit Rule: Tax Models for Gambling Losses and the Forgiveness of Gambling Debts, 45 Tax L. Rev. 697 (1990); Shaviro, supra note 90. But see Babette B. Barton, Legal and Tax Incidents of Compulsive Behavior: Lessons From Zarin, 45 Tax Law. 749 (1992) (supporting taxation of Zarin); Joel S. Newman, Five Will Get You Ten: You Haven't Heard the Last About Zarin, 50 Tax Notes 188 (1991) (same).

*

4

Karen B. Brown

The Story of *Davis*: Transfers of Property Pursuant to Divorce

In March, 1955, Thomas Crowley Davis, an officer and director of E.I. du Pont de Nemours & Co. ("du Pont Co."), transferred 500 shares of du Pont Co. stock to his former spouse, Alice M. Davis, pursuant to a divorce decree. Upon audit of his tax return for that year, the Service determined that Mr. Davis owed a capital gains tax as a result of the transfer because the fair market value exceeded his adjusted basis in the stock.[1] The subsequent decision of the United States Supreme Court in 1962, *United States v. Davis*,[2] confirmed that a transferor of property to a former spouse realized gain or loss in the same manner as a seller of property. This resulted because the property was transferred in exchange for a release of marital property rights. Adopting the longstanding position of the Service,[3] the court also held that the transferee of the property, who relinquished marital rights in the exchange, received the property with an adjusted basis equal to its fair market value. This provided favorable treatment to the transferee who was not required to recognize gain on the transfer of the marital rights and obtained a "stepped-up" (fair market value) basis in property received in exchange for those rights.

---

[1] Mr. Davis' adjusted basis in the 500 shares of du Pont stock was $74,775, and the fair market value was $82,250. He was entitled to a deduction of 50% of the capital gain. This meant that $3,737 was subject to tax. The Service assessed a deficiency on the basis of this additional income and on the basis of the disallowance of a portion of the deduction claimed for attorney's fees.

[2] United States v. Davis, 370 U.S. 65 (1962), *rev'g in part & aff'g in part*, 287 F.2d 168 (Ct.Cl.1961).

[3] *See, e.g.*, Rev. Rul. 67–221, 1967–2 C.B. 63 (wife realizes no gain or loss on transfer of her dower rights in exchange for former husband's interest in apartment building, and basis of apartment building in her hands is its fair market value on date of transfer).

Background

Alice and Thomas Davis were married in 1941. On January 5, 1955, a Nevada state court granted Alice a final decree of divorce on the ground of extreme mental cruelty. The decree incorporated the separation and property settlement agreement of the parties. Under this agreement, Thomas agreed to make a cash payment to Alice representing the value of certain personal furnishings, to transfer certain life insurance policies to her, to make cash payments for her maintenance and support, to establish an irrevocable trust for their son, and to transfer a total of 1,000 shares of du Pont Co. to her. The transfer of 500 shares of du Pont Co. stock in January, 1955, generated the primary controversy later resolved by the Supreme Court.

Thomas was an employee, vice president, member of the executive and finance committees, director, and a shareholder of the du Pont Co. Before the divorce, he acquired as many as 3,416 shares of du Pont Co. stock as bonus awards. Consequently, the du Pont Co. stock transferred to Alice was owned solely by Thomas. Delaware, a common law state, accorded no present interest in Thomas' stock to his wife. However, Alice had an inchoate interest in her husband's property by way of dower and rights under testacy and intestacy laws.

The du Pont Co. expected Thomas, as a director and vice-president, to retain his stock unless he needed to sell it to purchase a home or pay taxes resulting from the bonus award. In Thomas' view, the holding of a certain amount of shares in the company constituted a significant factor in his nomination to the board of directors and his subsequent re-election. Consequently, Thomas was reluctant to reduce his holdings below 3,000 shares.

When marital troubles led Alice to begin negotiations for a property settlement, Thomas resisted, but he eventually transferred a small amount of shares to appease her. By late 1953, the marriage had deteriorated to the point of constant quarreling and immense unhappiness. Alice retained an attorney to assist in negotiating a separation agreement. The final property settlement, which was incorporated into the Nevada divorce decree detailed above, resulted from a series of negotiations. It provided that:

> [It settled the] respective rights and obligations [of the parties] against and to one another by (1) making a division of their property; (2) providing in lieu of alimony in the event of a decree of divorce for the support and maintenance of the wife; (3) making an arrangement and provision for the support and maintenance of Stephen [their minor child]; and (4) defining the rights of custody, maintenance, support and education of [Stephen].

Thomas paid attorney's fees to Young, his own attorney, and to Morford, Alice's attorney. The fees were for services rendered in structuring the property settlement as well as in providing tax advice.

Thomas remarried in 1955 and filed a federal income tax return for 1955, which claimed a deduction for attorney's fees paid to Young and Morford. After an audit of that return, the Service assessed a federal income tax deficiency that was based upon disallowance of the deduction for attorney's fees in the sum of $5,000 and addition of long term capital gain in the sum of $3,737. This total equaled the tax on one-half of the gain realized on transfer of the 500 shares of du Pont Co. stock to Alice in exchange for relinquishment of her marital rights.

Mr. Davis paid the deficiency, plus interest, and filed a claim for refund in 1958. The refund claim disputed the disallowance of the attorney's fees paid to Young and Morford regarding tax matters arising out of the divorce and asserted an additional deduction for attorney's fees relating to the property settlement. The claim also objected to the inclusion in income of gain from the transfer of the stock to Alice. The Service disallowed the claim in full by letter dated September 23, 1958. Thereafter, Thomas filed suit in the Court of Claims.

The Court of Claims allowed a deduction for the portion of attorney's fees relating to tax advice provided to Thomas and held that Thomas realized no taxable gain upon transfer of the stock to Alice. After issuance of a writ of *certiorari* to the Court of Claims, the Supreme Court affirmed the lower court's decision regarding deductibility of attorney's fees but reversed its holding that Thomas realized no taxable gain as a result of the stock transfer.

Before the Supreme Court's decision in *Davis*, many taxpayers argued that a transfer of property between spouses, or former spouses, amounted to a reconfiguration of ownership within a single economic unit, which was not a realization event. They maintained that imposition of an income tax in connection with property settlements incident to a divorce complicated and impeded resolution of these matters. While the courts had confirmed that equal divisions of community property or partition of jointly held property were not taxable events, considerable confusion existed regarding the tax consequences of other divisions of property.[4] Regarding transfers of separately-owned property between spouses incident to a divorce, courts reached different results. Two courts of appeals held that the transfer of such property in satisfaction of marital obligations was a taxable event resulting in recognition of gain.[5]

---

[4] For the Service's pronouncement that equal divisions of community property are nontaxable, see Rev. Rul. 74–347, 1974–2 C.B. 26.

[5] *See* Commissioner v. Halliwell, 131 F.2d 642 (2d Cir.1942), *cert. denied*, 319 U.S. 741 (1943); Commissioner v. Mesta, 123 F.2d 986 (3d Cir.1941), *cert. denied*, 316 U.S. 695 (1942).

One held that such a transfer was nontaxable due to the difficulty of valuing the marital rights received in exchange.[6]

The tax treatment of a transfer of property in a divorce settlement also depended upon state law ownership rights. If a spouse had a present interest in marital property, as in the case of a community property state, a transfer of such property might constitute a nontaxable division of jointly owned property. In common law jurisdictions, it was more likely that a transfer of property under a divorce decree would result in gain recognition by the transferor because the recipient spouse had no present interest in property amassed during the marriage.

The Supreme Court's decision in *Davis* failed to harmonize the results of property transfers incident to divorce in community and non-community property states. In addition, in the wake of *Davis*, litigants whipsawed the government in divorce matters when the transferor of property did not report gain and the transferee claimed a basis in the property equal to fair market value at the time of the transfer. If both successfully maintained these positions, gain would never be taxed.

Acknowledging the problems unresolved or created by *Davis*, Congress enacted § 1041 in 1984. Section 1041 treats transfers of property pursuant to divorce (as well as those between married persons) as nontaxable events. It provides that no gain or loss is recognized on the transfer of property to a spouse or former spouse if the transfer is incident to divorce. In these cases, the property is treated as acquired by gift, and the transferee takes the property with the adjusted basis of the transferor.

By enacting § 1041, Congress reversed the result in *Davis*. *Davis* required that Thomas recognize gain on the transfer of the stock pursuant to divorce and gave Alice a fair market value basis in the stock that she received. If the § 1041 regime had applied, Mr. Davis would have recognized no gain on the transfer, and Mrs. Davis would have taken a transferred basis in the stock, which was Mr. Davis' lower-than-fair-market-value adjusted basis.[7] Under the § 1041 regime, a transferred basis ensures that the gain not recognized by the transferor eventually will be recognized by the transferee for federal income taxation purposes on a subsequent sale to a person other than a spouse or a former spouse incident to a divorce.

Although § 1041 reversed the result in *Davis* and significantly diminished the tax complexities accompanying settlement of property in

---

[6] *See* Commissioner v. Marshman, 279 F.2d 27 (6th Cir.), *cert. denied*, 364 U.S. 918 (1960).

[7] § 1041(a), (b); *see also* § 7701(a)(43) (defining "transferred basis property" as property having a basis determined under any income tax provisions if that basis is determined in whole or part by reference to basis in hands of the transferor).

a divorce, *Davis* remains authoritative in the case of property transfers between non-spouses, between former spouses when the transfer is not incident to divorce, and in other situations described later in this chapter. Before we get to the end of the story, however, we first turn to the lower court and Supreme Court decisions in *Davis*. We then examine both the immediate impact of *Davis* on the development of tax law and the continued importance of *Davis* today.

Prior Proceedings

Mr. Davis filed suit in the Court of Claims after the Service denied his claim for refund. The refund claim had two bases. First, Davis sought to claim a deduction for attorney's fees paid for services rendered in the divorce action on behalf of both parties. Second, he sought a refund of the capital gains tax he paid as a result of the transfer of his du Pont Co. stock to his former wife. The Court of Claims partially resolved the attorney's fees claim in favor of Mr. Davis by allowing a deduction for the portion of the payment representing tax advice to Mr. Davis. This holding was affirmed by the Supreme Court. The Court of Claims resolved the second claim concerning nontaxability of the stock gain in favor of Mr. Davis. The Supreme Court reversed this portion of the decision.

Regarding the deductibility of attorney's fees, the Court of Claims' decision broke no new ground. It held that the fees were deductible under § 212(3) only to the extent that they related to tax advice on behalf of Mr. Davis in connection with the divorce settlement. Fees paid on behalf of Mrs. Davis to secure tax advice were not deductible. In addition, rejecting Mr. Davis' claim concerning the balance of the fees relating to property settlement, the Court of Claims held that they were not deductible. The court found that the fees were not deductible under § 212(2) despite a connection to Mr. Davis' position as stockholder, director, and officer of the du Pont Co. The court was not persuaded that Mr. Davis' position with the du Pont Co. was jeopardized by his disposition of shares. It concluded that the major portion of the fees related to the marital break-up and an effort to minimize the amount of property transferred (on Mr. Davis' behalf) or to maximize the amount transferred (on Mrs. Davis' behalf).

Absent a showing that the fees resulted from more than Mr. Davis' general desire to conserve his property or to minimize his financial obligations, the court found the balance of the fees for attorneys representing both parties to the divorce, which related to the property settlement, were not deductible. In particular, the court found no evidence that Mr. Davis needed to retain the stock in order to maintain his positions as officer and director of du Pont Co.

Here the Court of Claims simply followed the Supreme Court's decision in *Lykes v. United States*,[8] which held that a deduction for attorney's fees under § 212 was intended for income-producing activities of a commercial nature and not for any expense that might help a taxpayer retain property. The Court of Claims found inapplicable decisions that departed from the *Lykes* rule, for example, in which a taxpayer needed to retain stockholdings in order to retain his position with the company or in which a taxpayer might lose control of a company and salary if other parties obtained control.[9]

The Court of Claims' holding in *Davis* that the attorney's fees related to determination of property settlement in the divorce proceeding are nondeductible was affirmed without significant discussion by the Supreme Court.[10] In a subsequent decision, *United States v. Gilmore*,[11] the Supreme Court squarely addressed the issue, holding that a husband could not deduct legal expenses incurred in divorce proceedings because the fees related to claims arising entirely out of the marital relationship.

In *Gilmore*, the Court enunciated what is now known as the "origin of the claim" test. It stated: "The principle we derive from these cases is that characterization, as 'business' or 'personal,' of the litigation costs of resisting a claim depends on whether or not the claim *arises in connection with* the taxpayer's profit-seeking activities."[12]

Under this test, legal expenses are deductible if they arise in connection with profit-seeking activity. Consequences potentially resulting to income-producing property from the failure to defeat a claim are immaterial if the origin of the claim is in a personal relationship. Applying this standard, the Court found that the husband's legal expenses of the divorce proceeding in *Gilmore* were nondeductible even though loss of a substantial part of his assets would have resulted in loss of his corporate positions and loss of dealer franchises, which the husband owned. The decision of the Court of Claims in *Davis* predicted, and was consistent with, the Supreme Court's subsequent decision in *Gilmore*.

The more significant question decided by the Court of Claims in *Davis* related to Mr. Davis' second claim that a transfer of property to

---

[8] 343 U.S. 118 (1952).

[9] *See* McMurtry v. United States, 132 Ct.Cl. 418 (1955); Baer v. Commissioner, 196 F.2d 646 (8th Cir.1952).

[10] The Supreme Court found the question a simple one. It considered only the question whether the portion of the fees for tax advice paid to Mrs. Davis' attorney were deductible. It concluded that they were not deductible because they did not relate to tax advice directed to Mr. Davis' tax problems.

[11] 372 U.S. 39 (1963).

[12] *Id.* at 48.

his former wife in exchange for relinquishment of her marital rights was not a taxable event. On this issue, the court held in favor of Mr. Davis. As discussed below, the Supreme Court reversed the Court of Claims on this ground.

Mr. Davis argued that the transfer of stock to Mrs. Davis was not a taxable event for two reasons. First, the transfer was a nontaxable division of property. Second, the transfer was not in satisfaction of Mr. Davis' obligation to support his former wife.

The Court of Claims held that Mr. Davis did not recognize gain on the transfer of stock because there was no measure of the amount of gain. The court found that § 1001, which determines the amount of taxable gain upon a sale or disposition of property, required that a transferor receive property with an ascertainable fair market value. In this case, Mr. Davis received in exchange for the stock a relinquishment of his wife's rights to maintenance and support, which could not be measured. No value could be placed on those rights because the factors governing their determination were uncertain.

The court rejected the established tax axiom providing that in an arm's length transaction the fair market value of what is received is presumed to be the same as the fair market value of the property given up.[13] If that rule had been applied, it would have been presumed that Mr. Davis received a relinquishment of rights equal in value to the stock that he exchanged, resulting in a disposition of the property—a deemed sale—for its fair market value. The Court of Claims was reluctant to posit equivalent value in the context of a divorce proceeding because concessions are made and transfers occur out of a personal desire to resolve marital troubles and not out of any determination of fair value.

The Court of Claims' decision in *Davis* accorded with that of the Court of Appeals for the Sixth Circuit in *Commissioner v. Marshman*.[14] *Marshman* previously had held that a husband's relinquishment of an option to reacquire stock from his former wife was not taxable because the fair market value of the marital rights relinquished in exchange could not be determined.[15] The Sixth Circuit's decision in *Marshman* conflicted with those of the Second and Third Circuits.

---

[13] *See* Philadelphia Park Amusement Co. v. United States, 126 F.Supp. 184 (Ct.Cl. 1954).

[14] 279 F.2d 27 (6th Cir.), *cert. denied*, 364 U.S. 918 (1960).

[15] There was an additional question in *Marshman* concerning the extent of the husband's option to reacquire the stock. The Sixth Circuit was concerned that the husband might be taxed on the disposition of an option to repurchase the full number of shares when there was a genuine dispute as to the number of shares he was entitled to repurchase. The Service placed a value on the option equal to the full fair market value of the shares involved.

In *Commissioner v. Mesta*,[16] the Third Circuit held that a husband realized gain on the transfer of stock to his former wife in a divorce proceeding in satisfaction of his support obligation. The Third Circuit found a Congressional intention to tax the gain in the value of the stock in the event of realization, which supported treating the husband as though he had received his money's worth (fair market value) for the property. Although the fair market value of what the husband received (relief of a support obligation) might be difficult to ascertain, the Third Circuit felt it proper to take it to be equivalent to the fair market value of what was given up. The Second Circuit in *Commissioner v. Halliwell*[17] agreed with the *Mesta* decision.

In light of the conflicting views of the Second and Third Circuits, which found the transfer of property in a satisfaction of marital obligations to be a taxable event, and the Sixth Circuit and Court of Claims, which found such a transfer to be nontaxable because the fair market value of marital rights was not ascertainable, the Supreme Court granted *certiorari* in *Davis*.

The Supreme Court Decision

The Briefs and Oral Argument

In his brief in support of the government's petition for a writ of *certiorari*, the Solicitor General, Archibald Cox, presented two critical reasons to reverse the Court of Claims' decision holding that Mr. Davis' transfer of property was not a taxable event. First, he argued that the transfer was similar to numerous other situations in which courts recognized that a transfer of appreciated property in exchange for "unliquidated claims, inchoate rights or other species of property not readily susceptible of appraisal" was taxable.[18] The *Mesta* and *Halliwell* cases, which the Solicitor General found to be "indistinguishable from the case at bar," supported this point because the Courts of Appeals in those cases found transfers of appreciated property in a divorce proceeding to be taxable events.[19] Other cases, such as *International Freighting Corp. v. Commissioner*,[20] holding that an employer recognizes gain on the transfer of appreciated property to pay undetermined bonus awards,

---

[16] 123 F.2d 986 (3d Cir.1941), *cert. denied*, 316 U.S. 695 (1942).

[17] 131 F.2d 642 (2d Cir.1942) (holding that husband's transfer of securities to wife in discharge of his obligations to support her and their child allowed him to realize enhancement in value of securities during his ownership), *cert. denied*, 319 U.S. 741 (1943).

[18] Petition for Writ of *Certiorari* at 5.

[19] Petition for Writ of *Certiorari* at 4.

[20] 135 F.2d 310 (2d Cir.1943).

illustrated that a transfer of property for an unliquidated claim is a taxable event.

Mr. Cox contended that "one who exchanges property of known value for an unliquidated claim [should be presumed to] receive[] money's worth."[21] The integrity of the federal income tax base depended upon inclusion of realized appreciation. Consequently, the Court should not fail to confirm that gain is subject to tax even if it is difficult to evaluate the value of the property (such as release of marital rights) received because value could be presumed to be equivalent to what was given in exchange.

The government's second point referred to the need for uniformity in treatment of transfers incident to divorce property settlements. Finding the transfer to the wife the event marking appropriation of the gain by the husband, the government argued that these transactions should be taxed. Given the frequency of these transfers, a revenue-maximizing rule was important. Additionally, because the wife received a fair market value basis in property received in exchange for release of her marital rights, appreciation in these assets would never be taxed if it were not taxed in the hands of the husband. Finally, the government viewed the Court of Claims' decision as a potential threat to the tax base if it were extended to other non-divorce situations in which there was no means of assessing the value of rights released.

Converse Murdoch, in Mr. Davis' Brief in Opposition to Petition for Writ of *Certiorari*, first claimed that the transfers between the Davises differed from those in *Mesta* and *Halliwell* because Mr. Davis was not discharging an obligation to support and maintain Mrs. Davis. In cases in which the transfer of property was pursuant to a distribution of marital property (as opposed to in satisfaction of alimony or support and maintenance rights), no taxable event occurred and the transferee of the property took a basis equal to that of the transferor.[22] Marshaling support for Davis' claim that the Court should defer tax at the time of the transfer and preserve gain for later recognition by holding that Mrs. Davis retained his basis in the property, Murdoch cited one case, *Swanson v. Wiseman*, in which the government had contended that the wife's basis in the property received was not "stepped-up" (fair market value).[23] Murdoch failed to state that it was likely that the Service took this position in *Swanson* in order to avoid being whipsawed. In order to

---

[21] Petition for Writ of *Certiorari* at 5.

[22] Brief in Opposition to Petition for Writ of *Certiorari* at 4–5.

[23] Swanson v. Wiseman, 61–1 U.S.T.C. ¶ 9264 (W.D.Okla.1961) (holding that a divorce decree in 1943 effected a division of property that did not entitle the transferee-wife to a new fair market value basis in stock received). The issue in *Swanson* arose in 1952, nine years after the divorce, when the wife sold stock received from her husband pursuant to the decree.

protect the fisc, the Service asserted that the wife had a carryover basis when it could not collect tax on the gain in the property from the husband.[24]

Mr. Davis pointed to other areas in tax law in which a distinction was made between transfers of property in satisfaction of a fixed obligation and a mere distribution of property. He provided the example of the infamous, but now repealed, *General Utilities* rule. In *General Utilities and Operating Co. v. Helvering*,[25] the Supreme Court held that a corporation recognized no gain when it distributed appreciated property to its shareholders with respect to their stock. Davis contrasted the *General Utilities* rule of nonrecognition with the rule that a corporation does recognize gain when it distributes property in satisfaction of a dividend of a fixed amount.

Mr. Davis' efforts to characterize the transfer of property to his former wife as a nontaxable transaction warrant further exploration. The point goes to the heart of the controversy in *Davis*, which was the determination of the appropriate moment to tax appreciation in the value of property. As the government noted in its brief, the question was "whether a property settlement incident to divorce should be treated as a taxable event at all—i.e., whether it is the kind of 'sale or disposition of property' in which an accounting of gain or loss is required."[26] Mr. Davis urged deferral of taxation by, in effect, shifting the burden to pay tax to the recipient of property:

> If in situations of this kind a gain is to be recognized either at a time when the husband transfers property to his wife or when the wife later sells the property, it seems far preferable to impose the tax in the second event rather than at the time of the transfer from the husband. At the time the husband transfers the property he is depleting his estate and is realizing no cash which will furnish a fund from which an income tax can be paid. On the other hand, if the tax is imposed at the time when the wife sells the property, the tax will be imposed at a time when the taxpayer has realized a cash

---

[24] A post-*Davis* decision, Wiles v. Commissioner, 499 F.2d 255 (10th Cir.1974), discussed *infra* note 47, explained the Service's approach when there is the potential for it to collect no tax when the parties take inconsistent positions and each wins. In that case, the taxpayer complained that the Service had improperly taken inconsistent positions by asserting a claim against the wife on the basis of the settlement transaction (which would require her to use a carryover basis instead of a fair market value basis in computing gain on any subsequent sale of the property) when it was also contending that the transfer was a taxable event to the husband. The Tenth Circuit noted that this is "an administrative practice for the protection of the revenues." It indicated that it was "confident that the Commissioner will not attempt to collect double taxes and, if he does, the liability of the divorced wife can then be considered." *Id.* at 259.

[25] 296 U.S. 200 (1935).

[26] Brief for the United States at 9.

gain which will furnish the funds for payment of the tax. This seems to be the better result.[27]

Deferral of taxation was appropriate in his case, Mr. Davis argued, because the transfer of the shares was analogous to a nontaxable division of property between two co-owners. He contended that this characterization of the transfer would eliminate disparity in treatment of married couples in common law and community property jurisdictions. In a common law jurisdiction, the wife's rights to a husband's property are not equivalent to those of a co-owner but depend upon a determination of her entitlement to a portion under state law. In a community property jurisdiction, the wife's rights in certain of her husband's property placed her in the position of co-owner. Thus, under community property law, a transfer of property between spouses would be viewed as a nontaxable reconfiguration of jointly owned property.

Both the government and Mr. Davis urged consistency in treatment of transfers of marital property with different outcomes. The government essentially argued that transfers of marital property (whether or not in satisfaction of support obligations) should be immediately taxable in the same manner as all other exchanges for value. The Solicitor General maintained:

> It is accordingly important to the revenue that there be a uniform rule of law for purposes of determining whether the husband realizes taxable gain when he transfers such property to the wife. The transfer, we emphasize, marks "the last step ... by which he obtains the fruition of the economic gain which has already accrued to him[.]"[28]

Mr. Davis contended that consistency of treatment required that taxation of appreciation in marital property be deferred, as in the case of spouses residing in community property jurisdictions, until the transferee spouse later sold the property and possessed the sales proceeds with which to pay the tax.[29]

The Opinion

The Supreme Court viewed the critical questions to involve whether and when Congress intended to tax the appreciation in value of Mr. Davis' stock. Because there was no doubt that Congress intended to tax the economic growth in the stock, the more significant question related to timing. The Court queried whether tax on the gain should be imposed upon Mr. Davis or upon Mrs. Davis when she subsequently sold the

---

[27] Brief in Opposition to Petition for Writ of *Certiorari* at 9.

[28] Petition for Writ of *Certiorari* at 6.

[29] Brief for Petitioner at 9.

stock. If taxation were to be deferred until the occurrence of a later sale by Mrs. Davis, her basis in the shares received would be equal to Mr. Davis' basis, placing her in his shoes for gain measurement. If Mr. Davis were taxed upon transfer of the shares, Mrs. Davis' basis in the stock would equal fair market value.

Calling upon Congress, if it so chose, to correct the disparity created by different legal regimes, the Supreme Court nonetheless felt obligated to acknowledge that the transfer of separately-owned property between former spouses in a common law jurisdiction was a taxable event. It found that the rights granted a wife in her husband's property under Delaware law did not rise to the level of co-ownership. Those rights were founded upon the husband's obligation to support and were not premised upon any right to manage or dispose of her husband's property.[30]

Having concluded that Mr. Davis' transfer was a taxable event, the Court held that Mr. Davis must be treated as receiving in exchange for the stock marital rights of equal value. It viewed the transfer as an arm's length transaction in which, absent a readily ascertainable value, the two properties exchanged are presumed to be of equal value. Although it was sympathetic to the argument that divorce negotiations are seldom at arm's length, the Supreme Court found it consistent with Congressional intent to broadly tax gains to make a rough approximation of the gain realized once a transfer is recognized as a taxable event.

Regarding the wife's basis in the property received from her husband, the Court held that it is a cost basis measured by the fair market value of the property received.[31] This ensured that the wife was never taxed on the appreciation in value of the property that occurred during the period of ownership by the husband.

The holding achieved a generous result for the wife (or transferee spouse generally) because, in keeping with administrative practice of the Service, she was permitted to treat the transfer of her marital rights as a nontaxable event.[32] As a consequence, she recognized no gain on the

---

[30] The Court found that the wife's rights to the husband's property did not descend to her heirs or beneficiaries. In addition, she was entitled to only such property as a court deemed reasonable in connection with dissolution of the marriage.

[31] The Court expressed concern that the determination by the Court of Claims that the transfer was a taxable event for which gain could not be measured (due to the uncertain fair market value of the relinquished marital rights received by the husband) left open the question of the wife's basis in the property received. This would place the wife in the difficult position of receiving property in a taxable exchange for which there was no presumed value. She would have the burden of proving the value of the property received in order to establish her basis or be required to pay tax on the difference between the lower value that she could prove and the subsequent appreciation in value after receipt of the property.

[32] *Davis*, 370 U.S. at 73, n.7.

transfer of marital rights with a value presumed to be equal that of the property received but took a fair market value basis in that property.

The win-win situation for the transferee spouse was an important departure from the general rule that a taxpayer received a fair market value basis in property only if it is received in an exchange that is taxable to the taxpayer. Because administrative practice considered the wife's relinquishment of marital rights to be a nontaxable event to her, the wife's basis in the property received should have been equal to her basis in the marital rights.[33] This basis, now known as an exchanged basis, would have placed the wife in a position to recognize the gain built into the property, which is normally the rule applied in tax-free transactions.[34] A simple example demonstrates this point. Pursuant to a divorce, H transfers property worth $10,000 (with a $2,000 basis) to W in exchange for her relinquishment of marital rights in which she has a $0 basis. If the transaction is taxable to H, he recognizes $8,000 gain. If the transaction is taxable to W, she recognizes $10,000 gain and takes a $10,000 basis in the property. If the transaction is not taxable, neither H nor W recognizes gain on the transfer. Under normal tax rules, W would take a $0 basis in the property received (her basis in the property exchanged (the marital rights)). In *Davis*, it was assumed that the wife's adjusted basis in the property received would be either fair market value or the husband's basis. As discussed below, this result was reversed by the enactment of § 1041, which automatically requires the transferee spouse to take a carryover basis in the property received because it treats all transfers incident to divorce as nontaxable.[35]

It is likely that the Service's administrative practice and the Supreme Court's imprimatur rested upon the understanding that the wife would in most cases have no basis in her marital rights because they are not purchased or otherwise acquired in a transaction that would provide basis. Treatment of her relinquishment of marital rights as a taxable event would guarantee that she would include in gross income the full fair market value of the property received. This would result in a hardship to the wife, who would be required to sell the property in order to pay the taxes and who would be left with diminished resources after the divorce. It would also depart from the general rule, derived from the

---

[33] Where a transfer results in nonrecognition of gain, the party takes a basis in the property received equal to the basis that she had in the property given up in the exchange. This rule allows eventual taxation of the gain not taxed at the time of the transfer. *See* Philadelphia Amusement Park Co. v. United States, 126 F.Supp. 184 (Ct.Cl.1954).

[34] Section 7701(a)(44) defines "exchanged basis property" as property having a basis determined in whole or in part by reference to other property held at any time by the person for whom basis is to be determined.

[35] § 1041(a), (b).

Supreme Court's decision in *Gould v. Gould*,[36] that support to a former spouse is not taxable income. The Supreme Court in *Davis* acknowledged that the wife's rights to her husband's property in a common law jurisdiction on termination of the marriage derived in substantial part from the husband's obligation of support and alimony.

The second matter considered by the Supreme Court in *Davis* concerned the deductibility of the attorney's fees for tax advice rendered by Mrs. Davis' attorney. Because that advice did not relate to Mr. Davis' tax problems, the Court affirmed the Court of Claims' disallowance of the deduction.

The Immediate Impact of *Davis*

Although the Supreme Court's decision in *Davis* may have reached a technically correct conclusion regarding exchanges of property in connection with divorce, it did not have a salutary effect on the development of tax law. The disadvantages have been summarized as follows:

> [The *Davis* decision] frequently imposed a heavy tax burden at the worst possible time—when a couple's finances were in disarray and every available dollar was needed to finance the transition from one household into two. The taxable transfer was essentially involuntary because it was compelled by marital property law. Finally, the transfer produced no cash with which to pay the tax.[37]

An additional problem created by *Davis* was that the differing marital rights accorded to a divorced spouse in common law and community property jurisdictions resulted in different tax consequences for substantially similar transactions. The co-ownership of property created in community property jurisdictions allowed couples to avoid taxation of gain in transfers incident to divorce. However, a transfer of property in exchange for relinquishment of the inchoate interest of a spouse in a common law jurisdiction would result in taxation. Thus, the Supreme Court achieved uniformity in treatment of transfers of appreciated property, other than relinquishment of marital rights, but created inconsistency in treatment of marital property settlements based upon the residence of the taxpayers in a common law or a community property state.

---

[36] 245 U.S. 151 (1917). The rules of §§ 71 and 215, which provide for inclusion of alimony payments in the gross income of the recipient and for a deduction for the payor, were adopted as an income-splitting device to accord relief to husbands subject to high taxes during World War II. *See* Laurie L. Malman, *Unfinished Reform: The Tax Consequences of Divorce*, 61 N.Y.U. L. Rev. 363, 380 (1986).

[37] Michael Asimow, *The Assault on Tax–Free Divorce: Carryover Basis and Assignment of Income*, 44 Tax L. Rev. 65, 67 (1988) (footnotes omitted).

In order to avoid taxation of property transfers pursuant to divorce, common law jurisdictions contemplated or adopted changes in divorce law in an attempt to achieve non-taxation of property settlements incident to divorce. This entailed efforts to accord state law marital rights in the separate property of a spouse akin to co-ownership. In addition, state courts strained to avoid taxation of marital property settlements by interpreting a common law equitable distribution statute to provide rights amounting to co-ownership, resulting in tax-free dispositions.[38]

In the Tenth Circuit, for example, two cases interpreting the divorce law of Colorado and Oklahoma found that property settlements were not taxable events. Another case in the Tenth Circuit reached the opposite result regarding Kansas law. The three cases demonstrate the complexity created by *Davis*.

In *Collins v. Commissioner*,[39] the Tenth Circuit relied on the Supreme Court of Oklahoma's determination of the interest of a wife in property acquired during marriage to conclude that a transfer of stock to her pursuant to a divorce was a nontaxable division of property. This conclusion was reached at the end of a long chain of decisions that exposed the problems created by the Supreme Court's decision in *Davis*. The Tenth Circuit initially determined that the property transfer was a taxable event, relying on a previous Tenth Circuit decision, *Collins I*.[40] Shortly thereafter, the Oklahoma Supreme Court in *Collins II* found the interest of the wife "similar in conception to community property of community property states, and [] regarded as held by a species of common ownership."[41] The United States Supreme Court granted *certiorari* (*Collins III*) to review *Collins I* but vacated the judgment in *Collins I*, remanding it for reconsideration in light of the Oklahoma Supreme Court's decision in *Collins II*.[42] In its final decision (*Collins IV*), the Tenth Circuit reversed its original decision and held, as noted above, that the stock transfer pursuant to divorce was nontaxable.[43]

In *Imel v. United States*,[44] the Tenth Circuit held in accordance with *Collins IV* that a transfer of stock to a wife pursuant to a property settlement incident to divorce governed by Colorado law was not a taxable event. Although it agreed with the argument of the government

[38] *See* Malman, *supra* note 36, at 384–85.

[39] Collins v. Commissioner, 412 F.2d 211 (10th Cir.1969).

[40] Pulliam v. Commissioner, 329 F.2d 97 (10th Cir.), *cert. denied*, 379 U.S. 836 (1964).

[41] Collins v. Oklahoma Tax Comm'n, 446 P.2d 290, 295 (Okla.1968).

[42] Collins v. Commissioner, 393 U.S. 215 (1968).

[43] Collins v. Commissioner, 412 F.2d 211 (10th Cir.1969).

[44] 523 F.2d 853 (10th Cir.1975).

that state law may not dictate federal tax consequences, the Tenth
Circuit found that the federal tax determination depended upon interpretation of state law. The Colorado Supreme Court determined the
state law issues when it answered certified questions posed by the
federal district court regarding the nature of the wife's interest in
marital property.[45] Accordingly, based upon the state court's determination that the wife's interest was a species of common ownership, the
Tenth Circuit held that the stock transfer was not a taxable event.

Applying the law of Kansas, the Tenth Circuit found that the rights
of a wife in the property of her husband did not rise to the level of co-
ownership. Consequently, it held in *Wiles v. Commissioner*[46] that the
husband recognized gain on a transfer of his separate property to her
pursuant to divorce. The Tenth Circuit acknowledged the discrepancy in
law in the Tenth Circuit created by the decisions in *Collins IV* and *Imel*,
which held, as described above, that the transfers were not taxable
events. It noted the inapplicability of the Colorado and Oklahoma
decisions to a matter of Kansas law:

> The Oklahoma and Colorado decisions . . . are noted in recognition
> of the disparities which exist in the application of federal tax
> statutes to transactions occurring in the states which compose the
> Tenth Circuit. We are bound by *Davis*, which comments that al-
> though Congress has alleviated disparities in many areas "in other
> areas the facts of life are still with us." *Davis* requires us to follow
> Kansas law. We are convinced that under the pertinent Kansas
> statutes and decisions the wife has no vested co-ownership in the
> property of the husband during the marriage.[47]

One commentator noted that the law after *Davis* concerning property settlements caused many states to take actions similar to those taken
in the early 1940s to minimize tax consequences to married couples in
non-community property jurisdictions before Congressional adoption of
the joint return. She observed:

> The state of the law regarding property settlements was reminiscent
> of the attempts by common law states in the 1940s to achieve
> income splitting between spouses. The states were unsuccessful in
> their attempts, however, unless they made fundamental substantive
> changes in their property law principles. The confusion caused by
> such efforts was a factor in the enactment of the joint return

---

[45] *In re* Question Submitted by the U. S. Dist. Court, 517 P.2d 1331 (Colo.1974).

[46] 499 F.2d 255 (10th Cir.1974).

[47] *Id.* at 259 (citation omitted).

provisions in 1948. Similarly, the confusion caused by the *Davis* rule provided the impetus for the 1984 divorce tax legislation.[48]

Even when one could navigate the confusion to discern state law rights to marital property, *Davis* exacerbated the complexity attending property settlements. Post-*Davis* decisions illustrated that the tax law in this area could be successfully negotiated only by the most sophisticated tax attorneys. For example, the Tax Court in *Pennington v. Commissioner*[49] demonstrated that the result in *Davis* was limited to the situation in which a spouse released her dower rights in exchange for an interest in the separate property of the husband. If the wife exchanged her interest in property owned jointly with her husband during the marriage for his separate property, she would recognize taxable gain. If she relinquished her interest in jointly held property for other jointly held property, the exchange was considered a nontaxable division of property.[50]

A ruling issued by the Service after *Davis* further evidenced a potential trap for tax planners. In *Revenue Ruling 74–347*, the Service held that while equal division of property jointly owned under a non-community property regime was not taxable, unequal division of such property was a taxable exchange.[51] In that situation, an award of more than half of the jointly-owned property to the wife constituted a taxable exchange of a portion of the husband's jointly owned property for his wife's marital rights in his separately owned property. There the total assets owned by the couple had a fair market value of $110,000. The wife was awarded jointly-owned property with a value of $55,000. The husband was awarded jointly-owned property with a value of $15,000 and his separately-owned property with a value of $40,000. The Service held that he effectively transferred a portion of his separately-owned property for his wife's marital rights in the excess portion of the jointly-owned property that she received. This transfer was taxable to the husband.[52]

The complexity of the tax result arising from *Davis* forced the structuring of divorce settlements in inappropriate ways in order to minimize tax consequences.[53] Many unwittingly negotiated taxable prop-

---

[48] Malman, *supra* note 36, at 386 (footnotes omitted).

[49] 60 T.C.M. (CCH) 559 (1990).

[50] *See also* Carrieres v. Commissioner, 64 T.C. 959 (1975) (holding that exchange of husband's separate property for wife's interest in community property is a taxable event, but exchange of community property for community property is not taxable).

[51] Rev. Rul. 74–347, 1974–2 C.B. 26. *See also* Rev. Rul. 81–292, 1981–2 C.B. 158 (equal division of jointly-owned property in non-community property state is a nontaxable division of property); Rev. Rul. 76–83, 1976–1 C.B. 213 (approximately equal division of community property is nontaxable where some assets go to one spouse and others go to the other).

[52] The Service did not find the transfer by the wife a taxable event.

[53] Professor Asimow notes that "[p]roperty settlement negotiations turned heavily on tax considerations, rather than on the needs of the spouses. Costly tax counsel participated

erty settlements but failed to report them.[54] Gain from these transactions was not reported while the transferees were claiming a stepped-up basis in the property received. As a result, absent an audit by the Service, gain was never taxed.[55] As noted by one observer, this state of affairs was a strong factor in the effective repeal of *Davis* by enactment of § 1041:

> Competent tax counsel were puzzled by the state of the law, but they made the most of it. Since wholly plausible arguments supported the conclusion that many divisions were taxable or tax free, transferors sometimes claimed nonrecognition treatment, while transferees claimed a stepped-up basis. The government was relentlessly whipsawed. Davis was likely a net money loser for the Treasury, a factor which must have contributed heavily to the Treasury's decision to support a legislative abrogation of *Davis*.[56]

A further ground for repeal of the *Davis* result was its failure to reflect changing views of marriage as an economic partnership. State marital dissolution laws were increasingly resting upon equitable distribution principles, which involved disposition of marital property on the basis of each spouse's contribution to the marriage enterprise rather than on the basis of wrongdoing or fault. This development was explained, as follows:

> The conceptual rationale of equitable distribution is that a marriage is a shared enterprise or partnership and, since each spouse contributes to the marital enterprise, assets of the enterprise should be allocated on bases other than technical title ... Advocates of equitable distribution-type statutes argue that spouses in functioning marriages generally pool their assets and earnings to satisfy the family's needs ... Thus, one spouse may temporarily put aside individual career goals for the sake of the family, use individual earnings to finance the other's education or career, interrupt a career or switch jobs to follow the other spouse, or stop working to stay at home with children. These situations give rise to an expecta-

---

in planning even the most straightforward property divisions. Often, for example, the parties would substitute alimony for property division, even though this unnecessarily prolonged the dependence of the supported spouse." Asimow, *supra* note 37, at 68.

[54] *Id.*

[55] *Id.*

[56] *Id.* at 68–69 (footnotes omitted). *See also* Staff of Jt. Comm. on Tax'n, 98th Cong., *General Explanation of the Revenue Provisions of the Deficit Reduction Act of 1984* 711 (Comm. Print 1984) ("The Congress believes that to correct these problems, and make the tax laws as unintrusive as possible with respect to relations between spouses, the tax laws governing transfers between spouses and former spouses should be changed.").

tion that assets will be shared during the marriage. The law should protect that expectation when the marriage dissolves.[57]

Settlement of marital property according to the equitable contributions of the partners to the enterprise would result in nontaxation of transfers. Under this scenario, a spouse would not be taxed on the transfer of appreciated property because the "transferee spouse [would] be viewed as receiving property that he or she previously owned, albeit in a different form."[58]

Davis also departed from equitable principles. Commentators routinely tout equity and efficiency as foundational principles of federal income taxation. Efficiency promotes economic growth while equity provides the appearance of fairness necessary to ensure taxpayer compliance. *Davis* illustrated a circumstance in which it was all but impossible to serve both these goals and other social policy ends at the same time. Horizontal equity is served when the tax system treats similarly situated taxpayers similarly. A proponent of horizontal equity might argue that *Davis* reached an unfair result.

Horizontal equity would dictate that a taxpayer who falls within a defined group entitled to prescribed tax benefits must be taxed in the same manner as other members. Application of this test is frequently complicated by a determination of the appropriate group. In *Davis*, for example, if Mr. Davis were placed in the group of spouses transferring property pursuant to divorce, the Supreme Court's holding that he must recognize gain would cause him to be treated differently than former husbands residing in community property jurisdictions who transferred property without gain recognition. If, however, Mr. Davis were placed in the group of transferors of appreciated property, he would be treated the same as those in *International Freighting* and *Philadelphia Park Amusement* who were required to recognize gain.

On the other hand, Mrs. Davis was accorded better treatment than similarly situated persons. The Supreme Court held that she recognized no gain on relinquishment of her marital rights in exchange for the stock, affirming a longstanding Service administrative rule. Other transferors of appreciated property were required to recognize gain. The Supreme Court in *Davis* apparently felt that it could find either gain recognition by the husband upon the transfer of property to the wife or gain recognition by the wife when she subsequently sold the property received. A third option not taken by the Court was to tax both parties at the time of the exchange for relinquishment of marital rights. The decision not to tax the transferor of marital rights presumably was based

---

[57] Malman, *supra* note 36, at 373–374 (footnotes omitted).

[58] *Id.* at 387.

either upon the Court's determination not to impose a tax on the wife at the same time that she was undergoing the hardship of divorce or upon its determination that marital rights did not amount to property that could be transferred.

Although the decision in *Davis* to tax an exchange of property for marital rights supported a trend in modern tax law to broadly tax gains under an ability-to-pay rationale, the havoc that it wreaked in the domestic relations law world forecast its demise. As discussed below, Congress acted in 1984 to eliminate the *Davis* result. *Davis* nonetheless remains authority for the proposition that a disposition in satisfaction of an obligation is a taxable event. It is also determinative in the realm of non-spousal transfers of property and transfers between former spouses, which are not incident to divorce.

The Continuing Importance of *Davis* Today

In response to the complexities and confusion created by the decision to tax certain transfers incident to a property settlement arising out of divorce, Congress effectively repealed *Davis* in 1984 with the enactment of § 1041.[59] Under the statutory regime, no gain or loss is recognized on any transfer of property (even a sale) between spouses and between former spouses when the transfer is incident to divorce. Such property is treated as having been acquired by gift. As a result, the transferee spouse takes a basis in the property received equal to the transferor's adjusted basis.

Section 1041 thus shifts the incidence of taxation onto the transferee spouse. If appreciated property is transferred, the recipient will recognize gain on a subsequent disposition. If property that has depreciated in value is transferred, the recipient will recognize loss on a subsequent disposition. A simple example will demonstrate the application of § 1041 to transfers of property between former spouses incident to divorce. Assume that W transfers property to her former husband H in accordance with the terms of their divorce decree issued after 1984. W has a $25,000 basis in the property, which has a $100,000 fair market value at the time of transfer. Section 1041(a) provides that W does not recognize gain as a result of the transfer. Section 1041(b) provides that H receives the property as a gift and takes W's $25,000 basis. If H later

---

[59] § 1041 is effective for transfers of property after July 18, 1984. For an article urging that divorce tax law remains "needlessly complex" even after enactment of § 1041, especially regarding resolution of assignment of income issues, see Deborah A. Geier, *Simplifying and Rationalizing the Federal Income Tax Law Applicable to Transfers in Divorce*, 55 Tax Law. 363 (2002).

sells the property to a third party for its $100,000 fair market value, he recognizes $75,000 of gain.[60]

Despite the massive overhaul of divorce settlement transfers resulting from the adoption of the § 1041 rules, *Davis* was not overruled and retains vitality in four areas: (1) taxable exchanges where one of the properties lacks an ascertainable fair market value, (2) transfers of property in exchange for relief of an obligation or relinquishment of any non-marital right having value, (3) transfers of property between non-spouses or to a spouse who is a nonresident alien, and (4) transfers of property between former spouses which are not incident to divorce.

1. *Exchange of Property Having No Ascertainable Fair Market Value*

The Supreme Court's articulation of the rule that the fair market value of property received in a taxable exchange is presumed to be equivalent to the value of property relinquished is of particular importance to a student of federal income taxation. If, in such an exchange, the value of one of the properties is not known or ascertainable, equivalent value is presumed. On this issue, courts continue to rely on *Davis*.[61] Thus, for example, if as a result of an arm's length negotiation, A agrees to transfer Property 1 (with a fair market value of $1,000) in exchange for B's Property 2 (with an unascertainable fair market value), it is presumed that Property 2 is worth $1,000.

Two consequences flow from *Davis'* equivalent value rule. First, taxation of gain is accelerated, occurring even if only one of the exchanged properties has an ascertainable value. Second, in a taxable exchange when equivalent value is presumed, the recipient of the property will have a basis equal to the deemed fair market value. This is necessary to prevent double taxation because the fair market value of the property must be treated as an amount realized under § 1001(b) in computing property disposition gain. In the example of A and B above,

---

[60] This would result even if H purchased the property from W for its $100,000 fair market value. On a purchase of the property for $100,000, H nonetheless would take W's $25,000 basis. *See* Treas. Reg. § 1.1041–1T, Q–2 & A–2. This is a result that H would seek to avoid. An alternative to a purchase for fair market value would be a purchase for an amount equal to adjusted basis (in this case, $25,000) or a sale of property by W (resulting in gain recognition by her) and transfer of the proceeds of sale to H (perhaps net of taxes—that is, sales price minus tax paid by W.) In a property transfer covered by § 1041, the transferee's basis is always the same as the transferor's. This departs from the rule for transfers of property by gift. *See* § 1015(e). For a gift transfer, if a loss is built into the property at the time of the gift (transferor's adjusted basis exceeds fair market value at that time), the donee takes a basis equal to fair market value at the time of the gift for purposes of determining loss. This rule disallows deduction of the built-in loss.

[61] *See, e.g.*, Davis v. Commissioner, 210 F.3d 1346 (11th Cir.2000) (holding that Service failed to establish that neither property involved in hypothetical exchange had an ascertainable value in taxable year for which assessment would be barred by statute of limitations); Framatome v. Commissioner, 118 T.C. 32 (2002) (citing *Davis* for proposition that "the value of two properties exchanged in an arm's-length transaction is presumed to be equal").

both A and B must report $1,000 as the amount realized on the sale. The amount of property disposition gain is determined by subtracting each person's basis in the property given up in the exchange from the amount realized. (Realized loss is determined by subtracting the amount realized from the basis.) If A and B each has a basis of $100 in their respective properties, each will report a gain of $900. Finally, each will have an adjusted basis equal to fair market value, or $1,000, in the property received.

2. *Transfers of Property for Non–Marital Rights*

Davis continues to support the proposition that an exchange of property for any valuable right is a taxable event. Thus, it is authority for the proposition that a case like *Farid-Es-Sultaneh v. Commissioner*[62] remains good law. In *Farid-Es-Sultaneh*, the Second Circuit found a taxable exchange in a pre-marital transaction. In that case, Mr. Kresge transferred 2500 shares of S.S. Kresge Co. stock to his intended bride. Considering that Mr. Kresge was married to another person at that time, the transfer protected the intended bride in the event that Mr. Kresge were to die before the expected marriage. After Mr. Kresge's divorce from his previous wife, but before his marriage to Farid-es-Sultaneh, the two executed an ante-nuptial settlement acknowledging that the transfer of stock was in consideration of her promise to marry and of her release of her dower and other marital rights to which she was entitled under New York law, including her right to support.

Even though the ante-nuptial settlement referred to the transfers as gifts, the Second Circuit found that Farid-es-Sultaneh acquired the shares for a fair consideration. As a purchaser of the property, she obtained a fair market value basis in the shares that was higher than Mr. Kresge's basis at the time of transfer.[63] While the Second Circuit did not address the tax consequences to Mr. Kresge, the logic of the decision dictated that the transfer be considered a taxable event—a transfer of appreciated stock in exchange for the intended bride's release of her state law marital rights.

Consequently, a transfer in exchange for a valuable right before marriage is a taxable event. Section 1041 does not change this result because it applies only to transfers between spouses and former spouses. In general, § 1041 may be viewed as an exception to the general rule of taxation of exchanges where, as in the case of divorce matters, there is a strong public policy reason to seek to avoid the complication of taxation. This means that the results in cases like *International Freighting Corp.*

---

[62] 160 F.2d 812 (2d Cir.1947).

[63] With a higher basis, Farid-es-Sultaneh recognized less gain on the subsequent sale of the stock.

v. Commissioner[64] (holding that an employer realizes gain on the transfer of property to employees in satisfaction of bonus awards) and *Kenan v. Commissioner*[65] (holding that a transfer of securities in satisfaction of a specific bequest is taxable), which are outside of the marital transfer arena, continue to find support in *Davis*.

3. Transfers of Property Between Nonspouses or to a Nonresident Spouse

The *Davis* rule of taxation of exchanges also continues to apply in the case of transfers between persons who are not married but who retain a close personal relationship, such as unmarried couples who live together. Thus, *Davis* would continue to apply to transfers of property in exchange for services between unmarried individuals or transfers in satisfaction of a common law obligation of support, such as the so-called "palimony" right.

In addition, in order to avoid complete escape of taxation, § 1041(d) renders the rule of nonrecognition of gain inapplicable to a transfer to a nonresident alien spouse. As a general rule, nonresident aliens are not subject to tax in the U.S. on gain from the sale of property other than real property located in the United States.[66] Section 1041(d) requires the transferor spouse to recognize gain on transfer of appreciated property to a nonresident alien spouse because the gain, which is preserved by a transferred basis regime when the transferee is subject to United States' income taxation, would not be subject to United States' income tax if the property were subsequently sold by the transferee.

4. Non-Divorce–Related Transfers of Property Between Former Spouses

Finally, *Davis* continues to apply to transfers between former spouses in one limited circumstance. It applies to transfers not covered by § 1041, such as transfers between former spouses which occur so far in the future as to be treated as not incident to the divorce. This situation could arise in the case of transfers occurring outside of the six-year, safe-harbor period provided for in Reg. § 1.1041–1T Q & A–7.

Reg. § 1.1041–1T Q & A–7 provide that a property transfer is presumed to be incident to a divorce (related to the cessation of the marriage) if it occurs not more than six years after the date of divorce. A transfer after that six-year period is presumed not to be related to the cessation of the marriage unless the taxpayer overcomes the presumption. The taxpayer may rebut the presumption by establishing that the transfer occurred outside of that period because of legal, business, or

---

[64] International Freighting Corp. v. Commissioner, 135 F.2d 310 (2d Cir.1943).

[65] Kenan v. Commissioner, 114 F.2d 217 (2d Cir.1940).

[66] I.R.C. §§ 2(d), 871(a), 865(a).

other impediments. Although it may be unlikely that a transfer arising
out of divorce would not fit within the six-year, safe-harbor period, or
that a delay in transfer of more than six years could not be justified by
the circumstances, the rare case not covered by § 1041 would be subject
to *Davis*.

Conclusion

Divorce unfortunately is an all-too-common story in the United
States. In *Davis*, the Supreme Court provided needed certainty in
clarifying the tax consequences of transfers of property incident to a
divorce. But the Court's approach—penalizing the transferor spouse by
taxing any appreciation in the transferred property and rewarding the
transferee spouse with a fair market value basis in the property—
resulted in differing tax consequences for divorcing couples depending on
whether they lived in common law or community property states. Moreover, if the transferor spouse misreported the transaction, the Service
often found itself in an untenable position when it first examined the
transaction on the transferee spouse's later sale of the property, at which
point the statute of limitations frequently had run on the transferor
spouse's return. Congress responded by equalizing the tax treatment of
divorcing couples throughout the fifty states and by empowering the
Service to effectively police compliance. The § 1041 regime lets the
transferor spouse off the tax hook and shifts the tax burden to the
transferee spouse through a carryover basis in the transferred property.
Since in most cases the transferor spouse is the husband and the
transferee spouse is the wife, and post-divorce the ex-husband often is in
a higher tax bracket than the ex-wife, the consequences of § 1041 can be
critiqued on feminist grounds. But that is another story. The impact of
Davis continues to be felt in the tax law in the many contexts not
covered by § 1041.

5

Joel S. Newman

The Story of *Welch*: The Use (and Misuse) of the "Ordinary and Necessary" Test for Deducting Business Expenses*

Of course business expenses should be deductible. To see why, contrast a retailer with a trust beneficiary. When a retailer receives $100 of sales profits, she must use most of it to pay expenses like building rent, employee salaries, and advertising before she can even think about spending any of it on herself. In contrast, when a trust beneficiary receives a $100 distribution of income, she can spend every penny of it any way she wants. It could not possibly be fair to tax the retailer's $100 the same as the trust beneficiary's $100. As it happens, we don't. The trust beneficiary is taxed on all of it, but the retailer is allowed to deduct the business expenses.

Of course, personal expenses should be nondeductible. If personal food, clothing and shelter expenses were deductible, then the taxpayers with the most extravagant lifestyles would pay the least tax. Personal lifestyle choices should have no impact on the taxes people pay.

Therefore, business expenses are generally deductible; personal expenses are generally nondeductible. Accordingly, the distinction between business expenses and personal expenses is very important. *Welch v. Helvering*[1] deals with that distinction. So why was the decision not reported at all in the *New York Times*?

---

* I previously mined some of this material in Joel S. Newman, *On the Tax Meaning of "Ordinary": How the Ills of* Welch *Could Be Cured Through Christian Science*, 22 Ariz. St. L.J. 231 (1990).

[1] 290 U.S. 111 (1933).

Even within the category of legitimate business expenses, not all business expenses are treated equally. Timing can be hugely important. An ordinary expense can be deducted in full, immediately. A capital expense cannot. Capital expenses must be added to basis, and at best, deducted over the useful life of the asset. At worst, as was the case in *Welch*, they will only have a tax impact when the entity or asset is sold.[2]

The distinction between ordinary business expenses and capital business expenses is therefore a very important one for the tax law. *Welch v. Helvering* says quite a bit about that, too. So why was there not a single law review case note on the decision? Perhaps if only the opinion had been better written . . .

Background

In the late nineteenth and early twentieth centuries, starting a business in Minnesota was not for the faint of heart. Many businesses failed. In fact, many businesses, which since have become household names, failed once, or perhaps more than once, before they succeeded. The Northern Pacific Railroad went bankrupt in 1873 and again in 1893. Pillsbury failed in 1907.[3] Cargill almost went under in 1909 and did not recover fully until 1917.[4] Hormel came within "inches" of bankruptcy in 1921.[5]

Then there was International Multifoods. It started life as Polar Star Milling Company when Francis Atherton Bean, Sr. took over his father's flour mill in 1872. The firm collapsed in 1890. It owed $100,000 and had no assets. Bean tried again in 1892. This time he succeeded well enough to acquire another company in 1908.

Just before Christmas in 1911, Bean decided to pay off the debts of the defunct Polar Star Milling Company even though they had been discharged in bankruptcy. The first creditor he called was the Bemis Brothers Bag Co. At Bean's insistence, Bemis Brothers dug through old records and found that they had written off a $900 debt from Polar Star in 1890. Bean calculated six per cent interest on the debt for 21 years and wrote them a check for $2,000. Then he went to every other creditor and repaid all of his debts. With interest, he paid more than $200,000.

Wherever he went, he made his former creditors promise not to tell anyone what he had done. He would have pulled it off, too, but for one

---

[2] In *Welch*, the payments improved goodwill, which at the time of the case was unamortizable. The payments presumably increased basis, which could be subtracted from the amount realized if and when the asset was sold.

[3] Don W. Larson, *Land of the Giants: A History of Minnesota Business* 30 (1979).

[4] *Id.* at 62–63; Wayne G. Broehl, Jr., *Cargill: Trading the World's Grain* ch. 4 (1992).

[5] *Id.* at 17.

slip. On one of his last repayment trips, he told friends that he was off on a business trip to Moose Jaw, Saskatchewan. He said that he might not make it back by Christmas, but that even if he didn't, he was going to enjoy the happiest holiday of his life. His friends were intrigued. They did some digging and figured it out.

The story was picked up in the papers. As reported in the *Minneapolis Journal*:

> Penniless and $100,000 in debt 21 years ago, a northwestern miller is observing the 1911 Christmas season by distributing $200,000 among men who have absolutely no legal claim against him, but to whom he owed money when the crash came which left him stranded at middle age. The miller is now 71 years old.
>
> The story of F.A. Bean of New Prague, Minn., reads like a business romance with a Dickens Christmas tale ending. It is a story of a man who lost his fortune, only to give $200,000 away because of a sense of business honor. Not a cent of the $200,000 which Mr. Bean has distributed among his former creditors could have been collected and for every cent of the $100,000 which he originally owed he has paid six percent interest for the entire 21 years. And the best part of the story is that Mr. Bean has enjoined secrecy on every man to whom he has paid money, has said that he didn't want the news to get out that he was paying back the money, that he just wanted to think about it himself, that he owed money no matter what the law was and that no thanks are due him from the people who are sharing the $200,000 distribution.[6]

For all we know, Thomas Welch and his father, E.L. Welch, knew what Bean had done. The Welches were certainly in the right place at the right time. They had been in the grain brokerage business in Minnesota since 1906, doing business as the E.L. Welch Company, and they were still there in 1911. Thomas was the secretary of the corporation and the owner of ten shares. His father was president and owned the bulk of the stock. Thomas was the outside man, spending most of his time on the road, dealing with the customers. E.L. was the inside man, in charge of finances.[7] Presumably, in 1911 when Bean was repaying his debts, things were not too bad.

Then came World War I and its aftermath. During the war, agricultural production in Europe dropped to almost nothing, and American farmers got rich making up the shortfall. However, with the peace,

---

[6] Minneapolis Journal, December 21, 1911, *quoted in* Larson, *supra* note 3, at 16–17.

[7] Record at 10, 28, 29.

European agricultural production quickly returned to pre-war levels. Prices plummeted. Many American farmers lost their farms.[8]

Middlemen were in even worse shape. From the top, the big railroads used their monopolistic power over freight rates and terminal elevators to gouge the farmers. From the bottom, the farmers fought back by banding together to establish cooperative grain elevators. Middlemen like the Welches were, well, caught in the middle.[9] Both the E.L. Welch Company and Thomas Welch, as an individual, went bankrupt in 1922. The final liquidation of corporate assets took place in 1926; customers lost some $170,000 in discharged debts.[10]

Even before 1922, Thomas Welch could see trouble coming. He contemplated bankruptcy, but he was afraid that the local business community might never trust him again. Accordingly, he asked the advice of the President of the First National Bank of Minneapolis, C.T. Jaffray. Jaffray's advice: "[I]f a man went through bankruptcy with the idea of beating his creditors and avoiding paying his just debts that all bankers considered him absolutely crooked, but if a man went through bankruptcy with the idea of getting a new start and making up his claims, that they considered him 100 per cent."[11] Thomas, apparently a thorough man, went to three bankers, asked the same question, and received the same advice.[12]

Accordingly, after the bankruptcy, when Thomas Welch went back into the grain brokerage business, he began repaying the debts of the E.L. Welch Company, even though they had been discharged. He made the payments for the following reasons: "[t]o re-establish my credit for one thing, reestablish my business, and, further, it was a matter of moral obligation."[13]

The new business prospered, and Thomas Welch had taxable income. With the income came the need for deductions. He deducted the

---

[8] *See* Van L. Perkins, *Crisis in Agriculture* 19 (1969); Theodore Saloutos & John D. Hicks, *Agricultural Discontent in the Middle West: 1900–1939* 105 (1951); Clarence Alton Wiley, *Agriculture and the Business Cycle Since 1920* (1930); David Friday, *The Course of Agricultural Income During the Last Twenty–Five Years*, 13 Am. Econ. Rev. 147 (1923). *See generally* United States Federal Trade Commission, *The Report of the Federal Trade Commission on the Grain Trade* (1920–26).

[9] Saloutos and Hicks, *supra* note 8, at 75.

[10] Record at 10, 28.

[11] Record at 31.

[12] *Id.* C.T. Jaffray was experienced in such matters. He was the chairman of the Creditor's Committee formed in 1909 at the time of the Cargill company's financial difficulties. Broehl, *supra* note 4, at 162.

[13] Record at 31.

debt repayments from the income in the tax years 1924 ($4,000) and 1925 ($11,968).

The Commissioner of Internal Revenue balked. Business expenses, then and now, had to be "ordinary and necessary" to be deductible.[14] He said that the repayments were neither. He characterized them as more like gratuities. He noted that the payments were apparently new obligations since there was neither an agreement between Thomas and the bankrupt corporation nor between Thomas and the old customers. Finally, he said that the payments were more in the nature of capital expenditures.[15]

Prior Proceedings

The Board of Tax Appeals

The matter went to the Board of Tax Appeals.[16] The Board ruled in favor of the Commissioner.[17] It noted that the payments, even if they related at all to the "carrying on a trade or business," could still not be allocated as an expense of a particular year. It also cited two of its own recent decisions, both holding that "the payment of discharged obligations for the purpose of re-establishing credit resulted in the acquisition of an intangible capital asset, in the nature of goodwill, which had a probable useful life co-extensive with the business."[18]

The Board of Tax Appeal's second citation was to A. Harris & Co v. Lucas.[19] In Harris, a retailer in financial difficulties reached a "composition" with its creditors per state law, under which the creditors settled their claims for fifty cents on the dollar. After the composition, the retailer attempted to resume normal business relationships but discovered that none of his suppliers would deal with him, except on a cash basis—an impossible situation. The retailer, just like Welch, sought the advice of his local banker. The banker told him that no one would give him any credit until he repaid the debts, which had been extinguished in the composition. So, he did. The Board of Tax Appeals in Harris held that the debt repayments were nondeductible capital expenditures, but the Fifth Circuit reversed that decision. Nonetheless, the Board of Tax Appeals in Welch was not concerned because it distinguished Harris:

---

[14] § 162(a).

[15] Record at 6, 10.

[16] By this time, the dispute had been expanded to cover tax years 1924 through 1928.

[17] Welch v. Commissioner, 25 B.T.A. 117 (1932).

[18] Id. at 119 (citing A. Harris & Co. v. Lucas, 48 F.2d 187 (5th Cir.1931), and Herbert Brush Mfg. Co. v. Commissioner, 15 B.T.A. 673 (1929)).

[19] 48 F.2d 187 (5th Cir.1931).

There [in *Harris*] a mercantile establishment, which had been discharged from its debts in a compromise settlement, reimbursed its former creditors in an effort to re-establish its credit so that it could buy without having to pay cash for each order. Here the bankrupt corporation is no longer in business and an individual is seeking to *build up* a business by reimbursing creditors of the corporation who have lost money.[20]

Whether or not *Harris* was distinguishable from *Welch* turned out to be an important issue for some. It was clearly important at the circuit court level and to the parties' briefing in the Supreme Court. The Court itself did not seem to care about it, but subsequent cases would care a lot.

The crucial factual distinction between *Harris* and *Welch* was that *Harris* involved a state law composition with creditors while *Welch* involved a federal law bankruptcy. In both cases, debts that were previously enforceable became unenforceable. One would think, therefore, that in both cases repayments of those debts were equally repayments of voluntary obligations.

Yet, there is a relevant distinction. In bankruptcy, the bankrupt entity dies. We are told in so many words that the E.L. Welch Company was no more: "Final liquidation of the assets was made on July 2, 1926."[21] In a composition with creditors, in contrast, the debts are partially discharged, pursuant to a unanimous agreement by the creditors. However, the entity that owed the debts lives on.[22] This distinction is relevant, if at all, for two reasons.

First, there is the timing. When one goes back into business after a bankruptcy, one is necessarily beginning a brand new business. Payments made at the beginning of an enterprise tend to be capital. In this sense, the repayments made by Thomas Welch were intended to *create* goodwill. Conversely, when one goes back into business after a composition with creditors, one is resuming operations of an ongoing concern. Payments made during the middle of the life of a business concern tend to be ordinary. In this sense, the payments made by A. Harris & Co. were made to *maintain* pre-existing goodwill.

Second, there is the identity of the parties. If bankrupt entities are indeed dead, then the one repaying their debts (presumably an entity which is still alive) cannot possibly be the same as the entity that owed

---

[20] 25 B.T.A. at 119 (emphasis in original).

[21] Record at 10.

[22] I have discussed this matter with a few bankruptcy professors. Although they were willing to talk with me in general terms, no one was willing to get too specific about the precise differences between federal bankruptcies and state law compositions with creditors because they occurred some eighty years ago.

them originally. In contrast, when one repays the debts which were the subject of a composition, it is likely that the payor of the debts is indeed the same entity as the entity that incurred them. Why, indeed, would anyone ever pay debts that were (1) incurred by some other entity, and (2) not legally owed any more by anyone?

The Eighth Circuit

Welch appealed to the Eighth Circuit, which affirmed the Board of Tax Appeals.[23] The Eighth Circuit commented that the expenses might have been "necessary" under some interpretations: "It would be rather clear that they would be helpful in a business way and that helpfulness might approach or reach necessity...."[24] However, the Eighth Circuit found "no possible basis upon which payments of this character can be treated as 'ordinary.' ... In fact, they are very extraordinary payments, and not expenses of the business at all."[25] The payments in *Harris* were distinguished because the *Welch* payments somehow were more voluntary.

The Supreme Court Decision

The Briefs

1. *The Taxpayer's Brief*

Welch appealed to the Supreme Court, citing an irreconcilable conflict between the Fifth Circuit's opinion in *Harris* and the Eighth Circuit's opinion in *Welch*. In their brief, Welch's lawyers demonstrated the conflict by setting out language from the Eighth Circuit's opinion in the left-hand column to be compared with language from the Fifth Circuit's opinion in the right-hand column.[26]

The were two main conflicts: (1) *Welch* had ruled that "ordinary and necessary" were conjunctive requirements, so both had to be satisfied; *Harris* had found them to be disjunctive; and (2) *Welch* had found the expenditures in question to be capital; *Harris* had found them to be ordinary. On appeal, Welch's lawyers preferred *Harris*.

Welch's lawyers argued that "ordinary and necessary" were disjunctive requirements, so only one of them had to be met. Nevertheless, they argued that both elements were satisfied. To satisfy "ordinary," they asked whether, "in the particular circumstances shown to have existed, it would be common, or usual, or 'ordinary' to have made the expendi-

---

[23] 63 F.2d 976 (8th Cir.1933).

[24] *Id* at 977.

[25] *Id.*

[26] Petitioner's Brief at 8–9.

ture."[27] Of course, they answered "yes." As to necessary, they inferred "convenient" or "suitable."[28] Once again, they managed to pass their own test.

They argued that the payments could not have been capital since the payments in *Harris* were not distinguishable in any meaningful way, and those payments had been found to be ordinary. Moreover, they argued that the payments were at least as business-related as other payments that had been held deductible in other cases.

2. *The Government's Brief*

The government's brief defined "ordinary" as "common, usual, often recurring," and "necessary" as "essential, needful, requisite, or indispensable," conceding, however, that in some cases "necessary" had been construed more broadly.[29] Mere business expedience, the government argued, was not enough, especially given that these payments were both voluntary and gratuitous. The payments "had no necessary connection with the petitioner's individual business and were not current operating expenses incident to the normal conduct of his business. Admittedly, the payments had some effect upon his business, but they were too indirect to justify the deduction...."[30]

As to *Harris*, the government's brief did not distinguish it in so many words: "Even though expenditures for the purpose of reestablishing credit may be deductible [citing *Harris*], there would seem to be no doubt that expenditures for the purpose of building up a business are in the nature of a capital expenditure, since a continuing benefit inures to the taxpayer throughout future years."[31]

As to whether ordinary and necessary were conjunctive or disjunctive requirements, the Government merely noted: "The statement in the *A. Harris & Co.* case, *supra,* to the effect that the statute is not to be construed as requiring a deductible expense to be both ordinary and necessary is contrary to the weight of authority."[32]

The Opinion

Justice Cardozo wrote the opinion for the Supreme Court.[33] He found the debt repayments to be "necessary," in that they were "appro-

---

[27] *Id.* at 6.

[28] *Id.* at 17.

[29] Respondent's Brief at 6.

[30] *Id* at 4.

[31] *Id* at 9–10.

[32] *Id.* at 12.

[33] 290 U.S. 111 (1933).

priate and helpful."[34] However, he found that the payments were not ordinary. Therefore, he found for the government. Perhaps we should have known that the opinion would not be terribly enlightening when Justice Cardozo started whining:

> Here, indeed, as so often in other branches of the law, the decisive distinctions are those of degree and not of kind. One struggles in vain for any verbal formula that will supply a ready touchstone. The standard set up by the statute is not a rule of law; it is rather a way of life. Life in all its fullness must supply the answer to the riddle.[35]

Why did Justice Cardozo find for the government? There are three strands running through the opinion: the expenses were (1) too "personal" to be deductible, (2) too bizarre to be "ordinary," and (3) "capital" and thus nondeductible.

1. *Personal*

Were the expenses too personal? Remember that the debts were not legally enforceable. Welch paid them off at least in part as a matter of "moral obligation." After so many years of close business relationships, many of his former creditors had in fact become his friends. Justice Cardozo's opinion reflected this point of view. He worried that to allow deductions for Welch's repayments

> would open the door to many bizarre analogies. One man has a family name that is clouded by thefts committed by an ancestor. To add to his own standing he repays the stolen money, wiping off, it may be, his income for the year. The payments figure in his tax return as ordinary expenses. Another man conceives the notion that he will be able to practice his vocation with greater ease and profit if he has an opportunity to enrich his culture. Forthwith the price of his education becomes an expense of the business, reducing the income subject to taxation. There is little difference between these expenses and those in controversy here.[36]

What would be wrong with allowing a deduction for repaying the stolen money or enriching one's culture? At least in part, these payments simply are too personal to be deductible business expenses.

---

[34] *Id.* at 113.

[35] *Id.* at 114–15.

[36] *Id.* at 115. Justice Benjamin Cardozo's mention of "a family name that is clouded by thefts committed by an ancestor" is personally revealing. In 1872, Albert Cardozo, then a New York Supreme Court judge, resigned in disgrace, amid allegations of corruption. Some sixteen years later, Albert's son Benjamin decided to become a lawyer. "He felt that he had to clear up the disgrace to his family name and could do this only as a lawyer." Andrew L. Kaufman, *Cardozo* 40 (1998). Mr. Justice Cardozo's bizarre analogy was, therefore, "painfully close to Cardozo's own personal situation." *Id.* at 41.

2. *Bizarre*

Were the repayments simply too bizarre? Note that Justice Cardozo used that term in his opinion.[37] Surely, people do not normally repay debts that have been extinguished in bankruptcy. Much of Justice Cardozo's opinion spoke to this point. Consider the definition of "ordinary" in the opinion: "Now, what is ordinary, though there must always be a strain of constancy within it, is none the less a variable affected by time and place and circumstance."[38] The opinion went on:

> Men do at times pay the debts of others without legal obligation or the lighter obligation imposed by the usages of trade or by neighborly amenities, but do not do so ordinarily, not even though the result might be to heighten their reputation for generosity and opulence. Indeed, if language is to be read in its natural and common meaning, we should have to say that payment in such circumstances, instead of being ordinary is in a high degree extraordinary. There is nothing ordinary in the stimulus evoking it, and none in the response.[39]

3. *Capital*

Were the payments capital expenses? As such, they would have been nondeductible when incurred and instead would have had to be added to basis and perhaps amortized. As Justice Cardozo explained, "the problem is not solved when the payments are characterized as necessary. Many necessary payments are charges upon capital."[40] Later, he observed: "The Commissioner of Internal Revenue ... found that the payments in controversy came closer to capital outlays than to ordinary and necessary expenses in the operation of a business. His ruling has the presumption of correctness, and the petitioner has the burden of proving it to be wrong."[41]

Return to those two bizarre analogies that so concerned Justice Cardozo: (1) repaying the thefts committed by an ancestor, and (2) the enrichment of a man's culture through education. Surely, they are both highly personal, but they are something more: "Reputation and learning are akin to capital assets, like the goodwill of an old partnership."[42]

---

[37] 290 U.S. at 115.

[38] *Id.* at 113–14.

[39] *Id.* at 114.

[40] *Id.* at 113.

[41] *Id.* at 115. As will be seen, Justice Cardozo's statement about the presumption of correctness is by far the most heavily cited passage of the entire opinion.

[42] *Id.*

4. *Conflict Between the Fifth and Eighth Circuits*

But what of the conflict between the Fifth Circuit in *Harris* and the Eighth Circuit in *Welch*? Although this conflict seemed so important in the opinions below and in the briefs, Justice Cardozo did not mention it. Instead, there is an oblique reference in the concluding paragraph of the opinion: "Many cases in the federal courts deal with phases of the problem presented by the case at bar. To attempt to harmonize them would be a futile task. They involve the application of particular situations, at times with border-line conclusions. Typical illustrations are cited in the margin.[43] With that, Justice Cardozo unfurled a string cite of ten cases, five labeled "Ordinary expenses" and five labeled "Not ordinary expenses." Justice Cardozo listed *Harris* in the "ordinary" group with the comment: "payments of debts discharged in bankruptcy, but subject to be revived by the force of a new promise."[44] That is the Court's only mention of *Harris*.

The Immediate Impact of *Welch*

1. *Was the Supreme Court Right?*

Justice Cardozo was right to whine in his *Welch* opinion. On the facts, he was wrong on the personal versus business issue, and he was wrong on the ordinary versus bizarre issue. As to ordinary versus capital, he was right, but his opinion gave us very little guidance.

A. Personal

As to personal versus business, it is true that Welch felt a moral obligation to do what he did. However, he also had sound business reasons. The fact that one of a person's motivations relates to individual morality does not necessarily tilt an expenditure to the personal side of the ledger. True, many of Welch's former creditors also were his friends. Surely, all of us would hope that some of our business associates will eventually come to like us as people, too. However, even if they do, that affection does not turn business expenses into personal expenses. The crucial question is: where did Welch get his advice? Did he turn to his minister? No, he turned to three bankers. He sought business advice, not moral advice. Clearly, the expenditure was predominantly business-oriented.

B. Bizarre

Justice Cardozo characterizes Welch's repayments as bizarre. But they were not unique in Minnesota. We know that Welch did not act on his own personal whim. Rather, he asked three prominent bankers what

---

[43] *Id* at 116.

[44] *Id*.

to do, and then he took their advice. What better way could there have been to determine the business morays of that community at that time? What is more, we know that Francis Atherton Bean did exactly the same thing some years before. If we distinguish common from bizarre in light of time, place, and circumstance, we must conclude that Welch's payments were not bizarre.

C. Capital

Were Welch's repayments capital expenses? They probably were. Viewed from a more modern perspective, the repayments were intended to generate increased earnings for far more than one year. Therefore, in order properly to match up expenses with income, the expenses should have been capitalized and spread out of the period during which the projected income would be earned.

However, even if Justice Cardozo was correct that the expenses should have been capitalized, his opinion is not very persuasive on the point. According to the Court, the expenses were capital because (1) the Commissioner said so, and (2) they were akin to reputation and learning, which appear to be capital assets. Justice Cardozo could have said something about the distinction between *Harris* and *Welch* below, but he did not.

D. A Scorecard

The Supreme Court was wrong on personal, wrong on bizarre, and right on capital. In effect, the Court did not say anything about the conflict between the Fifth and Eighth Circuits. The score, therefore, is two "wrong," one "right," and one "no decision." Unfortunately, Justice Cardozo's opinion gave us scant guidance on the relative weights of these factors. Not surprisingly, all of them figured to some extent in post-*Welch* jurisprudence. Early on, the one with the most impact was the one Justice Cardozo said the least about.

2. *Capital Expenditures: The Conflict Between the Fifth and Eighth Circuits*

Despite the short shrift given by the Court to the distinctions between the *Welch* and *Harris* opinions below, these distinctions were very important to the early, post-*Welch* cases. Cases finding nondeductible, capital expenditures cited *Welch*. Cases finding deductible, ordinary expenditures cited *Harris*, *Welch* notwithstanding.

A. Capital Expenditures: Cases Following *Welch*

Foye Lumber & Tie Co. v. Commissioner[45] was a capital expenditure case. In *Foye*, as in *Welch*, the taxpayer's predecessor went bankrupt in the early 1920s. The taxpayer wanted to go back into business and asked

---

[45] 33 B.T.A. 271 (1935).

its former banks to extend credit. Not surprisingly, the banks refused unless the taxpayer would compensate them for their earlier losses in bankruptcy. The taxpayer did so and deducted the payments, citing *Harris*. The government disallowed the deductions, citing *Welch*. The Board of Tax Appeals held for the government, also citing *Welch*.

A number of cases followed *Foye Lumber*.[46] For example, in *Carl Reimers Co. v. Commissioner*,[47] the taxpayer's predecessor, an advertising agency in New York City, went bankrupt. The taxpayer attempted to reenter the business. To do so, it was essential to be recognized by the Publishers' Association of New York City. Without such recognition, Reimers would have had to pay cash up front for newspaper ads and would not have been entitled to the standard fifteen percent commission. After Reimers duly applied, the Publishers' Association advised him to repay the predecessor's debts to local newspaper publishers. Reimers demurred, noting that he was not legally obligated to pay them. The Association told him that they would not recognize him unless he paid. After consultation with his lawyer, he paid. The Tax Court held the repayment expenditures to be capital and nondeductible, citing *Welch*.

---

[46] *See* Portland Gasoline Co. v. Commissioner, 181 F.2d 538 (5th Cir.1950); Carl Reimers Co. v. Commissioner, 19 T.C. 1235 (1953), *aff'd*, 211 F.2d 66 (2d Cir.1954); Eskimo Pie Corp. v. Commissioner, 4 T.C. 669 (1945), *aff'd*, 153 F.2d 301 (3d Cir.1946); Levitt & Sons, Inc. v. Commissioner, 5 T.C. 913 (1945), *aff'd*, 160 F.2d 209 (2d Cir.1947).

Mitten Mgmt. Inc. v. Commissioner, 29 B.T.A. 569 (1933), is on all fours with *Welch* and denied the deduction. As a 1933 decision, however, it cited the circuit court opinions in *Welch* and *Harris* and only briefly noted that *Welch* had just been affirmed by the Supreme Court.

Donnelley v. Commissioner, 68 F.2d 722 (7th Cir.1934), is difficult to categorize. A brokerage partnership was going through federal bankruptcy proceedings when a third party reached a composition with the creditors by paying them amounts ranging from $.26 on the dollar to full payment. The third party made these payments in exchange for an assignment of their claims against the brokerage company. One of the partners of the now defunct brokerage later came into some money and repaid those old creditors of the partnership who had not been fully paid in the composition with creditors. His motivations were apparently moral. The Seventh Circuit denied the claimed loss deduction. The Seventh Circuit pointed out that taxpayer might have had a better argument for a trade or business deduction but noted that, with no apparent business motive for the repayment, the taxpayer had an even weaker argument than Welch, who also lost his case. *Donnelley*, ironically, was the subject of a note in the University of Chicago Law Review. Recent Cases, 1 U. Chi. L. Rev. 818 (1934). Note that this law review had not been founded in time to comment on *Welch*.

[47] 19 T.C. 1235 (1953), *aff'd*, 211 F.2d 66 (2d Cir.1954).

B.   Ordinary Deductions: Cases Following *Harris*

The weight of decisions, however, allowed deductions and followed *Harris*.[48] In *First National Bank of Skowhegan v. Commissioner*,[49] the taxpayer ("Bank") had invested in the Skowhegan Trust Company ("Trust"). Trust got into trouble and asked for help. Bank refused to merge with Trust, but it did pay $10,000 to persuade another bank to do so. The taxpayer deducted the payment, but the Commissioner disallowed the deduction. Before the Board of Tax Appeals, both sides cited *Welch*. The Board distinguished *Welch* and allowed the deduction, noting that Bank had "acquired no capital asset by the disbursement."[50]

In *Miller v. Commissioner*,[51] the taxpayer was an independent insurance agent representing twelve different companies. One of those companies failed. In order to retain their business, the taxpayer paid the claims of his customers against the failed insurance company out of his own pocket. The Commissioner disallowed the claimed deduction. The Board of Tax Appeals reinstated the deduction, distinguishing *Welch* by noting: "There [in *Welch*] the expenditures were made to acquire, and not to retain or protect and promote the taxpayer's business. *Cf. First National Bank of Skowhegan* . . . "[52]

In *Dunn & McCarthy, Inc. v. Commissioner*,[53] the president of the taxpayer corporation lost heavily at racetracks and borrowed money from his employees. The president ultimately committed suicide, leaving a hopelessly insolvent estate. The corporation reimbursed its employees for the bad debts. The government denied a deduction for the repayments, citing *Welch*. The Second Circuit, however, distinguished *Welch* on the ground that the taxpayer there had "made a capital outlay to acquire goodwill for a new business. In the present case, the payment was an outlay to retain an existing goodwill, that is, to prevent loss of

---

[48] *See* McGee v. Nee, 113 F.2d 543 (8th Cir.1940); Snow v. Commissioner, 31 T.C. 585 (1958); Dinardo v. Commissioner, 22 T.C. 430 (1954); Scruggs–Vandervoort–Barney, Inc. v. Commissioner, 7 T.C. 779 (1946); Miller v. Commissioner, 37 B.T.A. 830 (1938); First Nat. Bank of Skowhegan, Me. v. Commissioner, 35 B.T.A. 876 (1937). *See also* Mountain Paper Prods. Corp. v. United States, 287 F.2d 957 (2d Cir.1961); Dunn & McCarthy v. Commissioner, 139 F.2d 242 (2d Cir.1943); Macy v. Commissioner, 19 T.C. 409 (1952), *aff'd*, 215 F.2d 875 (2d Cir.1954); Cannon Valley Milling Co. v. Commissioner, 44 B.T.A. 763 (1941), *aff'd*, 129 F.2d 642 (8th Cir.1942).

M.L Eakes Co. v. Commissioner, 686 F.2d 217 (4th Cir.1982), is a curious case, involving a composition with creditors. In Tax Court, both sides characterized the issue as whether the payments were intended to create goodwill for a new business or to maintain goodwill for an existing business. The Tax Court held that the expenses were intended to maintain goodwill and were therefore deductible. T.C. Memo. 1981–429. The Fourth Circuit, however, rejected this approach and found the expenses to be deductible because they were common to the industry.

[49] 35 B.T.A. 876 (1937).

[50] *Id.* at 885. *See also* Robert Gaylord, Inc. v. Commissioner, 41 B.T.A. 1119 (1940).

[51] 37 B.T.A. 830 (1938).

[52] *Id.* at 833.

[53] 139 F.2d 242 (2d Cir.1943).

earnings that might result from destroying such goodwill by failing to recognize the company's moral obligation."[54]

Scruggs-Vandervoort–Barney, Inc. v. Commissioner[55] reached a similar result. Scruggs–Vandervoort–Barney Dry Goods Co. was a large department store in St. Louis. In 1911, it established the Scruggs–Vandervoort–Barney Bank, a subsidiary corporation. The Bank was placed inside the department store. The Bank went under in 1933. Pursuant to the advice of three St. Louis bankers, the department store paid off the bank's depositors in merchandise certificates from the store in order to maintain the store's goodwill. The Commissioner disallowed the deduction, citing *Welch*. The Tax Court allowed it, distinguished *Welch,* and cited *Skowhegan, Miller*, and *Dunn & McCarthy*.[56]

Note that in all four of these cases following *Harris*, the taxpayer itself had not gone bankrupt. Therefore, in each, it could truly be said that the payments were intended to maintain the goodwill of an existing business rather than to create goodwill for a new business. Also, the payments in all four of the cases could be characterized as intended for the benefit of the payor's business, not someone else's business. Thus, *Welch* could be distinguished, and *Harris* could be followed.

3. *Bizarre*

Over time, a number of cases followed the bizarre versus ordinary theory. Recall Justice Cardozo's comment that "what is ordinary . . . is none the less a variable affected by time and place and circumstance."[57] Business expenses, if common enough in the given industry at that time and place, were deductible. However, some expenses simply were not.

In *Goedel v. Commissioner*,[58] the expenditures were the premiums paid on a life insurance policy on the life of President Franklin Roosevelt. The taxpayer was a partner in a large New York brokerage house. In 1933, he had invested heavily in the stock market, largely inspired by his confidence in President Roosevelt's economic policies. He was fearful that, were President Roosevelt to die, the market would decline as it had upon the deaths of Presidents McKinley and Garfield. The Board of Tax Appeals denied a deduction for the premium payments. The Board was not impressed with the taxpayer's reference to *Harris*, noting that *Welch* was contrary to *Harris*. The insurance premiums were not ordinary in the sense of being customary or usual. Further, the Board distinguished *Skowhegan* as the payment there represented an attempt to deal with a current emergency while the

---

[54] *Id*. at 244.

[55] Scruggs-Vandervoort–Barney, Inc. v. Commissioner, 7 T.C. 779 (1946).

[56] *Id*. at 786–88.

[57] *Welch*, 290 U.S. at 113–14.

[58] 39 B.T.A. 1 (1939).

insurance in *Goedel* was purchased to protect against a very remote contingency.

A. Giurlani & Bro. v. Commissioner[59] involved the four Giurlani brothers. Two were the principal shareholders of Gaetano Giurlani, S.A., an Italian corporation ("Giurlani–Italy"), and the other two were the principal shareholders of the taxpayer, a California corporation ("Giurlani–USA"). More than one-third of Giurlani–USA's business was derived from the sale of Star Brand olive oil, supplied exclusively by Giurlani–Italy. Star Brand olive oil became unavailable during a strike, so Giurlani–USA tried to substitute another brand. It didn't work; many customers angrily demanded their money back. This experience convinced Giurlani–USA that Star Brand olive oil was unique and crucial to its business. Accordingly, when Giurlani–Italy faced bankruptcy, Giurlani–USA paid almost $33,000 to Giurlani–Italy's creditors to prop it up.

Giurlani–USA asserted that it made this payment to maintain its supply of the crucial Star Brand olive oil. The Board denied the deduction on the ground that payment was "distinctly out of the ordinary."[60] The Board again distinguished *Skowhegan*, this time on the basis that the Depression had not caused the strain in *Giurlani* as it had in *Skowhegan*. The Board obviously was unimpressed with the alleged uniqueness of Star Brand olive oil.[61] Although it did not mention it, could it be that the Board was influenced by the fact that the payments were effectively made from brother to brother, inserting a very personal element into an otherwise business transaction?[62]

Then there are *Amend*[63] and *Trebilcock*.[64] Both cases involved the expenses of hiring religious ministers to help businessmen. In the first case, Fred W. Amend was the founder, major stockholder, officer, and later chairman of the board of his corporation. The minister was a certified Christian Science practitioner[65] who helped Amend to invoke

---

[59] 41 B.T.A. 403 (1940), *aff'd*, 119 F.2d 852 (9th Cir.1941).

[60] *Id.* at 407.

[61] *But see* M. Visser, *Much Depends on Dinner* ch. 7 (1986) (containing valuable insights on why all olive oils are not created equal).

[62] In United Draperies v. Commissioner, 340 F.2d 936 (7th Cir.1964), *cert. denied*, 382 U.S. 813 (1965), the Seventh Circuit held that kickbacks to drapery purchasing agents were not common in the industry and thus were not deductible, distinguishing Lilly v. Commissioner, 343 U.S. 90 (1952) on the ground that the kickbacks there were common in the optical industry and thus deductible.

[63] Fred W. Amend Co. v. Commissioner, 55 T.C. 320 (1970), *aff'd*, 454 F.2d 399 (7th Cir.1971).

[64] Trebilcock v. Commissioner, 64 T.C. 852 (1975), *aff'd*, 557 F.2d 1226 (6th Cir.1977).

[65] *Amend*, 454 F.2d at 401. I confirmed Reverend Halverstadt's status by telephoning the mother church. To be certified, Reverend Halverstadt had to cite three successful cures,

the spirit of the Divine Mind in order to make better business decisions. The matters discussed were undeniably business matters;[66] the president's personal consultations with the minister were accounted for separately. Yet, the deductions for the business consultations were disallowed under § 262 as inherently personal.[67] The Seventh Circuit did not cite *Welch*.[68]

Mr. Amend's case was hurt by the fact that Reverend Halverstadt did not give specific answers to Amend's business questions.[69] This is not surprising. Whether dealing with medical problems or business problems, Christian Science practitioners routinely do not give specific answers to specific questions. Rather, they engage in dialogue.[70] Is it not a

---

confirmed by investigators from the Mother Church. Telephone Interview with Marcia Kopang, Legal Department, First Church of Christ, Scientist, Boston, Massachusetts (Oct. 13, 1988).

[66] Amend consulted with the minister about:

matters of freight charges in relation to the territory served and package sizes; of the shrinking market and introduction of a new product line; of a new union contract and labor negotiations, particularly women's wage scales relative to men's; of offers from other businesses; of machine production in relation to large packages; of adopting a new costing method and machine production schedules; [and] of internal harmony and dissatisfactions among executive personnel.

Petitioner–Appellant's Brief at 10.

Mr. Amend testified in Tax Court about a production problem:

Well, I can tell you what I was bellyaching about, but I cannot give you his (Halverstadt's) reply. We were getting about 325 cases a day out of one of those big machines and we should have been getting 700. Every time we did everything, we would just about get it up to running right and then something would happen. I don't know whether we had a jinx or not. I kept going to him on that, and I know within a short, a very short time, we were getting out 800 cases a day.

Id at 24.

I reached Reverend Halverstadt by telephone, read the above quote to him about the 325 cases per day, and asked if he had performed a miracle. Reverend Halverstadt objected that a miracle is unnatural or supernatural. In contrast to a miracle, he had simply realigned the machine with the Divine Mind—the most natural thing in the world. Telephone Interview with Reverend Halverstadt (Jan. 13, 1989).

[67] 454 F.2d at 402, 403. In Vitale v. Commissioner, T.C. Memo. 1999–131, the taxpayer wrote books about prostitution and sought to deduct the money he paid to prostitutes as research expenses for his book. The Tax Court disallowed the deductions as inherently personal, citing *Amend* with approval.

[68] However, the Tax Court below cited *Welch*: "To characterize as vexatious the task of determining whether an expenditure is 'ordinary and necessary' to a taxpayer's business is to define in mild terms a problem as convoluted as the scope of human experience is wide." 55 T.C. at 325.

[69] "The practitioner offered no specific or concrete solutions. His procedure was to interrogate Amend so as to bring out the different elements involved and thus clarify Amend's thinking.... The Tax Court found that through the insight provided by Halverstadt's interrogation, Amend was enabled to approach problems with detachment and a new understanding, but Halverstadt never offered concrete solutions to any of the matters discussed." 454 F.2d at 401, 402.

[70] Telephone Interview with Marcia Kopang, Legal Department, First Church of Christ, Scientist, Boston, Massachusetts (Oct. 13, 1988).

bit surprising that the judge, who presumably went to law school, should question the effectiveness of a Socratic dialogue?

In *Trebilcock*, a minister again was hired to help a business. In one respect, however, *Trebilcock* was a better case for the taxpayer: this time the minister gave specific answers.[71] Reverend Wardrop would listen to the question and then pray for an answer. Having received the answer through prayer, he would then report back to the business. But the Tax Court denied any deduction for the expenses of providing that advice. It pointed out that Reverend Wardrop had no expertise.[72] If Reverend Wardrop was not himself a business expert, didn't he consult one? The Tax Court cited *Welch* only for the burden of proof proposition.

4. *Cases Combining Multiple Threads*

Over the years, more often than not, one case would combine two or more of *Welch's* multiple threads. *Deputy v. du Pont*[73] was an early example. The Du Pont Company established a nine-member executive committee in 1919 and decided that its members would be more effective if they were shareholders of the company. Since the company was unable to sell them the shares directly, the taxpayer, a major shareholder, undertook to do so. He incurred some expenses and attempted to deduct them.

---

[71] Albert Thomas, a salesman for Litco Products, testified:

Q: ... In direct examination, you testified that you contacted Reverend Wardrop with respect to customers that you were concerned about. You also spoke of lost customers. What sorts of advice or help would Reverend Wardrop give you when you contacted him about those subjects?

A: Well, I'd call him and I'd ask him to reach out and touch God, to look for answers, for guidance and give me through his prayer, help in answering the problem to regain that lost customer or to better do my work. To face my day with more confidence ...

Q: When you posed a business or a personal problem, to Reverend Wardrop, did he offer a specific solution, a course of action that you should take?

A: You must understand, that when I would ask him, I would tell him about a specific problem, he would not give me an answer, he would take it to God in prayer. The next day or later on in the week, he would give an answer, advice through his prayer. He might be on his knees, several hours seeking for an answer.

Record at 86–87 (statement of Albert Thomas), Trebilcock v. Commissioner, 557 F.2d 1226 (6th Cir.1977).

[72] "The solutions [Reverend] Wardrop offered were not based upon his expertise in the brokerage of wood products; he admits he had no such expertise. Rather, his solutions came through prayer from God. ... Petitioner has offered no proof that his payments to Wardrop for solutions to business problems, considering the method that Wardrop used, were 'ordinary' in his type of business. We hold that petitioner has failed to carry his burden of proof." 64 T.C. at 855.

[73] 308 U.S. 488 (1940).

The Supreme Court disallowed the deduction was for two reasons: (1) the expenses proximately resulted not from the taxpayer's business but from the corporation's business,[74] and (2) the expenditures were far too extraordinary to be deductible.[75] The Court quoted *Welch* at length.

In *Friedman v. Delaney*,[76] a lawyer for a respected Boston firm worked out a composition with creditors for his client. When the client failed to make the agreed payments, the lawyer made them himself. Since the lawyer had personally represented to the creditors that the payments would be made, he felt morally obligated to keep his client's promise. The district court denied the deduction for two reasons: (1) the payment "was closer to a capital outlay,"[77] and (2) "in the absence of any evidence as to what is the custom in the legal profession, there is no basis for a court assuming or finding that it is usual."[78] The First Circuit affirmed.[79]

Canton Cotton Mills v. United States[80] involved a processing tax of doubtful legality. The taxpayer paid the tax, passing on the cost to customers. However, most of taxpayer's contracts with its customers provided that, if the Court invalidated the processing tax, the taxpayer would then credit its customers' accounts for those taxes. The Court subsequently invalidated the tax in *United States v. Butler*,[81] and the taxpayer dutifully credited its customers' accounts in the amount of $79,300 and successfully deducted the credits on its income taxes. However, the taxpayer went further. It also credited an additional $26,300 for invalidated taxes passed on to customers, even though, for various reasons, it was not contractually obligated to do so. The taxpayer credited these additional amounts, both to avoid potential arguments and because its competitors were doing so.

---

[74] *Id.* at 494. Note that this argument places *Deputy v. du Pont* in the *Welch* line of cases. Part of the reason *Welch* distinguished *Harris* was that, since Welch's predecessor was bankrupt, it was a totally different entity from the new grain brokerage business. Therefore, in paying off the bankrupt's debts, Thomas Welch was paying someone else's expenses, not his own.

[75] The Court cited the District Court's opinion with approval: "[the payments were] 'beyond the norm of general and accepted business practice' and were in fact 'so extraordinary as to occur in the lives of ordinary businessmen not at all.' " 308 U.S. at 495.

[76] 75 F.Supp. 568 (D.Mass.) *aff'd in part & vacated in part*, 171 F.2d 269 (1st Cir.1948), *cert. denied*, 336 U.S. 936 (1949).

[77] *Id.* at 570.

[78] *Id.* at 571.

[79] 171 F.2d 269 (1st Cir.1948).

[80] 94 F.Supp. 561 (Ct.Cl.1951).

[81] 297 U.S. 1 (1936).

The government, citing *Welch*, argued that the payments were nondeductible, capital expenditures. However, the Court responded: "[t]he rule of *Welch v. Helvering, supra,* does not apply to expenditures to retain or protect existing goodwill."[82] The government argued that the payments were not ordinary because they were too bizarre, and the Court seemed to agree:

> To be ordinary, payments need not be habitual or normal in the sense that the taxpayer will have to make them often. However, a payment made "without legal obligation or the lighter obligation imposed by the usages of trade or by neighborly amenities" is not ordinary, but is "in a high degree extraordinary." [citing *Welch*].[83]

However, the Court ultimately ruled for the taxpayer:

> Here, there was no legal obligation; but the obligation "imposed by the usages of trade" and the requirements of good business was compelling. As a matter of commercial reality plaintiff had no alternative to following the course taken by its competitors. The realities of the situation cannot be ignored. Such payments may not have been ordinary before the *Butler* decision, but they speedily became ordinary; in fact they were general in the trade. Under the circumstances existing at the time, the refunds of $26,300[] were ordinary and necessary expenses of doing business.[84]

In *Polak's Frutal Works, Inc. v. United States,*[85] a Dutch corporation formed the taxpayer, a New York subsidiary, to handle United States sales. During World War II, the taxpayer took over the parent's business, receiving its secret formulae, technical know-how, and customer list. In 1944, it decided to pay its parent for the use of these assets, even though it was under no obligation to do so. The district court denied a deduction for the payment because it was "most extraordinary and completely unnecessary.... If more were necessary we agree with the government that even if the accrual was legitimate it represented the payment for a capital asset."[86] The Second Circuit affirmed, commenting that "payments must be tested by normal business standards and practices."[87]

Harold L. Jenkins v. Commissioner,[88] a true trifecta, considers capital expenses, bizarre expenses, and personal expenses, thus touching

---

[82] 94 F.Supp. at 564.

[83] *Id.* at 565.

[84] *Id.*

[85] 176 F.Supp. 521 (S.D.N.Y.1959), *aff'd,* 281 F.2d 261 (2d Cir.1960).

[86] *Id.* at 523.

[87] 281 F.2d 261, 263 (2d Cir.1960).

[88] T.C. Memo. 1983–667, 47 T.C.M. (CCH) 238.

every factor that might have been important in *Welch*. Conway Twitty (nee Harold Jenkins), a popular country music entertainer, formed a chain of fast food restaurants called "Twitty Burger" and persuaded some seventy-five of his friends in the country music business to invest with him. The venture failed. Twitty, concerned about adverse publicity and feeling a moral obligation to his investors, reimbursed them for their losses, even though he was under no legal obligation to do so.[89] The Tax Court allowed the deduction. It began its analysis by referring to "[t]he general rule [] that a shareholder may not deduct a payment made on behalf of the corporation but rather must treat it as a capital expenditure. However, the payment may be deducted if it is an ordinary and necessary expense of a trade or business of the shareholder."[90] The Tax Court further explained: "There is no suggestion in the record that any of the payments were made in order to protect petitioner's investment in Twitty Burger or to revitalize the corporation."[91]

The situation indeed was much closer to *Harris* than to *Welch*. Twitty Burger was dead; there was no hope of reviving it. Therefore, Conway Twitty's payments to his co-investors were never intended to re-establish credit or goodwill in the fast food franchise business. Such a repayment might well have been a nondeductible, capital expenditure under *Welch*. Instead, the repayments were to maintain his goodwill in his continuing business as a country music entertainer. Thus, *Welch* is easily distinguishable, and *Jenkins* can be, and was, justified by following the *Harris* line of cases.

The *Jenkins* opinion, however, also dealt with ordinary v. bizarre. More than a page of the opinion is devoted to a report by William Ivey, then Director of the Country Music Foundation in Nashville, Tennessee.[92] Dr. Ivey claimed that moral reputation is much more crucial to the business success of a country music entertainer than it might be in some other field.[93]

Why does the opinion go to such lengths to quote Dr. Ivey, preceded by an equally long quotation from the testimony of Conway Twitty? Surely, the judge was having fun. However, he also had a legitimate reason to quote Ivey and Twitty: to show how these repayments could have been "ordinary" in the country music business in the 1970s. This case, therefore, touches on what is common and what is bizarre.

---

[89] 47 T.C.M. (CCH) at 243–44.

[90] *Id*. at 241–42.

[91] *Id*. at 244. The Tax Court cited Scruggs–Vandervoort–Barney, Inc. v. Commissioner, 7 T.C. 779 (1946).

[92] 47 T.C.M. (CCH) at 245–46. Dr. Ivey is now head of the National Endowment for the Arts.

[93] *Id*.

Finally, *Jenkins* touches upon the personal-business dichotomy. The Tax Court ended its opinion with the following Ode to Conway Twitty:

Ode to Conway Twitty
Twitty Burger went belly up
But Conway remained true
He repaid his investors, one and all
It was the moral thing to do.
His fans would not have liked it
It could have hurt his fame
Had any investors sued him
Like Merle Haggard or Sonny James.
When it was time to file taxes
Conway thought what he would do
Was deduct those payments as a business expense
Under section one-sixty-two.
In order to allow these deductions
Goes the argument of the Commissioner
The payments must be ordinary and necessary
To a business of the petitioner.
Had Conway not repaid the investors
His career would have been under a cloud.
Under the unique facts of this case
Held: The deductions are allowed.[94]

The Service raised the business-personal distinction in its non-acquiescence:

Ode to Conway Twitty: A Reprise
Harold Jenkins and Conway Twitty
They are both the same
But one was born
The other achieved fame.
The man is talented
And has many a friend
They opened a restaurant
His name he did lend.
They are two different things
Making burgers and song
The business went sour
It didn't take long.
He repaid his friends
Why did he act
Was it business or friendship
Which is fact?

---

[94] *Id.* at 247, n.14.

> Business the court held
> It's deductible they feel
> We disagree with the answer
> But let's not appeal.[95]

Note the three mentions of "friends" in the reprise, including what must be in Service's view, the crux of the case: "Was it business or friendship?" Indeed.[96]

Thus, all three threads that appeared in the Court's opinion in *Welch*, and even in the arguments before the Court, can be found in subsequent case law. However, although *Welch* certainly remains in the case law gene pool, it is increasingly difficult to find concrete influences in the more recent cases, as discussed below.

The Continuing Importance of *Welch* Today

As befits a major Supreme Court case, *Welch* has been cited thousands of times. Most of the citations are recent.[97] However, the overwhelming majority of them cite the opinion for only one sentence: "His [the Commissioner's] ruling has the support of a presumption of correctness, and the petitioner has the burden of proving it to be wrong."[98] So much for the multiple threads. In fact, of those threads, the Court now seems to believe that only one is truly significant. In 1954, the Supreme Court stated that "[t]he principal function of the term 'ordinary' in section 162(a) is to clarify the distinction, often difficult, between those

---

[95] A.O.D. 1984–022 (March 23, 1984).

[96] For more on Conway Twitty's influence on this issue, see Dietrick v. Commissioner, 881 F.2d 336 (6th Cir.) (denying deduction to taxpayer who paid costs of his filtration equipment business's unsuccessful attempt to develop high performance aircraft), *cert. denied*, 493 U.S. 1003 (1989); Mohn v. United States, 2001 U.S.T.C. (CCH) ¶ 50,709 (E.D.Mich.2001) (denying government's summary judgment motion where insurance broker father and son deducted repayment of family members, friends and fellow country club members who invested in "prime bank instruments" promising a 300–600 percent return on a ten-day investment of $600,000); H. Kalicak Constr. Co. v. Commissioner, T.C. Memo. 1984–552 ("a shareholder payment which is motivated by . . . personal considerations will not qualify for deductibility under the rational applied in *Jenkins*"). For the unraveling of a tax shelter involving Conway Twitty's recordings, see Fritz v. Commissioner, T.C. Memo. 1991–176. For more on the tax problems of country and western legends, see Paul L. Caron, *Tax Myopia, Or Mamas Don't Let Your Babies Grow Up To Be Tax Lawyers*, 13 Va. Tax Rev. 517 (1994) (stretching for a way to cite the Editor of *Tax Stories*).

[97] Shepardizing the case on Westlaw, there appear to be 6668 citations, of which 2531 occurred since 1990 and 959 in the last three years. The numbers from Lexis are slightly different. I have no earthly idea why this is so.

[98] 290 U.S. at 115. I have randomly checked a few pages (100 cites per page) of the 2531 citations, which, according to Westlaw, have occurred since 1990. In the pages I checked, fully 90% of the *Welch* citations were only to this proposition.

expenses that are currently deductible and those that are in the nature of capital expenditures."[99]

The remaining influence of *Welch* on that "principal function" has been minimal. Consider how three recent, significant cases on capital expenses—*INDOPCO, Inc. v. Commissioner*,[100] *PNC Bancorp, Inc. v. Commissioner*,[101] and *A.E. Staley Mfg. Co. v. Commissioner*[102]—use *Welch*. *INDOPCO* uses *Welch* on capital expenses mostly to whine. The Court cites *Welch* for the propositions that "decisive distinctions" between current expenses and capital expenditures "are those of degree and not of kind,"[103] and that the cases are "difficult to harmonize."[104] In a footnote, *Welch* appears at the bottom of a string cite with the notation, "payments of former employer's debts are capital expenditures."[105]

PNC adds that the capitalization versus deductibility inquiry is heavily fact-based, and cites *INDOPCO* with the note "citing *Welch*."[106] That's it. *Staley* notes that "distinguishing between expenses that can be deducted under § 162 and those that must be capitalized under § 263 is not an easy task" and cites *Welch*.[107] More whining.

As to the less important, non-capital issues, all three cases cite *Welch* for the proposition that "necessary" means "appropriate and helpful."[108] *PNC* cites *Welch* for the propositions that ordinary is a variable affected by time, place, and circumstance,[109] and that one should not stray from the moorings of the "natural and common meaning" of

[99] Commissioner v. Tellier, 383 U.S. 687, 689–90 (1966).

[100] 503 U.S. 79 (1992). *See* Chapter 6 of *Tax Stories*.

[101] 212 F.3d 822 (3d Cir.2000).

[102] 119 F.3d 482 (7th Cir.1997).

[103] 503 U.S. at 86.

[104] *Id.*

[105] *Id.* at n.5.

[106] 212 F.3d at 833.

[107] 119 F.3d at 487. Clearly, there has been little progress. In announcing a new proposed rulemaking, Mark Weinberger, Treasury Assistant Secretary (Tax Policy) commented, "Currently, the IRS spends a substantial and disproportionate amount of its examination resources involving capitalization issues. Recently, much of the uncertainty and controversy in the capitalization area has related to expenditures that create or enhance intangible assets." The ANPRM (advanced notice of proposed rulemaking) goes on to say, "The difficulty of translating general capitalization principles into clear, consistent, and administrable standards has been recognized for decades. *See Welch v. Helvering.*" Treas. Dept. New Release PO–933 (Jan. 17, 2002), *CCH Standard Federal Tax Reports* ¶ 46, 272.

[108] 503 U.S. at 85; 212 F.3d at 828; 119 F.3d at 487.

[109] 212 F.3d at 828.

the term "ordinary."[110] *Staley* cites *Welch* for the proposition that expenses can be ordinary even if they only occur once in a lifetime.[111] Both *Staley* and *PNC* quote the "life in all its fullness" paragraph.[112] Nobody whines like Justice Cardozo.

How ironic. *Welch* was probably right on the capital expense issue even if Justice Cardozo did not tell us why. Yet, it is essentially not cited by recent cases on that important issue. Those cases, instead, cite it for its definition of ordinary as opposed to extraordinary. On that point, it was surely wrong.

Moreover, it was more than wrong; it was pernicious. *Welch* teaches that alleged business expenses that are not common to the relevant industry in the relevant time and place are far too extraordinary to be ordinary. In fact, such expenses are so bizarre in the business context that they can be explained only by the weird, personal predilections of those incurring them. As such, perhaps they are not business expenses at all.

Can any religious expenses pass muster under this doctrine? Those in *Amend* and *Trebilcock* did not. However, perhaps other religious expenditures are more common. For example, it used to be fairly common to have a minister bless the community fishing fleet before the first expedition of the season. Many communities still do this although they may well be thinking more of luring tourists than fish. Presumably, some of the ministers charge for their time. Are these expenses common enough to be deductible?

In Hawaii, construction sites must be blessed, or no one will work on them. If a serious accident happens at a site, it must be reconsecrated, or the workers will all stay away. Surely, any fees paid to the local Kahunas are necessary.[113] Are they not also ordinary, given the time, place, and circumstance?

For many years, there was a religious chapel in the corporate headquarters of R. J. Reynolds.[114] Does anyone imagine that Reynolds accountants carefully measured the square footage of chapel space so that they could carve out its maintenance costs as nondeductible, bizarre expenses?

---

[110] *Id.*

[111] 119 F.3d at 488.

[112] *Id.* at 487; 212 F.3d at 828.

[113] I have confirmed with a former colleague at University of Hawaii Law School that this practice continues.

[114] Telephone Interview with R.J. Reynolds, audit staff person (Jan. 10, 1989).

Different people may well reach different conclusions as to the deductibility of these various business-related, religious expenditures. But does *Welch* ask the right question? Should the deductibility of these expenditures turn upon how many businesses incur them?

Consider other, perhaps odd business expenditures. One normally would not consider trashing a hotel room as an ordinary and necessary component of a business trip. Yet, some rock musicians trash their hotel rooms during concert tours so routinely that their fans have come to expect it.[115] Arguably, the behavior is part of their group persona and is a contributing factor to their business success. Should it be deductible?[116]

Banks compete fiercely with one another to attract customers who bank on-line. To accommodate these new customers, the banks need user-friendly websites. To build good websites, they must hire people who would not normally want to work for a bank. To attract them, one bank in the Southeast has converted a large room in its building into a Meditation Room, complete with thick carpets, very little furniture, and New Age music. Meditation Rooms are not common in bank offices, at least not yet. Should they be deductible?

The difficulty is to balance two legitimate interests of the tax system. One legitimate interest is to have a system that is easily administered, one which places obstacles in the path of those who would abuse the system by claiming deductions that they do not deserve. This interest would be furthered by a bright-line rule disallowing business deductions for expenditures which are not common to the relevant industry.

The other legitimate interest is to achieve fairness in individual cases and to reward creativity and innovation. This interest would be furthered by allowing individuals with uncommon expenses to make their case. Hearing them out might complicate tax administration, and it might occasionally let an unwarranted deduction slip through. But it also might give proper encouragement to the best and the brightest among us.

---

[115] See Brian Cady, History of the Who at http://www.thewho.net/history/. Perhaps the members of the Who are not U.S. taxpayers, but who is to say that their example would not be followed by those who are?

[116] For another odd case, see Heineman v. Commissioner, 82 T.C. 538 (1984). A CEO of a corporation headquartered in Chicago built himself an office in Sister Bay, Wisconsin. The office was a 20 foot by 20 foot single room, suspended from a limestone cliff in a cantilevered steel frame. It cost some $250,000. The CEO used the office every August for long-range planning. He said he needed it to think. The Tax Court held the expenses of the office to be deductible. The issue was whether or not the expenses were necessary. Citing *Welch*, the Tax Court said that they were; it was reluctant to substitute its judgment for that of the taxpayer.

The first time a businessperson gets a new idea, she will incur expenditures that are not at all common because no one else will be doing it. If those new ideas succeed, however, then others will copy them. Ultimately, expenditures which at first appeared extraordinary will become quite ordinary.

Under the *Welch* rule, the creative soul with the new idea will be forced to try it out with nondeductible dollars. Only when the ideas have proven so successful that even the totally unimaginative business clods are doing it will the expenditures be ordinary enough to be deductible. Should the tax laws punish innovation in this way?[117]

It is not that Justice Cardozo's opinion necessarily struck the wrong balance of these two interests. Rather, the opinion hardly even addressed the question. Perhaps it is just as well that it is cited most often for its throwaway line on burden of proof.

Conclusion

The question of what expenses can be legitimately deducted by a business is one of the most fundamental in our tax system. The legacy of *Welch* is that it has needlessly confused subsequent courts (as well as tax practitioners and students) as they grapple with this question in many different business contexts. Although it long ago should have been consigned to the judicial scrap heap, *Welch's* spirit lives on in the unfortunate doctrine stifling business innovation at the very time that the twenty-first century global economy demands more, not less, business creativity. Perhaps a better approach for the Court would have been to say that "ordinary" means the opposite of "capital" and nothing more. Of course, that may have been asking too much of Justice Cardozo—indeed, one wag has recently applauded Justice Cardozo's "willingness to abandon legal precedent" and his "willingness to abandon an archaic, verbose style," emblematic of his desire to "break with tradition, a rejection of convention (in both style and substance)."[118] Well, that explains it.[119]

---

[117] As argued in Petitioner's Brief at 10:

It will not, we think, be disputed as a general proposition that business men should have a free hand to adopt such means as will result in increased business and increased income, resulting in increased revenue to the Government, and that the Government should not exercise a supervisory power over the methods adopted, or determine after the event whether the course adopted was wise or unwise, advisable or inadvisable, prudent or imprudent, so long as no law is violated. It is the taxpayer, whose investment is at stake, who should determine ways and means and not the Government.

[118] Brady Coleman, Lord Denning & Justice Cardozo: The Judge as Poet–Philosopher, 32 Rutgers L.J. 485 (2001).

[119] *See also* William Powers, Jr., *Thaumatrope*, 77 Tex. L. Rev. 1319, 1319 (1999) ("A common theme among Cardozo's detractors is that he sometimes substitutes rhetorical

> ### A Concluding Limerick
>
> Thomas Welch paid a debt which he didn't owe
> with hopes that his business would really grow.
> "His act wasn't ordinary;
> in fact 'twas extraordinary.
> No deduction," said Justice Cardozio.

---

flourish for analysis.''). Of course, most of the voluminous studies of Justice Cardozo do not mention his *Welch* opinion—it did not even make it on *Cardozo's Baseball Card*, 44 Stan. L. Rev. 899 (1992) (review essay by James D. Gordon III).

6

Joseph Bankman

The Story of *INDOPCO*: What Went Wrong in the Capitalization v. Deduction Debate?

INDOPCO v. Commissioner[1] is the most recent decision in this *Tax Story* volume, and in part for that reason, *INDOPCO* is the most frequently discussed case in the tax world. A case such as *Knetsch v. United States*[2] exerts its influence subtly, forming the basis for today's economic substance doctrine. Lawyers can (and do) debate the merits of that doctrine, and in so doing comment upon *Knetsch*, but the decision itself has faded into the background. *INDOPCO*, by contrast, is still very much alive. Industry has lined up an (anti) "INDOPCO Coalition,"[3] headed by the former Commissioner of the Internal Revenue Service who pursued the case; the government has recently issued *INDOPCO* regulations; and the decision (and its aftermath) is discussed in today's tax and business journals. The case is important, then, for its practical significance. It is the most recent Supreme Court pronouncement on the deductibility of business expenses that do not produce or enhance tangible assets.

In time, of course, *INDOPCO* will lie under, and help give shape to, newer cases and regulations. At that point, the case will be worth studying less for its practical import than for the light it sheds on the administration of an income tax, or more speculatively, on any tax or set of rules shaped by the political process. The judge, legislator, or adminis-

---

[1] 503 U.S. 79 (1992).

[2] 364 U.S. 361 (1960).

[3] *See* INDOPCO Coalition, *Proposed Capitalization Principles*, 2001 Tax Notes Today 198–42; Lee A. Sheppard, *The* INDOPCO *Grocery List*, 93 Tax Notes 320 (2001).

trator must balance competing goals: uniformity, certainty, practicality, and so on. In *INDOPCO*, that balancing act failed: the opinion is widely seen as making a bad situation worse. What makes this failure particularly sobering is that the case fell into seemingly able hands. The opinion was written by the most knowledgeable tax jurist ever to sit on the Court. The opinion was solicited by an administration whose leadership opposed everything the opinion came to stand for. The leadership of the Service was thwarted by career employees, its limited autonomy, and the difficulty of the balancing act itself.

Background

The Big Picture

The treatment of business expenditures under a "pure" Haig–Simons income tax[4] is clear: expenses that produce benefit beyond a year comprise an investment that must be capitalized. The capitalized expense is amortized or depreciated as the asset declines in value; the remaining basis is deducted when the asset is sold or declared worthless. For tangible investments, this regime perhaps works well enough. But for intangible investments, this regime is problematic. A primary difficulty is that there is no natural line of demarcation between expenses that produce lasting benefit and those that do not. A marketing campaign, for example, may yield sales in the current and future years. A secondary difficulty is that it is often difficult even to estimate the proper amortization of capitalized expenses. Cases involving corporate taxpayers sometimes raise yet another issue: whether an expense benefits the corporation or its shareholders.

These problems go away if one departs from the normative goal of taxing income. The leading non-income based tax is a cash-flow or consumption tax; a common observation is that our income tax system already incorporates many cash-flow elements. A cash flow tax can be implemented by taxing all salary and capital proceeds but allowing a deduction of all business expenses. For example, an individual who earns a $100,000 salary but pays out $70,000 for business expenses is taxed only on the $30,000 available for personal consumption. The $70,000 that goes to business expenses is deducted in full. There is no need to determine whether the expenses produce long-term benefit. Moreover, because all business expenses are deducted rather than capitalized, there is no need to determine the proper amortization period or rate.

It is possible, of course, to want a tax system to do something other than correctly measure income or consumption. Suppose one wished a tax system to maximize economic welfare, as conventionally defined.

---

[4] *See* Chapters 1 and 2 of *Tax Stories*.

What would be the most efficient treatment of expenses that produce or create intangible assets? Starting on a clean slate, one might as a rough approximation opt for the full deductibility that is part and parcel of the cash-flow tax. A cash flow tax is generally thought more efficient than an income tax because it defers tax on amounts saved or invested. This, in turn, reduces the tax burden on investment.[5] Economic models that incorporate this and other effects generally show that social wealth grows under a cash-flow tax.[6] Full deductibility of intangible business expenses offers another advantage as well: it will no longer be necessary to determine whether an intangible expense produces long-term benefit, or to determine the amortization schedule of an intangible expense that is found to produce such long-term benefit.

But of course we do not start on a clean slate. Business purchases of tangible assets, such as property, must be capitalized. If all intangible business expenditures are deductible, while expenditures on tangible assets must be capitalized, we will (inefficiently) favor the former over the latter. Dissimilar treatment of tangible and intangible expenditures will also introduce administrative costs as taxpayers and the government quibble about whether a particular expense is best tied to a tangible or intangible asset. If all this begins to sound indeterminate, it is. We may be able to usefully guess as to which of two proposed treatments will be more efficient. One treatment may impose tremendous administrative costs, for example, and be rejected for that reason. But we cannot come up with anything approaching an optimal rule in this area.

The State of the Law

As noted above, under a pure income tax, a business expense that produces benefit beyond the year it is incurred must be capitalized. This is true for intangible as well as for tangible investments. In fact, the "life span" of the investment or expenditure-related benefit is a key fact in the determination of whether an outlay must be capitalized. Outlays that do not produce benefit beyond the year in which they are incurred are deductible, usually as an ordinary business expense. As the term of the benefit increases, capitalization becomes more and more the rule. The term of benefit has played a particularly strong role in capitalization decisions in Tax Court cases. However, the term of the benefit is not the only factor relevant to the deduction/capitalization decision. A significant percentage of outlays tied to intangible assets are deductible notwith-

---

[5] Under certain assumptions, a cash-flow tax also reduces the social costs of the tax labor income as well. *See* A.B. Atkinson & J.E. Stiglitz, *The Design of Tax Structure: Direct versus Indirect Taxation*, 6 J. Pub. Econ. 55 (1976).

[6] *See, e.g.*, Ken Judd, *The Impact of Tax Reform in Modern Dynamic Economics*, in *Transition Costs of Fundamental Tax Reform* 5–53 (Kevin A. Hassett & Glenn Hubbard eds., AEI Press 2001).

standing a long useful life. Deduction rather than capitalization becomes more likely as the link between the outlay and a readily identifiable asset decreases, and as the asset to which the outlay is linked becomes less and less tangible. Deduction also becomes more likely for expenses that are recurring, or fit within a commonsense definition of ordinary and necessary. As might be expected, in time both courts and the Service tend to come to agreement on the treatment of certain categories of expenditures. Advertising, for example, is deductible. Only the expenditures that do not fit into established categories are litigated.

Because many expenses that produce long-term benefit are nonetheless deductible, the law here must be described as pro-taxpayer, at least when measured against a pure income tax. Once an investment is capitalized, however, the pro-taxpayer feature of the law goes away. Not only do taxpayers lose the up-front deduction, they often find themselves unable to amortize the capitalized expense.

There is something inescapably arbitrary about any of the countless decisions handed down in this area. Cases are litigated only if they fall between settled categories, offering each litigant its choice of precedents. The present law is inconsistent with a pure income (or cash-flow) tax, and efficiency analysis gets us nowhere. The most that can be said is that the pro-taxpayer, category-by-category approach produces some certainty over time and eliminates the difficulties inherent in the pure income tax treatment of these sorts of expenditures.

Consider, for example, *General Bancshares v. Commissioner*,[7] which concerned the deductibility of costs incurred in issuing stock dividends. The corporate taxpayer argued that the issuance of stock dividends was similar in relevant respect to the issuance of cash dividends. Courts had long held the ancillary costs (e.g., postage) of issuing cash dividends deductible. This determination, while hardly required as a matter of tax logic, is consistent with the factor analysis above. The ancillary costs of issuing cash dividends are recurring, comport with an everyday definition of ordinary and necessary, and are not tied too closely with any tangible corporate asset. The government argued that the costs were most similar to those incurred in issuing stock or rearranging corporate capital structure. These forms of costs had long been held non-deductible. With perhaps some stretching, this determination, too, can be fit within the factor analysis above: corporate restructuring is a rare rather than recurring event and results in the corporation buying back a tangible asset (e.g., securities) or issuing stock for consideration, thereby obtaining an obvious long-term benefit. The court, in a brief opinion, held that the costs fit within the corporate restructuring category and therefore had to be capitalized.

---

[7] 326 F.2d 712 (8th Cir.1964).

General Bancshares, an otherwise completely unremarkable case, is useful for our purposes for three reasons: (1) it illustrates the category-by-category approach that dominates case law and the rough relationship between category characterization and the factors described above; (2) the opinion was written by Harry Blackmun, the author of the opinion in *INDOPCO*; and (3) the opinion itself is quite conventional. The case is decided by analogy with other cases; what would be required under a pure income tax is touched upon only obliquely. In later decisions, Blackmun would be less restrained, and no effort would be spared to interpret (and over-interpret) his language.

Lincoln Savings *and its Aftermath*

Blackmun's next capitalization case, *Commissioner v. Lincoln Savings & Loan Ass'n*,[8] came after his elevation to the Supreme Court. At issue was the proper characterization of annual payments the taxpayer had made to the then-provider of federal deposit insurance. The payments were in some events creditable against insurance premiums due in later years, were refundable in the event the taxpayer withdrew from the federal deposit insurance program, and were treated as assets on the taxpayer's balance sheet. The government characterized the payments as non-deductible capital investments. The taxpayer argued that the payments provided current rather than future value. Without the payments, the taxpayer could not separately purchase (heavily subsidized) federal deposit insurance, and without the insurance, the taxpayer could not stay in business. The payments therefore were best thought of as an additional insurance cost, and like such costs, ought to be deductible. The taxpayer also argued that the payments were recurring as well as ordinary and necessary.

Lincoln Savings thus seems a typical capitalization case: difficult to resolve but narrow in scope. A narrow reading of the case is consistent with the *certiorari* petition filed by the government, which argued that the conflict between the Tax Court (which had ruled in favor of the government) and the Ninth Circuit (which had ruled in favor of the taxpayer) would affect the tax positions taken by over 4,000 thrift institutions. The petition does not claim any effect on capitalization issues outside of the savings and loan industry.

The larger issues of capitalization policy were raised on brief. The government argued that "[t]he essence of an ordinary business expense is that the benefit from the expense is derived and exhausted within the taxable year." In contrast, the taxpayer argued that the payment was ordinary and necessary, and that the "the possibility of a future benefit

---

[8] 403 U.S. 345 (1971).

does not convert an ordinary and necessary business expense into a capital expenditure."

Justice Blackmun, writing for the Court, held that the payments produced an asset of benefit apart from and unrelated to insurance coverage and therefore were appropriately characterized as contributions to capital:

> [T]he presence of an ensuing benefit that may have some future aspect is not controlling; many expenses concededly deductible have prospective effect beyond the taxable year.
>
> What is important and controlling, we feel, is that the payment serves to create or enhance for Lincoln what is essentially a separate and distinct additional asset and that, as an inevitable consequence, the payment is capital in nature and not an expense, let alone an ordinary expense, deductible under § 162(a).[9]

Judging without the benefit of hindsight, we might conclude that Blackmun intended these sentences to limit, rather than expand, the impact of the decision. This is obviously true with respect to the first sentence, which rejects the argument that any expense that provides future benefit must be capitalized. But what about the second sentence? From the context, the most reasonable explanation is that it offers the payment as an example of an easy case for capitalization because it comprised the whole of a separate asset. Under this interpretation, Blackmun did not intend that only "separate and distinct" assets be capitalized. From the standpoint of judicial deference, the most egregious mistake would be to adopt the pure "future benefit" test. A lesser evil would be to write an opinion that could be read to support that test. Blackmun's language ensured that would not happen.

More speculatively, we might surmise that Blackmun would not have been emboldened to add anything to the narrow wording required in the case had he not been comfortable with his own capabilities and expertise in the field. Blackmun had spent over a decade as a tax lawyer prior to his appointment to the bench; he had also taught the subject at the University of Minnesota Law School and what is now William Mitchell College of Law.[10] He was smart (summa in math at Harvard) and by all accounts a stickler for details. One can imagine that he felt an almost aesthetic distaste for the government's somewhat deceptive statement that equated future benefit with capitalization. The truth—at that time and today as well—is that future benefit is a necessary but not sufficient condition for capitalization. Blackmun gave the government the victory but added language to prevent an expansive reading of the holding.

---

[9] *Id.* at 354.

[10] These details are taken from Robert Green's informative article, *Justice Blackmun's Federal Tax Jurisprudence*, 26 Hastings Const. L.Q. 109 (1998).

The immediate reaction to the case was muted. In the four-year period beginning with the granting of *certiorari*, only a single article can be found in *The Index to Legal Periodicals* discussing the case. In time, however, the decision became quite important for two reasons. First, the number of reported cases on the deductibility of intangible expenses grew, presumably in part because the government pursued the issue more aggressively.[11] Second, the limiting language inserted to prevent an expansive reading of the future benefit requirement became instead a significant weapon in the taxpayer's arsenal.

This revisionist interpretation of *Lincoln Savings* first became apparent in *Briarcliff Candy Corp v. Commissioner*.[12] After watching its urban customer base flee to the suburbs, Briarcliff attempted to retain those customers by placing its candies in suburban drug stores. The company entered into franchise agreements with the drug stores and deducted its up-front costs associated with the franchise program. The government on audit held that the franchise costs were non-deductible capital outlays. The Second Circuit described the Tax Court opinion, and relevant precedent, as follows:

> The Tax Court rests its decision squarely on the fact that some of the agency agreements continued in effect for terms exceeding a year, and therefore that the expenses connected with the procuring of the agreements were not ordinary but capital in nature ...
>
> Prior to 1971, this was an often repeated and generally accepted standard. The Supreme Court, however, in the case of *Lincoln Savings* held "the presence of an ensuing benefit is not controlling; many expenses concededly deductible have prospective effect beyond the taxable year. What is important and controlling, we think, is that the ... payments serve to create or enhance for the taxpayer what is essentially a separate and distinct asset."
>
> This has brought about a radical shift in emphasis and directs the inquiry in the present case to whether or not [the taxpayer], in advertising and soliciting drug stores ... created or enhanced for itself what is essentially a separate and distinct asset.[13]

The court went on to hold that the franchise-related costs did not create or enhance separate and distinct assets and therefore were deductible in the year incurred.

It is possible to read *Briarcliff* sympathetically to the taxpayer. The franchise agreements did not require the franchisee to sell or even

---

[11] Another factor contributing to this growth may have been the increased importance of intangible expenses in an expanding economy.

[12] 475 F.2d 775 (2d Cir.1973).

[13] *Id.* at 782.

market candy beyond the close of the taxable year, and as it happened, the franchise program did not create significant long-term value.[14] The Second Circuit's reading of *Lincoln Savings* in *Briarcliff*, however, was followed by other courts in cases that did involve future benefits. A representative case is *NCNB Corporation v. Commissioner*.[15] At issue was the proper treatment of market studies and other costs related to expansion but not directly connected to any building or tangible assets. The taxpayer had deducted these costs; the government claimed the costs must be capitalized. The Sixth Circuit at the time had a "one-year" rule that had the same effect as the future benefit test (i.e., required capitalization of any expenditure whose benefits extended beyond the close of the taxable year). In an en banc decision, the Sixth Circuit in *NCNB* overturned a panel decision and held that the expenses were deductible. In so doing, the Sixth Circuit rejected the one-year test and instead adopted part of Blackmun's limiting language as an affirmative test for deductibility: "[C]osts incurred in expanding a business are not considered capital costs unless they meet the *Lincoln Savings & Loan* 'separate and distinct additional asset' test. And this test holds whether or not the expenditures have benefits beyond the current taxation period."[16]

The transformation of Blackmun's dicta in *Lincoln Savings* was now complete. As noted above, it seems likely that Blackmun used the separate and distinct nature of the asset as a characteristic of a capital expenditure, or perhaps as a definitive marker that an expenditure must be capitalized. *NCNB* thus established a "separate and distinct" threshold for capitalization. What in *Lincoln Savings* seemed at most a sufficient grounds to uphold capitalization now seemed to be necessary for capital characterization. Decisions in three other circuits read the "separate and distinct asset" language in a similar manner.[17]

The elevation of 'separate and distinct' into a requirement for capitalization did not meet with uniform approval. The Bittker and Lokken treatise, for example, opined that the decision in *Briarcliff* "overstates the significance of the use in *Lincoln Savings* of the phrase 'a separate and distinct additional asset.' "[18] In a case whose facts were

---

[14] In a sale of the taxpayer's business at the end of the decade, the franchise rights for all years were valued at only $10,000.

[15] 684 F.2d 285 (4th Cir.1982).

[16] *Id.* at 291.

[17] *See* Campbell Taggart v. United States, 744 F.2d 442 (5th Cir.1984); First Sec. Bank of Idaho v. Commissioner, 592 F.2d 1050 (9th Cir.1979); Colorado Springs Nat'l Bank v. United States, 505 F.2d 1185 (10th Cir.1974).

[18] Boris I. Bittker & Lawrence Lokken, *Federal Taxation of Income, Estates and Gifts* ¶ 20.4.4, n.86 (3d ed. 1999).

nearly identical to those in *NCBC*, *Central Texas Savings & Loan Ass'n v. United States*,[19] the Fifth Circuit held that expenses of bank expansion were properly characterized by the government as capital. The Fifth Circuit in *Central Texas Savings & Loan*, like the Tenth Circuit in *NCBC*, held that capitalization was required only for expenses that created a "separate and distinct asset." However, the Fifth Circuit in *Central Texas Savings & Loan* went on to hold that the costs of permits and marketing studies incurred in expansion constituted such an asset, both because the costs were ultimately tied to the physical assets of branch banks and because the rights obtained through permits constituted an intangible asset. *Central Texas Savings & Loan* thus suggested one way around the "separate and distinct" asset hurdle was to simply expand the definition of asset to encompass the long-term value created by any particular expenditure. A more direct approach to the issue was taken by the Tax Court, Third Circuit, and Supreme Court in *INDOPCO*.

Prior Proceedings

The issue in *INDOPCO* was straightforward. Taxpayer had paid and deducted $2 million to Morgan Stanley in connection with the "friendly" acquisition of the company by the Unilever Group. The government on audit treated the expenditure as a non-deductible capital asset. The Tax Court rejected the taxpayer's interpretation of *Lincoln Savings* and held without much discussion that the expenses produced future benefits and were therefore capital. The Third Circuit reached the same decision on somewhat similar grounds.

The Supreme Court Decision

The Briefs and Oral Argument

As presented to the Court, the case revolved around three major (though related) arguments. The first argument concerned the proper interpretation of *Lincoln Savings*. The taxpayer contended that the decision made "separate and distinct" a necessary condition for capital asset characterization: the Morgan Stanley payment had not created or enhanced any such asset and was therefore deductible. The government argued that under *Lincoln Savings*, the creation of a "separate and distinct additional asset" was at most a sufficient, rather than necessary, condition for capital asset characterization.

The second argument was precedential as well, but here the appeal was to the broader categories of case law or doctrine. Both sides

---

[19] 731 F.2d 1181 (1984).

acknowledged that the law had developed a category-by-category approach to the issue. The taxpayer relied on the precedents created by the lower courts that made the creation of a separate and distinct asset a necessary condition for capitalization. The government relied on a line of cases (including *General Bancshares*) which, it asserted, required capitalization of expenses associated with restructuring corporate capital structure.

In response, the taxpayer argued that the capital structure cases established no special rule but simply required capitalization for expenses that were properly tied to particular assets. Here, the taxpayer argued, the expenses were tied to no particular asset, and the company was not meaningfully enhanced in any way by the expenses or the merger. Instead, the expenses arose from the company's legal obligations to its shareholders, including the board's obligation to make an informed judgment about the adequacy of the merger. The taxpayer argued that these fiduciary duty-related expenses, like other shareholder relationship expenses, were commonly and appropriately deducted.

The argument that the merger-related expenses did not significantly benefit the company was a bit of a two-edged sword. It raised the possibility—as noted by the government in oral argument—that the expenses were best characterized as a non-deductible constructive dividend to the shareholders.[20] The government also argued that the expense produced long-term corporate benefit,[21] and the fact that a long-term investment was legally required did not preclude capitalization.

Finally, and most significantly, each side marshaled the policy arguments that favored its position. The government led off with the argument, maintained consistently in cases as far back as *General Bancshares*, that proper reflection of income required the capitalization of expenses that provide future benefit. The government acknowledged that it would often be difficult to categorize an expense (referring to the task as an "elusive, fact-intensive inquiry"), and that some expenses would offer both current and future benefits (stating that "the analysis properly focuses on whether income will be *better* reflected by deducting or by capitalizing the amount in question").

The taxpayer replied with a proper reflection of income argument of its own: capitalization properly matched income only where it was accompanied by amortization. The taxpayer argued that the government

---

[20] The dividend would be taxable to the shareholders as well, though presumably added to basis so as to reduce the capital gain (or increase the capital loss) recognized upon sale of stock.

[21] The government claimed that the merger presented operating and financial synergies, and that it removed the depressing effect on the stock price created by the eventual sale of stock by the controlling shareholders.

had no adequate theory of how the expenses in question would be recovered. On brief and oral argument, the taxpayer went further and argued that common forms of cost recovery—through sale or loss or depreciation—required the creation (or presumably enhancement) of a separate and distinct asset. Expenses that did not meet the separate and distinct asset test but were nonetheless capitalized could therefore never be recovered.[22]

At oral argument, the government's time was spent largely responding to questions concerning the amortization of the Morgan Stanley fee. The government's response to the baseline case seemed to satisfy the Court: so long as the company continued operations as part of the Unilever Group, the expenditures would have an indefinite duration and were appropriately not amortizable. The government had a harder time describing how costs would be recovered in other situations. It stated that the costs incurred by a would-be acquirer in an unsuccessful takeover could be deducted in the year the takeover failed. However, the costs incurred by a target company in unsuccessfully fending off a takeover would be non-deductible. The treatment of expenses incurred in a successful takeover upon sale of the stock or assets of the acquired company was in the opinion of the government "[a] very difficult question."

Finally, the taxpayer argued that the government's test could not be easily applied (many expenses produce both current and future benefits) and was inconsistent with accepted treatment of certain expenses (e.g., advertising).

The Opinion

In an unanimous decision authored by Justice Blackmun, the Court affirmed the decision of the lower courts. Blackmun took the opportunity to correct what seems to have been an obvious misinterpretation of his ruling in *Lincoln Savings*:

> *Lincoln Savings* stands for the simple proposition that a taxpayer's expenditure that "serves to create or enhance ... a separate and distinct" asset should be capitalized under § 263. It by no means follows, however, that only expenditures that create or enhance separate and distinct assets are to be capitalized under § 263. We had no occasion in *Lincoln Savings* to consider the tax treatment of expenditures that, unlike the additional premiums at issue there, did not create or enhance a specific asset, and thus the case cannot be read to preclude capitalization in other circumstances. In short, *Lincoln Savings* holds that the creation of a separate and distinct

---

[22] At oral argument, this argument put the taxpayer in an odd position. The government, when pressed, stated that under certain conditions the costs at stake could be deducted as a capital loss (or offset against sales proceeds). The taxpayer then was forced to argue that the government could not do what it had just said it would do.

asset may be a sufficient, but not a necessary, condition to classification as a capital expenditure.[23]

Blackmun then held the expenses fell into the category of corporate restructurings, and under settled case law were therefore non-deductible. He explained that "[c]ourts long have recognized that expenses such as these, 'incurred for the purpose of changing the corporate structure for the benefit of future operations are not ordinary and necessary expenses.' "[24]

Blackmun could have stopped at this point. The case had arisen in part because of an over-reading of dicta in his last opinion on the subject. A chastened Blackmun might have suppressed any urge to expand upon the decision or the issue in general; indeed, Blackmun might have specifically included language warning against a similar misreading of, or overreaction to, his decision. Yet Blackmun went on to discuss the relevance/importance of future benefit:

> Nor does our statement in *Lincoln Savings* that "the presence of an ensuing benefit that may have some future aspect is not controlling" prohibit reliance on future benefit as a means of distinguishing an ordinary business expense from a capital expenditure. Although the mere presence of an incidental future benefit—"*some future aspect*"—may not warrant capitalization, a taxpayer's realization of benefits beyond the year in which the expenditure is incurred is undeniably important in determining whether the appropriate tax treatment is immediate deduction or capitalization.... Indeed, the text of the Code's capitalization provision, § 263(a)(1), which refers to "permanent improvements or betterments," itself envisions an inquiry into the duration and extent of the benefits realized by the taxpayer.[25]

What are we to make of this part of the decision? The paragraph can be read to require capitalization of any expense with a more than incidental future benefit. The paragraph also can be read (with largely similar effect) to suggest that the Court would uphold the Service if it were to insist upon capitalization in such cases, but not that it would require the Service to do so. This expansive reading of the future benefit language is consistent with a string of pro-government decisions already cited—*General Bancshares*, *Lincoln Savings*, and *INDOPCO*—and with another case, *Commissioner v. Idaho Power Co.*,[26] decided four years after *Lincoln Savings*.

---

[23] 503 U.S. 79, 86–87 (1992).

[24] *Id.* at 89.

[25] *Id.* at 87–88.

[26] 418 U.S. 1 (1974). At issue in that case was the proper depreciation of transportation equipment used to construct a transmission line. The taxpayer had depreciated the

Support for this interpretation also can be found in Blackmun's decision in *Newark Morning Ledger Co. v. United States*,[27] decided the year after *INDOPCO*. The taxpayer had paid $325 million for a daily newspaper and had allocated $70 million of the purchase price to an intangible asset called "paid subscribers." The taxpayer had commissioned studies showing that the subscriber base would be reduced (through death, relocation, and other factors) over a given number of years and had taken an annual amortization deduction to reflect this decline in value. The government argued that the $70 million constituted non-depreciable goodwill. Blackmun, writing for the Court, upheld the deduction. A persistent bugaboo with capitalization of intangibles has been the uncertain amortization of those assets. Indeed, one of the principle arguments against capitalization in *INDOPCO* was the lack of any mechanism for depreciation or recovery of the capitalized costs. *Newark Morning Ledger* can be read as a limited rebuttal to this objection. In this case, at least, the Court was willing to accept a taxpayer's estimation of useful life and grant amortization over that life.

Should we assume then that Blackmun intended his discussion on future benefit to override existing precedent and institute, in this arena, a pure income tax? Probably not. Blackmun's language and arguments, considered in isolation, are unexceptional. It is obvious that future benefit is necessary to capital asset characterization. An expenditure with no future benefit cannot be capitalized. Blackmun's language here may simply be restating that fact and, going one step further, may acknowledge that the degree of future benefit will be relevant in deciding whether an expense ought to be capitalized. Presumably, other relevant factors might be the difficulty of making that determination, established precedent as to the type of expense at issue, and the presence or absence of amortization.

What is surprising, and a bit disappointing, is that Blackmun left the meaning of that paragraph unclear. Blackmun might have told us whether future benefit was a sufficient, or simply a necessary, condition for capital asset treatment, and if the latter, what the other factors were to be considered. Of course, he might have been unsure of his own position on the matter, or felt he could not get a consensus on the Court on the matter, or felt it was the one issue that was properly left to the legislature or bureaucracy to resolve. If that were the case, though, why say anything about future benefit? The decision in *INDOPCO* had come about in part because of a misreading of unnecessary language in

---

equipment for tax purposes over the useful life of the equipment; for accounting purposes, the equipment had been depreciated over the useful life of the transmission line. The government argued—and the Court held—that the equipment must be depreciated over the longer life of the transmission line.

[27] 507 U.S. 546 (1993).

Lincoln Savings. Why risk a similar misreading here? Indeed, if Blackmun had not have wanted to take a position on whether future benefit was sufficient or merely necessary, why not say that, or at least write a decision that explicitly abjured anything but category-by-category judicial determination in the area?

The Immediate Impact of *INDOPCO*

The fact that the decision in *INDOPCO* was ambiguous did not mean that it had no effect. As noted above, Blackmun's language could be read as affirming present law, as requiring capitalization of all expenses with non-incidental future benefit, or as falling anywhere between those two extremes. If the decision did anything, it moved the status quo toward a pure income tax, with capitalization of intangible outlays more the rule than the exception.[28]

Predictably, the decision emboldened IRS agents to challenge longstanding deductions. The new-found aggressiveness of agents was described in almost unfailingly unflattering terms. *The Agents Run Riot*[29] ran as a headline in Forbes, presenting the business world's reaction to events. *INDOPCO*, wrote a prominent lawyer, "is a tattoo on the wrist of every revenue agent, with the result being a hemorrhage of fashionable, new capitalization issues with no foreseeable end in sight."[30]

The ambiguity of the decision, together with the change in auditor behavior, led to a spate of articles, bemoaning both the decision and the audit behavior. Headlines of tax articles tell the story: *Doping Out Capitalization Rules After* INDOPCO;[31] *Panel Wrestles with Impact of* INDOPCO;[32] INDOPCO: *The Still Unsolved Riddle*;[33] *ABA Tax Section Meeting:* INDOPCO *Issues Continue to Perplex Practitioners and IRS*;[34] *IRS Has No Answers to Sticky Audit Issues Emerging Under* INDOP-

---

[28] *See* Peter Faber, INDOPCO: *The Still Unsolved Riddle*, 47 Tax Law. 607, 623 (1994) ("The language of the Court's opinion in *INDOPCO* is broad and it leans in the direction of capitalization. Capitalization is described as the normal rule, and deduction provisions are to be narrowly construed. Although the Court stopped short of saying that anything that creates a substantial future benefit must be capitalized, it did not stop too short.").

[29] Laura Saunders, *The Agents Run Riot*, Forbes, Nov. 9, 1992, at 144.

[30] Irving Salem & John Clair Jr., *Emerging Post-*INDOPCO *Issues: Rationale and Strategies*, 78 Tax Notes 1419 (1998).

[31] John W. Lee, 57 Tax Notes 669 (1992).

[32] Brian McConville, 59 Tax Notes 861 (1993).

[33] Peter Faber, 47 Tax Law. 607 (1994).

[34] Sheryl Stratton, 71 Tax Notes 992 (1966).

CO.[35] Interestingly, the decision attracted greater and more critical attention as the decade wore on.

The primary criticism, consistent with the analysis and evidenced by the headline titles above, was that the decision cast into doubt long-standing practices in countless settings. A mid-decade report by the American Bar Association listed over fifty *INDOPCO*-related issues.[36] These included issues raised in oral argument in the case itself (e.g., treatment of expenses incurred in unsuccessful efforts to thwart or accomplish takeovers), issues raised in earlier cases seemingly overruled by *INDOPCO* (e.g., treatment of business expansion costs), and the effect of the decision on the repair v. deduction issues (e.g., those in connection with environmental remediation).

Other criticisms were those inherent in any move toward a future benefit standard for capitalization. Commentators argued that the compliance and accounting costs of conceptual rigor outweighed the benefits, and that capitalization without adequate amortization would move the tax system away from, rather than towards, more accurate measurement of income.[37] The decision created arbitrary categories in which capitalization was required (and implicitly left untouched other categories in which it was not required). This, in turn, encouraged taxpayer dissembling and/or socially unproductive planning.[38]

From the (perhaps overly) detached perspective of the tax scholar, the primary criticism of the case seems apt. The secondary criticisms, directed against capitalization in general, seem not so much incorrect as one-sided or brief-like. A rule requiring capitalization of long-lived intangibles might (all else being equal) be praised for treating intangible assets in the same manner as tangible assets; instead it was criticized as inconsistent with the treatment of advertising expenses. In general, commentators critical of the decision made little effort to support key assertions, such as that capitalization without amortization would on balance distort accurate measurement of income.

The brief-like nature of the criticism may in some respect be a product of what might be called the political economy of case-related tax scholarship. Most of the commentators were practitioners whose clients were adversely affected by *INDOPCO* and any move toward greater capitalization; at least one significant *INDOPCO*-related report was paid by industry.[39]

---

[35] Sheryl Stratton, 78 Tax Notes 659 (1998).

[36] ABA Sect. of Tax'n Comm. on Tax Accounting, *Report on Capitalization Issues Raised under Sections 162 and 263 by* INDOPCO, Inc. v. Commissioner, 50 Tax Law. 181 (1996).

[37] Both criticisms were voiced in Kenneth W. Gideon's 1998 Woodworth Lecture, *Tax Law Works Best When the Rules Are Clear*, 81 Tax Notes 999, 1003 (1998).

[38] *See, e.g.*, Salem & Clair, *supra* note 30, at 1421.

[39] *See* INDOPCO Coalition, *supra* note 3.

It would be a mistake, however, to write off (so to speak) the reaction to *INDOPCO* as a product of self-interest or identification with clients. Among those writing critical commentary were reporters not identified with pro-taxpayer perspectives,[40] a group comprised of members of and appointed by, the ABA Tax Section,[41] and officials in the government during the time the case was pursued, whose loyalties on this issue must be not so clear cut. Moreover, while there may have been a host of commentators writing somewhat overdrawn articles on one side of the issue, virtually no one was writing or arguing on the other side.

The lack of favorable commentary may be a reflection of the fact that those who are motivated to write on any public issue are those who are upset; it is more common to write to complain about, rather than to applaud, a decision. Numbers, too, may have played a story here. Academics comprise the most natural group to write articles endorsing a case favorable to the government; there are far fewer legal tax academics than tax lawyers, and many of us in the profession do not write on this topic. One suspects, though, that academics as a whole were (and are) less than enthusiastic about the decision—or at least about the opinion.[42] Many may agree with this essay that Blackmun should have been more explicit about the role of future benefit or not brought up the issue at all. Others may support a cash flow tax and/or find the proper measurement of income a wrong goal not worth the costs. This is not to say that academics as a whole found (or find) the holding or even the language of the opinion bad; just that academics did (and do) not find the opinion good enough to justify the time required to write a supporting article on the subject.

The Continuing Importance of *INDOPCO* Today

The Judiciary

INDOPCO remains the Court's latest pronouncement on the subject and for that reason cannot be criticized directly by lower courts. In addition, because the precise meaning of *INDOPCO* is unclear, it is impossible to be very precise about whether it is faithfully followed. That said, it is clear that subsequent courts have read the decision in its most limited form.

---

[40] *See* Lee A. Sheppard, *Is the IRS Abusing* INDOPCO, 56 Tax Notes 1110 (1992) (critical commentary on extension of *INDOPCO* to asbestos removal costs).

[41] *See supra* note 36.

[42] At least a few academics have come down firmly in support of the decision. *See, e.g.,* Sheryl Stratton, *ABA Tax Section Meeting:* INDOPCO *Issues Continue to Perplex Practitioners and IRS*, 71 Tax Notes 992 (1996) (noting that decision is supported by Professors Calvin Johnson and Marty McMahon).

Consider, for example, *PNC Bankcorp v. Commissioner.*[43] The tax-payer was in the business of loaning out money. Its loans were its primary assets; the loans generated interest income, which was its primary source of income. The cost of each loan obviously included the amount received by the borrower. For financial accounting purposes, the cost of the loan included internal and external costs associated with obtaining the loans, processing the loan, and checking the credit of the borrower (collectively, "processing costs"). These processing costs were capitalized and recovered as the loan was amortized. PNC deducted the costs for tax purposes and the Service disallowed the deduction, taking the position on audit and in litigation that the costs were appropriately treated as part of the costs of the loan, recoverable through amortization as the loan was repaid.

As a matter of economic logic, the Service's argument is irrefutable. The processing costs were as much a part of the cost of each loan as the cash received by the borrower. Moreover, neither of the bugaboos of capitalization—the difficulty of dividing between present and future benefit and the lack of a clear amortization schedule—were present here. The taxpayer argued that the recurring nature of the expense, together with the short-term benefit of some of the processing costs (such as the credit report), made the expense deductible. These arguments were rejected in a brief Tax Court opinion, which held the processing costs were part of the asset created, and that the recurring nature of the expense was irrelevant.

The Third Circuit opinion is foreshadowed by its opening section, which asks in an exasperated manner why the Service has bothered to pursue the issue and then answers its own question:

> The costs that the banks seek to deduct are the internal and external costs that they incur in connection with the issuance of loans to their customers. These costs, discussed in more detail below, are a routine part of the banks' daily business, and the services procured with these outlays have been integral to the basic execution of the banking business for decades.

> The general contours of banks' involvement in making loans have not changed dramatically in recent years, and the relevant sections of the Tax Code have remained largely unchanged. Histori-cally, the costs at issue have been deductible in the year that they are incurred; however, the Commissioner rejected this tax treatment by PNC. Why is the Commissioner now insisting upon capitalization of these costs?

---

[43] 212 F.3d 822 (3d Cir.2000).

There are two relatively recent developments that appear to have emboldened the Internal Revenue Service to pursue capitalization of such costs. One of these developments is the Supreme Court's opinion in *INDOPCO* ... *INDOPCO*, which signaled that the Supreme Court's previously announced tests for capitalization were not exhaustive, may well have been viewed by the IRS as a green light to seek capitalization of costs that had previously not been considered deductible.... This phenomenon has not escaped comment from observers.... Thus, *INDOPCO* ushered in an era of generally more aggressive IRS pursuit of capitalization....

The second development was the Financial Accounting Standards Board's promulgation of a new standard for ... loan origination costs....[44]

Given this introduction, the decision not surprisingly went in favor of the taxpayer. The court held that the processing costs were "associated with" but did not "create or enhance" the loan asset, that the costs did not comprise a "separate and distinct asset," and that shorn of their incorporation in the loan asset, the costs did not provide future benefit. The opinion in *PNC* is confusingly worded and for that reason difficult to parse or clearly summarize.[45] But the decision relies upon the reading of *Lincoln Savings*—that capitalization is required only where a separate and distinct asset is created—expressly rejected in *INDOPCO*.[46]

The *PNC* court did not, and could not, state that it had simply decided not to follow *INDOPCO*. Instead, it provided (or attempted to provide) a reading of the case consistent with its decision: "[W]e must remember that the future benefit analysis adopted in *INDOPCO* is not meant as a talismanic, bright-line test.... Rather, the *INDOPCO* analysis demonstrates the contextual, case-by-case approach to determining whether an expenditure better fits under the "ordinary and necessary" language of § 162(a) or the "permanent improvements or betterments" language of § 263(a)."[47]

A more nuanced—and responsible—interpretation of *INDOPCO* is

---

[44] *Id.* at 824–25.

[45] The decision also retains a key assertion—that the recurring nature of the expense ensures clear reflection of income—that, in present value terms, is clearly incorrect. A useful article discussing this and other aspects of the case is Jennifer Giannattasio & Jeremy Blank, *Wells Fargo (The Norwest Reversal)—Is it Just the Eye of the Storm*, 90 Tax Notes 107 (2001).

[46] The *PNC* court showed its approval of the "separate and distinct asset" test in other ways as well. For example, the court stated that, in its opinion, the line of cases following *Lincoln Savings* and preceding *INDOPCO*, in which expenditures were held deductible because they did not comprise separate and distinct assets, were still good law.

[47] 212 F.3d at 834.

found in *Wells Fargo v. Commissioner*.[48] The taxpayer had merged into what is now Wells Fargo & Co. The friendly merger required the best efforts of the taxpayer's employees. The Service sought to capitalize a portion of those employees' salaries.[49] The Tax Court, relying on *INDOPCO*, upheld the Service's position.

The Eight Circuit reversed. In a closely worded opinion, replete with mathematical symbols, the Eighth Circuit held that the deductibility of an outlay that produced a long-lived intangible or future benefit is a function of the relationship between the outlay and the benefit. Outlays that are directly linked to the future benefit must be capitalized; outlays that are indirectly linked may be deducted. Here, the Eighth Circuit ruled that the outlays had their origin in an employment contract, which was entered into prior to the merger, did not contemplate a merger and was not changed in any way due to the merger. The Eighth Circuit distinguished this situation from that in *INDOPCO*, where the outlay was made in direct anticipation of the upcoming merger.

It is easy to criticize the indirect/direct test—also referred to as the "origin of claim" test. It places weight on a determination that often—perhaps usually—will be difficult to make. The test will sometimes yield what seems to be the wrong answer. Suppose, for example, that the employment relationship began on January 2 and that between January 9 and the end of the year the employees worked exclusively on the merger. Does the fact that the merger was not anticipated on January 2 make the relationship between salaries and the merger indirect? Would the answer change if on January 2 the merger were thought likely? Unlikely but possible? The main virtue of the test is that it to some extent reflects and clarifies existing law, and that it offers one way to avoid the difficult issues raised under a pure income tax approach. What is important for our purposes is that the test owes nothing to the decision or opinion in *INDOPCO*.

The Bureaucratic Response

In general, one assumes that the actions of a bureaucracy's agents reflect the wishes of upper-level management—in this case, that the actions of the IRS agents in aggressively pursuing capitalization after *INDOPCO* reflected the instructions of their superiors. This common-sensical notion is supported here by the long period of time in which agents were said to have pursued the issue and by the fact that their actions on audit were in at least many cases supported in litigation.

---

[48] 224 F.3d 874 (8th Cir.2000).

[49] The Service also sought to capitalize a portion of the taxpayer's legal fees. The court's analysis of that issue revolved around the date on which the legal fees were incurred.

In fact, a persistent feature on the political landscape has been the apparent split between the field offices and agents, on the one hand, and the Treasury Department Office of Tax Policy and the upper echelons of the Service, on the other hand.[50] Complaints against government policy have almost without exception stated the problem as one of aggressive agents. Service or Treasury policy has been criticized primarily for its failure to constrain agents. The Clinton Administration, which took office shortly after the decision, announced that it did not believe that the decision broke new ground, issued a number of rulings that confirmed the deductibility of certain expenses,[51] solicited comments on how it might address issues raised by the decision,[52] and in a field service advice told a regional counsel's office to de-emphasize *INDOPCO* in arguing that expenses incurred in contract modification should be capitalized.[53] "We didn't try to capitalize (pun intended) on the decision, didn't see *INDOPCO* as justifying the capitalization of everything with future benefit, and went way out of our way to make that clear," said Glen Kohl, Deputy Assistant Secretary of the Treasury during that period.[54]

The Treasury Department in the (George W.) Bush Administration went even further. It approved additional pro-taxpayer interpretations of *INDOPCO*,[55] bemoaned the failure of IRS examiners to follow the constrained interpretations of *INDOPCO* put forth in revenue rulings,[56] and commented favorably upon a proposal put forth by the industry-comprised *INDOPCO* Coalition.[57] More significantly, in 2002, it issued an advance notice of proposed rulemaking that conceded most of the contentious issues arising out of *INDOPCO*.[58] The proposed rule would allow

---

[50] *See* Sherly Stratton, INDOPCO *Conference*, 86 Tax Notes 912, 913 (2000).

[51] *See, e.g.,* Rev. Rul. 2001–4, 2001–3 I.R.B. 295; Rev. Rul. 2000–7, 2000–31 I.R.B. 138; Rev. Rul. 2000–4, 2000–4 I.R.B. 331; Rev. Rul. 94–12, 1994–1 C.B. 36; Rev. Rul. 92–80, 1992–2 C.B. 57.

[52] *See* Stratton, supra note 34.

[53] *IRS Field Service Advice:* INDOPCO *Shouldn't Be Main Argument for Expense Capitalization*, 82 Tax Notes 982 (1999).

[54] Unfortunately, states Kohl, neither the Administration nor anyone else could develop a comprehensive approach to the issue: "People would say you've issued all these great rulings saying that things are deductible. Can you get us something principled? So we set out a request for comments and got absolutely nothing that even purported to be a generalized approach to the problem." Quotes are taken from a conversation with this author.

[55] *See, e.g.,* Rev. Rul. 2001–4, 2001–3 I.R.B. 295.

[56] *See* Sheppard, *supra* note 3, at 321–22.

[57] *See* Amy Hamilton, *Treasury Official Assesses* INDOPCO *Coalition Proposal*, 93 Tax Notes 745 (2001).

[58] *See IRS Describes Possible Rules on Capitalizing Costs of Intangibles*, 94 Tax Notes 453 (2002).

the deduction of employee compensation and other transaction costs associated with the creation of intangibles and suggests that a blanket deduction for recurring costs might be appropriate. The rule would allow deductions for costs incurred in connection with loan processing (thus abandoning the theory on which the government had argued *PNC Bancorp*) and for costs of employee compensation incurred in connection with corporate restructuring (thus abandoning the theory on which the government had argued *Wells Fargo Corp*). The proposed rule is widely seen as sympathetic to, and consistent with, the *INDOPCO* Coalition proposal.[59]

Whose Fault Is It, Anyway?

The discussion thus far has portrayed *INDOPCO* as a failure and Justice Blackmun as somewhat of a bumbler, tax-wise. He adds dicta to his opinion in *Lincoln Savings* that produces a meaningless search for "distinct" assets. In *INDOPCO*, he corrects his *Lincoln Savings* opinion but adds dicta that gives the government a victory that its appointed officers did not want and eventually undid. This portrait is accurate but incomplete. In Blackmun's defense, he issued the correct holding, not just in *Lincoln Savings* and *INDOPCO*, but also in the other cases mentioned—*General Bancshares*, *Idaho Power*, and *Newark Morning Ledger*. Moreover, it wasn't that Blackmun said anything wrong, even in dicta—just that he failed to anticipate how others would read his decisions. Blackmun was presented with a difficult task. As noted at the beginning of this chapter, determining the right degree of capitalization—and the right amortization schedule—for each business expenditure is impossible. The best that can be done is to come up with some workable rules that balance administrative ease against the distorted effects inherent in misclassifying an expenditure (as a deductible expense or capital investment) or adopting the wrong amortization schedule. It would have taken a judge with the rhetorical savvy of Federal Reserve Chair Alan Greenspan to come up with language that was interpreted in the right way so as to push the system towards that elusive balance.

It would have been better, to be sure, had Blackmun said less. One of the ironies of the case is that it was his knowledge of the tax law and his own intellect that gave him confidence to say as much as he did. A lesser judge would have said less and done better. But it would have been better even still had the question not been presented to the Court. Why not instead leave the issue to the other branches of government? The appropriate balance clearly requires line-drawing across a large number of areas. Each line, in turn, requires some consideration of the administrative costs involved and the distorted effect of getting things

---

[59] *See* David Lupi–Sher, *Proposed IRS Capitalization Rule Raises Questions*, 94 Tax Notes 804 (2002).

wrong. No jurist, however well informed, is equipped to perform such a task. Indeed, the nature of judicial decision-making precludes resolving these issues through case law. Why, then, was the case litigated, and why were such one-sided arguments made by the government in litigation?

What makes this question particularly interesting, perhaps, is that the litigation was brought by an administration whose ideological position ran counter to the case and counter to the arguments the government made in the case. During the period in question, the Republican Party campaigned, and to some extent voted, to reduce taxes in general, to reduce taxes on capital, and to reduce corporate income taxes. The Republican Party also led the charge—at least in rhetoric—against complex tax rules. *INDOPCO*, of course, runs against all of these themes. Capitalization requires an allocation of expenditures between short-and long-lived benefits and raises nearly insoluble amortization issues: it is undoubtedly more complicated than deduction. Capitalization moves the law closer to a pure income tax, and in so doing, increases the tax burden on capital and corporations.

Indeed, it is not just that one would expect the appointed officials in the Bush Administration to have reacted to *INDOPCO* with dismay; many of those officials have in fact publicly criticized the decision and its aftermath. Fred Goldberg, who was the Chief Counsel and Commissioner of the Internal Revenue Service during much of the period in which the case was litigated, has served as co-chair of the *INDOPCO* Coalition. Kenneth Gideon, the Assistant Secretary of the Treasury for Tax Policy during the later part of the Administration, used the opportunity of the Woodworth Lectures to bemoan both the decision and its affect on revenue agents.[60] In informal conversation, if not public statement, most of the other leading appointees express similar positions as to the case and its consequences. So what happened?

The answer—anticipated I am sure by those who have spent time in Washington—is multi-faceted. First, the ideology of the Bush appointees was not shared by the agency's career employees, and there were many more of the latter than the former. Career employees were less likely to worry about overburdening capital, more attracted to a pure income tax, and more likely to resolve the tension between taxpayer and government in favor of the government. The INDOPCO audit and the early years of litigation would have been managed by career employees. Only a few appointees would have been aware of, let alone focused on, the matter until it came to the Third Circuit on appeal.

The appointees who looked at the case might not have seen anything amiss. As noted earlier, under tax theory or then-present law, INDOPCO's payment to Morgan Stanley should have been capitalized. It

---

[60] *See* Gideon, *supra* note 37, at 1003.

created long-term benefit, posed no allocation issues, could not be characterized as ordinary and necessary, and was not recurring. The problem then was not the government's position on audit or the Supreme Court's holding, but the ambiguous and expansive language in a Supreme Court opinion, as interpreted by agents, and the actions of agents as interpreted by industry and the tax community. It would have taken a great deal of foresight for anyone who was informed of the case to anticipate this string of events. Finally, in part because they were so outnumbered, appointees who had qualms about the case would have had to balance those concerns against the intra-agency political ill created by quashing the matter.

By the time the Court granted *certiorari*, the case had risen in importance and it would be reasonable to suppose that the government had thought out the implications of its position. Here, the structure of arguments made on brief and in oral argument have to be considered mistaken. The government argued flatly that an income tax required capitalization and did not acknowledge difficulties with enforcing this view of the income tax. The government might have both maximized its chance of winning the case and limited the danger of an overly expansive opinion by stating what the case did not involve difficult allocation issues or recurrent or ordinary and necessary expenditures. The government might have also down-played its pure income tax arguments and/or beefed up its reliance on existing precedent. Had the government taken this tack, it seems likely that the opinion would have restated the government's narrow interpretation of the matter. Of course, the government might have gone further, explicitly eschewing greater ambition; it might have issued announcements as to its position at the time of the litigation or victory; or it might have dropped the case altogether.

Part of the reason this was not done was described above: the unhappy outcome of the case was not anticipated. More speculatively, the Treasury may have been hurt by the peculiar rules that transfer control of Supreme Court cases to the Solicitor General's Office of the Justice Department. Attorneys with that office write the briefs and argue the cases. Those attorneys invariably consult with officials in the Office of Tax Policy or in the Service, and the briefs are sent to the General Counsel and Chief Counsel before filing. But there is a world of difference between drafting and signing off on a document. A consequence that goes unnoticed when reviewing a brief someone else has written may become apparent when faced with the more intense responsibility of writing the brief. It is possible that had the Treasury, rather than the Justice Department, handled the case before the Court, it would have realized that its arguments on the theoretically correct treatment of an expenditure might give it a victory it did not wish.

Conclusion

Where does all this leave us? The opinion in *INDOPCO* looks best to those who favor a pure income tax. Even for those with that view, however, *INDOPCO* must be seen as a failure. It is confusingly worded, and its attempt (if that motive can be ascribed to a decision) to move the law in the direction of a pure income tax did not succeed. For those with other priorities (e.g., cash-flow tax, efficiency), the failure is even more clear cut.

Some of the responsibility for the failure rests on Justice Blackmun's shoulders. He confused the tax world with unnecessary dicta in *Lincoln Savings* and then repeated the mistake in *INDOPCO*. His opinions would have been better had they been shorter. Paradoxically, they also might have been better had they been longer, with greater clarity as to the standards for deductibility.

The bureaucracy contributed to the failure, though not in any way that implicates any one set of individuals or is easily remedied. Career employees interpreted Blackmun's ambiguous opinion in an overly aggressive manner. Not much can be done, however, about the split between career employees and political appointees. It will sometimes occur and is not in all cases undesirable. Sometimes the law will be best served by the interpretation of the career employees rather than political appointees. The Solicitor General's Office seems anachronistic—a throwback to a time when an educated lawyer was capable of handling cases in any area—but that office no doubt has its defenders. More to the point, it is uncertain whether the government's arguments would have been any different had the case been argued "in-house" or whether different arguments would have led to a different opinion.

Ultimately, the problem with the opinion is rooted in the income tax itself, which requires that outlays that provide long-term benefit be capitalized, rather than deducted, and that each class of capitalized outlay be amortized over its useful life. The capitalization and amortization rules are difficult to apply to outlays that produce or enhance intangible assets. It is hard to determine whether an asset will produce long-term benefit, and amortization of intangible assets is purely speculative. Many outlays, such as salaries, will go toward the creation of multiple intangible assets, thus further increasing the difficulty of the allocation and amortization determinations.

What of the future? Outlays associated with human capital, intellectual property and service businesses are certain to increase—in absolute terms and as a proportion of total outlays. This will make the proper administration of the capitalization requirement even more difficult.

7

George K. Yin

The Story of *Crane*: How a Widow's Misfortune Led to Tax Shelters

Beulah Crane's story is a tax classic. Something about this widow's predicament, a rather unremarkable one given the time of her story, stirred the government to achieve what many believe to be its most pyrrhic tax victory. The precedent it urged upon the Supreme Court is said to have "laid the foundation stone of most tax shelters."[1] And in the process, the Court crafted the "most famous footnote in tax history."[2] This chapter describes Mrs. Crane's story, explains how it came about, and considers whether it deserves all of this notoriety.

Background

In 1924, Beulah Crane's husband, William, purchased for roughly $1 million the De Witt Clinton apartment house located at 395 Clinton Ave., Brooklyn, NY. A picture of the apartment house reveals a distinguished looking six-story brick-and-stone building that was recently completed at the time of Mr. Crane's purchase. The 182–room building potentially housed 30 families and was described as located in one of the most fashionable sections of Brooklyn. According to an advertisement, it offered "exceptionally large light rooms," "large foyer halls," "day and night elevator service," and "individual telephone service." Mr. Crane owned and operated this apartment house as an investment until his death in 1932. In addition, in 1927, he purchased a large, residential

---

[1] Boris I. Bittker, *Tax Shelters, Nonrecourse Debt, and the* Crane *Case*, 33 Tax L. Rev. 277, 283 (1978).

[2] *Id.* at 277.

waterfront estate in Westchester County, N.Y. known as "Shore Acres," where one of Mrs. Crane's activities was to host charity bridge events.

The economic shock of 1929 apparently took its toll on the Crane family's finances. When Mr. Crane died in 1932, his estate included about $360,000 in gross assets but only about $80,000 in net assets. The principal asset of the estate was the Clinton Ave. property, which had lost about three-quarters of its value since its acquisition eight years earlier and was worth about $262,000. Furthermore, the property was encumbered at that time by a $255,000 mortgage and a liability to pay $7,000 in accrued interest.

Mrs. Crane was the executrix and sole beneficiary of her husband's estate. Shortly after his death, Mrs. Crane contacted the Bowery Savings Bank, the mortgagee of the Clinton Ave. property, to advise it of her inability to repay any of the mortgage principal or accrued interest. She explained, however, that the property was "of vital importance to me." The bank agreed to permit her to continue operating the property if she would remit to the bank each month the net rental payments (after operating expenses), which were applied to the payment of interest.

The estate was finally settled at the end of 1936 and all of its assets, including the Clinton Ave. property, were distributed to Mrs. Crane. She took the property subject to the debts encumbering it but without any personal obligation to repay them. Thus, this debt was "nonrecourse" to Mrs. Crane. The mortgagee retained the right to enforce its claim for repayment by foreclosing on the Clinton Ave. property, which served as security for the claim, but had no right to proceed against Mrs. Crane personally or against her other assets if the proceeds from the foreclosure sale turned out to be insufficient to cover the full amount owed. She continued operating the property for two more years but got further and further behind in the payment of interest. Indeed, the mortgage debt was in default for the entire period the estate and Mrs. Crane owned the property. Eventually, in late 1938, the bank threatened foreclosure. To avoid such action, Mrs. Crane sold the property, subject to the still outstanding $255,000 mortgage and an almost $16,000 liability for interest in arrears, to the Avenue C Realty Corp. for $3,000. According to the contract of sale, the $3,000 was "for the equity conveyed by the seller." Throughout the period the estate and Mrs. Crane owned and operated the property, they reported the rentals as gross income and claimed deductions for interest, taxes, operating expenses, and depreciation. The total depreciation deductions claimed during this period was $25,500.

The tax law at the time required taxpayers to calculate their gain or loss from the sale of property in virtually the same way as they do today. Section 111(a) of the Revenue Act of 1938, the predecessor to current

§ 1001(a), provided that gain from the sale or other disposition of property was equal to the excess of the "amount realized" over the taxpayer's "adjusted basis" in the property, and loss was equal to the excess of adjusted basis over amount realized. Section 111(b) of the 1938 Act, identical to existing § 1001(b), provided that the "amount realized" was equal to the sum of any money received plus the fair market value of property received other than money. Similar to existing §§ 1012 and 1014(a)(1), § 113(a)(5) of the 1938 Act defined the "basis" of property as the taxpayer's cost, except that the basis of property acquired by bequest, devise, or inheritance was equal to the fair market value of the property at the time of acquisition. The regulations specified that the pertinent valuation time was the date of the decedent's death. Finally, similar to §§ 1011(a) and 1016(a)(2), § 113(b)(1)(B) of the 1938 Act defined "adjusted basis" as the taxpayer's initial basis as adjusted for, among other things, the deduction for depreciation to the extent allowed but not less than the amount allowable.

On her 1938 income tax return, Mrs. Crane reported a $2,500 capital gain from the sale of her equity interest in the Clinton Ave. property. Her position was that she had inherited and then sold a mere equity in the property whose value was zero at the time of her husband's death. Accordingly, she claimed that she received a zero basis in the equity interest. Her gain from the sale was therefore equal to the $3,000 purchase price, less $500 in sale expenses, and less the zero basis in the interest sold, or net gain of $2,500.

The Commissioner asserted that Mrs. Crane had inherited and sold the entire interest in the Clinton Ave. building and land, and not just the equity. Therefore, the taxpayer's initial basis in the property was $262,000, the fair market value of the apartment house at the time of Mr. Crane's death. According to the Commissioner, the taxpayer's amount realized from the sale was $257,500, representing the sum of the net cash received after sale expenses ($2,500) plus the principal amount of the mortgage indebtedness encumbering the property at the time of sale ($255,000). The Commissioner then allocated both the amount realized and basis between the land and the building, and adjusted the building's basis by the allowable amount ($28,000) of depreciation during the almost seven years the building was owned and operated by the estate and the taxpayer, to determine that she had a $24,000 gain from sale of the building and a $500 loss from sale of the land. The Commissioner asserted that the $24,000 gain should be reported as ordinary income and the $500 loss was a capital loss:

Commissioner's position	Entire property	Land	Building
1. Amount realized	$257,500	$54,500	$203,000
2. Initial basis	262,000	55,000	207,000
3. Basis adjustments: depreciation	28,000	–0–	28,000
4. Adjusted basis (2–3)	234,000	55,000	179,000
5. Gain (loss) (1–4)	$23,500	($500)	$24,000

Although the tax positions of the parties might initially seem to be quite different, in fact they were very similar. If we ignore the character of the income or loss recognized by Mrs. Crane, an issue she ultimately did not contest, and therefore disregard the Commissioner's allocation between the land and building, the similarity of the two positions can be easily shown. The positions were identical with respect to the *total amount* of income or loss that Mrs. Crane was required to report as a result of inheriting, owning, and then disposing of the property. The only difference was in the *time* the tax items had to be reported.

To see this, let us simplify the facts in slight ways by assuming that Mrs. Crane (1) received her inheritance of the Clinton Ave. property in 1932 when it was worth $262,000; (2) took the property subject to a mortgage debt with a principal amount of $262,000 but without any personal obligation to repay the debt; (3) owned and operated the property during the next almost seven years, with her income from the property exactly equaling her expenses except for total depreciation deductions of $28,000; and (4) sold the property subject to the still existing $262,000 mortgage debt and received net cash proceeds of $2,500 from her buyer.

These simplified facts indicate that, as a purely economic matter, Mrs. Crane obtained a slight benefit from owning the property. During her period of ownership, the income from the property exactly equaled her cash expenses from operating the property. Furthermore, she paid nothing for the property and received $2,500 cash upon its sale. Thus, regardless of whether she is viewed as having acquired a mere equity in the property or the land and building, Mrs. Crane obtained a $2,500 economic benefit from having owned the property.

But how much *taxable* income or gain had to be reported by her based on the position of the parties in her case? As shown by the following table, the parties were in agreement that under the simplified facts, Mrs. Crane was required to report net taxable income of $2,500 from having owned the property, the same amount as her economic benefit:

Comparison of tax positions (simplified facts)	Mrs. Crane	Commissioner
1. Amount realized	$2,500	$264,500
2. Initial basis	-0-	262,000
3. Depreciation	-0-	28,000
4. Adjusted basis (2–3)	-0-	234,000
5. Taxable gain on sale (1–4)	2,500	30,500
6. Net taxable income from property (5–3)	$2,500	$2,500

Under the taxpayer's position, her initial basis in the equity was zero, its fair market value in 1932 (line 2). She claimed that during her years of ownership, she was not entitled to any depreciation deductions because her starting basis was zero (line 3).[3] Finally, at sale, her amount realized was $2,500, which therefore represented her gain from the sale (lines 1 and 5). Her net taxable income from owning the property was therefore $2,500 (line 6).

Under the Commissioner's position, Mrs. Crane's initial basis in the entire property was $262,000, its fair market value in 1932 (line 2). She was entitled to claim depreciation deductions of $28,000 during her years of ownership, thereby reducing her basis to $234,000 at the time of sale (line 3 and 4). Her amount realized from the sale was the $2,500 in cash plus the $262,000 mortgage debt, or $264,500 (line 1). Thus, her gain from the sale was $30,500 (line 5). Taking into account, however, the $28,000 in depreciation deductions previously allowed to her (and disregarding the character of the items involved), the Commissioner's position also required her to report net taxable income of $2,500 from owning the property ($30,500 tax gain from sale less $28,000 depreciation deductions during ownership) (line 6).

Thus, the two parties were in agreement regarding the total amount of taxable income that Mrs. Crane had to report from owning the Clinton Ave. property. Where they differed, though, was in the time the income had to be reported. And here we see the first peculiar aspect of this case: the Commissioner advocated a position that permitted Mrs. Crane to defer reporting her income. Indeed, even though she recognized $2,500 of taxable income from owning the property, the Commissioner's position permitted her to claim $28,000 in tax *deductions* during her almost seven years of ownership. Only at the very *end* of her ownership of the property, when she sold it, did the Commissioner require her to report enough taxable gain ($30,500) to net out to $2,500 of taxable income after the prior depreciation deductions were taken into account.

---

[3] In her opening brief to the Supreme Court, the taxpayer conceded that the depreciation deductions actually taken by her and the estate had been wrongly permitted by the government. *See* Taxpayer's Brief at 10, 42.

By the same token, Mrs. Crane also seems to have taken the "wrong" position. Under her position, she was not allowed to claim any tax depreciation deductions at all during her years of ownership. Her taxable gain upon sale was less than the Commissioner's, but this difference would not ordinarily compensate her for the lost tax deductions when the timing of the items is taken into account.

So, why did the parties appear to argue against their interests? The answer, of course, lies in the fact that although Mrs. Crane's position did not allow her to take any depreciation deductions, she (and her husband's estate) had in fact taken such deductions during the period they owned the property. Thus, she was trying to have it both ways and "whipsaw" the government. She wanted the tax deductions when she owned the property and then wanted, in effect, to "forget" that she had taken them in calculating her taxable gain upon sale of the property. As we have seen, she experienced an economic benefit of $2,500 from owning the property, but her inconsistent tax positions entitled her to report a net tax *loss* of $23,000 ($25,500 tax depreciation deductions actually claimed less $2,500 taxable gain upon sale). The Commissioner, therefore, presumably took his position as a way to "remind" her of what she had forgotten and thereby prevent the attempted whipsaw. But in fact, as we shall see shortly, there was actually more going on in this case than all of this.

With this little background, let us turn to see how the courts resolved the dispute.

Prior Proceedings

The Tax Court

In a 14–2 decision, the Tax Court agreed with Mrs. Crane's calculation of gain.[4] Approaching the matter as a straightforward case of statutory interpretation, the court began by considering whether the taxpayer's "amount realized" included the principal amount of the mortgage encumbering the property, as contended by the government. It concluded that the statutory definition of that term—"the sum of any money received plus the fair market value of the property (other than money) received"—was simply not broad enough to include the mortgage debt, the repayment of which was not a personal liability to Mrs. Crane: "As she was never under any personal obligation to pay the mortgage debt she received no consideration whatever when she sold and conveyed the property subject to the mortgage, except the $2,500 in money. . . . Except for the $2,500, the petitioner thus did not receive money, or the

---

[4] Crane v. Commissioner, 3 T.C. 585 (1944) (reviewed by the court).

equivalent of money, or property (other than money)...."[5] The court contrasted Mrs. Crane's situation with one where the seller *is* personally liable for the debt; in the latter case, assumption of the liability by the buyer is the equivalent of money received by the seller.

The court then determined Mrs. Crane's initial basis in the property sold. As noted, the basis of property acquired by bequest, devise, or inheritance was equal to the fair market value of the property at the date of death. The court conceded that the fair market value of the apartment house was $262,000 at the time of Mr. Crane's death. Nevertheless, the court found that Mrs. Crane's basis must take into account the encumbrances, which were equal to this fair market value. Thus, her unadjusted basis in the property was zero.

The court recognized that normally a taxpayer's unadjusted basis is reduced by any deductions for depreciation to ascertain the taxpayer's adjusted basis. In Mrs. Crane's case, however, such an adjustment could not be made because her unadjusted basis was zero. Thus, the court concluded that her adjusted basis in the property was also zero, and that her calculation of $2,500 gain from the sale was correct. In view of its holding, the court disallowed the $3,200 depreciation deduction claimed by Mrs. Crane in 1938 but found it "unnecessary" to resolve the propriety of prior year depreciation deductions, presumably because those years were not before it.[6]

The Second Circuit

In a split decision, the Second Circuit reversed the Tax Court.[7] Writing for the majority, Judge Learned Hand began by considering Mrs. Crane's basis in the property sold. Right away, the Second Circuit identified a problem with her position. The court observed that "if the value of mortgaged property at the time of its devise is the value of the equity, as the taxpayer asserts, [then] the annual allowance for depreciation must be computed upon that value, and ... will represent only that fraction of the actual 'wear and tear' suffered by the buildings which their proportion of the equity bears to their actual value."[8] As the court further explained, the concern was not that she would be unable to claim a tax deduction for any actual loss in economic value. Rather, the concern was the *mistiming* of that deduction. The court noted that if the property really suffered economic depreciation, any purchaser would reduce the purchase price to reflect that loss, thereby giving the seller

---

[5] *Id.* at 590.

[6] *Id.* at 591. The taxpayer did not challenge the disallowance of her 1938 depreciation deduction on appeal.

[7] Commissioner v. Crane, 153 F.2d 504 (2d Cir.1945), *rev'g* 3 T.C. 585 (1944).

[8] *Id.* at 505.

the equivalent of a tax deduction at the time of sale. But a deduction at that time would still be inadequate to the seller: "Yet, so far as the mortgagor has not been allowed for depreciation by progressive installments, the allowance will all come in one year, which is clearly contrary to the intent of the act—Sec. 23(*l*)—and to the uniform practice of the Treasury."[9]

Judge Hand seems to have envisioned the following scenario: Taxpayer inherits a building worth $200,000 but subject to a nonrecourse debt of that amount, and the building proceeds to depreciate in value to $140,000. If taxpayer's depreciation allowance is determined based on her equity in the building (which is zero), then she is not permitted any depreciation deductions during her period of ownership. Her basis, therefore, remains at $200,000 and upon sale of the building for $140,000, she recognizes a tax loss of $60,000, an amount exactly equal to her economic loss. Still, taxpayer is treated inappropriately because she should have been able to deduct that loss in value in "installments," *i.e.*, when it actually occurred.

But this scenario is different from the position taken by Mrs. Crane. She claimed that she obtained a zero basis in her property and therefore was not entitled to any tax depreciation deductions when she inherited the property subject to a nonrecourse liability equal to its value. If during her period of ownership, the building had declined in value by, say, $60,000, with no change in the amount of the mortgage principal, she presumably would have received no cash upon disposition and therefore, under her position, would have had no amount realized. Thus, she would not have recognized any loss upon disposition either. The absence of any tax deduction at all to her to match the economic decline in value, however, would have been perfectly consistent with her position because she claimed that she did not suffer that loss—it was the mortgagee's. In short, Crane's position asked the court to decide whether she should obtain any tax deductions at all for economic losses exceeding her equity in the property. Judge Hand failed to address this point; instead, he seems to have assumed that she should get such deductions, with his only concern being that they would be allowed in one lump amount and too late.

Judge Hand then noted that if the taxpayer's basis for depreciation is determined by the taxpayer's equity interest in the property, there would have to be "repeated recomputations ... introduc[ing] administrative complication and confusion extremely undesirable."[10] He concluded from these points that "the right 'basis' for depreciation is the actual

---

[9] *Id.* Section 23(*l*) of the 1938 Act authorized the deduction for depreciation.

[10] *Id.*

value of the buildings."[11] In other words, her starting basis in the property for purposes of depreciation was $262,000.

Having determined the taxpayer's *un*adjusted basis, Judge Hand appeared to turn to the question of "adjusted basis." But here, his opinion took a bit of a detour. For immediately following his conclusion about Mrs. Crane's starting basis, he began a new paragraph with three very puzzling sentences. Quoted below is the final sentence of the paragraph just discussed followed by the three puzzling new ones:

> We cannot doubt ... that the right "basis" for depreciation is the actual value of the buildings.
>
> If so, unless the "adjusted value" of the buildings is not computed upon the same value in finding the subtrahend in the equation of gain, the taxpayer gets a double deduction. By hypothesis he will have been allowed deductions seriatim, based upon the actual value of the buildings; and he will in addition have got a reduction in his gain to the extent to which actual "wear and tear" has reduced the selling price. Manifest justice demands that he must surrender one or the other, and the only question is whether the language of the statute forbids that result.[12]

Hand's mistaken use of the term, "adjusted value," and his cryptic reference to the "subtrahend in the equation of gain" make the precise meaning of the first sentence of the new paragraph almost impossible to decipher.[13] If we assume that he was referring to "adjusted *basis*," then one conceivable meaning is that "basis" for purposes of calculating gain must similarly reflect the actual value of the building, including adjustments for any decline in such value. To return to the earlier example, suppose after inheriting a $200,000 building subject to a nonrecourse debt of that amount, the taxpayer claims tax depreciation deductions of $60,000 equal to the economic depreciation in the building. Hand may have been saying that for purposes of determining the amount of gain or loss upon sale of the building, the basis of the building must also begin at $200,000 and then be adjusted downward to $140,000 to reflect the decline in value. Otherwise, taxpayer will receive a double deduction: the $60,000 in depreciation deductions (the "deductions seriatim") and *another* $60,000 loss deduction upon sale of the building for $140,000.

One cannot be certain whether this is what Hand was trying to say, but if it is, it seems quite irrelevant to the issue in the case. No one was

---

[11] *Id.*

[12] *Id.*

[13] A little refresher: The difference between two numbers is equal to the minuend less the subtrahend. Thus, in the "equation of gain" contained in § 1001(a), the minuend is "amount realized" and the subtrahend is "adjusted basis."

claiming that "basis" for purposes of depreciation and for calculating gain should not initially be the same, or that basis should not be adjusted in the manner described. Indeed, the statute mandated both outcomes.[14] (As a technical matter, the statute required basis to be adjusted for prior tax depreciation deductions and not for actual declines in value of property, but Judge Hand in this part of the opinion assumed that the two were the same.) Why then did Hand create and then reject this straw argument?

One possible answer is revealed by an unpublished, draft opinion prepared by him about five days after the oral argument and about six weeks prior to issuance of the court's decision.[15] As we have seen, Mrs. Crane *did* make an inconsistent argument. Her legal position did not entitle her to claim any depreciation deductions with respect to the Clinton Ave. property, yet she and her husband's estate had, in fact, claimed such deductions throughout their ownership of the property. Thus, she in effect claimed a $262,000 basis for purposes of determining depreciation but a zero basis for purposes of calculating gain. As noted, this inconsistency was not overlooked by the Tax Court, nor was it missed by Judge Hand. Indeed, this factor appears to have been a critical one in deciding his view of the case.[16] In the draft opinion, Judge Hand first recited the taxpayer's and Tax Court's technical argument based on the meaning of the terms, "basis" and "amount realized," and seemed to agree with it, but then he concluded otherwise:

> Verbally there is no escape from [the taxpayer's and the Tax Court's] position: the "amount realized" was the sum received; the "basis" was the value at the death of the devisor, and being zero nothing could be deducted from it. It is true that the taxpayer has either taken, or could have taken, deductions for depreciation and that, as the Commissioner argues, this results in a double allowance, if the buildings did in fact equally depreciate, for that lowered the sum received and with it the gain. Thus she received again an allowance for the same depreciation.

> I think this argument must prevail, in spite of the verbal difficulty. The taxpayer has already received the benefit of the

---

[14] *See* §§ 113(b)(1)(B) and 114(a) of the Revenue Act of 1938, comparable to existing §§ 1011(a) and 1016(a)(2).

[15] This draft, along with draft opinions prepared by the other members of the Second Circuit panel (Judges Frank and Swan), all dated within a day of one another, were found among Judge Hand's papers at the Harvard Law School library and are on file with the author. The timing of the drafts coming so soon after oral argument suggests that they represent the initial impression of the judges to the case.

[16] In her brief to the Supreme Court, Mrs. Crane indicated that "the point which really disturbed the Second Circuit" was the failure to disallow the prior depreciation deductions claimed by her and the estate. *See* Taxpayer's Brief at 41.

deduction (or she has been entitled to it, which is the same thing). She gets it again in the putative reduction of the "amount realized," which reflects that depreciation. Thus she gets a double deduction for the same depreciation. I cannot see the injustice of taking away the second deduction. . . .

We should not read too much into the meaning of this draft because the historical record is so incomplete. But the draft does seem to provide a possible explanation for the "double deduction" argument that appears in the Second Circuit's opinion. Mrs. Crane *was* attempting to obtain the equivalent of a double deduction (more precisely, a *single* deduction for which there was no equivalent loss in value) although not exactly in the way described in the opinion.

Interestingly, at the conclusion of his draft opinion, Judge Hand revealed how he would have prevented Mrs. Crane's "double deduction." Taking up a suggestion by the Commissioner, Hand indicated a willingness to consider negative basis: "I find no objection to deducting depreciation from zero; minus quantities merely indicate an operation, and in this case the statute demands the operation."[17] Under this view, Mrs. Crane would have started with a zero basis in her property interest (as she claimed) and then reduced the basis to a negative number to reflect the depreciation deductions actually taken during the years of operating the property. Thus, upon disposition, even if her amount realized were only $2,500, she would still have had to recognize gain equal to that amount plus the previously claimed depreciation deductions. But the court's opinion ultimately adopted a different approach.

Following this little detour, the court strung together three final points. First, the court stated that the mortgagee was a mere preferred creditor and was not the owner of the property. Rather, Mrs. Crane was the owner of the property who had the right to manage it, receive income from it, sell it, benefit from any increase in value, and suffer from any decrease in value at least until the value fell below the amount of the mortgage. Certain of these claims seem a little questionable, given the economic arrangement Mrs. Crane had worked out with the mortgagee to remit all rental payments after expenses.

Second, Judge Hand argued that Mrs. Crane *did* benefit when her buyer took the Clinton Ave. property from her subject to the mortgage debt: "When therefore upon a sale the mortgagor makes an allowance to the vendee of the amount of the lien, he secures a release from a charge upon his property quite as though the vendee had paid him the full price on condition that before he took title the lien should be cleared. . . . "[18] As

---

[17] *See supra* note 15. The statutory provision "demanding" this reduction was presumably § 113(b)(1)(B) of the 1938 Act, comparable to existing § 1016(a)(2).

[18] Commissioner v. Crane, 153 F.2d 504, 506 (2d Cir.1945).

Hand noted, had Mrs. Crane's purchaser paid cash in this manner, there would have been no question that her amount realized from the sale included the full amount of the cash. Curiously, this analogy, which Hand did not explain further, is the closest statement in the Second Circuit's opinion to its holding that Mrs. Crane's amount realized must include the full amount of the nonrecourse debt.

Finally, Judge Hand conceded that the court's holding might subject a taxpayer in Mrs. Crane's situation to some hardship. Such a taxpayer may have to pay "a tax upon a gain which is out of all proportion to what he in fact receives; . . . a tax which may indeed be greater than the whole consideration received."[19] He offered two responses to this complaint. First, he suggested that the consequence was optional to the taxpayer and arose only when the taxpayer continued to own the property and tried to profit from its sale: "He is not charged with gain except upon a 'sale or other disposition' of the property—[§ 1001(a)]— and *if he abandons it to the mortgagee there is no gain*."[20]

This last statement is very surprising because it seems so sharply inconsistent with other parts of his opinion. Why could not an abandonment be treated the same as a transfer for cash conditioned upon a clearing of the mortgage lien? Should the seller's tax consequences be affected so dramatically by whether or not the buyer happens to pay a little consideration? And if the taxpayer recognizes no gain upon abandonment, despite the prior claiming of depreciation deductions, does not the taxpayer thereby obtain the equivalent of a "double deduction"?

Judge Hand added a second response at the very end of the Second Circuit's opinion. He stated that taxpayers in Mrs. Crane's situation were being taxed simply to take into account prior advantages they obtained from depreciation allowances.

Neither of the other two judges on the panel chose to elaborate much on their view of the case. Judge Frank joined the majority without offering a separate opinion and Judge Swan simply dissented for the reasons stated in the Tax Court's opinion. Interestingly, from their draft opinions written shortly after the oral argument, we know that they *both* were prepared at that time to side with Mrs. Crane and to affirm the Tax Court's holding. Had they stuck with their initial reactions, Judge Hand would have been in the minority.[21] In their drafts, both judges recognized

---

[19] *Id.*

[20] *Id.* (emphasis added).

[21] Unfortunately, I have been unable to discover anything in the papers of either Judges Hand or Frank that might help to explain this change of heart on the part of Judge Frank. According to Professor Gunther, the friendship between Judges Hand and Frank was "one of the court's most affectionate and intimate." Gerald Gunther, *Learned Hand: The Man and the Judge* 524 (A.A. Knopf 1994).

that a holding in Mrs. Crane's favor permitted her whipsaw to occur but neither thought that it could properly be prevented in the case before it. As stated in Judge Swan's draft: "I think the Tax Court was right in holding her basis zero. Hence she was entitled to no adjustment for depreciation under [§ 1016(a)(2)]. Apparently she and the testator claimed depreciation in earlier years. It was a mistake to allow it but I don't see on what theory that can give her income in 1938."

The Supreme Court Decision

On April 14, 1947, in a 6–3 decision, the Supreme Court affirmed the Second Circuit.[22] Writing for the majority, Chief Justice Vinson determined Mrs. Crane's initial and adjusted basis in the Clinton Ave. property and her amount realized upon its sale in 1938.

Initial Basis and Adjusted Basis

The Court began its analysis by stating that Mrs. Crane's unadjusted basis in the property was "[l]ogically" the first matter to determine. Although the Court may well have believed that logic required consideration of the basis question first, there was also a strategic explanation to this point of departure. Each of the courts, as well as both of the parties, understood the need for a consistent interpretation of basis and amount realized. Yet the statutory language and the precedents were quite favorable to the taxpayer's interpretation of the latter term. It is not obvious that the amount of an unassumed mortgage should properly be treated as either "money received" or the "fair market value of the property (other than money) received," and two Circuit Courts had disagreed with the Second Circuit on this point.[23] In contrast, "basis" presented a murkier question for the taxpayer because it was linked to the nature of the property interest she acquired. It is not surprising, then, that the taxpayer's briefs to the Second Circuit and the Supreme Court consistently discussed the "amount realized" issue first whereas the government's briefs always started with the question of "basis." Moreover, the Tax Court resolved the "amount realized" question with little discussion of "basis," and the Second Circuit did essentially the opposite.

At various points in her briefs, the taxpayer tried to finesse this problem by suggesting that "amount realized" was the *only* thing that had to be decided. This position might seem strange since the equation for gain or loss clearly involves a comparison of amount realized and

---

[22] Crane v. Commissioner, 331 U.S. 1 (1947), *aff'g* 153 F.2d 504 (2d Cir.1945).

[23] *See* Hilpert v. Commissioner, 151 F.2d 929, 933 (5th Cir.1945); Polin v. Commissioner, 114 F.2d 174, 176 (3d Cir.1940).

basis. But the taxpayer asserted that gain from the sale of property *cannot exceed* the amount realized, and she conceded that she had the lowest possible basis, or zero.[24] Hence, she argued that the "amount realized" *was* the gain in her case. As a technical matter, her statement was correct only if one accepts the impossibility of negative basis, but neither of the lower courts had shown any willingness to venture into that territory. In any event, the Court refused to follow the taxpayer's invitation to ignore "basis."[25] To those who were closely following this case, the Court's decision to begin with the basis question essentially announced that the taxpayer had lost the case.

Because § 113(a)(5) of the 1938 Act provided that the basis of property acquired by bequest, devise, or inheritance was the fair market value of such property at the time of acquisition, the Court indicated that the basis question depended upon the meaning of the term, "property," in this provision. For several reasons, the Court concluded that the term should be construed as meaning the entire Clinton Ave. land and building and not the mere equity interest. First, three standard dictionaries defined the term in that way and, according to the Court, "the words of statutes . . . should be interpreted where possible in their ordinary, everyday senses."[26]

The Court's endorsement of an "ordinary, everyday" construction of statutory words is a bit strange given its subsequent, strained interpretation of the words "amount realized."[27] More importantly, in footnote 30 of its opinion, the Court seemed to nullify the entire significance of this first point: "Obviously we are not considering a situation in which a taxpayer has acquired and sold an equity of redemption only, *i.e.*, a right to redeem the property without a right to present possession. In that situation, the right to redeem would itself be the aggregate of the taxpayer's rights and would undoubtedly constitute "property" within the meaning of s. 113(a). . . ."[28] But if "property" for purposes of

---

[24] *See* Taxpayer's Brief at 13; Taxpayer's Reply Brief at 1, 4.

[25] In his draft opinion, Judge Frank of the Second Circuit explicitly accepted the taxpayer's argument: "[T]he taxable gain shall be the excess of 'the amount realized over the adjusted basis.' The gain cannot, therefore, exceed the 'amount realized.' . . . Here the 'amount realized' consisted solely of money in the amount of $2500 (after deducting expenses of the sale). Consequently, no matter what may be said to be the 'basis,' the taxable gain cannot be said to be more than $2500." *See supra* note 15.

[26] *Crane*, 331 U.S. at 6 (footnote omitted).

[27] One commentator has suggested that in view of how it interpreted "amount realized," the Court should have said, "[e]veryday meanings are of only secondary importance when construing the words of a tax statute and are very seldom given any weight when a more abstruse and technical meaning is available." D. Nelson Adams, *Exploring the Outer Boundaries of the* Crane *Doctrine: An Imaginary Supreme Court Opinion*, 21 Tax L. Rev. 159, 164 (1966).

[28] *Crane*, 331 U.S. at 10, n.30.

§ 113(a) of the 1938 Act is "undoubtedly" broad enough to encompass a mere equity of redemption, despite an "ordinary, everyday" meaning to the contrary, then what is the relevance of the latter usage? The parties, after all, were in disagreement as to the exact nature of the property interest acquired by Mrs. Crane, and the Court never resolved *that* question.

One reason for the inconsistency is that footnote 30 was added towards the end of the opinion preparation process. This fact is revealed by internal Supreme Court correspondence between Chief Justice Vinson and Justice Jackson, who wrote the dissenting opinion in *Crane*.[29] Footnote 30 was added in response to criticism contained in Justice Jackson's draft dissent,[30] the substance of which is reflected in the following note:

> I am unable to see that the widow was left anything but an equity of redemption. The mortgage was in default, the mortgage debt was as large as the value of the mortgaged property. The only thing that she had was an equity to redeem from forfeiture by paying the mortgage debt. But by deferring the forfeiture she managed to find a purchaser—and she sold him precisely what she inherited—an equity to redeem. She received a legal right—worth zero—she sold it at a profit.

> I am a little disturbed about defining "property" as used in the Revenue Act to exclude such a right. I think an equity of redemption such as we have here is a property right and is property as surely as the land and building were property. Such equity are bought and sold—and if they are not property I should wonder about leases and other intangibles.[31]

---

[29] This correspondence was found in the collection of Chief Justice Vinson's papers at the University of Kentucky and Justice Jackson's papers in the manuscript division of the Library of Congress; it is on file with the author.

[30] Among Chief Justice Vinson's papers is an unsigned and undated typewritten note stating, "I suggest that if you think it desirable to make some addition to our draft opinion in this case as an answer to the criticism made in Justice Jackson's dissent, the following sentence be added as a footnote...." Beneath the note is a draft of the text of footnote 30 with a few handwritten changes that conform it to the final version of the footnote. On March 24, 1947, about three weeks prior to the issuance of the final opinion, the Chief Justice circulated a "Memorandum for the Conference" in which he indicated his intention to add the text of footnote 30 to his draft opinion in the *Crane* case.

[31] This handwritten note was found among Justice Jackson's papers. *See supra* note 29. The note is marked *to* Mr. Justice Jackson, *from* The Chief Justice, and circulated March 3, 1947. However, due to the substance of the note and its wording, portions of which are identical to Justice Jackson's dissent, I believe that this note was prepared *by* Justice Jackson and may be a draft of his dissent. Professor Stark has interpreted this document in the same way. *See* Kirk J. Stark, *The Unfulfilled Tax Legacy of Justice Robert H. Jackson*, 54 Tax L. Rev. 171, 241 (2001).

As noted, footnote 30 concedes Justice Jackson's point regarding the breadth of the term, "property," but disagrees with his premise that she only acquired an equity of redemption. Nowhere in the opinion, however, did the Court explain *why* this premise was incorrect.

The Court further found that its interpretation of "property" was consistent with how the term was used in the estate tax law and regulations and in the rest of the 1938 Act and supporting regulations. The regulations under § 113(a)(5) linked the value of property acquired by bequest, devise, or inheritance to the appraised value of the property for estate tax purposes.[32] The Court, therefore, drew support for its construction of the term, "property," from the fact that Mrs. Crane had included the full $262,000 value of the land and building as part of her husband's gross estate. But this inclusion by Mrs. Crane—required by the law and regulations at the time—was simply a reporting mechanism; in another estate tax schedule, she reported the amount of the estate's liabilities, including the Clinton Ave. mortgage, and reduced the gross estate by the sum of these liabilities to ascertain the amount of the net estate. And the *taxable* amount of her husband's estate, of course, was the *net* amount, *i.e.*, the value of the equity interest (if any), not the gross amount. Thus, it is difficult to see how the reporting scheme mandated for estate tax purposes lent much support for the Court's construction.

Moreover, this estate tax reporting requirement was *changed* in subsequent years. Beginning in 1937, an estate was required to include only the value of the equity interest in the gross estate, with of course no further reduction for the amount of the lien, in cases where the estate was not liable for the amount of the debt.[33] This change was inapplicable to Mr. Crane's estate because he died in 1932. (It was also unclear whether he and his estate were liable for the debt.) But the mere existence of the change should have given the Court pause before relying upon the particular estate tax reporting methodology mandated by the Commissioner to help resolve its statutory construction question.

Finally, the Court found that construing "property" to mean "equity" was not in harmony with the depreciation provisions of the tax law. Although this reason was mentioned last, one senses that it was of primary importance to the Court in its determination of the taxpayer's basis. The Court began by making the same point made earlier by Judge Hand:

---

[32] *See* Reg. 101, Art. 113(a)(5)–1. The current regulations provide for the same linkage. *See* Reg. § 1.1014–1(a).

[33] *See* T.D. 4729, 1937–1 C.B. 284, 289, *amending* Art. 38 of Reg. 80 (1934 ed.). The Court was aware of this change. *See Crane*, 331 U.S. at 8, n.25.

> [I]f the mortgagor's equity were the [unadjusted] basis, ... and if the amount of the annual allowances were to be computed on that value, as would then seem to be required, they will represent only a fraction of the cost of the corresponding physical exhaustion, and any recoupment by the mortgagor of the remainder of that cost can be effected only by the reduction of his taxable gain in the year of sale.[34]

As with Judge Hand, the concern appears to be only the *mistiming* of the taxpayer's tax deduction. But the Court then proceeded to reject the taxpayer's position more directly:

> If, however, the amount of the annual allowances were to be computed on the value of the property, and then deducted from an equity basis, we would in some instances have to accept deductions from a minus basis or deny deductions altogether.[28]

---

[28] So long as the mortgagor remains in possession, the mortgagee can not take depreciation deductions, even if he is the one who actually sustains the capital loss, as [§ 167(a)] allows them only on property "used in the trade or business."[35]

Thus, the Court was concerned that under the taxpayer's view, *no* taxpayer would be entitled to claim the tax depreciation deductions as the property physically exhausted. Finally, the Court indicated that the taxpayer's position would create "a tremendous accounting burden" and would permit the mortgagor to "acquire control over the timing of his depreciation deductions."[36]

In this discussion, the Court was trying to make sure that its conclusion with respect to basis was compatible with the overall statutory scheme. But in so doing, it might be criticized for unduly emphasizing depreciation and placing the depreciation "cart" before the basis "horse." The Court seems to be making the following line of argument: (1) when property economically depreciates, someone must be entitled to claim tax depreciation deductions equal to the amount of economic depreciation; (2) because the law precludes the mortgagee from obtaining such deductions, then they must belong to the mortgagor; and (3) because negative basis is not possible, the mortgagor must begin with a large enough positive basis to support the later claim of depreciation

---

[34] *Id.* at 9 (footnotes omitted).

[35] *Id.* at 9–10.

[36] *Id.* at 10. The Commissioner argued in his brief that if the taxpayer's depreciable basis were her equity in the property, then the taxpayer might make a large repayment of principal when there was relatively little depreciable period left in the property, thereby permitting the taxpayer to obtain large depreciation deductions over a short period. *See* Government's Brief at 20–21.

deductions. Yet, as the Court recognized, tax depreciation deductions represent a recovery of the taxpayer's investment or basis. In the absence of basis (and assuming negative basis is not permitted), a taxpayer is not entitled to tax depreciation deductions, regardless of the existence of economic depreciation. Thus, investment or basis determines the existence of the tax deductions, and not vice-versa.

Moreover, the Court's analysis was premised on the existence of economic depreciation. If there were no such depreciation, then under the court's reasoning, there were no tax depreciation deductions that *had* to be awarded to someone and that necessitated a sufficiently large starting basis. Yet at least in Mrs. Crane's case, as the Court later conceded perhaps unwittingly, there apparently was *no* economic depreciation in the Clinton Ave. land and building during the time she and the estate owned it:

> Petitioner urges ... that she was not entitled to depreciation deductions ... because the law allows them only to one who actually bears the ... loss, and here the loss was not hers but the mortgagee's. We do not see, however, that she has established her factual premise. There was no finding of the Tax Court ... to the effect that the value of the property was ever less than the amount of the lien. Nor was there evidence in the record ... that this was so. The facts that the value of the property was only equal to the lien in 1932 and that during the next six and one-half years the physical condition of the building deteriorated and the amount of the lien increased, are entirely inconclusive, particularly in the light of the buyer's willingness in 1938 to take subject to the increased lien and pay a substantial amount of cash to boot.[37]

But if there was no evidence of any loss suffered by the mortgagee, there likewise was no evidence of any loss suffered by Mrs. Crane. Thus, the entire rationale for making sure Mrs. Crane had enough basis to claim the tax depreciation deductions collapses.

Having resolved the amount of Mrs. Crane's unadjusted basis, the Court then quickly determined that such basis must be adjusted for the allowable amount of tax depreciation deductions. In an important caution, the Court observed that it was *not* deciding the allowable amount of depreciation to a taxpayer who acquires property when its value is clearly less than the amount of an unassumed mortgage encumbering it.[38]

Amount Realized

"At last," the Court announced, it was able to turn to the question of the taxpayer's amount realized. Here, we see the critical importance of

---

[37] *Id.* at 11–12 (footnote omitted).

[38] *Id.* at 12.

the Court's resolution of the basis question first. Given its conclusion with respect to basis, treating the $2,500 of net cash as the only amount realized would produce "the absurdity that she sold a quarter-of-a-million dollar property for roughly one per cent of its value, and took a 99 per cent loss.... [W]e find that the absurdity is avoided by our conclusion that the amount of the mortgage is properly included in the 'amount realized' on the sale."[39] Of course, had the Court first determined that the amount realized was only $2,500, it would have been equally absurd for it to conclude that Mrs. Crane's starting basis in the property was $262,000.

The absurd result having been avoided, the Court nevertheless felt compelled to explain further how and why Mrs. Crane's amount realized had to include the amount of the mortgage debt for which she was not personally liable:

> [W]e think that a mortgagor, not personally liable on the debt, who sells the property subject to the mortgage and for additional consideration, realizes a benefit in the amount of the mortgage as well as the boot. If a purchaser pays boot, it is immaterial as to our problem whether the mortgagor is also to receive money from the purchaser to discharge the mortgage prior to sale, or whether he is merely to transfer subject to the mortgage—it may make a difference to the purchaser and to the mortgagee, but not to the mortgagor. Or put in another way, we are no more concerned with whether the mortgagor is, strictly speaking, a debtor on the mortgage, than we are with whether the benefit to him is, strictly speaking, a receipt of money or property. We are rather concerned with the reality that an owner of property, mortgaged at a figure less than that at which the property will sell, must and will treat the conditions of the mortgage exactly as if they were his personal obligations. If he transfers subject to the mortgage, the benefit to him is as real and substantial as if the mortgage were discharged, or as if a personal debt in an equal amount had been assumed by another.[40]

In a cautionary note, the Court added the following, famous footnote 37. We can see Judge Hand's fingerprints in this footnote for it echoes his dictum that no gain is recognized upon a mere abandonment:

> Obviously, if the value of the property is less than the amount of the mortgage, a mortgagor who is not personally liable cannot realize a benefit equal to the mortgage. Consequently, a different problem might be encountered where a mortgagor abandoned the property or

---

[39] *Id.* at 13.

[40] *Id.* at 14 (footnotes omitted).

transferred it subject to the mortgage without receiving boot. That is not this case.[41]

This explanation has come to be known as the "economic benefit" theory of *Crane*. The Court asserted that if a purchaser of property pays additional consideration (or "boot") on top of taking the property subject to an existing mortgage debt unassumed by the seller, then the seller must treat such debt as if it were a liability for which the seller is personally obligated to repay. Only by treating the conditions of the nonrecourse debt as if it were recourse debt (and thereby preventing the mortgagee from foreclosing on the property) can the seller realize the economic benefit of the boot. Hence, in that circumstance, a transfer of property subject to the nonrecourse debt should have the same tax consequences to the transferor as a transfer of property in which the seller is relieved of a personal obligation. Both liabilities should be included in the transferor's amount realized.

In explaining its economic benefit theory, the Court discussed two phenomena interchangeably. One is the receipt of boot by the seller. The other is the existence of an "equity cushion" in the property when it is sold, *i.e.*, the amount by which the value of the property at that time is greater than the amount of nonrecourse debt encumbering it. The Court apparently *assumed* that these two phenomena must necessarily arise together. According to the Court, if the seller receives boot, then it must be because there is an equity cushion in the property. And if there is no equity cushion, then the seller will not receive any boot. Thus, the Court warned in its footnote 37 that if there were no equity cushion, a seller "cannot realize a benefit equal to the [nonrecourse] mortgage" *because the seller would not receive any boot.*

Yet it is important to recognize that these two phenomena need not always occur together. A buyer might pay boot even in the absence of an equity cushion at the time of acquisition. The boot might simply represent the cost to the buyer of acquiring the right to benefit from a *subsequent* increase in the value of the property. Option rights like this are commonly bought and sold. Assuming that the buyer is not personally liable for the debt encumbering the property, the buyer would stand to lose at most the amount of the boot if there were no subsequent increase.

Or, the buyer might pay boot for a different reason altogether. For example, Mrs. Crane's buyer presumably understood that if it paid her $3,000 cash and took the Clinton Ave. property subject to a $262,000 mortgage indebtedness, it would obtain a starting depreciable basis of $265,000 in the property.[42] Thus, the $3,000 boot may simply have been

---

[41] *Id.*, n.37.

[42] Obviously, Mrs. Crane's purchaser did not know how the Court was going to come out in her case (or even that there would be a case) and, in any event, her case involved an

payment for the *tax savings* the buyer expected to receive from depreciating the property in the future. This explanation provides a reason to pay boot quite apart from the existence of any equity cushion in the property or any prospect of a future increase in its value.[43]

But if one phenomenon can occur without the other, which is more important? If that question had been posed to Chief Justice Vinson, it seems likely that he would have identified the receipt of boot as critical to the Court's economic benefit theory. So long as the seller receives some boot—for whatever reason—the Court's theory provided a rationale for requiring the seller to treat nonrecourse debt the same as recourse debt. Only by so treating the nonrecourse debt could the seller prevent foreclosure and thereby realize the benefit of the boot. Conversely, what difference would it make to the seller if there were an equity cushion in the property but no boot received upon its disposition? In that circumstance, why would the seller have a reason to treat the nonrecourse debt like recourse debt? A transfer of the property for no boot would leave the seller in largely the same position as a foreclosure of the property by the mortgagee. As we shall see, the Court's conflating of the boot question with the presence or absence of an equity cushion not surprisingly managed to confuse some subsequent courts.

At the end of its opinion, the Court responded more directly and articulately than Judge Hand to the taxpayer's complaint regarding the hardship and unfairness of the Court's holding:

> Petitioner contends that the result we have reached taxes her on what is not income within the meaning of the Sixteenth Amendment.... If it is because the entire transaction is thought to have been "by all dictates of common-sense ... a ruinous disaster," as it was termed in her brief, we disagree with her premise. She was entitled to depreciation deductions for a period of nearly seven years, and she actually took them in almost the allowable amount. *The crux of this case, really, is whether the law permits her to exclude allowable deductions from consideration in computing gain.* We have already showed that, if it does, the taxpayer can enjoy a double deduction, in effect, on the same loss of assets. The Sixteenth

---

acquisition by devise rather than by purchase. Nevertheless, it was longstanding Treasury practice at the time to permit taxpayers in the situation of Mrs. Crane's buyer to obtain a basis that included the mortgage debt and to use that amount for depreciation purposes.

[43] One might wonder why, for the same reason, Mrs. Crane did not try harder to hang onto the property. After all, she and the estate had been claiming depreciation deductions during their period of ownership. The answer, as we shall see, is that the deductions may not have been very valuable to her given her tax situation. Thus, the transaction may simply have been a sale of the deductions to a taxpayer who could use them more efficiently.

Amendment does not require that result any more than does the Act itself.[44]

We cannot tell exactly how much influence the taxpayer's inconsistent position—"[t]he crux of this case, really"—had on the Court's view of the case.[45] Did that factor, alone, persuade the Court to hold against her, with the rest of the opinion simply providing the necessary legal analysis to justify that conclusion? Or was the Court persuaded as a matter of statutory interpretation that the government was right and Mrs. Crane was wrong, and that this last statement was merely a way of explaining to her why the end result was not unfair? What does seem evident from the foregoing excerpt is that Mrs. Crane's inconsistency played *some* role in the decision-making process.

Justice Jackson's Dissent

In his brief dissent, Justice Jackson argued that, consistent with the *Dobson* case,[46] the Court should defer to the Tax Court's judgment regarding whether Mrs. Crane had acquired the entire land and building or a mere equity interest. As he noted, an equity interest qualifies as "property" under the Revenue Act. As to the taxpayer's attempted whipsaw, he said, "[w]e are not required in this case to decide whether depreciation was properly taken, for there is no issue about it here."[47] Justices Frankfurter and Douglas joined in the dissent.

Recapitulation of the Judicial Opinions

A clear majority of the jurists who passed on Mrs. Crane's case held in her favor.[48] Nevertheless, the government got the votes needed to prevail. Perhaps the key vote was provided by Judge Frank of the Second Circuit. His switch enabled Judge Hand to write for the majority of the Circuit Court, and Hand's influence on the Supreme Court is legendary.[49] The Supreme Court's holding resolved both Mrs. Crane's basis in the Clinton Ave. property and her amount realized upon its sale, and we

---

[44] *Crane*, 331 U.S. at 15–16 (footnotes omitted) (emphasis added).

[45] The Court alerted the reader early on about the existence of the inconsistency. *See id.* at 4, n.2.

[46] Dobson v. Commissioner, 320 U.S. 489 (1943).

[47] *Crane*, 331 U.S. at 16.

[48] For those counting, 18 of the 28 jurists sided with the taxpayer.

[49] *See* Gunther, *supra* note 21; Marvin A. Chirelstein, *Learned Hand's Contribution to the Law of Tax Avoidance*, 77 Yale L.J. 440 (1968). Perhaps the most famous tax case in history, *Gregory v. Helvering*, 293 U.S. 465 (1935), followed the same judicial path as *Crane*, with Judge Hand reversing the decision of the Board of Tax Appeals and the Supreme Court affirming (and closely tracking) Hand's opinion.

can think of the *"Crane* rule" as representing both aspects of the holding.

The technical merits of the Supreme Court's decision are pretty debatable. The Court was surely correct in deciding to avoid the absurd result, described towards the end of its opinion, that would have arisen from an inconsistent interpretation of basis and amount realized. But on that point, no one disagreed. The question before the Court was exactly *how* to avoid the absurdity: should it agree with the taxpayer's or the government's theory? This question was much more difficult, with each party's position seemingly requiring no small stretch of the applicable statutory language.

Given that setting, it might be easy to conclude that Mrs. Crane lost because of her attempt to whipsaw the government. If the merits are closely balanced, why not hold against the party who is trying to gain an undeserved advantage? As we have seen, there is some evidence to suggest that this line of thinking had an important influence on Judge Hand's view of the case, and it may have been equally significant to the Supreme Court. The problem with this explanation is that Mrs. Crane apparently gained very little "undeserved advantage." From the beginning, she described to the various courts the insignificant amount of tax savings she and the estate were able to obtain as a result of taking the $25,500 in depreciation deductions during the years 1932–1938. In her petition to the Tax Court, she claimed that all of those deductions produced a tax savings for her and her husband's estate of only about $122.[50] The government never stipulated to these claims, but the income tax returns were received into evidence so that the claims presumably could have been easily verified. We further know that the Tax Court's denial of her $3,200 depreciation deduction in 1938 produced a tax deficiency of only $27.77.[51]

The absence of any significant, undeserved advantage to Mrs. Crane if she had won her case is very important because it suggests that all of the concern expressed by both the Second Circuit and the Supreme Court about "double deductions" was, for the most part, an illusion. Bear in mind that the *position* she urged upon the courts did not authorize any double deduction. Thus, the *only* reason to raise the specter of a double deduction was from the circumstances of her particular situation, and the personal advantage she might have gained from a holding in her favor. But if there was such little advantage, why be so influenced by it? In that regard, the reminder of both courts that their

---

[50] *See* Tax Court Petition at 6–7. She made similar representations in her brief to the Supreme Court. *See* Taxpayer's Brief at 3, 46.

[51] *See* Tax Court's Decision, Crane v. Commissioner, 3 T.C. 585 (1944) (No. 110361), *reprinted in* Transcript of Record, Supreme Court of the United States, Oct. Term, 1946, No. 68, at 45.

holdings were merely offsetting the advantages to the taxpayer of the prior depreciation deductions must have seemed like an especially bitter pill for Mrs. Crane to swallow.

Of course, at bottom, both appellate courts were simply following the lead of the government. Why did the government urge its position so strenuously? One possible explanation is that the government was simply being tunnel-visioned. Mrs. Crane had taken an inconsistent position, albeit with little tax advantage to herself, and the government's role was to set her straight. In its briefs to the Second Circuit and the Supreme Court, the government repeatedly brought Mrs. Crane's inconsistency to the attention of the court.[52] Under this view, winning the case and maximizing the amount of revenue the government could collect from her were of paramount importance, with larger tax policy considerations being of only secondary concern.

The government had arguably demonstrated this same attitude five years earlier when it litigated *Virginian Hotel Corp. v. Helvering*,[53] a case eerily similar to Mrs. Crane's. The facts of that case, as simplified and with illustrative numbers, were as follows. The taxpayer acquired property in 1931 for $1,000 and depreciated its investment on a straight-line basis over ten years, thereby claiming a $100 deduction ($1,000/10) each year. In 1938, after allowing these deductions for seven years, the Commissioner asserted that the property actually should have been depreciated over 20 years and the taxpayer agreed to this change. The question was how much depreciable basis the taxpayer had remaining in 1938 in order to calculate its depreciation deduction in that year. The statute at the time required that basis be reduced by the amount of depreciation allowed, but not less than the amount allowable.[54] Accordingly, the government contended that the taxpayer's remaining basis in 1938 was, after reduction for the "allowed" amount of depreciation, only $300 ($1,000—($100 x 7)).

The taxpayer conceded that the government's position was correct if the earlier, erroneous deductions had provided it with a tax benefit. But the taxpayer argued that since no tax benefit had been obtained from the deductions in 1931–37, it should only have to reduce its basis by the "allowable" amount of depreciation in those years, or $50 per year ($1,000/20). Thus, its remaining basis in 1938 was $650 ($1,000—($50 x 7)). The taxpayer asserted that the term, "allowed," should be interpreted as meaning, in effect, "claimed *and* used to reduce taxable income." According to the taxpayer, this interpretation was consistent with the

---

[52] *See* Government's Second Circuit Brief at 15–16; Government's Supreme Court Brief at 21, 33.

[53] 319 U.S. 523 (1943).

[54] This continues to be the rule today. *See* § 1016(a)(2).

purpose of the rule, which was to prevent a double deduction, something the taxpayer was not trying to obtain. In a 5–4 decision, the Supreme Court refused to agree with the taxpayer.

From a policy standpoint, the taxpayer's position was not an unreasonable one. After all, if it had depreciated the property correctly from the beginning, its remaining depreciable basis in 1938 would have been $650. Thus, the taxpayer was merely trying to rectify a mistake which had had no effect on prior taxes in order to determine its future ones correctly. It is difficult to understand why the government did not permit this, other than a desire to collect a windfall from the taxpayer.[55] Congress eventually saw the merits of the taxpayer's position and enacted the predecessor to current § 1016(a)(2)(B) in 1952 to reverse the effect of the *Virginian Hotel* case. The new statutory rule was made retroactively applicable to all open years after 1931.[56]

Like the taxpayer's position in *Virginian Hotel*, Mrs. Crane's position might be characterized as an effort to correct a mistake that had had little or no effect on her prior taxes so that her future ones could be calculated correctly. The government's decision to resist her may therefore have been no more thoughtful than the stance it took in the earlier case.

Alternatively, the government may have had a broader concern. Although there was little undeserved benefit obtained by Mrs. Crane, the same might not be true for countless other taxpayers in her similar situation. If Mrs. Crane had prevailed in the Supreme Court, it might have opened the door wide for similar taxpayers to assert that their gain or loss upon disposition of debt-financed property did not have to take into account prior depreciation deductions allowed in years now closed. The government had previously experienced this very phenomenon—a Supreme Court pro-government "victory" with unintended consequences to the fisc, and an eventual government-requested reversal by the Congress of the decision. Perhaps the lessons of that hard experience were still reverberating in the government's ears when it formulated its litigation strategy in *Crane*.[57]

---

[55] Bernard Wolfman et al., *Dissent Without Opinion: The Behavior of Justice William O. Douglas in Federal Tax Cases* 25 (U. Pa. Press, 1975). According to Professor Stark, Justice Jackson, one of the dissenters in *Virginian Hotel*, was suspicious of the government's litigating position and believed, perhaps, that the government was "not playing fair." Stark, *supra* note 31, at 212–13. It is noteworthy that Justice Jackson also dissented in *Crane*.

[56] *See* Act of July 14, 1952, ch. 741, § 3, 66 Stat. 629.

[57] The earlier case was United States v. Hendler, 303 U.S. 564 (1938), *reh'g denied*, 304 U.S. 588 (1938), and its holding was legislatively reversed by the predecessor to current § 357(a). Congress even passed a law to refund the taxes upheld in the *Hendler* case itself. See Boris I. Bittker & James S. Eustice, *Federal Income Taxation of Corporations and*

If so, the government may have been excessively cautious. As just described, the tax statute required taxpayers to adjust their basis in property for depreciation deductions allowed, even though in excess of the allowable amount. Thus, even if Mrs. Crane's theory had prevailed in the Supreme Court, the government would still have retained a potential response to other taxpayers trying to get her same whipsaw advantage. As discussed by Judge Hand in his draft opinion and as endorsed three years later by Judge Magruder in his concurring opinion in the case of *Parker v. Delaney*,[58] the government could have argued that those taxpayers had a negative basis at the time of disposition of the property due to the previously allowed (though not allowable) depreciation deductions from a small or zero starting basis. Nothing in the statute specifically precluded negative basis. Thus, upon disposition of their property, those taxpayers would have had to recognize gain equal to the prior depreciation deductions allowed. Indeed, instead of fighting Mrs. Crane, the government conceivably could have accepted her position but still asserted the same deficiency against her based on this negative basis theory.

A final, possible explanation for the government's strategy is simply the belief that its position, though "taxpayer-favorable," represented the most administrable way to tax debt-financed property transactions. Contrary to Mrs. Crane's view, the government's position provided a clear, predictable outcome: the mortgagor would be entitled to claim all of the depreciation deductions with respect to such property. In addition, it avoided some of the accounting difficulties described by both appellate courts. The position had been a longstanding one in terms of the government's administrative practice—it was one reason why the depreciation deductions claimed by Mrs. Crane and the estate had gone unchallenged—and presumably, tax policy concerns had driven adoption of that practice. In short, the underlying reason for the *Crane* rule may have been a goal of administrative simplicity.[59]

But the "best laid schemes of mice and men often go astray." The following section describes the immediate aftermath of Beulah Crane's case and its longer term effect on the tax law.

The Impact of *Crane*

Immediate Aftermath

Immediately after the Supreme Court case was decided, there was some confusion in the popular press as to exactly what the Court had

---

Shareholders ¶ 3.06[1] (6th ed. 1998); Stanley S. Surrey, *Assumption of Indebtedness in Tax-Free Exchanges*, 50 Yale L.J. 1, 10–14, 28 (1940).

[58] 186 F.2d 455, 459 (1st Cir.1950), *cert. denied*, 341 U.S. 926 (1951).

[59] *See* Government's Second Circuit Brief at 10, 16–17; Government's Supreme Court Brief at 18–21.

held. Six days after the decision, *The New York Times* published a lead story about the case in its business section that was captioned, "Equity in Realty Held Not Property." Below it was a subheadline which read "No Depreciation Possible."[60] As we know, the first caption was technically correct but hardly the crux of the decision. The second caption was demonstrably false, as the government's victory *permitted* depreciation to be taken. It was the *taxpayer's* position that might have precluded depreciation.

Headlines are sometimes written by editorial staff who are not very familiar with the substance of the underlying story. But the following lead paragraph of the story suggests that the author also may not have fully appreciated the significance of the case: "Equity in real estate is held by the United States Supreme Court not to be 'property' either for the purpose of computing depreciation or for determining gain or loss resulting from its sale." Other stories contained in the popular press provided more accurate descriptions of the decision. Shortly after the decision was issued, *The Wall Street Journal*'s "Tax Report" column described the facts and holding and then stated:

> The Supreme Court decision was a defeat for this particular taxpayer. But it was good news for many others in that it reaffirmed long-established Treasury practices. Under these, taxpayers can continue to calculate depreciation on the full value of property owned for income purposes without reduction for mortgage indebtedness.[61]

The initial, published commentary about the case focused mostly on the uncertain scope of the rule established by the Court. Because Mrs. Crane inherited her property, one question was whether the Court's rule would apply equally to taxpayers who *purchase* property subject to a nonrecourse mortgage. Other questions concerned the tax consequences of transactions where the amount of the nonrecourse mortgage exceeds the value of the underlying property. One commentator who was critical of the Court's rule suggested that it might be limited to situations where it is necessary to prevent unfair tax avoidance, such as the whipsaw attempted by Mrs. Crane.

A number of commentators discussed the tax consequences of an abandonment of encumbered property. As you recall, Judge Hand suggested that a taxpayer in Mrs. Crane's situation could avoid recognizing any gain by simply abandoning the property, and the Supreme Court did not disagree with that conclusion. Some commentators were disturbed

---

[60] N.Y. Times, Apr. 20, 1947, at F–1.

[61] *Tax Report*, Wall St.J., Apr. 23, 1947, at 1; *see also* N.Y. Herald Trib., Apr. 15, 1947, at 26.

by the policy implications of Hand's dictum whereas others, while recognizing the logical reasons to tax an abandonment like a sale, nevertheless viewed such an outcome as harsh to taxpayers like Mrs. Crane who had not obtained any significant tax benefit from the prior depreciation deductions.

Several commentators were concerned about the tax avoidance potential of the Court's rule. One worry was that the gain upon disposition of depreciable property might be taxed at low capital gains rates and therefore not fully compensate for the ordinary income deductions provided by depreciation. At least one author seemed to recognize the tax deferral opportunity provided by the Court's rule.

Subsequent Case Law

Subsequent cases built on *Crane* to elaborate on the extent to which nonrecourse debt is included in both basis and amount realized.

1. *Inclusion of Nonrecourse Debt in Basis*

Blackstone Theatre Co. v. Commissioner,[62] decided just two years after *Crane*, involved a taxpayer who purchased a building in 1941 for about $37,000. At the time of the purchase, the building was encumbered by liens of about $121,000 for accrued but unpaid property taxes. In the purchase, the taxpayer took the building subject to the liens but without any personal liability to repay them. Five years later, in 1946, the taxpayer was able to satisfy the liens through a payment of about $50,000. The issue was the amount of the taxpayer's basis in the property for purposes of depreciation. The taxpayer contended that its initial "cost" basis included the full amount of the liens encumbering the property when it was acquired. The Commissioner argued that the taxpayer's initial basis had to be retroactively reduced to reflect the amount actually paid by the taxpayer to satisfy the liens. Drawing upon *Crane*, the Tax Court agreed with the taxpayer: "From *Crane* we can deduce the following applicable principles: (a) The basis for given property includes liens thereon, even though not personally assumed by the taxpayer; and (b) the depreciation allowance should be computed on the full amount of this basis. These principles ... are controlling...."[63]

It is interesting to see how quickly the holding in *Crane* began to be stretched beyond its original limits. As we know, *Crane* involved an acquisition of property by devise, not by purchase. The Supreme Court found that Mrs. Crane's initial basis in her property was $262,000 because that amount was the fair market value of the land and building at the time of her husband's death. Narrowly read, therefore, the

---

[62] 12 T.C. 801 (1949).

[63] *Id.* at 804.

decision did not say anything about whether nonrecourse liabilities are included in a taxpayer's cost basis upon a purchase of property. Nevertheless, because the Supreme Court reasoned backwards from depreciation to basis, it is easy to understand why the Tax Court reached the conclusion that it did. If one reasons backwards, there is no reason to differentiate between an acquisition by devise and one by purchase. The taxpayer's initial basis in the two cases must be the same because the depreciation deductions from the property are the same in each case. Thus, there is no need to determine the amount of the purchaser's investment or exactly *why* nonrecourse liabilities should be treated as part of his "cost." The Tax Court may also have been influenced by *Crane*'s inclusion of nonrecourse debt in the amount realized. Given that conclusion, it would have been nonsensical not to include the same debt in basis.

The Tax Court limited its holding to situations where the value of the property is not less than the amount of the liability at the time of the acquisition. It inferred that this requirement had been met in the present case since the taxpayer had paid boot in addition to taking the property subject to the tax liens.[64] But the payment of boot did not really reveal anything about the value of the property because there was no finding that the tax liens were still worth their face amount of $121,000 when the taxpayer acquired the property. Presumably, the liens were worth that amount when they were first placed on the property but, as evidenced by the taxpayer's later satisfaction of the liens for only $50,000, their value may have subsequently declined.

The importance of knowing the value of property at the time of acquisition is illustrated by the case of *Mayerson v. Commissioner*.[65] In that case, the taxpayer acquired some commercial real estate by providing the seller with a purchase-money note of $332,500 secured by the property. The note was not due for 99 years and, other than $10,000 promptly paid by the taxpayer at the time of the purchase, no payments of principal had to be made prior to the due date. In the event of default, the seller's only recourse was to foreclose on the property. About five years after the purchase, the parties agreed to discharge the obligation through a $200,000 payment by the taxpayer.

The issue was whether the taxpayer was entitled to claim depreciation deductions from the property based on an initial basis of $332,500, the full face amount of the note. The Commissioner argued that the taxpayer had merely acquired a 99–year leasehold interest in the property for the $10,000 initial payment and, therefore, limited the taxpayer's deductions to an amortization of the $10,000 over the 99 years. Relying

---

[64] *Id.* at 805, n.8.

[65] 47 T.C. 340 (1966), *acq.* Rev. Rul. 69–77, 1969–1 C.B. 59.

largely upon *Crane*, the Tax Court held for the taxpayer. It first described exactly why a "cost" basis should include the amount of the purchaser's purchase-money debt obligation:

> [I]t is well accepted that a purchase-money debt obligation for part of the price will be included in basis. This is necessary in order to equate a purchase-money mortgage situation with the situation in which the buyer borrows the full amount of the purchase price from a third party and pays the seller in cash. It is clear that the depreciable basis should be the same in both instances.[66]

The court then explained why this general treatment of debt should extend to indebtedness for which the taxpayer is not personally liable:

> Taxpayers who are not personally liable for encumbrances on property should be allowed depreciation deductions affording competitive equality with taxpayers who are personally liable for encumbrances or taxpayers who own unencumbered property. The effect of such a policy is to give the taxpayer an advance credit for the amount of the mortgage. This appears to be reasonable since it can be assumed that a capital investment in the amount of the mortgage will eventually occur despite the absence of personal liability.[67]

While drawing important analogies among cash, recourse indebtedness, and nonrecourse indebtedness to help explain the rationale for the *Crane* doctrine, the Tax Court failed to recognize some of their potential differences. For example, the court did not discuss at all the adequacy of the interest obligation included in the taxpayer's note.[68] A cash payment of $332,500 is considerably different from a mere promise to pay that amount in 99 years' time with an inadequate amount of interest due in the interim, even if the promise to pay is absolutely certain. Thus, there is no reason for those different investments to result in the same consequences for tax depreciation purposes.

Furthermore, investments financed by recourse or nonrecourse debt may be different if there is not an equal likelihood that the amounts borrowed will eventually be repaid. The Tax Court "assumed" that the amount of a nonrecourse liability will eventually be satisfied, but did not consider under what conditions that assumption is a realistic one.

Crane did not address these issues directly but it did provide a clue as to how they might be resolved. In order to equate investments financed with cash, recourse debt, and nonrecourse debt, it is important to determine whether the *amount* of the investment is the same. There

---

[66] *Id.* at 349.

[67] *Id.* at 352.

[68] The note required a payment of interest but there was no discussion of whether the terms were consistent with market conditions at the time.

is little uncertainty regarding the amount of a cash investment. But because there is uncertainty in the case of debt-financed ones, particularly transactions involving nonrecourse debt, one of *Crane*'s lessons is that the *value* of the property being acquired might be a helpful proxy to gauge the amount of the debt-financed investment.[69] Yet in contrast to *Blackstone Theatre*, the Tax Court in *Mayerson* failed to determine or even discuss the value of the property acquired by the taxpayer. As in *Blackstone Theatre*, the taxpayer's discharge in *Mayerson* of his entire obligation with a $200,000 payment five years after the acquisition at least raised the possibility that the amount of the taxpayer's initial investment was something less than the full amount of the $332,500 nonrecourse liability.[70]

What *Mayerson* did consider were the circumstances surrounding the acquisition. The court found "no hint of a sham transaction.... [It was] an arm's-length transaction entered into between knowledgeable strangers for business motives."[71] But the court overlooked the fact that two knowledgeable strangers, bargaining at arm's length and with sound business motives, might nevertheless find it in their *mutual* best interests to overstate the amount of a nonrecourse obligation and thereby create an inflated tax basis in the property. The potential benefit to the buyer is obvious. The seller might go along so long as the seller receives some additional, "real" consideration from the buyer for doing so.

In *Estate of Franklin v. Commissioner*,[72] decided about ten years after *Mayerson*, the government finally succeeded in challenging the amount of the taxpayer's depreciable basis resulting from an acquisition financed by nonrecourse debt. Charles Franklin was a partner in a partnership which acquired the Thunderbird Inn, a motel property, from the Romneys. The Romneys had purchased this property earlier that same year for about $660,000. The partnership, however, paid $75,000 in cash and also provided a $1,224,000 note to the Romneys to acquire the property. Concurrent with the purchase, the partnership leased the property back to the Romneys for ten years in exchange for annual rental payments that approximated the principal and interest payments due from the partnership on its note. Thus, during the first ten years, no cash was required to change hands between the partnership and the Romneys other than the $75,000 cash downpayment. The lease was a net

---

[69] *See supra* note 38 and accompanying text.

[70] In its grudging acquiescence to the court's decision, the Service noted that "the fair market value of the property was not put in issue in the case," and stated that the case would be relied upon only "in situations where it is clear that the property has been acquired at its fair market value." Rev. Rul. 69-77, 1969-1 C.B. 59.

[71] *Mayerson*, 47 T.C. at 350.

[72] 544 F.2d 1045 (9th Cir.1976), *aff'g* 64 T.C. 752 (1975).

lease, meaning that the entire burden of owning and maintaining the property during the ten-year term of the lease fell upon the Romneys, the lessees. At the end of ten years, a balloon payment was due on the note equal to the remaining, unpaid principal amount of the debt at that time. The note, however, was nonrecourse to the partnership; in the event of default, the Romneys' only recourse was to take back the property.

Under the tax law, a partnership is generally not treated as a separate taxpayer in its own right. Instead, each partner is required to report for tax purposes the partner's share of the partnership's income and deductions. The partnership calculated its interest and depreciation deductions based on the full amount of the $1,224,000 note, and Franklin reported losses after taking into account his share of the partnership's income and deductions.

The Tax Court agreed with the government's disallowance of Franklin's losses. The court concluded that the partnership paid the $75,000 cash down payment in exchange for a mere option to acquire the property in ten years' time. The court noted that during the ten years, no cash would change hands and that the use of, and responsibility for, the property would remain with the Romneys. Moreover, because the note was nonrecourse, the partnership was not obligated to make the balloon payment after ten years. If the value of the property did not exceed the remaining principal amount after ten years, the partnership could simply walk away from the transaction, which would be equivalent to forfeiting its option. As a mere option holder, the partnership was neither the owner of the property nor an obligor of real indebtedness, and therefore not entitled to either interest or depreciation deductions.

The Ninth Circuit affirmed the Tax Court's holding but on a slightly different theory. The Ninth Circuit indicated that if the partnership had engaged in a genuine sale-leaseback transaction, then it would have been entitled to interest and depreciation deductions. The fatal flaw in this case, however, was the partnership's failure to show that the purchase price "was at least approximately equivalent to the fair market value of the property."[73] If the price reflects that value, then the purchaser's investment will "rather quickly yield an equity in the property which the purchaser could not prudently abandon."[74] In the absence of that showing, the court concluded that no sale had occurred, and the partnership had neither made an investment in the property nor obligated itself to pay real indebtedness.

---

[73] *Id.* at 1048.

[74] *Id.*

2. *Inclusion of Nonrecourse Debt in Amount Realized*

In *Parker v. Delaney*,[75] the taxpayer acquired in the mid–1930's various apartment buildings from a bank that had foreclosed on the properties. The taxpayer took the properties subject to the bank's mortgage liens of $273,000 but without any personal obligation to repay them. During his ownership of the properties, the taxpayer repaid $14,000 of the mortgage debt and also claimed depreciation deductions of about $45,000. Eventually, in 1945 when the mortgages were in default, he surrendered the properties back to the bank. The question was the amount, if any, of the taxpayer's gain at the time of the surrender. The First Circuit agreed with the government that the taxpayer's amount realized included the remaining mortgage principal of $259,000 ($273,000 − $14,000). Therefore, the taxpayer recognized gain of $31,000, the excess of the $259,000 amount realized over the taxpayer's adjusted basis of $228,000 ($273,000 − $45,000).

Parker supplements *Crane* in two ways. First, the court rejected Judge Hand's dictum that no gain is recognized upon an abandonment of property. Hand's conclusion was based on the view that an abandonment does not constitute a "sale or other disposition" within the meaning of the predecessor to current § 1001(a). The First Circuit rejected this position, and concluded without discussion that a "disposition" of the properties had clearly occurred. This holding continues to be the law today.

In addition, the court applied the *Crane* rule to include the nonrecourse debt in the amount realized even though the taxpayer did not receive any boot upon surrendering the property. The court explained that the case did not present one of the situations reserved by footnote 37 in *Crane*:

> The added factor [in *Crane*], not present here, that boot was paid over and above the mortgage, is not material so long as the value of the properties was not less than the liens. Boot served to show this in the *Crane* case, but the payment of boot is of course not the only means of showing whether or not value is equal to or more than the liens on the property disposed of.... [Taxpayer's] statement [that the *Crane* doctrine does not apply] is predicated upon a situation where the value of the property when disposed of is less than the mortgage. There is no evidence to that effect in this case. The District Court treated the value as equal to the mortgages and we have no basis for doing otherwise. The critical point is that the value equaled the mortgages, not that it exceeded them....[76]

---

[75] 186 F.2d 455 (1st Cir.1950), *cert. denied*, 341 U.S. 926 (1951).

[76] *Id.* at 458.

The court's factual premise regarding the relationship between the value of the properties and the amount of the liens at the time of the surrender is somewhat dubious.[77] More importantly, the First Circuit appears to have misunderstood the Supreme Court's economic benefit theory. Under the *Parker* view, the existence of an equity cushion in the property was enough to justify the *Crane* rule's inclusion of the nonrecourse debt in the taxpayer's amount realized. Indeed, the court went one step further, concluding that it was sufficient to show that the value of the property was *at least equal to* (though not necessarily greater than) the amount of the mortgage when the surrender occurred. But what difference did that make to the taxpayer? If there was no boot paid—and the taxpayer received none upon surrendering the properties—then where was his "economic benefit"? What was the rationale in this case for requiring the taxpayer to treat the nonrecourse debt like recourse debt for tax purposes? The court simply ignored these questions. It is unclear whether the court was genuinely confused about the meaning of the economic benefit theory or whether this case represents an early judicial effort to distance itself from that theory altogether.

The confusion was compounded two years later when the same issue arose in the case of *Woodsam Associates, Inc. v. Commissioner*.[78] In that case, a bank foreclosed on the taxpayer's property when it was encumbered by a nonrecourse debt of $381,000. The taxpayer claimed that because the value of the property at foreclosure was not more than $320,000, her amount realized should be limited to the value of the property. Oddly, the Tax Court stated that the value of the property was "immaterial," disregarded the taxpayer's requested finding of fact regarding value, and therefore rejected the taxpayer's position, largely on the basis of a Tax Court case decided *prior to* the Supreme Court's opinion in *Crane*.[79] The court did not think that the absence of boot or the reservation contained in *Crane's* footnote 37 had "any application" to this question. Even more strangely, the taxpayer did not pursue this argument in the Second Circuit, which cited *Parker v. Delaney* for the proposition that the taxpayer's capitulation on this issue was well-

---

[77] Although not completely clear, the district court's finding that the amount of the mortgage equaled the value of the properties seems to relate to the time of acquisition and not to the time of surrender. *See* Parker v. Delaney, 50–2 U.S.T.C. ¶ 9416 (D.Mass.1950). Given the circumstances of the surrender for no cash consideration when the mortgage was in default, it seems unlikely that the value of the properties remained equal to the mortgage amount when the properties were surrendered. One commentator has described the court's explanation as "sheer dishonesty" and "disingenuous." Note, *Federal Income Tax Treatment of Nonrecourse Debt*, 82 Colum. L. Rev. 1498, 1504–05 (1982).

[78] 198 F.2d 357 (2d Cir.1952), *aff'g* 16 T.C. 649 (1951).

[79] *Woodsam Assoc.*, 16 T.C. at 654. The case relied upon by the court was Lutz & Schramm Co. v. Commissioner, 1 T.C. 682 (1943).

advised.[80] But as just discussed, in *Parker v. Delaney*, the First Circuit tried to side-step this issue altogether by asserting that the value of the property at disposition was not less than the amount of the encumbering mortgage.

Two later cases eventually clarified the extent to which nonrecourse debt must be included in the amount realized. In *Estate of Levine v. Commissioner*,[81] Mr. Levine made a gift of some commercial real estate to a trust for the benefit of his grandchildren. At the time of the gift, the property was worth $925,000 but it was encumbered by mortgage liabilities of $786,000 for which Levine was not personally obligated but which the trust assumed. In addition, Levine incurred expenses of about $124,000 mostly to improve the property, and the trust also agreed to pay these expenses as part of the transfer. Thus, the net value of Levine's gift to the trust was about $15,000, the amount the value of the property ($925,000) exceeded the two liabilities assumed by the trust ($910,000 = $786,000 + $124,000).

The Commissioner asserted that upon making the gift, Levine recognized gain of $425,000, the excess of the liabilities ($910,000) over Levine's $485,000 basis in the property. Levine argued that a gift transfer is not a realization event and that, in any case, he did not receive anything upon making the gift. Instead, the donee should take the donor's basis in the property, thereby preserving any gain for future recognition.[82]

The Tax Court agreed with the government. The court stated that it would be "ludicrous" if the donor did not recognize any gain, and the donee simply inherited the donor's basis in the property. In that case, if the donee promptly sold the property, the donee would have to pay taxes on $440,000 of gain ($925,000 value less $485,000 transferred basis) even though the net value of the gift to the donee was only $15,000.[83] But the court struggled to find a rationale for its holding consistent with *Crane*. The court tried to fit the case within *Crane*'s economic benefit theory by repeatedly emphasizing that Levine had received a "tangible economic benefit" from making the gift, but nowhere did the court identify exactly what that benefit was.

Affirming the Tax Court, the Second Circuit did not encounter the same difficulty. Writing for the court, Judge Friendly agreed with the Tax Court that a gift constitutes a "disposition" of property in which gain may be recognized. As to the donor's amount realized, Friendly

---

[80] *Woodsam Assoc.*, 198 F.2d at 358, n.1.

[81] 634 F.2d 12 (2d Cir.1980), *aff'g* 72 T.C. 780 (1979).

[82] *See* § 1015(a).

[83] *See Estate of Levine*, 72 T.C. at 791, n.6.

noted that although Levine was not personally liable for the mortgages, he *was* personally liable for the $124,000 in other expenses which were assumed by the trust. Thus, the assumption of these other expenses constituted the "boot" to Levine, which justified under *Crane*'s economic benefit theory the inclusion of the nonrecourse mortgage liability in his amount realized. The court reserved on whether the same result would apply had Levine simply transferred the property subject to the nonre-course mortgages *without* the additional assumption of expenses by the donee.[84]

Judge Friendly, however, proceeded to make quite clear how he would have decided the latter case. He analyzed Levine's gain in the transaction and determined that it consisted of essentially three ele-ments. One element was the expenses incurred by Levine and assumed by the donee. Under well recognized tax principles,[85] that amount clearly represented income to Levine. The other two elements were the recap-ture of tax depreciation deductions taken by Levine (but not reflected in loss in property value) and the proceeds of post-acquisition debt received and pocketed by Levine (but not taxed to him as a result of the *Woodsam* holding, discussed below). Friendly concluded that taxing these benefits to Levine was "scarcely harsh."[86] This case helped to set the stage for a complete rethinking of *Crane*'s economic benefit theory in *Commissioner v. Tufts*.[87]

In *Tufts*, the taxpayer was a partner in a partnership which con-structed an apartment complex. The construction was financed by an approximately $1,851,000 nonrecourse mortgage loan provided by a commercial lender and about $44,000 in cash provided by the partners. After the complex was built, the partnership operated it unsuccessfully for about one year, during which time it claimed depreciation deductions of about $440,000. At the end of the year, the property was sold to Fred Bayles in exchange for $250 in cash plus Bayles' assumption of the mortgage debt, which remained at $1,851,000. The apartment complex was worth no more than $1,400,000 when it was sold.

The taxpayer and the government were in agreement that at the time of the sale, the partnership's adjusted basis in the property was about $1,455,000, determined as follows:

---

[84] *Estate of Levine*, 634 F.2d at 16–17.

[85] *See* Old Colony Trust Co. v. Commissioner, 279 U.S. 716 (1929), in which the Supreme Court concluded that an employer's satisfaction of its employee's obligation constituted income to the employee.

[86] *Estate of Levine*, 634 F.2d at 18.

[87] 461 U.S. 300 (1983), *rev'g* 651 F.2d 1058 (5th Cir.1981), *rev'g* 70 T.C. 756 (1978).

Partnership's Adjusted Basis

1.	nonrecourse mortgage	$1,851,000
2.	cash	44,000
3.	unadjusted basis ((1) + (2))	1,895,000
4.	depreciation deductions	440,000
5.	adjusted basis ((3) − (4))	$1,455,000

The parties disagreed, however, as to the amount realized from the sale. The taxpayer contended that *Crane*'s footnote 37 limited the amount realized to the fair market value of the property, or $1,400,000, and that therefore the transaction resulted in a loss of about $55,000. The government countered that the amount realized must include the full amount of the nonrecourse liability still outstanding, or $1,851,000, and that the sale thus produced a gain of about $396,000 ($1,851,000 − $1,455,000).

Writing for a unanimous Supreme Court, Justice Blackmun agreed with the government. He stated that *Crane* "ultimately does not rest on its limited theory of economic benefit."[88] Instead, he indicated that the *Crane* holding was based on a theory of symmetry or consistency. The exclusion of loan proceeds from income, and the inclusion of the amount of a loan in a taxpayer's basis in a debt-financed acquisition of property, are both predicated on the assumption that the debtor has an obligation to repay the loan which he will eventually honor. Furthermore, in these situations, no distinction is drawn between recourse and nonrecourse debt:

> When encumbered property is sold or otherwise disposed of and the purchaser assumes the mortgage, the associated extinguishment of the mortgagor's obligation to repay is accounted for in the computation of the amount realized.... Because no difference between recourse and nonrecourse obligations is recognized in calculating basis, *Crane* teaches that the Commissioner may ignore the nonrecourse nature of the obligation in determining the amount realized upon disposition of the encumbered property. He thus may include in the amount realized the amount of the nonrecourse mortgage assumed by the purchaser. The rationale for this treatment is that the original inclusion of the amount of the mortgage in basis rested on the assumption that the mortgagor incurred an obligation to repay. Moreover, this treatment balances the fact that the mortgagor originally received the proceeds of the nonrecourse loan tax-free on the same assumption. Unless the outstanding amount of the mortgage is deemed to be realized, the mortgagor effectively will have received untaxed income at the time the loan was extended and

---

[88] *Id.* at 307.

will have received an unwarranted increase in the basis of his property.[89]

The Court therefore concluded that the amount realized had to include the full amount of the nonrecourse liability. That the amount of the loan exceeded the fair market value of the property at the time of the sale was "irrelevant."

The weakness of the taxpayer's position is revealed by the fact that although the partners together invested and lost a mere $44,000 in the real estate venture, they were attempting to claim net tax losses of $495,000 ($440,000 depreciation deductions plus $55,000 loss upon sale). The difference between those two figures, or $451,000, had in fact been lost (there was a decrease in the value of the complex from at least $1,851,000 to $1,400,000, a $451,000 loss, during the time the property was owned by the partnership), but not by the partners. Instead, it was a loss suffered by the mortgagee. Indeed, because the mortgage loan was federally insured, the loss was actually borne by taxpayers generally. There was, therefore, simply no justification for the taxpayer's position in the case, and the Court gave it short shrift. The Court's holding provided the partners with a net tax loss of $44,000 ($440,000 depreciation deductions less $396,000 gain upon sale), the amount equal to their economic loss.

Interestingly, despite the absence of any equity cushion in the apartment complex when it was sold, Bayles *did* pay a little bit of boot. Thus, at least in theory, the Court could have decided the case narrowly within the bounds of *Crane*'s economic benefit doctrine. Instead, quite wisely, the Court concluded that it was time to lay that theory to rest. There was no reason to allow a seller's tax consequences potentially to vary so significantly depending upon whether the buyer happened to pay a small amount of boot.

But by identifying symmetry as the sole basis for the *Crane* decision, the Court made plain that the holding in that case was just a matter of choice. There was no independent ground in the statute that mandated the particular outcome in *Crane* or *Tufts*. According to Justice Blackmun, the Court in *Crane* approved the government's decision not to distinguish between recourse and nonrecourse debt in the determination of basis. Once that choice had been made, the resolution of the amount realized question became a foregone conclusion.

3. *Tax Treatment of Post–Acquisition Nonrecourse Debt*

One final issue, which was the main focus of *Woodsam Associates, Inc. v. Commissioner*,[90] concerns the proper tax treatment of nonrecourse

---

[89] *Id.* at 308–10.

[90] 198 F.2d 357 (2d Cir.1952).

debt incurred subsequent to the acquisition of the property securing the debt. The facts of *Woodsam*, as simplified, were as follows. Mrs. Wood purchased some real property in 1922 for $296,000 by paying $101,000 in cash and incurring mortgage indebtedness of $195,000. She subsequently borrowed additional amounts that were secured by the property, and consolidated all of the debts in 1931 into a single nonrecourse mortgage liability of $400,000. The issue was the amount of her gain in 1943 when the bank foreclosed on the property with the remaining consolidated debt being $381,000.

Mrs. Wood's principal argument related to her basis in the property at the time of foreclosure. She agreed that her initial basis was $296,000, which included the amount of the mortgage debt used to finance the acquisition. She made the novel argument, however, that the receipt of the additional mortgage proceeds in 1931 represented income to her to the extent the proceeds exceeded her adjusted basis in the property, and that she therefore was entitled to increase her basis in the property at that time by the amount of her gain:

> The contention of the petitioner ... is that, when the borrowings of Mrs. Wood subsequent to her acquisition of the property became charges solely upon the property itself, the cash she received for the repayment of which she was not personally liable was a gain then taxable to her as income to the extent that the mortgage indebtedness exceeded her adjusted basis in the property. That being so, it is argued that her tax basis was, under familiar principles of tax law, increased by the amount of such taxable gain ...[91]

For example, suppose a taxpayer purchases property for $10,000 and subsequently sells it for $100,000. Taxpayer must clearly report $90,000 of gain at the time of the sale. Suppose, however, that sometime prior to the sale, taxpayer borrows $40,000 on a nonrecourse basis, with the property used as security for the loan. Mrs. Wood's argument was that the borrowing of the $40,000 is an income realization event. The nonrecourse nature of the borrowing assured the taxpayer that she would never have to repay the money borrowed, no matter what might subsequently happen to the property. Thus, the taxpayer should be treated as realizing $40,000 at that time and having a gain of $30,000, the amount realized in excess of the taxpayer's basis. Moreover, having recognized the $30,000 in gain, the taxpayer must then increase her basis in the property to $40,000 to make sure that she is not taxed again on the same gain. Hence, upon later sale of the property for $100,000, the taxpayer's gain would be only $60,000 and not $90,000. In summary, Mrs. Wood's theory went to the timing of the income item. Did all of the gain have to be reported in 1943 or should some of it have been reported

---

[91] *Id.* at 359.

at an earlier time when the post-acquisition borrowing took place? Moreover, just as we saw in the *Crane* case, the parties argued against their usual best interests. Mrs. Wood's theory accelerated the reporting of the gain to a time earlier than the government was contending.

Of course, like Mrs. Crane before her, Mrs. Wood was probably trying to have it both ways. Presumably, she did not actually report any gain in 1931, and that year was likely out of the reach of the government by 1943. To be sure, because income tax rates were considerably higher in 1943 than they were in 1931,[92] her attempted whipsaw may not have been as objectionable as first appears. Still, the government may have been concerned that if Mrs. Wood's theory had prevailed, other taxpayers would claim that the amount of their present gains should be reduced because of gains that should have been (but were not) reported by them in earlier, now closed years. We do not know how common Mrs. Wood's fact pattern was back then and whether the government could have somehow imposed upon those other taxpayers a rule of consistency.

In any event, the government contested Mrs. Wood's theory, and the Second Circuit chose not to accept it. Instead, relying primarily upon Judge Hand's opinion in *Crane*, the court observed that the mortgagee of the post-acquisition debt was a "mere creditor." The mortgagee was not an owner or co-owner of the property, and Mrs. Wood did not dispose of any property interest in 1931. The court seemed to think that this meant she could not recognize any gain in that year. Accordingly, there was no increase in her basis in the property prior to 1943.

4.   *Summary of Post-*Crane *Case Law*

The post-*Crane* case law reveals the influence of that case on the important questions of whether nonrecourse debt used to acquire property is included in basis and amount realized. *Crane* did not directly answer the basis question because Mrs. Crane acquired her property by devise. Nevertheless, the case's most lasting influence is in resolving the basis issue. By reasoning backwards from depreciation to basis and by holding that nonrecourse debt must be included in the amount realized, the Supreme Court in *Crane* invited the conclusion reached by subsequent courts that the basis of property acquired with nonrecourse debt should also include such debt.

Although the Court's holding with respect to amount realized continues to be the law today, the analysis it used to reach its conclusion did not stand the test of time. Subsequent courts very quickly either misunderstood or began to disregard the Supreme Court's economic

---

[92] In 1931, the normal income tax rate ranged from 1–1/2% to 5% with fairly flat surtax rates rising to 20% for incomes of over $100,000. By 1943, the normal tax rate was a flat 6% with sharply graduated surtax rates rising to 82%. Incomes of over $100,000 were subject to a surtax of 79%. *See* 2002 CCH Std. Fed. Tax Rptr. ¶¶ 140–41.

benefit theory. This process culminated with *Tufts*, where Justice Blackmun, in a bit of revisionist history, announced that the economic benefit theory really had not been critical to the *Crane* holding after all. Instead, Blackmun articulated a symmetry argument which in effect placed the entire resolution of the amount realized question on the back of the basis determination. *If* nonrecourse debt is included in the taxpayer's basis in property upon acquisition, then the same debt must be taken into account in determining the taxpayer's amount realized when the property is sold. There is clearly some circularity here if the conclusion regarding basis was determined in part by the *Crane* Court's holding with respect to amount realized.

The *Crane* decisions, and more particularly Judge Hand's opinion, also had an important influence on the outcome in *Woodsam*. As a result of that case, the proceeds of post-acquisition nonrecourse borrowing are not treated as income to the borrower and do not affect the borrower's basis in the property securing the debt. Many view the Second Circuit's decision in *Woodsam* as a missed opportunity to adopt a sounder rule from a tax policy standpoint.[93]

Finally, recall that one possible explanation for the government's litigating position in *Crane*—perhaps the only reason that seems justifiable in retrospect—was a goal of administrative simplicity. The expectation was that the *Crane* rule would permit a clear, predictable outcome: The mortgagor would be entitled to claim the depreciation deductions with respect to property acquired with nonrecourse debt. The later case law makes clear, however, that this objective is not always achieved. If the amount of the debt exceeds the value of the property at the time of acquisition, there is uncertainty regarding the buyer's basis in the property for depreciation purposes. According to the Ninth Circuit in *Estate of Franklin*, the buyer's basis may be *zero* in that situation, thereby precluding anyone from getting the depreciation deductions. At least one other court has indicated that the buyer's basis in that case should be the fair market value of the property.[94] Under either rule, the buyer's entitlement to depreciation deductions depends upon the often uncertain determination of fair market value.

In short, in transactions involving property financed with nonrecourse debt, the value of the property remains important under current law but only to the buyer (in determining basis) and not to the seller (in determining amount realized). This asymmetry makes the determination of value an especially challenging undertaking. There may not be any

---

[93] *See, e.g.*, Marvin D. Chirelstein, *Federal Income Taxation* ¶ 13.03 (9th ed. 2002); Alvin D. Lurie, *Mortgagor's Gain on Mortgaging Property for More Than Cost Without Personal Liability (Contentions of Taxpayer's Counsel in a Pending Case)*, 6 Tax L. Rev. 319 (1951).

[94] *See* Pleasant Summit Land Corp. v. Commissioner, 863 F.2d 263 (3d Cir.1988).

bilateral agreement on value reached by parties bargaining at arm's length and with conflicting interests.

But these complications are minor compared to what Congress has done to the *Crane* rule. These changes are briefly summarized in the next section.

Crane's *Role in the Growth of Tax Shelters*

Beginning in the mid–1960s, tax shelter activity in this country started to increase dramatically. One small indication of this trend is reflected in statistics relating to partnerships engaged in real estate activities. Between 1965 and 1982, the number of such partnerships tripled and their number of partners showed a fivefold increase. In addition, receipts of such partnerships grew at an average rate of 15 percent per year. Despite these increases, the net income reported by such partnerships during this period *declined* by an average of 30 percent each year. Indeed, in only three of the years during this entire period did real estate partnerships in the aggregate report an increase in profits from the prior year. Presumably, if this absence of profit had been "real," there would not have been such growth in interest in real estate partnerships. Losses reported by all partnerships grew significantly throughout this period, and by all indications, tax shelter activity continued to increase until 1986.

There were many reasons for this increase in shelter activity, ranging from economic factors such as inflation and high interest rates, legal changes such as the deregulation of broker-dealer commissions, which caused brokerage houses to seek out new products to sell, and the Vietnam War and Watergate, which changed public attitudes towards government generally. But high tax rates and other aspects of the tax laws fueled the growth as well.

The *Crane* rule played an integral role in many tax shelters. To illustrate, let us return to the facts of *Tufts*. In that case, in exchange for committing $44,000 in cash to the venture, the partners (thanks to the *Crane* rule) obtained a depreciable basis in the apartment complex of $1,895,000 which entitled them to claim *$440,000* in depreciation deductions in the first year of operation alone. Assuming that income from the property offset any cash expenses, this meant that the partners were able to report losses from their partnership investment in the first year of $440,000. These losses were able to shelter their income from services, investments, or other profitable activities in that year. If the partners were on average in the 50 percent tax bracket, their first year tax savings were $220,000, or five times their cash investment.

True, as a result of the holding in *Tufts*, taxpayers in the partners' situation faced a sizable amount of income down the road when they eventually disposed of their investment. But this later gain was in certain circumstances taxed at preferential capital gains rates. Or, the tax situations of some taxpayers permitted them to avoid having to pay much tax on the subsequent gain. (Indeed, if taxpayers invested in a new tax shelter in the interim, losses from the new shelter could be used to offset the *Tufts* gain from the first shelter.) Some taxpayers simply "forgot" to report the later gain. Finally, even if forced to pay tax at full ordinary income rates on the eventual gain, taxpayers still gained the benefit of deferral. The tax shelter investment enabled them to defer paying the taxes on their services or other income in the first year of the investment until some later time. They received, in effect, an interest-free loan from the government for the period of the delay.

These same advantages arose whether or not the investment was financed by recourse or nonrecourse debt. The advantage of using nonrecourse debt was that it limited the risk of the investors. In *Tufts*, the partners may have hoped that their real estate investment would turn out to be an economic success. But they knew that no matter what, they would obtain the tax savings, and that *both* the possibility of an economic success *and* the tax savings would cost them at most the $44,000 in cash. Thus, the use of nonrecourse debt opened up the market for tax shelters to investors without sizable amounts of capital to commit or to put at risk in a venture.

The use of nonrecourse debt created one other possibility. As we saw in *Mayerson* and *Estate of Franklin*, some taxpayers tried to overstate the amount of such debt in seller-financed acquisitions in order to augment the buyer's basis for depreciation purposes. If the Service went along with this treatment (or, more likely, simply failed to scrutinize it at all), then the buyer stood to obtain tax benefits even greater than those provided by an "ordinary" tax shelter not involving an inflated basis in property. Sellers would typically go along as long as they received some consideration for doing so. As a result of *Tufts*, an overstated, nonrecourse liability increased the seller's amount realized and gain from the sale. But because of the installment sales provision applicable at the time, sellers were not required to report any of the "gain" attributable to the overstated obligation unless and until they actually received payments on the note.[95] Moreover, some sellers did not care about the amount of this gain because they were effectively tax-exempt.

The increased tax shelter activity had pervasive effects in this country. It was common in certain areas to see the construction of "see-through buildings," *i.e.*, buildings with no tenants, because the buildings were being constructed for tax purposes rather than as a result of

---

[95] *See* § 453. The law has now been changed in important respects.

economic demand. The real estate sector became so tax-favored that according to one Congressional study, exempting the sector altogether from income taxes would actually have *raised* revenue. Many other parts of the economy were also affected. In one widely-publicized incident, Florida legislators actually sponsored legislation to eliminate the tax breaks applicable to citrus growers because the tax advantages (and resulting shelter investments) had completely distorted the market for citrus products. There was also considerable concern about the adverse impact of tax shelters on voluntary compliance, a bedrock principle of the tax system. Popular magazines such as *Money Magazine* regularly published articles detailing how upper-and middle-income taxpayers could avoid paying income taxes altogether.

The Treasury Department and the Congress adopted many, many changes, large and small, in an effort to curb tax shelter activity. Indeed, one might even attribute as fundamental a change as the flattening of the tax rate structure to, in part, a desire to reduce incentives to engage in shelters. The changes most directly affecting the *Crane* rule were the enactment of the "at risk" rules in 1976, the expansion of those rules in 1986, and the enactment of the passive activity loss rules in the latter year.

The at risk rules prevent certain taxpayers from claiming a loss from an activity that is greater than the amount the taxpayer has at risk in the activity.[96] In general, "at risk" amounts only include cash investments and borrowed money which the taxpayer is personally obligated to repay. Thus, by generally excluding nonrecourse debt from the amount at risk, the rule is essentially an "anti-*Crane*" rule. Nonrecourse debt is still included in basis, but any losses arising from that portion of the investment cannot be deducted by the taxpayer. Rather, such losses are suspended indefinitely until the taxpayer has enough at risk in the activity to support the loss or until the taxpayer has income from the activity (including *Tufts* gain).

As originally enacted, the at risk rules applied to only a limited number of activities, but their scope was eventually expanded to include virtually all activities other than real estate. Then, in 1986, Congress extended the rules to real estate activities but also enacted an important exception which treats nonrecourse real estate financing as an amount at risk if the amount is borrowed from a third-party commercial lender.[97] The distinction being drawn by this exception is the difference between the lender in *Estate of Franklin* (or *Mayerson*) and that involved in *Tufts*. In the first two cases, the lender was the seller of the property who agreed to take the buyer's nonrecourse note for all or part of the

---

[96] § 465(a)(1).

[97] § 465(b)(6).

purchase price. As previously discussed, in these seller-financed situations, there was the potential for parties to try to overstate the amount of the liability to obtain and share additional tax benefits. The at risk rule therefore does not include seller-financed nonrecourse debt as an amount at risk. In contrast, in *Tufts*, the lender to the partnership was a third-party commercial lender which presumably had no reason to lend an amount greater than the value of the property because the lender's only recourse in the event of the borrower's default was to foreclose on the property. As a result of the statutory exception, the nonrecourse debt in *Tufts* would have been treated as an amount that the partnership had at risk.

Overlaying the at risk rules is another set of limitations, the passive activity loss (PAL) rules. In very general terms, these rules prevent certain taxpayers from using losses from so-called "passive activities" to reduce income from services or portfolio investments.[98] A passive activity is one in which the taxpayer does not materially participate and, in general, all rental activity is considered a passive activity. Thus, had these rules been in place, the partners in *Tufts* could not have used their partnership losses from the apartment complex to shelter their income from services, portfolio investments, or other non-passive sources. The PAL limitation is not limited to losses financed by nonrecourse debt. Losses from recourse debt as well as cash investment may all be restricted by the PAL rule. Like the at risk rules, losses not allowed by the PAL rules are suspended indefinitely until the taxpayer has enough passive activity income or disposes of the investment. As mentioned, these rules operate on top of the at risk rules; thus, losses that may be deducted because the taxpayer has a sufficient amount at risk may nevertheless be trapped by the PAL rules.

This brief summary of some of the principal provisions limiting the effect of the *Crane* rule does not begin to describe the additional level of complexity that they introduce to the tax system. The simple concept of "net income," in which a taxpayer merely nets together all income and all deductions in order to determine the taxpayer's tax base, has long eluded the system because of the existence of special categories of income, such as capital gains. The at risk and PAL rules move us further away from this simple ideal. Instead, the tax system now more closely resembles a form of "schedular" taxation in which income and deductions must first be separately classified and netted together as if they were on separate schedules before the taxpayer's tax base can be measured. Schedular taxation presents the obvious definitional problem of determining which income and deductions must appear on which schedule. In addition, once the categories are defined, rules then must be

---

[98] § 469(a), (c)(1), (d)(1), & (e)(1).

developed to prevent taxpayers from trying to redesign or recharacterize
their activities in order to shift their income or deductions from one
category to another. Further, because many deductions arise as a result
of a timing preference, additional rules have to be developed to make
sure that when the timing preference reverses, the taxpayer is not
unfairly disadvantaged. The one saving grace with respect to these rules
is that they apparently have been quite effective at curbing *Crane*-type
tax shelters.

In summary, we see that much of the tax law today, including a not
insignificant portion of its complications, can be traced back to the
decision involving Beulah Crane. The next section considers briefly the
continuing importance of her case today.

The Continuing Importance of *Crane* Today

The *Crane* rule continues to be the law today. In general, the basis
of property includes the amount of nonrecourse debt used to acquire it.
Further, the amount realized upon disposition of property secured by
nonrecourse debt includes the amount of the debt.[99] But the at risk and
PAL rules have dramatically altered the continuing significance of the
case. In many situations, deductions emanating from a *Crane*-supported
basis in property may not be used by the taxpayer because of either or
both of those rules. In those cases, the taxpayer may be in much the
same situation as if nonrecourse debt had not been included in basis in
the first place. This is, then, the ultimate irony of Mrs. Crane's saga: a
rule adopted in no small part to ensure the claiming of depreciation
deductions survives in the law, but without that consequence.

The *Crane* rule still provides an *internal* shelter for a taxpayer's
activities. The at risk and PAL rules only disallow the claiming of
"losses" from an activity in certain circumstances. Thus, any income
generated by an activity itself can be sheltered by depreciation deductions resulting from the *Crane* rule. The availability of internal (but not
external) sheltering places some pressure on the definition of an "activity." For example, if the ownership and operation of two rental buildings
are treated as separate activities for purposes of the at risk rules, then it
may not be possible for losses from one of the buildings to offset income
from the other.

In addition, the *Crane* doctrine continues to be significant in situations that are carved out of the usual application of the at risk or PAL
limitations. For example, as noted, nonrecourse debt provided by third-
party commercial lenders to finance real estate activities is treated as an
amount the taxpayer has at risk in the activity. Thus, the deduction of

---

[99] *See* Reg. § 1.1001–2(a)(1) & (4)(i).

losses arising from such debt would not be limited by the at risk rule. Of course, to be able to deduct the loss against income from a non-passive activity, the taxpayer would still need to navigate the PAL limitation, which has its own set of exceptions and special rules.

Finally, certain taxpayers, such as widely-held C corporations, are not subject to either the at risk or PAL limitations.[100] For those taxpayers, the *Crane* rule continues to apply with full force.

Epilogue—The *Crane* Rule in Retrospect

In her reply brief to the Supreme Court, Beulah Crane brought to the Court's attention a recently published student law review note critical of the Second Circuit's holding in her case.[101] The note suggested adoption of an alternate rule that would have limited an owner's depreciation deductions to the amount of equity the owner had invested in the property being depreciated. The amount of the deductions would have been computed based on the full value of the property, and not just the equity. But the owner's entitlement to use those deductions would have been limited by the amount of the owner's equity. In the absence of a sufficient unrecovered equity, the deductions would simply have remained unused; no other taxpayer would have been entitled to claim them. In other words, the note urged adoption of a rule that is essentially equivalent to the "at risk" limitation in the law today. What would have happened if the Court had heeded the advice of this note, or had reversed the Second Circuit and reinstated the holding of the Tax Court? Would we have avoided the 20–year war on tax shelters and all of its adverse effects on the economy and the tax system?

One can only speculate, but the answer may well be "no." The question is whether there would have been general acceptance of the Court's adoption of an anti-*Crane* rule. If not, the Congress and/or subsequent courts presumably would have tried to circumvent or limit the Court's holding. It is quite possible that an anti-*Crane* decision by the Court would have been viewed as "before its time."

To understand why, it is important to remember that, as explained by the Tax Court in *Mayerson*, there is a reason to treat cash and debt-financed investments in a similar way for tax purposes. As long as debt proceeds are not treated as income when received, a taxpayer who acquires property in exchange for a debt obligation should presumably bear the same tax consequences as one who makes a cash investment with borrowed funds. Part of the *Crane* rule, then, is simply establishing this basic equivalency between cash and debt.

---

[100] §§ 465(a)(1), 469(a)(2).

[101] *See* Taxpayer's Reply Brief at 7. The note was Note, 13 U. Chi. L. Rev. 510 (1946).

Crane, of course, extended the tax treatment of debt to include nonrecourse borrowing. But recourse and nonrecourse debt differ only in degree and not in kind. In the ordinary case, where the amount of the debt remains less than the fair market value of the property serving as security for the debt, nonrecourse debt is fully repaid by the borrower. Conversely, recourse debt may not be repaid in a variety of circumstances such as when the debtor becomes insolvent. If either recourse or nonrecourse debt is not repaid, the tax system in each case requires the debtor to recognize income equal to the amount of the debt discharged.[102] Thus, it is not obvious that a sharp distinction should be drawn for tax purposes between recourse and nonrecourse debt.

In addition, although the *Crane* rule was an integral part of tax shelters, the rule, on its own, was not the cause of shelters. Other tax rules—the allowance of tax depreciation deductions in excess of economic depreciation, the taxation of *Tufts* gain at preferential tax rates, the failure to distinguish interest from principal payments for tax purposes, the deferral permitted by the installment sale rules, to name a few— were necessary to produce the shelters in conjunction with the *Crane* rule. The flaw of the *Crane* rule—a not insignificant one in retrospect— is that it did nothing to *restrain* tax shelter activity once the economic, tax, and other conditions in this country made it ripe for such activity.[103] Instead, it magnified the inadequacies of the other tax rules. In order to prevent shelters, it relied upon a degree of perfection among the other rules, and a level of compliance among taxpayers, that were probably unrealistic expectations of any tax system.

But would this weakness have been generally recognized in 1947? The government did not demonstrate any particular awareness of it and it seems unlikely that the public would have been any more cognizant. Thus, adoption of an anti-*Crane* rule by the Court may well have encountered opposition because of its deviation from normative income tax principles and led to efforts to reverse or limit the effect of the Court's holding. As they say, some lessons simply have to be learned the hard way.

Note on Sources

The information contained in the first part of this chapter is derived from the Tax Court opinion, *Crane v. Commissioner*, 3 T.C. 585 (1944), court documents and other materials included in the Transcript of Record, Supreme Court of the United States, Oct. Term, 1946, No. 68,

---

[102] *See* United States v. Kirby Lumber Co., 284 U.S. 1 (1931), discussed in Chapter 3 of *Tax Stories*.

[103] *See* Chirelstein, *supra* note 93, at 304.

and articles appearing in the following editions of The New York Times: Jun. 24, 1923, p. RE1; Oct. 7, 1923, p. RE14; Feb. 26, 1924, p. 35; Jan. 3, 1926, p. E15; Feb. 6, 1927, p. RE1; Feb. 6, 1931, p. 23; Jun. 15, 1931, p. 14; Jan. 12, 1932, p. 20; Jun. 14, 1932, p. 19; Oct. 18, 1933, p. 39; Nov. 10, 1934, p. 20; and Sep. 14, 1935, p. 30.

Selected References

Adams, D. Nelson, *Exploring the Outer Boundaries of the* Crane *Doctrine; An Imaginary Supreme Court Opinion*, 21 Tax L. Rev. 159 (1966).

Andrews, William D., *On Beyond* Tufts, 61 Taxes 949 (1983).

Barton, Babette B., *Economic Fables/Tax–Related Foibles: On the "Cost" of Promissory Notes, Guarantees, Contingent Liabilities and Nonrecourse Loans*, 45 Tax L. Rev. 471 (1990).

Bittker, Boris I., *Tax Shelters, Nonrecourse Debt, and the* Crane *Case*, 33 Tax L. Rev. 277 (1978).

Braunfield, Fritz L., *Subject to a Mortgage*, 24 Taxes 424 (1946) (Part I); 24 Taxes 557 (1946) (Part II); 25 Taxes 155 (1947) (Part III).

Case Note, 37 O. O. 259 (1948).

Chirelstein, Marvin A., *Federal Income Taxation* (Foundation Press, 9th ed. 2002).

Chirelstein, Marvin A., *Learned Hand's Contribution to the Law of Tax Avoidance*, 77 Yale L. J. 440 (1968).

Comment, 33 Iowa L. Rev. 143 (1947).

Comment, *Depreciation of Property Subject to an Unassumed Mortgage: Implications of the* Crane *Decision*, 26 Tex. L. Rev. 796 (1948).

Coven, Glenn E., *Limiting Losses Attributable to Nonrecourse Debt: A Defense of the Traditional System Against the At–Risk Concept*, 74 Cal. L. Rev. 41 (1986).

Del Cotto, Louis A., *Basis and Amount Realized Under* Crane*: A Current View of Some Tax Effects in Mortgage Financing*, 118 U. Pa. L. Rev. 69 (1969).

Engel, Irving M., *Effects of the* Crane *Case*, Proceedings of NYU 6th Ann'l Inst. on Fed. Tax'n. 379 (1948).

Epstein, Richard A., *The Application of the* Crane *Doctrine to Limited Partnerships*, 45 S. Cal. L. Rev. 100 (1972).

Geier, Deborah A., Tufts *and the Evolution of Debt–Discharge Theory*, 1 Fla. Tax Rev. 115 (1992).

Ginsburg, Martin D., *The Leaky Tax Shelter*, 53 Taxes 719 (1975).

Green, Robert A., *Justice Blackmun's Federal Tax Jurisprudence*, 26 Hastings Const. L. Qtrly 109 (1998).

Gunther, Gerald, *Learned Hand: The Man and the Judge* (A.A. Knopf, 1994).

Halpern, James S., *Footnote 37 and the* Crane *Case: The Problem That Never Really Was*, 6 J. Real Est. Tax'n. 197 (1979).

Jensen, Erik M., *The Unanswered Question in* Tufts: *What Was the Purchaser's Basis?*, 10 Va. Tax Rev. 455 (1991).

Jensen, Erik M., *Nonrecourse Liabilities and Real Costs: A Reply to Professor Johnson*, 11 Va. Tax Rev. 643 (1992).

Johnson, Calvin H., *Play Money Basis: When is Nonrecourse Liability a Valid Cost?*, 11 Va. Tax Rev. 631 (1992).

Johnson, Calvin H., *The Liability Was Also Not a Cost to Bayles*, 11 Va. Tax Rev. 651 (1992).

Lurie, Alvin D., *Mortgagor's Gain on Mortgaging Property for More Than Cost Without Personal Liability (Contentions of Taxpayer's Counsel in a Pending Case)*, 6 Tax L. Rev. 319 (1951).

Lurie, Alvin D., *Taxing Transfers of Mortgaged Property*, 39 Cornell L. Qtrly. 611 (1954).

Lurie, Alvin D., *I Know* Crane *and BOSS Isn't* Crane *(An Historical Perspective)*, 86 Tax Notes 1932 (2000).

McKee, William S., *The Real Estate Tax Shelter: A Computerized Exposé*, 57 Va. L. Rev. 521 (1971).

Meyer, Richard, *Running for Shelter: Tax Shelters and the American Economy* (Public Citizen 1985).

Note, 13 U. Chi. L. Rev. 510 (1946).

Note, *Tax Consequences of the Disposition of Property Subject to an Unassumed Mortgage*, 49 Colum. L. Rev. 845 (1949).

Note, *Federal Income Tax Treatment of Nonrecourse Debt*, 82 Colum. L. Rev. 1498 (1982).

Note, *Taxation of Gain Resulting from Sales of Mortgaged Property*, 60 Harv. L. Rev. 1324 (1947).

Note, Estate of Levine v. Commissioner *and Treasury Regulation Section 1.1001–2: Toward a Comprehensive Application of the* Crane *Rule*, 1 Va. Tax Rev. 159 (1981).

Shaviro, Daniel N., *Risk and Accrual: The Tax Treatment of Nonrecourse Debt*, 44 Tax L. Rev. 401 (1989).

Simmons, Daniel L., *Nonrecourse Debt and Basis: Mrs.* Crane *Where Are You Now?*, 53 S. Cal. L. Rev. 1 (1979).

Sims, Theodore S., Debt, *Accelerated Depreciation, and the Tale of a Teakettle: Tax Shelter Abuse Reconsidered*, 42 UCLA L. Rev. 263 (1994).

Stark, Kirk J., *The Unfulfilled Tax Legacy of Justice Robert H. Jackson*, 54 Tax L. Rev. 171 (2001).

Sugin, Linda, *Nonrecourse Debt Revisited, Restructured and Redefined*, 51 Tax L. Rev. 115 (1995).

Surrey, Stanley S., *Assumption of Indebtedness in Tax–Free Exchanges*, 50 Yale L. J. 1 (1940).

Surrey, Stanley S., *The Tax Reform Act of 1969–Tax Deferral and Tax Shelters*, 12 B. C. Ind. & Comm. L. Rev. 307 (1971).

Tax Notes, 21 S. Cal. L. Rev. 112 (1947).

Wolfman, Bernard, Silver, Jonathan L.F., & Silver, Marjorie A., *Dissent Without Opinion: The Behavior of Justice William O. Douglas in Federal Tax Cases* (U. Pa. Press 1975).

Yin, George K., *Getting Serious about Corporate Tax Shelters: Taking a Lesson from History*, 54 SMU L. Rev. 209 (2001).

*

8

Russell K. Osgood

The Story of *Schlude*: The Origins of the Tax/Financial Accounting GA(A)P

Schlude v. Commissioner[1] is the third in a trilogy[2] of cases that established emphatically that tax accounting under the Internal Revenue Code may differ from generally accepted accounting principles ("GAAP"). Unfortunately, the principles to be applied in determining when such a divergence is permissible are not made clear in the *Schlude* trilogy, and indeed still have not been made clear forty years later. The *Schlude* trilogy thus forms part of a depository of cases embracing a common law approach to the matter.

Background

The Legal Background

Since the 1919 revenue act,[3] the income tax has required a taxpayer to report income "under the method of accounting on the basis of which the taxpayer regularly computes his income in keeping his books,"[4] unless that method "does not clearly reflect income."[5] These sensible and simple sounding words seem to establish linguistically, at a minimum, that tax accounting can differ from GAAP. But they do not

---

[1] 372 U.S. 128 (1963).

[2] The other two are American Auto. Ass'n v. United States, 367 U.S. 687 (1961) ("*AAA*"), and Automobile Club of Mich. v. Commissioner, 353 U.S. 180 (1957).

[3] Act of February 24, 1919, ch. 18, 40 Stat. 1057.

[4] § 446(a).

[5] § 446(b). Section 446(c)(2) permits a taxpayer to report his or her income on "an accrual method," as was the case with each taxpayer in the cases discussed in this chapter.

establish the theoretical basis for determining what clearly reflects income apart from some notion about how to account for or compute that income.

1. United States v. Anderson

There are several candidates to choose as the starting point for the odyssey that should have ended with *Schlude* but instead continues to this day (and in fact likely will continue until the end of the income tax as we know it). A good place to begin the story is with *United States v. Anderson*[6] decided along with *United States v. Yale & Towne Manufacturing Company*,[7] one of the several cases spawned by the sharp increases in rates of taxation during World Wars I and II. Such major rate changes are, of course, a likely venue for disputes about rules of accounting, inclusion, and deduction because the stakes in selecting one year versus another are so significant. The taxpayers were represented by John W. Davis, a distinguished Washington lawyer and the defeated Democratic presidential candidate in the 1924 election.

In *Anderson*, the Supreme Court, in an opinion by Justice Stone, held that munitions taxes owed by Yale & Towne Manufacturing for 1916 (but not assessed legally until 1917) were accruable expenses for 1916, contrary to the taxpayers' arguments. (Tax rates went up between 1916 and 1917.) Note that the Commissioner prevailed, as occurred in *every* case discussed in this chapter. Although the Court touched on some of the theoretical issues, such as whether "all events" necessary for a proper accrual occurred in the absence of a formal assessment of the tax, the most determinate sentence in the opinion indicates a knowing reliance on the presumptive correctness of a knowledgeable tax administration: "We think that the statute was correctly interpreted by the Commissioner and that his decision referred to was consistent with its purpose and intent."[8] Unfortunately, Justices Sutherland and Sanford dissented without opinions,[9] so there was little by way of contrapuntal elucidation of the majority's opinion. The Court reversed the Court of Claims, which had unanimously held for the taxpayers on the ground that the tax was not payable (or accruable) until assessed.[10]

Although *Anderson* concerned an expense (taxes), the remaining cases in the *Schlude* trilogy involved payments of income for matters

---

[6] 269 U.S. 422 (1926), *reversing* 60 Ct.Cl. 106 (1925).

[7] The lower court decision, also reversed, was Yale & Towne Mfg. Co. v. United States, 60 Ct.Cl. 440 (1925).

[8] 269 U.S. at 438.

[9] *Id.* at 443.

[10] Anderson v. United States, 60 Ct.Cl. 106 (1925).

that stretched over more than the taxable year of payment. As one begins to consider these cases, note that a significant quantum of business income payments (well beyond automobile or other club dues) are in fact made in advance of the full rendition of services, and that those services frequently extend beyond the year of payment.

2. Automobile Club of Michigan v. Commissioner

In *Automobile Club of Michigan v. Commissioner*,[11] the Supreme Court, in an opinion by Justice Brennan, considered for the first time an issue that bedeviled the Congress, the Commissioner, and the federal courts through several decades: when to include in the income of an accrual basis taxpayer prepaid dues for a club membership or service that extends across more than one fiscal year. Large amounts of revenue ultimately do not revolve around the resolution of this issue, as most such memberships or services spread over no more than two taxable years. *Michigan* raised two major issues: (1) could the Commissioner retroactively revoke its erroneous classification of the auto club as an exempt organization; and (2) was the club's reporting of prepaid membership income at a rate of 1/12 of an annual dues payment at the start of each month, extending frequently in a second year and thus causing reporting in a year later than the year of payment, consistent with the Code. The Court ruled in favor of the Commissioner on both issues. As to the latter, the Court explained that it could not "say, in the circumstances here, that the discretionary action of the Commissioner, sustained by both the Tax Court and the Court of Appeals, exceeded permissible limits."[12]

The *Michigan* opinion, although the shortest of the *Schlude* trilogy, in many ways is the most articulate in explaining why deference is appropriate to the Commissioner's determination that inclusion should occur in the year of payment rather than pro rata inclusion on a monthly or some other phased basis. The taxpayer's argument obviously was that it had to face the possibility of providing services in the later year and that there should be an effort to match the rate of inclusion with the possible rate of expense incurrence. Recall that the Club promised, in return for the dues, to provide maps, directions, and other membership services when requested rather than at fixed points in time.

Unfortunately for the taxpayers in each of these cases, because all services were to be rendered on demand or by mutual agreement on or at unspecified dates in the future, there was no certain way to set future points of liability or any definite amount of liability. Thus, in *Michigan*, Justice Brennan wrote that since "substantially all services are performed only upon a member's demand and the taxpayer's performance

---

[11] 353 U.S. 180 (1957).

[12] *Id.* at 189–90.

was not related to fixed dates after the tax year,"[13] the method of ratable inclusion was "purely artificial."[14] This tantalizing and interesting phraseology, which obviously captured something significant, provided a lead that ultimately proved to be a dead end to the litigants in the later cases. The use of "purely" before "artificial" suggested that if there were data to support the rate of later inclusion, data tied to likelihood of expense incurrence, then perhaps such ratable inclusion might be upheld.

In *Michigan*, Justice Harlan dissented on both the retroactive revocation and accounting issues. On the accounting issue, Justice Harlan focused on an argument that rattles around in all of these cases and debunked it. The Commissioner had argued below in *Michigan*, and repeated later in the Court of Claims in *AAA*,[15] that the taxpayer had to include the dues fully in income in the year of receipt under the "claim of right" doctrine of *North American Oil Consolidated v. Burnet*.[16] The Court of Claims rejected reliance on this doctrine and on this case,[17] echoing Justice Harlan's earlier and more precise description and treatment of this issue:

> However, that doctrine, it seems to me, comes into play only in determining whether the treatment of an item of income should be influenced by the fact that the right to receive or keep it is in dispute; it does not relate to the entirely different question whether items that admittedly belong to the taxpayer may be attributed to a taxable year other than that of receipt in accordance with the principles of *accrual* accounting.[18]

3.   American Automobile Association v. United States

In light of *Michigan's* tantalizing rhetoric about artificiality, and also taking into account certain weaknesses in the record in that case, similar taxpayers forged ahead, using a virtually identical accounting system, and tried to prevail over the Commissioner in other litigation. In *AAA*,[19] the taxpayer distinguished *Michigan* on three grounds: "[1]

---

[13] *Id.* at 189 n.20.

[14] *Id.* at 189.

[15] American Auto. Ass'n v. United States, 149 Ct.Cl. 324 (1960).

[16] 286 U.S. 417 (1932).

[17] 149 Ct.Cl. at 329 ("However, we do not find it necessary to resolve this issue, since we agree with the Government's contention that the method of treatment of prepaid automobile club membership dues employed by the plaintiff was dealt with by the Supreme Court in [*Michigan*.]").

[18] 353 U.S. at 191–92.

[19] 367 U.S. 687 (1961). The case was an appeal from American Auto. Ass'n v. United States, 181 F.Supp. 255 (Ct.Cl.1960). The Court of Claims opinion was consistent with an

[Their] record contains expert accounting testimony indicating that the system used was in accord with generally accepted accounting principles; [2] that its proof of cost of member service was detailed; and [3] that the correlation between that cost and the period of time over which the dues were credited as income was shown and justified by proof of experience."[20] The United States, represented by Assistant Attorney General and future judge Louis F. Oberdorfer, with the future Solicitor General and Harvard Law Professor, Archibald Cox, on brief, argued for inclusion of "the entire amount of membership dues actually received in the taxable calendar year."[21]

The Court, in a 5–4 decision written by Justice Clark, rejected AAA's arguments and restated its view that it would uphold the Commissioner's exercise of his discretion in this situation and reject ratable inclusion of income from prepaid dues. The Court found, as in *Michigan*, that virtually all services were performable "on demand":

> When their receipt as earned income is recognized ratably over two calendar years, without regard to correspondingly fixed individual expense or performance justification, but consistently with overall experience, their accounting doubtless presents a rather accurate image of the total financial structure, but fails to respect the criteria of annual tax accounting and *may* be rejected by the Commissioner.[22]

Interestingly and perhaps fatally, AAA had changed methodologies after the tax years in issue and adopted a revised methodology of including an unvarying one-half of such dues received in each of the two years in question, as opposed to ratably over the months in question, even if the dues covered two months in one year and ten months in the next.[23] Thus, it would appear to be almost impossible to produce statistical evidence of the predictability of expense incursion, which would lead the Court to overturn the Commissioner's exercise of discretion in this kind of case and that this is an instance in which the "clear reflection of income" language trumps good, sound, accurate financial accounting.[24]

---

earlier opinion on the same two issues in New Jersey Auto. Club v. United States, 149 Ct.Cl. 344 (1960), *cert. denied*, 366 U.S. 964 (1961).

[20] 367 U.S. at 691.

[21] *Id.* at 688.

[22] *Id.* at 692 (emphasis added).

[23] *Id.* at 693. "In addition, the Association's election in 1954 to change its monthly recognition formula to one which treats one-half of the dues as income in the year of receipt and the other half as income received in the subsequent year. Without regard to month of payment, only more clearly indicates the artificiality of its method, at least so far as controlling tax purposes are concerned." *Id.*

[24] *Id.*

The Court rejected additional AAA arguments that Congress' enactment, and then repeal in 1954 and 1955, of ameliorative provisions established that clubs like AAA should be allowed to use the method rejected by the Court in *Michigan*. The Court held that to read into legislative authorization followed by repeal a general approval of the technique was "sciamachy."[25] At the same time, the Court held that Congress' repeal left the Commissioner free to take the position he took in this case.

Justice Stewart, joined by Justices Douglas, Harlan, and Whittaker, dissented.[26] Justice Stewart resisted each determination in the majority opinion, including the refusal to read anything into the passage and quick repeal of ameliorative legislation. Perhaps the fierceness of this dissent, joined in by four justices, explained why *Schlude* made it to the Supreme Court two years later. Justice Stewart relied heavily on the numerous expense cases involving the "all events" standard, including *Anderson*, to support his position: "The net effect of compelling the petitioner to include all dues in gross income in the year received is to force the petitioner to utilize a hybrid accounting method—a cash basis for dues and an accrual basis for all other items."[27] Justice Stewart also reiterated Justice Harlan's rejection in *Michigan* of the "claim of right" doctrine as a basis for the Court's ruling and noted the Commissioner's abandonment of it.[28]

AAA established even more clearly than *Michigan* the Court's view that the timing of the inclusion of an item of prepaid income is a matter within the Commissioner's discretion, but that once the Commissioner exercises that discretion, there is no basis in law and on these facts to overturn it: "[T]he federal revenue cannot, without legislative consent, and over objection of the Commissioner, be made to depend upon average experience in rendering performance and turning a profit."[29]

The Factual Background

The long and multifarious *Schlude* litigation had commenced before the Supreme Court's decision in *AAA*. Indeed, the Tax Court decision, favorable to the Commissioner, was filed on September 28, 1959, well before the *AAA* decision.[30] *Schlude* involved a very different set of facts.

---

[25] *Id.* at 696. The Oxford English Dictionary defines a "sciamachy" as a "sham lighting."

[26] *Id.* at 698.

[27] *Id.* at 714.

[28] *Id.* at 690–91.

[29] *Id.* at 693.

[30] 32 T.C. 1271 (1959).

The Schludes operated an Arthur Murray dance studio in Omaha, Nebraska.[31] When an individual subscribed for lessons under a contract, he or she made a payment, signed a note, or made an unsecured promise to pay in the future that could, and frequently did, cover lessons to be given over more than one taxable year. Lessons were arranged individually, and it could not be precisely determined when any or all of them would or might occur. Although the lessons and contracts generally covered two taxable years, there also was a lifetime contract option, sold for $5,000, that provided 1,200 specified hours of lessons, and in addition, two hours of lessons per month and two parties a year for life.[32]

The Schludes, on the advice of their accountants, placed the entire subscription or contract amount paid in a deferred income account. Each lesson given in a taxable year (on a student-by-student basis recorded painstakingly on individual cards) was then costed, and that amount was backed out of the deferred income account and reported as taxable income for that year. The rest of the deferred income would carry over to the following year. Contracts could be cancelled either by direct action or by the passage of a year without activity. Occasionally, contracts were written down, meaning the number of lessons was reduced, and the obligation to make future payments was reduced. In addition, refunds (contrary to the terms of the contracts) occasionally were given in the event of a contract cancellation. The Schludes, in contrast to their method of reporting lesson income, immediately deducted the full salesman's commission and certain franchise fees owed to Arthur Murray. A fair number of contracts resulted in "forfeitures" (e.g., the contract period expired before some or all of the dancing lessons were ever given).[33]

Prior Proceedings

The Tax Court

The Tax Court held for the Commissioner in a sweeping decision that included in income all prepayments, the full face amount of any notes given for future lessons, and even the full amount of unsecured promises to pay for future lessons pursuant to contracts. The Schludes appealed to the Eighth Circuit.

The Eighth Circuit

The Eighth Circuit, in a learned opinion that discussed many decisions involving prepaid income and reserves for expenses, reversed

---

[31] A short three hours drive west of Grinnell, Iowa.

[32] 32 T.C. at 1274.

[33] *Id.* at 1272–75.

the Tax Court and approved the Schludes' accrual methodology.[34] The Eighth Circuit treated *Michigan* as inapposite on the ground that the Schludes' "obligation to provide services subsequent to the tax year was fixed, definite, and certain, thereby effectively rebutting any contention that petitioners' method of deferral was purely artificial."[35]

The Eighth Circuit's decision preceded the Supreme Court's decision in *AAA*, and therefore the Commissioner petitioned by writ of *certiorari* upon the rendition of that decision. The Court granted the petition,[36] vacating the Eighth Circuit's decision and remanding it back to that court for further consideration.[37] In a per curiam decision, the Eighth Circuit vacated its previous decision for the taxpayers.[38]

The Supreme Court Decision

The Petition for Certiorari

The Schludes, apparently not sensing the futility of a further appeal, or perhaps because of the erroneous inclusion in income of unsecured promises to pay for lessons due in the future, petitioned the Supreme Court to grant a writ of *certiorari*. The *certiorari* petition was well written and effective in getting the Court to take a case that perhaps it should not have taken. The petition contained three strong arguments: (1) there were significant factual differences between the Schludes' methods and those of the auto clubs;[39] (2) the decisions below finding for the Commissioner conflicted with *Anderson*;[40] and (3) the decision threatened to disrupt the affairs of many accrual taxpayers.[41]

The Oral Argument

On December 10, 1962, Carl F. Bauersfield and Louis F. Oberdorfer argued for the taxpayers and the government, respectively.[42] Unlike the

---

[34] 283 F.2d 234 (8th Cir.1960).

[35] *Id.* at 241. One might be inclined to say that when a federal judge says that something "effectively" rebuts something, rather than merely saying that it "rebuts" something, there may be more rhetoric and less substance in the former than in the latter.

[36] 367 U.S. 911 (1961).

[37] 368 U.S. 873 (1961).

[38] 296 F.2d 721 (8th Cir.1961).

[39] Taxpayer's Petition for *Certiorari* at 8. Not surprisingly, the petition does not discuss the inherent imperfections in the Schludes' methodology

[40] *Id.* at 11.

[41] *Id.* at 13 ("If the *American Automobile Association* decision is construed to mean, as the Courts below have construed it, that the full amounts of the contracts are income and taxable in the year the contracts are signed irrespective of when payment is made or due to be made, and irrespective of time of performance by the taxpayer under the contract it will raise havoc with American business.").

[42] 372 U.S. at 128.

majority opinion to come, the oral argument[43] was a fairly lively affair. The taxpayers' attorney was questioned less than the Assistant AG. No single colloquy is of particular note, but six interesting things occurred that perhaps presaged the result in the case: (1) the taxpayers' attorney emphasized, without comment from the bench, that the Schlude contracts involved a fixed number of lessons whereas the *Michigan* and *AAA* involved an indeterminate amount of services for club members; (2) members of the Court asked both counsel several probing questions about the lifetime contracts that promised to stretch over a number of years; (3) the Assistant AG emphasized that the contracts were cancelled at the relatively high rate of 17%, which made the two-year deferral look even less precise; (4) the Assistant AG conceded that although the case was not controlled by the claim of right doctrine, its insight was relevant to the proper understanding of the Commissioner's case; (5) the taxpayers' attorney exaggerated the stakes and significance of the case with respect to taxpayers like his clients if one considered the matter over a long period of time; and (6) the Assistant AG argued that the tax benefit of deferral (i.e., loss of the government's benefit of receiving the revenue) was at the heart of understanding the Commissioner's position.[44]

The Briefs

The briefs of both the government and the taxpayers do not reflect the shape of the ultimate opinion. The government's brief largely focuses on four arguments: (1) the "claim of right" doctrine is central to the proper resolution of the case;[45] (2) even with the greater definiteness of the service obligations in the *Schlude* contracts, the case was still controlled by *Michigan* and *AAA*;[46] (3) this case, like the two predecessors in the *Schlude* trilogy, was controlled by the annual tax accounting principle, and that tax and financial accounting clearly diverged in this regard;[47] and (4) *Anderson* was distinguishable.[48]

---

[43] Oral Argument lasted 1:00:45 and was interrupted by one recess.

[44] The full oral argument can be heard on the *Tax Stories* web site, www.law.uc.edu/TaxStories.

[45] Respondent's Brief at 30 ("The so-called 'claim of right doctrine' and its rationale lend strong support to the government's position."). This is contrary to the position taken by the Assistant AG at oral argument.

[46] *Id*. at 33–34.

[47] *Id*. at 36 ("The transactional or 'earnings' theory of tax accounting urged by taxpayer ignores the rationale of the annual accounting rule, to say nothing of the rule. As pointed out in *Sanford & Brooks*, . . . the annual accounting system is rooted in strong practical and policy considerations—the need of the government for an ascertainable amount of revenue at regular intervals, collectible through a system capable of practical operation.").

[48] *Id*. at 59 ("Nothing in [*Anderson*] may fairly be read as supporting the proposition that accrual of an item of gross income may be postponed from the taxable year in which it

The taxpayers' brief struggles in the face of *AAA*. The taxpayers argue strenuously that their individualized methodology in taking in income as individual lessons were given was so dissimilar to the method used in *AAA* that its case was not controlled by *AAA*: "It is submitted that this Court's decision in the [*AAA*] case does not prevent the use of an accrual accounting system for tax purposes which accurately and precisely matches revenues derived from services performed in a tax year with the cost of performing such services."[49] The taxpayers also argued that their methodology clearly reflected income and was consistent with *Anderson*.[50]

The Opinion

In a short and relatively lifeless opinion by Justice White, the Court upheld the result in a per curiam reversal of the Eighth Circuit and disallowed the taxpayers' method. The government had conceded that it was erroneous to include in income "future payments which were not evidenced by a note and which were neither due by the terms of the contract nor matured by performance of the related services."[51] As a result, the Court vacated that portion of the Tax Court and Eighth Circuit decisions. Justice Stewart, along with Justices Harlan and Douglas, and joined now by Justice Goldberg, dissented.

As to the main issue: "[W]e believe the problem is squarely controlled by [*AAA*]."[52] Not surprisingly, the Court based its decision on the deference principle: "[W]e invoke the 'long-established policy of the Court in deferring, where possible, to congressional procedures in the tax field,' and, as in that case, we cannot say that the Commissioner's rejection of the studio's deferral system was unsound."[53] As William Andrews has written: "In any event, one gets the feeling that the Court majority would like to be rid of the problem by deferring to either the

---

is received under claim of right and without restriction as to its use until some later year in which related expense items become deductible. To be sure, in *Anderson* the Court spoke of 'charging against income earned during the taxable period, the expenses incurred in and properly attributable to the process of earning income during that period.' ") (footnotes and citations omitted).

[49] *Id*. at 26.

[50] *Id*. at 11–13.

[51] 372 U.S. 128, 133 (1963).

[52] *Id*. at 134.

[53] *Id*. at 135

Commissioner or the Congress."[54] The Court also declined to make anything, one way or the other, of Congress' adoption and then repeal of specific statutory allowances of such accrual methods.

In a more fiery dissent than in *AAA*, Justice Stewart and his fellow dissenters complained of the "mutilation of a basic element of the accrual method of accounting."[55] Justice Stewart also wrote: "The most elementary principles of accrual accounting require that advances be considered reportable income only in the year they are earned by the taxpayer's rendition of the services for which the payments were made."[56] Although this certainly has a ring of plausibility, it sweeps a lot of transactions before it that probably make it significantly inaccurate. Specifically, what did Justice Stewart mean by an "advance"? Were the *Schlude* payments truly advances in view of the high rate of forfeitures and the unpredictability of service rendition?

The *AAA* litigation involved active participation by one amicus, the American Institute of Certified Public Accountants, ably represented by counsel led by Dean Acheson. In a formal statement, the AICPA reiterated its strong view that the Commissioner's position would convert accrual basis taxpayers to the cash method in this set of circumstances:

> The Court should be aware, however, that if the term 'right to receive' is given the meaning respondent urges, accrual accounting of advance receipts for income tax purposes will have been eliminated. Simply stated, the fundamental concept that underlies accrual accounting, insofar as it determines when receipts are to be recognized as income, is the taxpayer's earning of that income by performing services or providing goods as the case may be. That concept will lose all significance for tax purposes if respondent's position prevails.[57]

While undoubtedly hyperbolic, the brief does accurately capture the sense of despair in the accounting profession at the thought of diverging from the idea of pairing income with related expenses when possible.

The Immediate Impact of *Schlude*

At the end of the *Schlude* trilogy, it is hard to find articulable standards for when a business using the accrual method of accounting may be obligated to diverge from its method in order to "clearly reflect" income for tax purposes, except that it will occur when the Commission-

---

[54] William D. Andrews, *Basic Federal Income Taxation* 346 (4th ed. 1991).

[55] 372 U.S. at 143.

[56] *Id.* at 138.

[57] Statement of Amicus Curiae at 2.

er so insists. But this is, of course, unsatisfactory and would seem to give the Commissioner much more power than he has exercised since the *Schlude* trilogy. In trying to explicate these decisions, the task then would seem to be to identify what are the hidden factors or clues that will justify the Commissioner's fairly rare exercise of this power, or more precisely, what is it that motivates him or her to exercise this hard-to-define power?

There are several practical reasons why the Commissioner's power has not been widely exercised: (1) most accrual taxpayers probably report such payments fully in the taxable year of receipt if they are spread over a short period of time, even if the payments extend over two taxable years; (2) such allocations of income and expenses may not be administratively challenged or dislodged, either because auditors did not discover them or because little or no revenue is at stake in such a dislodgement; and (3) many of the most common situations in which this might have occurred have been dealt with by special statutory or regulatory provisions.[58]

But there are instances of continuing vitality of the doctrine, as illustrated by *Commissioner v. Indianapolis Power & Light* ("*IPL*").[59] In that case, the Commissioner sought to include in the regulated public utility's income certain security deposits required from customers viewed as credit risks. IPL sought such deposits from about 5% of its customers. The required security deposits were 200% of a customer's estimated monthly bill, were not physically segregated as a trust-type asset, earned interest payable to the customer or for the benefit of the account, and could be refunded on the determination that the customer was no longer a credit risk, the termination of service, or if a customer paid his or her bills on time for nine months in a row.[60] The Tax Court[61] and the Seventh Circuit[62] each found for the taxpayer without dissent. The well-reasoned Tax Court opinion sets out the task before the court: "[To determine the year of inclusion], we should continue to examine all of the facts and circumstance surrounding a deposit to evaluate the rights retained by the depositor and the rights acquired by the holder of the deposit."[63] The Seventh Circuit's decision was directly contrary to an

---

[58] *See, e.g.*, § 460 (special rules provided for accounting for long-term contracts—percentage of completion method).

[59] 493 U.S. 203 (1990).

[60] *Id.* at 204–05.

[61] 88 T.C. 964, 980 (1987).

[62] 857 F.2d 1162 (7th Cir.1988).

[63] 88 T.C. at 976.

earlier Eleventh Circuit decision, *City Gas Co. of Florida v. Commissioner*.[64]

The Supreme Court, in a unanimous opinion by Justice Blackmun, affirmed the result in the IPL decisions below and found for the taxpayer. The Court determined that the security deposits were in the nature of loans rather than advance payments for services, as in the *Schlude* trilogy. Looking to an economic substance test from *Commissioner v. Glenshaw Glass Co.*,[65] the Court held: "Under these circumstances, IPL's dominion over the fund is far less complete than is ordinarily the case in an advance-payment situation ... We hold that such dominion as IPL has over these customer deposits is insufficient for the deposits to qualify as taxable income at the time they are made."[66] In so holding, the Court was careful to note approvingly language from the Seventh Circuit's opinion that determining whether such a payment was an advance payment or a security deposit had to be made on the basis of the "facts and circumstances."[67] The Court distinguished the *Schlude* trilogy as being concerned with when the payments in question were income, whereas in *IPL* the question was whether they were income at all at the time for payment.[68]

The Continuing Importance of *Schlude* Today

This chapter has looked at only a few of the episodes in the occasional, and I would submit, thus far largely unsatisfactorily explained determinations about when tax accounting can and should differ from financial accounting for an accrual basis taxpayer. In the longest and most historically detailed treatment of the various corners of this universe, Deborah Geier concludes that tax lawyers should work to "debunk" the myths that for tax purposes we generally should "match" income and related deductions in the same accounting periods.[69] Although Professor Geier's article contains a lot of evidence that these

---

[64] 689 F.2d 943 (11th Cir.1982), *rev'g* 74 T.C. 386 (1980). The Tax Court holdings in *IPL* and *City Gas* thus were consistent.

[65] 348 U.S. 426, 431 (1955). *See* Chapter 1 of *Tax Stories*.

[66] 493 U.S. at 211, 214.

[67] *Id.* at 206–07.

[68] *Id.* at 203 n.3.

[69] Deborah A. Geier, *The Myth of the Matching Principle as a Tax Value*, 15 Am. J. Tax Pol'y 17 (1998). *See also* Deborah A. Geier, *Taxing Advance Payments: Choosing Among Imperfect Alternatives*, 93 Tax Notes 285 (2001). *But see* D. J. Gaffney, *Rotable Spare Parts: How Did a "Terrible" Accounting Method Become So Bad?*, 70 Tax Notes 1009 (1996); Alan Gunn, *Matching of Costs and Revenues as a Goal of Tax Accounting*, 4 Va. Tax Rev. 1 (1984).

myths are false, one comes away thinking that each exception discussed is slightly "odd" or difficult, and that in the vast array of accounting transactions over 90 years of income taxation, the real oddity is that this area is so little developed.[70]

Professor Geier's article, and the continued, if spotty, reliance on *Schlude*, has recently led to renewed and vigorous criticism of its outcome requiring inclusion of prepaid items of income that would not be properly accruable. Steven Willis has written a thoughtful exegesis of *Schlude* and the consequences that attend its conclusion.[71] Professor Willis demonstrates with some care that through a variety of techniques, a well-advised taxpayer may avoid the result ordained in *Schlude*. Professor Willis concludes that if a decision with such negative consequences for a taxpayer can be planned "around," then it should be reversed. At base, he believes that tax treatment should not diverge from accrual accounting results. Although this sentiment obviously has substantial support in the statute, it seems to render the words of § 446(b) meaningless. It also is perhaps a puzzling moment to assert that accrual accounting principles provide absolute, objective, compelling, and clear answers that should triumph over explicit statutory language that indicates that the revenue considerations may override accounting results. Professor Willis' article, in turn, has spawned several responses, including one by Daniel Halperin suggesting that "further study is needed."[72]

Although one can disagree with Professor Willis, the undeveloped nature of the rules in this area suggests that there remains substantial convergence between tax and financial accounting. Seen in this light, cases like *Schlude* reflect a common law grab bag of circumstances in which prepaid income or delayed deductions strain the revenue in situations of substantial factual uncertainty, hence supporting deference to an admittedly discretionary Treasury determination to require a tax accounting-financial accounting divergence.[73] This also may explain the occasional and not irrational eruptions against the very lean theory supporting the precise results in *Schlude* and its ancestors.[74] Is there a summative principle or two here? Perhaps these will do: (1) an accrual

---

[70] To be sure, it is true that the Code has been amended on occasion to reverse these results, as in the prepaid magazine subscription and dues cases *See* §§ 455 & 456. *See also* Rev. Proc. 71–21, 1971–2 C.B. (§ 549 permits accrual treatment for payments made within two taxable years).

[71] Steven J. Willis, *It's Time for* Schlude *to Go*, 93 Tax Notes 127 (2001).

[72] Daniel Halperin, Schlude: *Further Study is Needed*, 93 Tax Notes 1504 (2001).

[73] "The thrust of the Court's [three] decisions is thus to give the Commissioner very broad discretion in dealing with prepaid income situations." Paul R. McDaniel et al., *Federal Income Taxation: Cases and Materials* 1019 (4th ed. 1998).

[74] *See also* Steven J. Willis, *Show Me the Numbers ... Please*, 93 Tax Notes 1321 (2001).

basis taxpayer, if paid for services before the income is earned, will need to show with great specificity and detail why inclusion of that income should be deferred to a later tax year; and (2) an accrual basis taxpayer may well have to deduct expenses not legally (or "totally") incurred if all *substantial* events have transpired that will render them deductible. The first principle effectively places a heavy and perhaps insurmountable burden on a taxpayer if the Commissioner disallows such an effort (hence, all the talk in these opinions about deference to the Commissioner). The second principle suggests more obeisance to the norms of accrual accounting on the expense side because the principle itself reflects the accounting learning embedded in the "all events" test.

Conclusion

As this chapter goes to press, the media are full of reports of accounting scofflaws like Enron, Global Crossing, Tyco International, WorldCom, and Xerox. Although the precise nature of the malfeasance differ in these and other conflagrations through the years, the *Schlude* trilogy's sanctioning of departures in tax accounting from GAAP undoubtedly at least planted a seed that may have contributed to the subsequent flowering of accounting irregularities. However, the decoupling of tax accounting from financial accounting clearly makes sense in certain areas in light of the divergent purposes of each: in tax accounting, the pressure is to minimize taxable income (and thus tax liabilities) via decreasing income/increasing deductions; in financial accounting, the pressure is in the opposite direction to maximize book income (and thus stock prices) via increasing revenues/decreasing expenses. Yet one wonders about the cumulative effect as each generation's "masters of the universe"[75] search for new ways to take advantage of the opportunities afforded through the separation of the tax accounting and financial accounting regimes and the decreasing ability of the Internal Revenue Service and Securities and Exchange Commission (and other federal agencies) to reign in these abuses.[76] Indeed, one feature of the savings and loan debacle of the 1980s and early 1990s was the mortgage "swaps" in which S & Ls tried to have their cake (losses for tax purposes) and eat

---

[75] *See* Tom Wolfe, *Bonfire of the Vanities* (1987).

[76] *Cf.* J. Brent Vasconcellos, *Enron's Teresa Transaction: It's the Financial Disclosure, Stupid*, 95 Tax Notes 1829 (2002) (arguing that GAAP should adopt income tax business purpose and substance-over-form doctrines to empower SEC rather than IRS to monitor Enron-type transactions).

it too (no losses for financial purposes).[77] When the next tax/accounting two-step explodes onto the national scene, consider whether the move can be traced in part to an Arthur Murray dance studio in Omaha, Nebraska.

---

[77] *See* Cottage Savings Ass'n v. Commissioner, 499 U.S. 554 (1991).

9

Patricia A. Cain

The Story of *Earl*: How Echoes (and Metaphors) from the Past Continue to Shape the Assignment of Income Doctrine

In *Lucas v. Earl*, Justice Holmes, writing for the Court, held that a husband and wife could not split their earnings for tax purposes even though they were bound by contract to share all income equally. He wrote:

> There is no doubt that the statute could tax salaries to those who earned them and provide that the tax could not be escaped by anticipatory arrangements ... and we think that no distinction can be taken according to the motives leading to the arrangement by which the fruits are attributed to a different tree from that on which they grew.[1]

The *Earl* case is important for two central reasons. First, it is the most often-cited authority in cases that raise questions of assignment of income. Second, when coupled with *Poe v. Seaborn*,[2] decided just one term later, the case is responsible for the legislative creation of joint returns.

The Holmes opinion in *Earl* is especially famous for its "fruit and tree" metaphor. Although the metaphor is associated with Holmes, the concept of income as fruit borne by a tree was a familiar one in income

---

[1] Lucas v. Earl, 281 U.S. 111, 114–15 (1930).

[2] 282 U.S. 101 (1930).

tax cases. Justice Pitney had used it twice just ten years earlier.[3] In *Eisner v. Macomber*, he explained that "[t]he fundamental relation of 'capital' to 'income' has been much discussed by economists, the former being likened to the tree or the land, the latter to the fruit or the crop."[4]

Holmes often used metaphors in judicial opinions. Metaphors, after all, are analogies and the common law frequently relies on analogies to craft new rules for new fact situations. Remember that Holmes is the justice who relied more on experience than on logic in his legal reasoning.[5] He was first and foremost a common law judge. How fitting that he should pen the opinion that is known as creating a common law doctrine in taxation, an area of law that is usually controlled by statute.

How helpful is this particular metaphor? Not very, according to a number of tax scholars.[6] As one commentator explained, "More often than not, the metaphor is substituted for sound legal analysis."[7] The metaphor suggests that if the court is simply able to identify the tree that produces the fruit, the court can identify the correct taxpayer. In cases like *Earl*, the earner would be the tree that produced fruit in the form of earnings.[8] But sometimes earnings turn into property, as in the case of manuscripts and music scores. The "earner" is not taxed on all the earnings from the original effort unless the earner retains the property rights produced by his or her efforts.[9] And sometimes the true earner may not be entitled to the income, as when a junior associate in a law firm brings in earnings well in excess of his or her salary. In that case, we do not tax the "earner" of the income.

In cases that differ from *Earl*, the metaphor can be misapplied because the metaphor itself tells us nothing about how to identify the "tree." If the income-producing "tree" is property rather than a wage-

---

[3] Eisner v. Macomber, 252 U.S. 189 (1920); Shaffer v. Carter, 252 U.S. 37 (1920).

[4] 252 U.S. at 206. *See also* Chapter 2 of *Tax Stories*.

[5] "The life of the law has not been logic: it has been experience." Oliver Wendell Holmes, Jr., *The Common Law* 1 (1881).

[6] *See, e.g.*, Michael J. Graetz & Deborah H. Schenk, *Federal Income Taxation: Principles and Policies* 506 (3d ed. 1995).

[7] *See* Nick Marsico, Note, *Chopping Down the Fruit Tree:* Caruth Corp. v. United States *Applies Assignment of Income Doctrine to Gift of Stock Between Declaration and Record Dates*, 40 DePaul L. Rev. 845, 847 (1991).

[8] *See also* Saenger v. Commissioner, 69 F.2d 631 (5th Cir.1934). In holding that the taxpayer must pay taxes on the salary that he earned and that he could not legitimately argue that he had transferred himself (the "tree") to a corporation, the Fifth Circuit said: "The rule of the Earl Case, while made graphic by a figure, is more than a figure of speech. It is an expression of the simple truth that earned incomes are taxed to and must be paid by those who earn them ... " *Id.* at 632.

[9] *See* Nelson v. Ferguson, 56 F.2d 121 (3d Cir.1932) (rejecting the application of *Earl*'s principle of taxing the earner of income when a husband assigned all his right to future income from a patented invention to his wife).

earner, identification of the tree is insufficient unless the owner of the "tree" is also identified. Nor does the metaphor help us determine whether the thing that is producing the income is in fact property (i.e., capital) or services (i.e., a person). The current controversy over how to tax contingent legal fees is a prime example of a fact situation in which the metaphor is not particularly helpful. Consider, for example, the tax consequences to a plaintiff employee, who sues her employer for sex discrimination and recovers $1 million in taxable damages,[10] half of which is claimed by her attorney under a contract, entered into before litigation began. Most courts, applying assignment of income principles that date from the *Earl* case, view the full $1 million award as the income of the plaintiff. In their view, it is the plaintiff as employee who is the "tree." The contract assigning half of the award to the attorney, just like the contract between Mr. and Mrs. Earl, is not effective for tax purposes.[11] But other courts view both the plaintiff and the lawyer as trees, or as co-owners of an orchard (the claim) that produces the fruit (the damages).[12]

What did Holmes hope to accomplish by using the fruit and tree metaphor? However he viewed the analogy between trees and earners of income, he probably did not intend for the metaphor to translate into a rigid rule that earnings must be taxed to the tree that produced them. Holmes was, if anything, *not* rigid. He would undoubtedly be amused to learn of the many uses that the metaphor has experienced since it was first coined in *Earl*. Judges have referred at times to "ripe fruit," "green fruit," trees "barren of fruit," and, more recently, "cropsharing" in order to explain their holdings in assignment of income cases.[13] But the most vigorous extensions of horticultural imagery have come from teachers and students of tax law who insist on including references to trees, fruit, and orchards in titles to scholarly articles about the assignment of income doctrine.[14] Interestingly, Holmes himself never used the meta-

---

[10] Damages paid on account of discrimination, although personal in some ways, do not normally result from a physical injury. Section 104 exempts from gross income only damages received on account of "personal physical injuries."

[11] The plaintiff may be entitled to a deduction for the lawyer's fee, but because the deduction is subject to limitations as an itemized deduction, the plaintiff would be much better off if she could claim that the half paid to the lawyer was never her income in the first place. *See generally* Deborah A. Geier, *Some Meandering Thoughts on Plaintiffs and their Attorneys' Fees and Costs*, 88 Tax Notes 531 (2000).

[12] *See, e.g.*, Estate of Clarks v. United States, 202 F.3d 854, 858 (6th Cir.2000) ("Here the client as assignor has transferred some of the trees in his orchard, not merely the fruit from the trees. The lawyer has become a tenant in common of the orchard owner and must cultivate and care for and harvest the fruit of the entire tract.).

[13] *See, e.g.*, Cotnam v. Commissioner, 263 F.2d 119 (5th Cir.1959) (barren trees); Kenseth v. Commissioner, 114 T.C. 399 (2000) (cropsharing).

[14] *See, e.g.*, Traci A. Sammeth, Note, *Beyond the Fruit Tree: A Proposal for the Revision of the Assignment of Income Doctrine*—Caruth Corp. v. United States, 65 Wash. L. Rev. 229

phor again, even though the opportunity presented itself. Indeed, just one month after handing down the *Earl* decision, Holmes was faced with another assignment of income question, this time involving income from property rather than services. In *Corliss v. Bowers*,[15] he focused on an individual's *command* over the income (i.e., the power to revoke the trust) and held that one who commanded or controlled the income should be taxed even if the benefit of the income went to someone else. By extension, *Corliss* can be read to tax earners of income whenever they are in control of the earned income. Mr. Earl, for example, was the final decision-maker as to whether he would earn anything at all. And to the extent his earnings resulted from a negotiated salary, he was in full control of the salary and no more.

But then, surprisingly, several months later, Holmes joined the unanimous opinion in *Poe v. Seaborn*, endorsing a rule that allowed spouses in community property states to split the earned income of the spouses, regardless of who the earner was. The result in *Seaborn* was to tax the earned income of a husband to the non-earner wife, despite the fact that the husband had full control or command over all community property. The operative principle in *Seaborn* was *ownership* and not *control*, as the government had argued. The fact that Holmes joined the opinion against the government is surprising because Holmes almost always sided with the government in tax cases and he had suggested more than once that a husband's control might be a sufficient justification for taxing him on the full amount of community income.[16]

And then just one year later, Holmes participated in another tax decision, *Hoeper v. Tax Commission of Wisconsin*,[17] a case that challenged a Wisconsin statute on federal due process grounds. Wisconsin taxed the earned income of both spouses to the husband. The taxpayer argued that recently-enacted married women's property laws had given the wife control over her earnings. As a result, she *owned* those earnings under the common law. Thus to assess the tax on her earnings against her husband deprived him of property without due process of law. The Supreme Court agreed and held the statute unconstitutional. Holmes dissented. He would have upheld the statute, citing to the fact that the

---

(1990); Nick Marsico, Note, *Chopping Down the Fruit Trees:* Caruth Corp. v. United States *Applies Assignment of Income Doctrine to Gift of Stock Between Declaration and Record Dates*, 40 DePaul L. Rev. 845 (1991); Kristina Maynard, Comment, *The Fruit Does Not Fall Far from the Tree: The Unresolved Tax Treatment of Contingent Attorney's Fees*, 33 Loy. U. Chi. L.J. 991 (2002); Lauren E. Sheridan, Note, *Trees in the Orchard or Fruit From the Trees?: The Case for Excluding Attorneys' Contingent Fees from the Client's Gross Income*, 36 Ga. L. Rev. 283 (2001).

[15] 281 U.S. 376 (1930).

[16] *See* Robbins v. United States, 5 F.2d 690 (D.C.Cal.1925), *rev'd*, 269 U.S. 315 (1926).

[17] 284 U.S. 206 (1931).

wife's earnings had historically been subject to her husband's control. In his opinion, this fact was sufficient to justify the current tax. "Control" was not the determinative factor. And furthermore, it was appropriate to defer to legislatures on matters of tax law. Holmes was consistent in this respect. He believed that the Constitution granted a broad power to tax. Thus neither Congress nor state legislatures should be unduly constrained by the Constitution when exercising this power. His dissent in *Hoeper* is consistent with his dissent in *Eisner v. Macomber*.

But neither *Earl*, nor *Corliss*, nor *Seaborn* posed constitutional questions. These cases were concerned only with the interpretation of a statute that was somewhat murky in identifying the appropriate taxpayer in cases in which income was assigned by contract (or state law) from one person to another. One must have some operative rule to make that determination. If Holmes really believed that "control" was the trump factor in determining who should bear the tax, then his vote with the majority in *Poe v. Seaborn* seems misplaced and inconsistent with his opinions in *Earl* and *Corliss*. Given this remarkable evidence of conflicting positions by a remarkable justice, is it any wonder that mere mortal law students have difficulty deciding when to apply the holding in *Earl* to different fact situations? And if "tax the earner" or "tax the person in control" is not the lesson to be learned from *Earl*, then what is the lesson? After removing the proverbial "tree from the forest," I believe the core lesson to be learned from *Earl* is that there are some income-splitting arrangements that will be honored for tax purposes and some that will not. The task of the tax student is to distinguish the good income-splitting agreements from the bad.

Thus, tax students who read *Lucas v. Earl* should not focus on the "tree," but rather on the contract which attributed the fruits "to a different tree from that on which they grew." Guy C. Earl and his wife, Ella, signed an agreement in 1901 in Oakland, California in which they agreed, among other things, to split all of their earned income equally. There was no income tax in 1901 and so there was no assertion that the contract had been entered into for the purpose of reducing or avoiding tax. Holmes cryptically tells us only this: "[N]o distinction can be taken according to the motives leading to the arrangement by which the fruits are attributed to a different tree from that on which they grew."[18] This statement is perhaps more crucial in explaining the *Earl* opinion than the reference to trees and fruit. The government's concern in *Earl*, never explicitly mentioned by Holmes, was protection of the progressive rate structure. If an agreement to shift income results in the undermining of progressivity, that agreement should be ignored by the tax collector regardless of the taxpayer's innocent non-tax avoidance motives.

---

[18] Lucas v. Earl, 281 U.S. 111, 115 (1930).

What more do we know about this famous tax case? Who was Guy C. Earl? Why did he and his wife agree in 1901 to split property and income evenly? And what effect did California community property have on the litigation positions asserted in *Earl*? These are some of the factual inquiries that will help us put the litigation in context and better understand the story it tells.

A second set of questions addresses the place of *Earl* in tax jurisprudence generally. What effect did *Earl* have on income-splitting agreements between spouses? How did it contribute to the inequality between community property spouses and non-community property spouses? If *Earl* had come out differently, would we have needed the joint return, finally enacted in 1948? All of these questions will be addressed in turn.

Background

The Factual Context

1. *Who Was Guy C. Earl?*

All we learn from reading Justice Holmes's opinion is that Earl was an attorney, who, pursuant to an agreement signed in 1901, split his salary and attorney's fees for the years 1920 and 1921 with his wife. From the record we learn a bit more. Guy C. Earl and his wife, Ella F. Earl, were married in 1888. By 1901, he had "accumulated considerable property" and she "had about $30,000 worth of property."[19] They lived in Oakland, Alameda County, California, at 2914 McClure Street. Both of them "had an expectancy of inheritance."[20] Mr. Earl was an officer of the Great Western Power Company. In 1920, Earl's salary and fees totaled $24,839. In 1921, the total was $22,946.[21]

These amounts of earned income are quite high for 1920–21. Translated into 2002 dollars, the income is the equivalent of over $220,000 per year. In addition, the Earls received income from property they owned. In 1920, their income from property totaled $7,555, which they were allowed to split for income tax purposes, half to Guy and half to Ella. A lesser amount was split between them in 1921.[22]

Who was Guy C. Earl? He must have been someone of importance to earn so high a salary and hold so much income-producing property. Here's what the record does not tell us.

---

[19] Transcript of Record at 3.

[20] *Id.*

[21] *Id.*

[22] *Id.* at 5.

According to a 1931 account of the history of San Francisco, published one year after the Supreme Court handed down *Lucas v. Earl,* "No lawyer now practicing in San Francisco deserves greater credit for success achieved than Guy Chaffee Earl, now one of the most accomplished and popular lawyers of this city, with offices at 225 Bush Street."[23]

Guy Chaffee Earl was born in Red Bluff, California on May 7, 1860, the second son of Josiah Earl and Adelia Tobias Chaffee.[24] His older brother, Edwin Tobias Earl, was born two years earlier, May 30, 1858. A third brother, born in 1862, lived only one week. Josiah was from Indiana, where he used to operate a line of river barges, often navigating to New Orleans. A group of young men in New Orleans, strongly desirous of mining for gold in California, convinced Josiah to serve as their leader on the long and dangerous trip westward. In 1849, after battling hostile Indians by day and traveling by night, they arrived in southern California. Josiah stayed in Los Angeles and started a freighting business, the first of many successful ventures. In 1852, Adelia Tobias Chaffee, originally from Ohio and whom Josiah had met when he lived in Indiana, arrived in California by boat from New York. She made the trip to accept Josiah's proposal of marriage. They were married in San Francisco.

By the time Guy Earl was two years old, his father had made and lost at least four fortunes. Economic and natural disasters caused each loss. After each disaster, Josiah struck out anew undaunted.

One such disaster occurred shortly after Guy's birth. In the great floods of 1860–1861, Josiah Earl lost over $600,000.[25] Shortly thereafter, the family settled in the Owens River Valley, near Independence, California, located between the Sierra Nevadas and the Inyo Mountain Range. They farmed and raised cattle. Both sons worked on the homestead, learned to use guns at an early age to protect their home against hostile Indians, and attended an informal rural school for three months out of the year. Guy called the place of his boyhood "the enchanted valley" and often regaled his children and grandchildren with the magical stories from that era.[26]

---

[23] *History of San Francisco* 472 (Lewis Francis Byington ed., 1931).

[24] The information about Guy Chaffee Earl's life is derived from several sources. *See generally* Charles Coleman, *P.G & E. of California: The Centennial Story of Pacific Gas and Electric Company, 1852–1952* (1952); Guy Chaffee Earl, *The Enchanted Valley and Other Sketches* (1976) (privately published by his son, Guy C. Earl, Jr.); *History of San Francisco, supra* note 23.

[25] The equivalent of $13 million in 2002 dollars.

[26] *See* Earl, *supra* note 24.

The Earls were known as "black republicans" because they supported Lincoln and the abolition of slavery. Guy was quite proud of this stance and sometimes expressed fearful fascination when informed that a neighbor was a southern sympathizer. He thought his brother, two years his senior and later to become publisher of the Los Angeles Express, was much too serious. Therefore, Guy elected to spend much of his time with boys his own age, many of whom were Paiute Indians. He learned to speak their language fluently. Although his father told him never to ride a horse faster than a trot, Guy relished in galloping against his Paiute boyhood friends in races that he would usually win. A towhead, who bristled at the barbs directed at him by his playmates (how'd you get that cotton in your hair?), he once tried to blacken his locks only to emerge with a black and white spaniel look.

Guy and his family survived the raid of warring Indians, winters of subzero weather with little heat, and the earthquake of 1872. Guy counted at least 87 serious aftershocks as the family gathered outside the home that had been severely damaged by the earthquake. Rather than rebuild the damaged home, Josiah Earl decided that his boys needed to leave the Valley in order to become better educated and, in some sense, more civilized.

After scouting the options, Josiah determined that the family should move to Oakland, where the school system was highly touted. Another attraction of northern California was the fact that Berkeley was the site of the newly established University of California. Guy graduated from Oakland High School in 1879 and from the University of California at Berkeley four years later in 1883. Guy describes those days as follows: "We were poor. I was a rough specimen of youngster. I had to work to make my way and to help provide for the family."[27]

After graduating from college, Guy read law in the law offices of Estee and Boalt, in San Francisco. Three years later he was admitted to the bar. During this time, his father died on a business trip to Australia, forcing Guy once again to work to provide for his mother. He was determined to make something of himself. Ultimately, he served as assistant district attorney of Alameda County, entered private practice with S. P. Hall, who later became an appellate judge, and in 1893, one year after his mother's death, was elected as a state senator from Alameda County. In 1895, he joined Thomas Bishop and Charles Wheeler in the practice of law in San Francisco.

Guy's serious older brother, Edwin, was the founder of Earl Fruit Company, located in Los Angeles. To help sell his southern California fruit to consumers on the East Coast, Edwin invented the refrigerated rail car. He later sold both his fruit business and his railroad car line to

---

[27] *History of San Francisco, supra* note 23, at 474.

Armour and Company in Chicago. Brother Guy helped finalize the deal. Edwin died in 1919 with an estate in excess of $7 million.[28]

In 1920 and 1921, the tax years at issue in the case, Earl served as Vice–President and General Counsel of Great Western Power Company. He also served as Chairman of the Board of Regents of the University of California during these two years. By 1924, he would become President of Great Western Power.

In 1920, Great Western Power was serving 30,000 customers in approximately 15 counties of Northern California. The three largest energy suppliers in Northern California during the 1920s were Great Western Power, San Joaquin Light and Power, and Pacific Gas and Electric (PG & E). Rumors abounded that Great Western would soon merge with Pacific Gas and Electric Company. In 1930, the merger finally occurred, consolidating all three energy suppliers into a single utility company, PG & E. Great Western did not legally dissolve until 1935, at which time President Guy Earl was named to the Board of Directors of PG & E.[29]

Guy Earl was no ordinary taxpayer when the Service set out to audit him. He was one of the richest men in California, active in politics, and general counsel to a prominent utility company. He had both the resources and the stamina to fight the Commissioner all the way to the Supreme Court.

2. What Was the Purpose of the 1901 Agreement?

Guy married Ella J. Ford of Oakland in 1888. They had four children, Alice, Martha, Elinore, and Guy, Jr. In 1901, after thirteen years together and four children, one can presume that the Earls were secure in their marriage. Why then did Guy, a lawyer by trade, rearrange his affairs to convert all of his property (and his wife's) into joint tenancies rather than community property?

1901 was a big year in California and for the Earl family. Turn of the century California was ripe for talented entrepreneurs. The steam-driven motor car had recently joined the horse and carriage on the streets of Los Angeles and San Francisco. Henry Huntington established the Pacific Electric Railway Company that year, linking diverse parts of Los Angeles together through a network of rail cars. President William McKinley visited Los Angeles, the first U.S. President to do so. The renowned author Jack London returned to his home in Oakland and ran for Mayor as a socialist. He lost.

---

[28] The equivalent of $73.7 million in 2002 dollars.

[29] Guy Earl's connection with PG & E is detailed on the company's web page and a link to his photo appears on the *Tax Stories* web site at www.law.uc.edu/TaxStories.

In 1901, Edwin Earl, Guy's older brother, sold his fruit and rail car company for a small fortune and founded a Christian lecture series at the University of California. Guy Earl had recently started his own law practice. But the most important event of 1901 occurred when Julius Howells, an engineer, approached the Earl brothers for financial backing to develop what he believed would become the best hydroelectric site in California, Big Meadows basin in Plumas County at the north fork of the Feather River. For the next year, Howells, aided by then Oakland city auditor and Earl family friend, Arthur H. Breed, secured options on thousands of acres of land in Big Meadows. The purchases were made surreptitiously to avoid alerting any competitors to their plan. Breed even used code when he telegraphed messages about the option purchases back to Guy Earl. Finally they secured the necessary water rights. As one story has it, the rights were secured for Guy Earl by his agents who made it to the courthouse and filed the necessary papers just 40 minutes before the competition. They began developing the area and built Lake Almanor, named for Earl's three daughters, Alice, Martha, and Elinore. And they incorporated Western Power Company, later to become Great Western Power Company, which later merged with Pacific Gas & Electric.

While Guy Chaffee Earl has written stories about his early life and others have written about his important contributions to San Francisco history, none of these writings mention his contribution to federal tax law. Nor do any of these writings explain the reasons behind the famous 1901 agreement between Earl and his wife. We know they did not enter the contract for the purpose of avoiding taxes, for there was no income tax in 1901. Congress had passed an income tax in 1894, but the Supreme Court had declared it unconstitutional in 1895 because the tax on rents from property was considered a direct tax on property, which required apportionment among the states.[30] The Sixteenth Amendment authorizing Congress to pass an income tax, without apportionment, was not added to the U.S. Constitution until twelve years later in 1913. Nor, in 1901, was there any form of estate, inheritance or successions tax that might have been avoided by transferring property in the joint names of husband and wife.[31]

The sole clue to Earl's motives is contained in the Board of Tax Appeals opinion, which explains that "the petitioner was not very well and suggested to his wife that it might be wise for them to enter into

---

[30] Pollock v. Farmers' Loan & Trust Co., 157 U.S. 429 (1895).

[31] There was a federal inheritance or estate tax, enacted in 1898 and in force until 1902, but it exempted property left to a surviving spouse. *See generally* Knowlton v. Moore, 178 U.S. 41 (1900) (upholding constitutionality of the tax).

such an agreement, which would simplify affairs in case he died during her lifetime."[32] The agreement stated as follows:

It is now agreed and understood between us that any property either of us now has or may hereafter receive or acquire (of any and every kind) in any way, either by earnings (including salaries, fees, etc.) or any rights by contract or otherwise during the existence of our marriage, or which we or either of us may receive by gift, bequest, devise or inheritance, and all the proceeds, issues and profits of any and all such property shall be treated and considered and hereby is declared to be received, held, taken and owned by us as joint tenants and not otherwise with the right of survivorship.

The agreement thus was intended to serve as a simple estate planning tool. Under California law, then and now, a husband and wife could agree in advance how property to be acquired in the future would be held, e.g., as community, as separately owned by one spouse, or as separate joint tenancy property with right of survivorship. After the Earl agreement was signed, all property currently owned by them, as well as all property to be acquired, was converted into survivorship property. The effect of the agreement was to convert all community property into separate property. Community property could not be held with rights of survivorship. The survivorship feature was intended to make it easier for Ella to inherit Guy's wealth, much of which had been recently acquired in the form of land options. Had Guy Earl died, his wife, Ella, would have succeeded to full ownership in all the property without the need of a probate administration and without the need to probate a will.[33]

What a brilliant plan! The arrangement, if enforceable, accomplishes everything the modern day revocable trust accomplishes and more because it is effective not only as to all property currently owned and transferred into the trust, but also as to all property to be acquired in the future. While such spousal agreements are not generally used in modern day estate planning, they seem to have been somewhat common for California spouses during the early 1900s.[34] In 1915, the Supreme Court of California held that spousal agreements of this type effectively passed all the marital property to the surviving spouse upon death of the

---

[32] *See* Transcript of Record at 7–8.

[33] Another possible benefit to the Earls of passing property through a joint tenancy arrangement was that joint tenancy property would not have been available to any creditors of the deceased joint tenant. That is because the surviving joint tenant is entitled to full ownership so long as the joint tenancy is not severed. A creditor would have to execute a lien through a forced sale before the debtor's death in order to sever the tenancy and claim any interest in the property. See *Grothe v. Cortlandt Corp.*, 15 Cal.Rptr.2d 38 (Cal.App.1992), and cases cited therein. There was no evidence, however, that Guy Earl might have been trying to avoid creditors through this device.

[34] Krull v. Commissioner, 10 B.T.A. 1096 (1928) (tax case involving an agreement similar to the Earl agreement).

other spouse, even if the agreement was an oral one.[35] The effect of such agreements under the federal income tax was yet to be decided.

The Legal Context

1. *Tax Rates*

The Sixteenth Amendment authorizing an unapportioned income tax was adopted on March 1, 1913. That October, Congress passed an income tax statute that taxed income at the rate of 1%. A 1% surtax was applied to incomes above $20,000,[36] increasing in 1% increments to a maximum surtax of 6% on net incomes above $500,000.[37] Thus, from the beginning of the modern income tax, the rates were progressive. In the absence of progressive rates, income splitting would not be an attractive tax reduction tool. Indeed, with rates as low as 1% or 2%, taxpayers were unlikely to expend much effort to split income between family members.

In 1916, however, rates began to rise. The normal tax was raised to 2% with surtaxes increasing to 13% on incomes in excess of $2,000,000.[38] In 1918, a huge bump in rates occurred in order to help finance World War I. The normal tax was set at 6% on net income of $4,000, with a surtax of 12% on amounts in excess of $4,000.[39] Additional surtaxes were imposed ranging from 1% to 65%.

In 1913, there were no joint returns. Each taxpayer was expected to file a return based on his or her income. A 1914 pair of Treasury Decisions clarified that husband and wife were to file separate returns reporting their separate incomes.[40] An optional joint return was introduced in 1918.[41] The option allowed husbands and wives to file a single return and report aggregate income and deductions. This option provided a desirable convenience for those taxpayers whose combined income was below the amount that would trigger the surtax rate.[42] But with the increase in rates, joint returns that aggregated spousal incomes were not

---

[35] *See* In re Harris' Estate, 147 P. 967 (Cal.1915).

[36] The equivalent of $360,000 in 2002 dollars.

[37] The equivalent of $9 million in 2002 dollars. For a brief discussion of the history of early tax rates, see generally Vada Waters Lindsey, *The Widening Gap Under the Internal Revenue Code: The Need for Renewed Progressivity*, 5 Fla. Tax Rev. 1 (2001).

[38] The equivalent of $32.9 million in 2002 dollars.

[39] The equivalent of $47,500 in 2002 dollars.

[40] T.D. 2090 and T.D. 2137, discussed in George Donworth, *Federal Taxation of Community Incomes—The Recent History of Pending Questions*, 4 Wash. L. Rev. 145, 147 (1929).

[41] *See* Amy Christian, *Joint and Several Liability and the Joint Return: Its Implications for Women*, 66 U. Cin. L. Rev. 535, 538–39 (1998).

[42] It also allowed spouses to net their gains and losses, which could provide a benefit if one spouse had gains and the other had losses.

attractive to high-income taxpayers. The bump in rates encouraged high-income taxpayers to seek even more eagerly the benefit of splitting income between spouses. In community property states, spouses took the position that community income was owned equally by the spouses and thus could be split between them for purposes of reporting income.

2. Community Property and Income Splitting

A. Treasury Develops a Policy that Excludes California

In 1920, the Internal Revenue Service issued Office Decision No. 426, authorizing spouses in two community property states, Texas and Washington, to file separate tax returns, with each spouse reporting half of the income from community property.[43] Community earnings from spousal labor, however, were not to be split for tax purposes. Community property spouses were not satisfied with this limited ability to split income. They and their representatives complained. As a result, the Secretary of the Treasury asked the Attorney General to rule on the issue. In 1920, the Attorney General concluded that husbands and wives in Texas could split the husband's earnings equally between them in their separate tax returns.[44] Early in 1921, the Attorney General issued a further opinion, concluding that spouses in all of the eight community property states, other than California, could split the husband's earned income and allow the wife to report her half separately as her income.[45] This opinion was based on the fact that in all states other than California the wife had a vested present interest in all community income, whether derived from property or from her husband's labor.

This income-splitting device resulted in large losses to the Treasury, typically removing half of a husband's earnings from his higher brackets to the wife's lower brackets. Furthermore, the ability of some states to give their taxpayers this bracket-shifting benefit through community property laws created an inequality in the assessment of the tax burden among married couples from state to state. Now it was the spouses in non-community property states and the politicians representing them who complained. Almost immediately a bill was introduced in Congress that would have required community income to be included in the "gross income of the spouse having management and control of the community property."[46] In all of the community property states, husbands had powers of management over the community assets and income. Such a statute would have taxed all community income to the husband no

---

[43] O.D. 426, 2 C.B. 198 (1920).

[44] See Donworth, supra note 40, at 148 (discussing 32 Opinions of Attorneys General 229 (1920)).

[45] Id. at 150.

[46] Id. at 151 (discussing Revenue Act of 1921).

matter whose earnings created the income and no matter how vested the wife's rights were in the community property. Although introduced several times, this bill never passed.[47]

California spouses were the biggest losers in this competition to split income. First, they were specifically excluded from the income-splitting benefits authorized by the 1921 Attorney General opinion. Second, the management and control given to husbands under community property regimes led the Commissioner to argue that the husband was the appropriate taxpayer on 100% of community income. Thus, while California spouses argued that they were entitled to split community income in the same way that other community property spouses could, the Commissioner argued that, not only could they not split income, but the wife's earnings were appropriately taxable to the husband. In common law states, by contrast, the enactment of married women's property acts had sufficiently eroded the doctrine of coverture to give wives control over their own incomes. Thus, in those states, the Commissioner did not attempt to tax the husband on the wife's income. In California he did. One early Board of Tax Appeals decision noted the absurdity of the Commissioner's position, as applied to California spouses:

> It would be strange indeed if a wife who enjoys the supposedly more independent status provided by the community system were taxed upon a theory that her separate salary belonged to her husband, while the wife elsewhere is taxed upon the theory of independent ownership. Is the mere expectancy of the [California] wife in her husband's income less than or different from his interest in her independent earnings?[48]

The Board of Tax Appeals apparently did not understand California community property law. While a certain equality between the spouses had been achieved in the common law states through passage of married women's property legislation, there was no similar legislation in California.[49] The answer to the question posed above, if answered correctly in 1926, should have been, "Yes, the wife's mere expectancy in the husband's earnings is less than the husband's fully vested interest in her earnings." That is because the husband had full control of the expendi-

---

[47] *Id.* at 153 (discussing Revenue Acts of 1923 and 1924).

[48] *See* Estate of Randall v. Commissioner, 4 B.T.A. 679 (1926). Note that although the Board of Tax Appeals refers to the wife's "separate salary," the facts of the case involved *community* earnings produced by the wife's separate efforts. The earnings were not her *separate* property.

[49] In community property states generally, the husband was declared sole manager of all community property. Statutes giving management powers to wives in community property states were enacted as late as the 1960s and 1970s. In Louisiana, the husband was the sole manager of community property until 1981 when the United States Supreme Court struck down the provision as a violation of the equal protection clause. *See* Kirchberg v. Feenstra, 450 U.S. 455 (1981).

ture of all community assets, even those produced by the efforts of the wife. She controlled nothing except perhaps whether she would make the effort to create any earnings in the first place. But once she did make the effort to produce income, her husband would have full control and power over any money she earned. Because of this difference in power and control, the Board of Tax Appeals was soon reversed, and taxation of 100% of community income to the husband became the established rule for California spouses.[50] Only in California was the husband taxed on the wife's earnings since other community property states were allowed to split the earnings of both spouses.

B.   A California Taxpayer Brings a Test Case: *Robbins v. United States*[51]

California spouses reported their income on separate tax returns as early as 1918 and continued to do so into the 1920s, even after the Attorney General had ruled that California community property laws did not vest the wife with sufficient ownership over community income. Some spouses claimed that the community property laws entitled them to such a reporting position despite the Attorney General's decision to the contrary. Others accepted the law as laid down by the Attorney General and entered into spousal agreements that recharacterized all spousal earnings as the separate property of the earning spouse. Or, in some cases, spouses entered into a more limited agreement in which they agreed that the earnings of the wife would be her separate property. The Commissioner challenged these agreements between California spouses and continued to tax all community income to the husband. But the agreements were valid under state law. They did in fact transform what had once been community property into separate property. Based on the validity of these agreements under California law, the Board of Tax Appeals began to tax the wife's earnings to the wife rather than the husband, whenever the spouses had agreed that her earnings would be her separate property.[52]

i.   District Court

In 1918, California taxpayer Reuel D. Robbins and his wife, Sadie, filed separate tax returns, each reporting one-half of the community income. All income was derived from community property and the earnings of Mr. Robbins. The tax collector refused to accept the returns

---

[50] *See, e.g.*, Blair v. Roth, 22 F.2d 932 (9th Cir.1927) (holding 100% community income of California spouses taxable to the husband despite fact that portion of community earnings were attributable to labor by wife); Belcher v. Commissioner, 11 B.T.A. 1294 (1928) (acknowledging that *Randall* was wrongly decided).

[51] 5 F.2d 690 (C.D.Cal.1925), *rev'd*, 269 U.S. 315 (1926).

[52] *See, e.g.*, Harris v. Commissioner, 10 B.T.A. 1374 (1928); Gassner v. Commissioner, 4 B.T.A. 1071 (1926).

as filed and assessed a tax against Mr. Robbins for 100% of the community income. The taxpayer paid the tax and sued for a refund in Federal District Court. Judge Partridge, the Federal District Judge for Northern California, acknowledged at the outset that the suit was intended as a test case to challenge the Commissioner's differential treatment of California spouses. Income-splitting in seven community property states had been approved by the Treasury. The propriety of income-splitting between community property spouses in those states was not at issue. The only question in *Robbins* was whether or not California wives had an interest in community income that was as vested as that of wives in the other seven community property states.

The United States argued that California law controlled and that under California law, the wife had a mere expectancy. Thus, she could not be considered the "owner" of the income for tax purposes. Judge Partridge, in a lengthy and lucid opinion, explained that, although California courts had so described the wife's interest, the substance of the California law in fact created in the wife an interest just as vested as the interest of wives in the other seven community property states. Indeed, in some community property states, the wife's interest would appear to be less vested than in California. For example, husbands in Louisiana could convey community property without the consent of their wives. By contrast, a California husband could not convey community property by gift without his wife's consent.

No California court had ever determined that the wife was not a sufficiently vested owner to consider half the community income hers for federal tax purposes. Nor had the United States Supreme Court so ruled. Nor had the Court of Appeals for the Ninth Circuit. In the absence of binding precedent, Judge Partridge determined that California spouses were entitled to split community income for federal tax purpose, explaining that "[i]t is the marriage which creates ownership; death or divorce merely give possession." He ruled in favor of California taxpayers despite the government's plea that to do so would cost the federal fisc over $77 million in the form of tax refunds to California spouses.[53]

ii. Supreme Court

The case was appealed directly to the Supreme Court,[54] presenting the first opportunity for the Court to speak on the question of income splitting in community property states. The government argued narrowly that California wives were insufficiently vested in community income. Justice Holmes, writing for the majority, agreed, noting that California, unlike New Mexico, did not require the consent of both spouses to all

---

[53] The equivalent of $776 million in 2002 dollars.

[54] The United States appealed via a "writ of error," shortly before the Judiciary Act of 1925, which eliminated such direct appeals, went into effect.

conveyances of community property. He made no reference to any other distinctions between California and other community property states, totally ignoring the fifteen-page decision below that had detailed such distinctions, and concluded that the distinctions were more apparent than real. Holmes ended his brief, three-page opinion, with the following observation:

> Even if we are wrong as to the law of California and assume that the wife had an interest in the community income that Congress could tax if so minded, it does not follow that Congress could not tax the husband for the whole. Although restricted in the matter of gifts, etc., he alone has the disposition of the fund. He may spend it substantially as he chooses, and if he wastes it in debauchery the wife has no redress.... That he may be taxed for such a fund seems to us to need no argument.[55]

C.   The Aftermath

In the first Supreme Court opinion to address the issue of income-splitting in community property states, Justice Holmes appeared to be disagreeing with the position taken earlier by the Attorney General. He seemed to be saying that Congress had the power to tax the husband on the entire community income and that current law could be so construed, even though wives might have some vested rights in community income. This statement was clearly dictum as to any facts other than the facts before the Court. It could not be cited for the proposition that husbands in other community property states should be taxed on 100% of the community income. Yet shortly after the decision was handed down in January 1926, Treasury officials began to reconsider their position permitting income-splitting by spouses in the other seven community property states.

Not surprisingly, taxpayers from those seven states and their representatives in Congress responded quickly to the notion that Treasury would reconsider its policy. In response, Attorney General Sargent announced that he would hold public hearings on the matter at which time he would allow taxpayers and their representatives to state their views.[56] These hearings ultimately resulted in a new opinion by the Attorney General in which he acknowledged that all community property states were different, withdrew the earlier opinions in favor of the seven community property states, and indicated that the ability to split income on the basis of state law would be determined in a series of test cases that would eventually reach the Supreme Court.

---

[55] 269 U.S. at 327.

[56] See Donworth, supra note 40, at 164.

In addition, Congress passed § 121 of the Revenue Act of 1926, which provided as follows:

> Income for any period before January 1, 1925, of a marital community,⧫ in the income of which the wife has a vested interest, as distinguished from an expectancy, shall be held to be correctly returned if returned by the spouse to whom the income belonged under the state law applicable to such marital community for such period.[57]

This provision created a statute of limitations that prevented the Commissioner from challenging returns for tax years 1924 or earlier. Such a limitation was part of the agreement between Congress and the Treasury that the issue should ultimately be decided via litigation and appeal to the Supreme Court. The test cases would be confined to tax years 1925 or later.

Finally, the California legislature, eager to provide equal benefits for its spouses, amended the state's community property laws to provide that husband and wife had equally present vested interests in community property. Thus, California spouses would join the spouses from the other community property states in testing the income-splitting rule under the federal tax law.

Prior Proceedings

Robbins was handed down in 1926, just three months after Guy Earl had petitioned the Board of Tax Appeals to contest the Commissioner's refusal to recognize his income-splitting agreement with his wife. Earl's original petition was against then-Commissioner of the Internal Revenue Service, David H. Blair. The Earl agreement converted community property and community earnings into separate property and earnings. Thus, the issue in *Earl* did not directly involve the question of who was taxed on community income. Nonetheless, it is important to note that the *Earl* litigation occurred in the midst of a national rethinking of the role of community property in determining federal tax liability. Furthermore, the national rethinking had occurred because of a recent Supreme Court decision on the nature of California community property, the very type of property that the *Earl* agreement had converted into separate property, equally owned by the spouses.

Blair v. Roth[58] was another decision that would affect the *Earl* case. Decided initially by the Board of Tax Appeals in 1926, *Roth* involved an agreement between California spouses in which they had agreed to

---

[57] The statutory language is quoted in Donworth, *supra* note 40, at 162–63.

[58] 22 F.2d 932 (9th Cir.1927), *rev'g* 4 B.T.A. 834 (1926).

contribute their individual earnings to a joint account equally owned by them. The wife had substantial earnings of her own. The Ninth Circuit held that this agreement was in effect a mere assignment to the joint account of the wife's interest in community earnings and the husband's interest in community earnings. The assignment could not prevent the income from being community property the moment it arose. In other words, the effect of the agreement under California law was not to convert the community income of the wife into separate income, which under earlier Board of Tax Appeals decisions, should be taxed to her. Rather she had agreed to transfer her half of her earnings and her half of her husband's earnings into a joint account upon the understanding that he would do the same with his two halves. Since her earnings remained community, prior to the assignment, the husband was the appropriate taxpayer.

The Board of Tax Appeals

Earl argued that, under California law, the 1901 agreement with his wife was valid and served to convert all community income into equally-owned separate property the moment the income accrued: "There would be no instant of time when they [future earnings] could be considered as belonging to the husband before the agreement would take effect."[59] As to income from property, the Commissioner agreed. Early in the litigation he adjusted the spouses' incomes on their separate returns to reflect the fact that each should be reporting half of the income from jointly owned property.[60] Note that, in the absence of the agreement, the income from property would have been community income, all taxable to the husband under *Robbins*. Thus the only issue before the Board was whether the agreement was sufficient to convert the earned income of Mr. Earl into jointly owned income which could be split and reported separately by husband and wife.

The government stated its position as follows:

> In reporting income subject to taxation an individual may not reduce the amount of salaries, wages, fees, etc. received by him during a taxable year by an agreement or contract to pay over any amount thereof to another person.[61]

The Board of Tax Appeals agreed with the government. Citing to *Roth* and to *Robbins*, the Board held that Mr. Earl was the proper taxpayer on 100% of his earnings. The opinion was handed down on Valentine's Day (February 14) 1928.

---

[59] Transcript of Record at 3.

[60] *Id*. at 5.

[61] *Id*. at 6.

The Ninth Circuit

1. *The Government Lawyers*

Lawyers for the Commissioner at the Board of Tax Appeals proceeding were lawyers from the Bureau of Internal Revenue, as the Service was then known. On the appeal to the Ninth Circuit, the Commissioner was represented by attorneys from the Office of the Attorney General. The senior lawyer on the appeal was Mabel Walker Willebrandt, the first woman to head the Tax Division and a legend in her own right.

In 1921, President Harding appointed Mabel Walker Willebrandt as the first female Assistant Attorney General, a post she occupied until 1929. Willebrandt was the highest ranking woman in government office during these years, heading up the Justice Department division that was responsible for prohibition and prisons as well as taxation. She participated in over 200 cases before the Supreme Court. Willebrandt became quite unpopular for her enforcement of prohibition and was often labeled "Prohibition Portia" or "Deborah of the Drys." When she left the government in June of 1929, many speculated that it was primarily due to Hoover's refusal to nominate her for a federal judgeship. She was controversial because of her support of the "drys" and was criticized by the "wets" throughout the prohibition era. When President Hoover was pressed to appoint another women to replace Willebrandt as Assistant Attorney General, he responded: "It is not proposed to again put a woman in the position of having to deal with criminal elements, their supporters and the wet press throughout the United States. A woman may be appointed in the Department of Justice, but for some entirely different position."[62]

Willebrandt was something of a feminist heroine for her work on prison reforms that improved conditions for female prisoners. And when she left government service, she became counsel for the Aviation Corporation, where she had the opportunity to support women aviators such as Amelia Earhart. Before joining the Justice Department, she had practiced law in California, where she advocated on behalf of married women for more control over community property.[63] Ironically, she claimed in 1924 to have won the battle in favor of separate tax returns for California wives. She wrote to her mother:

> Hurrah—the most wonderful news. The A.G. has today just shown me his concurring opinion upholding my Com. Prop. Opinion. Isn't that a vindication of all those years of work that I spent on the Community Property Question in California ... His opinion, con-

---

[62] Dorothy M. Brown, *Mabel Walker Willebrandt : A Study of Power, Loyalty, and Law* 178 (1984).

[63] *Id.* at 42.

stantly refers to mine of March 8th and ends by reaffirming and reissuing it.... Aren't you just happy with me tonight? I feel you must know how grateful I am.[64]

She is referring to an opinion issued by Attorney General Daugherty on March 8, 1924, in which he concludes, on the basis of *Wardell v. Blum*, decided by the Ninth Circuit in 1921,[65] that California wives did have a sufficiently vested right in community income to warrant reporting half of the income as their own on separate returns. The opinion is described by Judge Partridge, the District Judge in the *Robbins* case, as follows:

> [O]n March 8, 1924, Attorney General Daugherty rendered an opinion, holding in effect that the same rule should be applied in California as in other community property states. The treasury (T.D. 3568), in accordance with this opinion, put this state in the same category as the others. However, on May 27, 1924, Attorney General Stone withdrew the opinion of Mr. Daugherty for further consideration. On the 9th of October, ... Stone gave his opinion, and on February 7, 1925, the treasury published T.D. 3670, applying the rule in the matter of estate taxes, but denying its application to income.[66]

Just two months after her "victory" on behalf of California wives, a new Attorney General, Harlan Fiske Stone, reversed the government's position. And one year later, when the *Robbins* case reached the Supreme Court, the government argued and the Supreme Court upheld Stone's ruling on the question. By that time, Stone was an Associate Justice on the Supreme Court and took no part in the *Robbins* opinion. That was in 1925 and the Solicitor General oversaw the briefing and arguments.[67]

In 1927, Attorney General Sargent ruled that all appeals from the Board of Tax Appeals would be handled by Willebrandt and her Tax Division at Justice. Since the *Earl* case was appealed during this period, she was given yet another opportunity to deal with California wives and separate tax returns. Although it is doubtful that Willebrandt personally participated in the numerous briefs in tax cases appealed during her tenure, *Earl* was appealed at a time in her career in which she had

---

[64] *Id.* at 141.

[65] 276 F. 226 (9th Cir.1921).

[66] *Robbins*, 5 F.2d at 691.

[67] The Solicitor General is primarily responsible for overseeing appeals of tax litigation to the Supreme Court, but attorneys in the tax division of the Department of Justice often do the detail work. Sometimes the Office of the Solicitor General drafts the government's brief, and sometimes the Solicitor General asks the Tax Division of the Justice Department to prepare the government's brief.

decided to provide more oversight on tax cases.[68] Thus, it is at least possible that she had her eye on the case.

2. *The Taxpayer's Brief*

Taxpayer Earl appealed the decision to the Ninth Circuit. His lawyers, Warren Olney, J.M. Mannon, Henry Costigan, and Robert Lipman, filed a nineteen-page brief on January 14, 1929, exactly 11 months after the Board of Tax Appeals decision was promulgated. They attacked the Board's characterization of the Earls' arrangement as one in which the earnings first vested in Mr. Earl and then in Mrs. Earl, as the assignee. In their view, the Board had misunderstood the effect of the agreement under California law. Their argument, reduced to its essential points, was as follows:

1. Under California law, the earnings of husband and wife are equally community property, under the control of the husband. No distinction is made between the wife's earnings and the husband's earnings.

2. Under California law, husband and wife can agree that the wife's earnings will be her separate property rather than community property. The effect of this agreement is that the earnings belong to her the instant they arise as her separate property and are never treated as community property.

3. Federal tax law follows state law in that it recognizes state rules of property ownership. Thus, when husband and wife agree that the wife's earnings will be her separate property, tax law recognizes her as the owner and taxes her rather than the husband.

4. The Earls made an agreement, valid under California law, which converts the husband's community earnings into separate earnings that are owned half by the husband and half by the wife. This agreement is valid under California law and has exactly the same effect as an agreement making the community earnings of the wife her sole separate property. That is, the moment the earnings arise, they are separate property, not community property.

5. Federal tax law follows state law and thus the California rules of ownership control. Mrs. Earl became the owner of half of Mr. Earl's earnings the moment they came into existence. Therefore she should be taxed on the half of the income that she owned and he should be taxed on the half that he owned.

The Board of Tax Appeals had cited *Blair v. Roth* to support its holding in *Earl*. Earl's brief to the Ninth Circuit, which had decided the *Roth* case, warned that anyone "not familiar with the community

---

[68] Brown, *supra* note 62, at 100–01.

property system" might mistakenly believe that the *Roth* agreement and the *Earl* agreement had the same legal effect. But, in *Roth*, husband and wife had agreed merely to put their earnings into a joint account and to share rights to the earnings once placed there. Thus, the earnings were correctly classified as community at the moment they came into being and only became the separate property of husband and wife as joint tenants once deposited into the joint account. Mr. and Mrs. Earl, by contrast, had agreed that the earnings of the spouses would be equally shared as separate property from inception, whether or not contributed to a joint account. Yes, the funds were deposited in a joint account, but the classification as separate property rather than community property arose the instant the income was earned and not later upon deposit in the joint account.

3. *The Government's Brief*

The government lawyers, led by Mabel Walker Willebrandt, head of the Tax Division of the Justice Department, agreed that the sole question before the court was "whether [the] agreement has the effect of making one-half of the salary and fees earned and received by the husband taxable to the wife, or whether the salary and fees were community income and as such were taxable to the husband."[69] The government lawyers made several important arguments, all focusing on the effect of the agreement under state law.

1. In response to the taxpayer's primary argument (outlined above), the government contended that the facts in *Earl* were quite different from the facts in the cases relied upon by the taxpayer. While taxpayer Earl relied on cases in which the husband and wife had agreed that the wife's earnings would be her separate property, the facts in the present case involve an agreement under which the husband's salary would not only become separate property, but would also belong half to him and half to her. The cases cited in the taxpayer's brief do no more than recognize the right of husband and wife to "nullify the effect of the community property law with reference to the wife's earnings which except for that law would have been her separate income and property"[70] in the first place. Thus, while the government might admit that a wife and husband can nullify community property laws to make her earnings hers and his earnings his, that principle cannot be extended to make his earnings *theirs*. To read the agreement as accomplishing this result would "not only nullify the provisions of the community property law but would go further and in effect establish by agreement that the

---

[69] Brief for Respondent at 2.

[70] *Id*. at 15.

earnings of the husband may become the earnings and income of the wife, a most anomalous situation."[71]

2 If, under California law, the Earl agreement vested half of Mr. Earl's income in Mrs. Earl *eo instanti* so that no tax could attach to Mr. Earl, then the same result would occur in any other state that allowed a person to assign his earnings to another before the earner's right to the earnings arose. Once an assignment contract like this is recognized for tax purposes, then any taxpayer might use such an arrangement to escape taxation altogether. Someone like Mr. Earl could make numerous assignments to various people, all in amounts below the exemption allowed, with the result that no tax would be paid. The result would be disastrous and would completely undermine the progressive tax system.

3. The assignment from husband to wife is similar to arrangements in which debtors assign their earnings to their creditors. Tax law clearly taxes the earner in this case even though the earner never actually receives the income.

4. The Earls' agreement is in fact no different from the agreement in *Roth* and is thus controlled by the Ninth Circuit opinion in that case. Mr. and Mrs. Earl, just like Mr. and Mrs. Roth, opened a joint account and deposited Mr. Earl's salary checks into that account. The checks were issued to Mr. Earl, and Mrs. Earl's rights in the monies only arose once they were deposited in the account. Even if she did have enforceable rights that attached prior to the deposit, those rights attached only after the community characterization had attached to the earnings.

5. Under California law such agreements, although valid, cannot take effect as to a person's earnings until the earnings come into existence.[72] Thus the Earl agreement is valid only as an agreement to convert Mr. Earl's earnings, once they are in his possession, into joint tenancy property. This "time delay" is sufficient to allow the earnings to be characterized first as community property, taxable in full to Mr. Earl.

6. Under general principles of common law, it is not possible to assign earnings from an employment contract until the employment contract is in existence. Because Mr. Earl signed this agreement in 1901, when he was in bad health and well before he was employed by Great Western Power, there was no employment contract that could be the subject of the assignment. In 1901, Guy Earl may have been participating in the acquisition of land that would later be owned by Great Western Power, but in 1901 no corporation existed and thus no employ-

---

[71] *Id.*

[72] Section 955 of the California Civil Code, included in an appendix to the government's brief, provided that "no assignment of . . . wages or salary shall be valid unless made in writing [and] . . . such wages and salary have been earned."

ment contract existed.[73] Since there was no contract to assign, the agreement to assign earnings was executory and gave Mrs. Earl no more than an enforceable right in equity. In the instant before her equitable lien can attach, the earnings are first "impressed with the status of community property,"[74] and thus taxable to the husband. "In any case, any equitable lien acquired under this agreement should ... be construed to be inferior to that of the Government for taxes."[75]

All of these arguments seem valid except for the third one. Mr. Earl gratuitously assigned his income to his wife and that is not the same thing as assigning one's income to a creditor who has provided the taxpayer with value. Indeed, when an employer pays a portion of a salary to a creditor of the employee rather than to the employee himself, income arises under the rule established in *Old Colony Trust*,[76] another key Supreme Court tax case of the 1920s litigated under the supervision of Mabel Walker Willebrandt. It is not the assignment alone that causes the income to be taxed to the employee, but rather the fact that the income was paid for the employee's benefit.

4. *The Opinion*

The Court of Appeals reversed the Board of Tax Appeals, holding that under California law the agreement gave Mrs. Earl a vested interest in half of the income from the instant the earnings came into being. The opinion is short. Judge Bean, writing for the panel, accepts the taxpayer's argument. The imaginary timeline of ownership was crucial to the court's determination. The government had argued that the Earl agreement, like that of the Roths, vested ownership of the earnings in Mr. Earl before ownership passed to the spouses jointly. The Ninth Circuit explained the positions of the parties as follows:

> The petitioner claims that by its terms his personal earnings become the joint property of himself and wife immediately upon being earned, while the position of the government is that, notwithstanding the language of the contract, there was an interval of time during which his earnings belonged to the community and were taxable as such. We are unable to agree with this latter view.[77]

---

[73] The government's brief does not explicitly mention Great Western or give its date of incorporation, but only relies on the argument that the employment contract did not exist in 1901. Based on the "outside the record" stories about Guy Earl and Great Western, we know that the corporation did not even exist in 1901.

[74] Brief for Respondent at 22.

[75] *Id.*

[76] Old Colony Trust v. Commissioner, 279 U.S. 716 (1929).

[77] 30 F.2d at 899.

The Supreme Court Decision

When Guy Earl first petitioned the Board of Tax Appeals in 1925, the Commissioner of Internal Revenue was David H. Blair, not Robert H. Lucas, whose name is now part of this historic decision. Lucas did not become Commissioner until June 1, 1929, just one month after the government petitioned the Supreme Court for a writ of *certiorari* in the case, which at that time was known as *Commissioner v. Earl*. Lucas held the office of Commissioner until August 15, 1930 and was never personally involved in the case. Mabel Walker Willebrandt participated in the Petition for a Writ of *Certiorari*, but left her position as Assistant Attorney General in 1929 before the final briefs and oral arguments in the case.

The Petition for Certiorari *and the Taxpayer's Response*

The government's Petition for a Writ of *Certiorari* stressed the importance of the case as follows:

> If the principle announced by the Circuit Court of Appeals becomes the settled law, then compensation for personal services may be divided into infinitesimal parts by agreements between any person having income from personal services and his immediate family so as to defeat the manifest intent of Congress to tax such income as a whole.[78]

In addition, the petition emphasized that the decision that husband and wife could split income was not limited to community property states. If California spouses could agree to split income, then spouses in non-community property states could do so as well. Such a result would pose a serious threat to the federal fisc as it would allow high-bracket income to be shifted to lower bracket taxpayers. It would allow taxpayers to "evade" the tax. Congress never intended to give taxpayers this much control over determining tax liability, but instead regarded "compensation for personal services as the sole income of the individual who performed the services."[79] The petition also claimed that the court of appeals decision ignored the doctrine of constructive receipt. And, the lawyers restated their argument that a salary not yet in existence cannot be validly assigned.

Guy Earl's lawyers responded by focusing on the narrowness of the decision below, stressing the fact that the decision would only affect agreements between spouses in California, where community earnings

---

[78] Petition at 5.

[79] *Id.* at 12.

were always taxed to the husband unless there was a valid agreement making the earnings the separate property of the wife, in whole or in part. The Ninth Circuit's decision had said nothing about other assignments of income, which in fact under California law would not be enforceable due to lack of consideration. Only husbands and wives can enter into such an agreement. Furthermore, the Earls surely did not enter this contract to "evade" taxes since the contract was entered into in 1901, well before there was an income tax. As to the alleged Congressional intent to tax the earner, Earl's lawyers replied that there was no statute so providing. The tax law merely provided for the taxation of "income derived from salaries," but did not say who the taxpayer was. Finally, as a matter of tax policy, the *owner* of the income, not the *earner*, was the person most able to pay the tax.

With respect to the government's argument that Mr. Earl was in constructive receipt, Earl's lawyers replied with a citation to *Old Colony Trust*, pointing out that the taxpayer there had received an economic benefit because the employer paid the employee's tax liability. By contrast, Mr. Earl received no such benefit and thus could not be considered in constructive receipt of anything of value.

Finally, in response to the government's argument that the agreement could not be effective to create a present vested interest in future earnings, Earl's lawyers again stressed the special provisions of California law that made such agreements valid between spouses. The facts of the case were thus *sui generis* and the principles applied had nothing to do with cases in which debtors might attempt to assign their wages to creditors before the wages arose. And what if the wife's claim was merely equitable? Owners of equitable rights to income are the appropriate taxpayer in the case of trust and partnership income, even though the income is legally owned by the trust or the partnership. In these cases, the tax is assessed on the beneficiaries and partners, despite the fact that all they own is an equitable interest in the income. Thus, even if Mrs. Earl's interest was merely equitable, she was still the correct taxpayer on her share of the income.

The Supreme Court granted *certiorari* on October 14, 1929. The New York Times reported that the "case involved an interpretation of the California community tax law."

The Government's Brief

In its brief to the Supreme Court, the government omitted the arguments it had made in the Ninth Circuit that the wife's interest in her husband's salary was merely an equitable interest, which vested only after the earnings had attained status as community. Instead, the brief focused on two primary arguments: (1) that income should be taxed to the earner, even if the earner does not receive it because that is what the statute requires, and (2) if taxpayers were allowed to assign their income to others, the tax laws could be evaded. The first case cited is *Old Colony Trust* and it is cited for the proposition that "gain can be *salary* only to the person who has performed the services."[80] At the end of the brief, the government lawyers renewed their argument that California law allowed spouses to agree only that the earnings of one spouse would become that spouse's separate property, a principle that should not be applied to validate an assignment of one spouse's earnings to the other spouse.

The Taxpayer's Brief

In response, the taxpayer first established the validity of the agreement under California law and described its effect. Two points are worth repeating. First, the California Supreme Court had specifically held that an agreement between husband and wife could in fact convert *ab initio* the payments for a husband's services into separate property owned by the wife.[81] Second, agreements between spouses did not operate as assignments. In support of this second point, the lawyers pointed to the fact that California law prohibited an individual from assigning a cause of action for personal injuries. Thus, a husband could not *assign* the right to sue for personal injuries to his wife. But a husband and wife could agree, under California law, that the status of any award that might result from the claim would be the separate property of the wife rather than community property.[82] Similarly, the Earl agreement was not an assignment. Rather it imposed the earnings with a particular characterization the moment they came into being, i.e., the separate property of husband and wife, jointly owned.

Relying on cases like *Old Colony Trust*, the taxpayer argued beneficial receipt of income is the necessary touchstone for taxation. Yes, the employee in *Old Colony Trust* was taxed on the salary that he earned even though he did not receive it. But the salary that he did not actually receive was applied for his benefit, to pay a tax that he owed. In support of the argument that beneficial receipt is the necessary touchstone, the brief states:

> The basic idea of the Income Tax is that it is a tax on incomes beneficially received. This is the economic justification for the law. It is the idea upon which primarily its provisions have been drawn. For example, the tax is not on incomes as such, that is, on all income,

---

[80] Brief for Petitioner at 6.

[81] Cullen v. Bisbee, 144 P. 968 (Cal.1914), is the case cited for this proposition. Brief for Respondent at 7.

[82] *Id*. at 5–6.

but on net income alone. The idea of net income is beneficial gain to the taxpayer.[83]

Examples of cases in which it is the beneficial receipt of income that triggers tax and not the entity earning the tax included: (1) personal service partnerships, such as law firms, (2) personal service corporations, which under then-existing law, were not taxed on their earnings, but instead passed the tax through to the stockholders in much the same way that partnerships were taxed, (3) wives in seven community property states (and in California as of 1927)[84] who were taxed on half of the earnings earned by their husbands, and (4) husbands in California, who for tax years before 1927 were taxed on their wives' earnings because community property law gave them sufficient beneficial enjoyment.

The Opinion

On March 17, 1930, less than a month after Guy Earl's brief had been filed, Justice Holmes delivered the opinion of the Court. The decision was unanimous with Chief Justice Hughes, who had recently been appointed, not participating. Without much explanation, Holmes merely tells us that earnings will be taxed to the earner husband despite the fact that by contract the wife has an enforceable right to possession of half of the earnings. In his own words: "[N]o distinction can be taken according to the motives leading to the arrangement by which the fruits are attributed to a different tree from that on which they grew."[85] He never says that earnings will be taxed to the earner. He never says that earnings will be taxed to the person who has the right to control the earnings. He merely says that *this* husband will be taxed on *these* earnings. Thus, some assignments of income, although valid under property and contract law, will not shift tax burdens from the earner/assignor to the assignee. And although Holmes never told us which assignments count and which do not, we do know that the *Earl* case involved an assignment for no consideration between family members. At its narrowest then, *Earl* stands for the proposition that *gratuitous* assignments of income will not be recognized for tax purposes.

---

[83] *Id.* at 11.

[84] In 1927, the California legislature added § 161(a) to the Civil Code, which provided that husband and wife had equally present vested interests in community property. The Commissioner responded with a revenue ruling that would allow California spouses to split community income and file two separate returns. I.T. 2457, C.B. VIII–9–4122 (1929) (discussed in Donworth, *supra* note 40, at 170–71).

[85] Lucas v. Earl, 281 U.S. 111, 115 (1930).

The Immediate Impact of *Earl*

The Road to Joint Returns

1. Poe v. Seaborn[86]

In August of 1928, when Guy Earl was appealing his case to the
Court of Appeals for the Ninth Circuit, spouses from the community
property states of Arizona, Louisiana, Texas, and Washington filed test
cases in federal district court. In every case, the spouses had reported
community income by allocating half to the husband and half to the wife.
This reporting position had been endorsed by the Attorney General as
early as 1920, but that opinion had been recently revoked. In every case,
the Service refused the returns and instead assessed a tax against the
husband, allocating 100% of the community income to him, whether the
income was from earnings or from property. The husbands in each case
paid the tax and sued the local Collector of Internal Revenue in federal
district court, claiming a refund in the amount of the additional tax that
had been assessed by the Collector.[87]

Ultimately these cases were consolidated and heard by the Supreme
Court. Briefs were filed in October 1930, just seven months after the
Supreme Court had handed down the *Earl* opinion. In the lead case, *Poe
v. Seaborn*, taxpayer/husband H.G. Seaborn sued Burns Poe, the Collector of Internal Revenue for the District of Washington.

The government argued in *Seaborn* that the community property
laws of the State of Washington gave the husband so much control over
both community property and income that he should be the one to bear
the tax on all community income. This position was a complete reversal
of the government's earlier position that all community property states,
other than California, gave the wife a sufficiently vested interest in
community property to tax her on half of the community income. The
Holmes opinions in *Robbins* and *Corliss v. Bowers*, emphasizing control,
supported the government's position in *Seaborn*. The Holmes opinion in
Earl could have been cited for the proposition that earnings should be
taxed to the earner, but that argument was not made on behalf of the
government in *Seaborn*. Instead, the government merely argued that
Earl supported *Corliss* and *Robbins* by requiring taxation of the husband.

The *Seaborn* briefs are a surprise in this respect. It appears that the
government had decided to go for broke, asking the Supreme Court to
extend *Robbins* to the other seven community property states. The
Robbins rule required that *all* community income, whether from personal service earnings or from property, be taxed to the husband because he
was the one in control of the income. Had the government relied
primarily on *Earl* rather than *Robbins*, it could have argued more

---

[86] 282 U.S. 101 (1930).

[87] *See* Harry C. Weeks, *The Community Property Income Tax Test Cases*, Nat'l Income
Tax Mag. 466, 468 (1929).

narrowly that earned income, as opposed to income from property, should be taxed to the "tree" that caused the earnings to exist in the first place, i.e., to the earner.

The government also argued that federal tax laws were intended to operate uniformly and that the tax burden should fall equally on similarly situated family units, regardless of the state of residence. Spouses in community property states should bear the same share of the tax burden as similarly-situated spouses in non-community property states.

While the government's primary purpose was to end the special benefit of income-splitting that had been available to community property spouses, its argument for uniformity was, in fact, flawed. If the government's position had been sustained by the Supreme Court, community property spouses not only would have lost their advantage, but they also would have been placed at a serious disadvantage. The Commissioner was not arguing for a tax on the earner, as the *Earl* holding suggested might be the appropriate rule. Instead, he was arguing in favor of taxing the husband on all community earnings, whether the earnings were attributable to the services of the husband or of the wife. Similarly, the government argued that the husband should be taxed on all income from community property, no matter how vested the wife's interest in that property might be.

Ultimately the Supreme Court agreed with the taxpayers in *Seaborn* that the tax should be borne by the owner of the income. Since wives had a vested property right in community property, they were co-owners with their husbands and thus should be taxed on half the community income from property. As to the earned income of the husband, the Court also held the wife taxable on half. In distinguishing *Earl*, the Court said:

> The very assignment in that case was bottomed on the fact that the earnings would be the husband's property, else there would have been nothing on which it could operate. That case presents a different question from this, because here, by law, the earnings are never the property of the husband, but that of the community.[88]

The case was decided primarily on grounds of statutory construction. The taxing statute provided for a tax on the "net income of every individual." The word "of" connoted ownership, not control. *Earl* was distinguished as a case in which ownership first vested in the husband. *Corliss* was similarly distinguished. There, the grantor had been the original owner of the income-producing property and, although he had transferred ownership, he had retained control, the power to revest the

---

[88] *Seaborn*, 282 U.S. at 117.

trust corpus in himself. By contrast, ownership of the wife's half of the community property had never vested in Mr. Seaborn.

A second ground for the holding in *Seaborn* was the fact of a "long and unbroken line of executive construction" of the tax law favoring the splitting of income between community property spouses in seven states, including Washington. The Court had deferred to the governmental interpretation of the tax law in *Robbins*, *Corliss*, and *Earl*. Now the government has changed its mind with respect to community property spouses in the state of Washington. But the Treasury had first gone to Congress in 1921 to ask for a statutory change that would tax the husband on community property income and Congress had refused to pass the bill. Instead, Congress continued to enact the same language that had been construed as authorizing community property spouses to split income. Given this action by Congress, it would be inappropriate for the Court now to change the statute. This alternative rationale, which gives deference to a Congressional decision not to change the administrative interpretation of the taxing statute may well have been sufficient for Justice Holmes, who in every other relevant tax case wrote a decision explicitly deferring to Congress and recognizing its broad power to tax.

The companion cases from Arizona,[89] Texas,[90] and Louisiana[91] all held in favor of the taxpayer on the same grounds. All were decided on November 24, 1930. Just two months later, on January 19, 1931, the Court extended the income-splitting rule to California spouses as to community property income derived in 1928 and later.[92]

2. *Legislative Response to* Earl *and* Seaborn

The net result of the Supreme Court opinions in *Earl* and *Seaborn* was to treat spouses in community property states more favorably with respect to earned income than spouses in common law states. Lack of uniformity was a major concern. The Supreme Court had answered the lack of uniformity argument, pressed by the government, by saying that the state law of Washington gave real rights to the wife which state law in non-community property states did not give. After all, said the *Seaborn* Court, any time income is earned by an entity such as a community or partnership, someone must be assigned responsibility for decision-making on behalf of the entity. The fact that the community property laws gave all such responsibility to the husband did not concern the Justices. In their view, he was acting as a special agent on behalf of

---

[89] Goodell v. Koch, 282 U.S. 118 (1930).

[90] Hopkins v. Bacon, 282 U.S. 122 (1930).

[91] Bender v. Pfaff, 282 U.S. 127 (1930).

[92] United States v. Malcolm, 282 U.S. 792 (1931).

the community. The agency was so special, that it could not be revoked. Yet, the wife could not sue the agent as other principals might, but this arrangement was required by public policy. "Public policy demands that in all ordinary circumstances, litigation between wife and husband during the life of the community should be discouraged."[93]

The tension created by the difference in tax treatment between spouses in community property states and spouses in other states continued. Congress had several options for correcting the imbalance: (1) overrule *Poe v. Seaborn* and tax earned income in community property states to the earner rather than allowing it to be split; (2) overrule *Lucas v. Earl* and tax income that spouses had agreed to share half to one spouse and half to the other; or (3) take some middle road that would reduce the difference between community and non-community property states.

In 1933, a subcommittee of the House Ways and Means Committee issued a preliminary report making no recommended change "in view of the legal difficulties involved." Acting Secretary of the Treasury Morgenthau then recommended consideration of compulsory joint returns for all spouses, but the recommendation was not enacted. In 1934, Representative Treadway introduced a bill similar to the one rejected by Congress in 1921 requiring community income to be taxed to the spouse with management and control. This solution was deemed simpler than a compulsory joint return. In 1937, President Roosevelt addressed the Congress on the issue of tax evasion, citing the division of community income as a primary cause of revenue loss. In 1941, the Treasury finally proposed a compulsory joint return for all spouses aimed at mitigating the community property problem as well as reducing the ability of other spouses to arrange their affairs in ways that would reduce tax revenues.[94] The proposal would have required spouses to pay a tax on their aggregate income at the same rate that a single person would have paid on the same amount of income. The result was to increase the tax burden on almost all married couples. As a tax on marriage, the proposal was attacked on moral grounds and was ultimately defeated.[95]

Common law states responded to the concerns of their citizenry by proposing community property legislation intended to gain for their spouses the same benefits available to spouses in the eight community property states. Oklahoma, Oregon, Hawaii, Nebraska, Michigan, and

---

[93] *Seaborn*, 282 U.S. at 112.

[94] E.g., using trusts, family partnerships, or closely held corporations to split income between spouses. For a discussion of these devices and the tax cases that held most of them invalid, see Stanley S. Surrey, *Family Income and Federal Taxation*, 24 Taxes 980, 981–82 (1946).

[95] *See* Boris I. Bittker, *Taxation and the Family*, 27 Stan. L. Rev. 1389, 1411–12 (1975).

Pennsylvania became, for at least a short time, community property states. In a 1944 case,[96] the Supreme Court, citing both *Seaborn* and *Earl*, determined that the Oklahoma system of community property would not be honored for income tax purposes. Why? Because the system was optional for Oklahoma spouses. If they elected into the system, community property rules would control. If they failed to elect, they remained within the common law separate property regime. An election into the system was analogized to the contract between Mr. and Mrs. Earl and considered a mere assignment of income, which, but for the agreement to opt in, would have belonged to the husband. The fact that California had changed its law after the *Robbins* case in order to obtain the benefit of income-splitting for tax purposes, and the fact that spouses in California could enter into agreements about property characterizations at will, were viewed as irrelevant to the Oklahoma decision. After all, as the Court noted, California at least had a history of community property derived from Spanish law. This notion that some states could be genuine community property states based on state history while others could not suggested that the Court would not be the best institution to maximize tax equality between spouses in different states.

Finally, in 1948, Congress responded to the problem with the enactment of the modern joint return. Under this approach, spouses would aggregate income, but the tax paid would be "equal to twice what a single person would pay on one-half" of such income.[97]

This option satisfied numerous concerns. For one thing, once the Supreme Court of the United States had held that half of all community earnings *belonged* to the non-earning spouse, some in Congress were afraid to tax those earnings to the non-owning spouse. Why? *Hoeper v. Wisconsin* was now on the books, holding that it was unconstitutional under due process analysis to tax one person on income that belonged to another. In addition, the eight community property states were quite populous and powerful. Thus, adopting an option that would have repealed income-splitting for community property spouses was simply not politically feasible. The joint return option should appeal to everyone because it had the effect of extending the benefit of income-splitting to all spouses.

The same result, giving all spouses the right to split income, could have been accomplished by reversing *Lucas v. Earl*. But reversing *Earl* would have required husbands in common law states to enter into binding agreements in which they gave half of everything they owned to their wives. The partnership ideas, the concept of equal sharing, might be understood in community property states. But in common law states,

---

[96] Commissioner v. Harmon, 323 U.S. 44 (1944).

[97] Bittker, *supra* note 95, at 1412.

with a history of coverture under which the husband was used to controlling all marital property even more than in community property states, equal sharing was a huge price to pay for mere reduction of taxes. Indeed, when community property was introduced in New York, the State Tax Commission issued a report warning against that option in part because of the interest in property that wives would acquire under such a system. Congress in effect stopped the community property revolution by allowing husbands to pay a reduced tax whether or not they actually shared income or property with their spouses.

The Continuing Importance of *Earl* Today

After the *Earl* decision, spouses in non-community property states attempted to shift income from one spouse to another using partnerships, corporations, trusts and similar devices. The principle in *Earl* continued to be applied to prevent assignment of earnings through such devices. *Corliss* was the more relevant authority for attempts to shift property income. But *Earl* did establish the rule that if spouses in common law states had current vested rights in income-producing property, that income could be split. *Earl*'s primary import then, is its prohibition of gratuitous assignments of income between spouses. Even if they can accomplish a valid assignment under state law, federal tax law will tax the earner.

As a result of *Earl*, couples whose income was primarily in the form of salary (typically that of the husband in those years) could not split their income for tax purposes, whereas couples, who were wealthy enough to live off of investment income rather than wages, could split their income for tax purposes. As Stanley Surrey of Harvard Law School, then serving as tax legislative counsel, explained:

> [T]he middle bracket family with stocks and bonds which has split its income equally between husband and wife, receives a tax holiday at least every fifth year while the family living on a salary or professional earnings must still work for Uncle Sam. One wonders whether the decision of Justice Holmes in *Lucas v. Earl* to prevent the fruits from being attributed to a different tree has not caused us to lose sight of the forest of tax equity.[98]

What if *Earl* had come out the other way? In that event, spouses in common law states would have been able to opt into income-splitting by entering into sharing agreements. And if states did not allow such contracts with respect to future earnings, as the government briefs suggested might be the case even in California, states would have been pressured to adopt enabling legislation. Otherwise their spouses would

---

[98] Surrey, *supra* note 94, at 983.

be denied the federal tax benefit of splitting income. Wives would have had vested rights in their husband's earnings and property as a result of such agreements. Indeed, a wife's rights under an Earl-type of agreement would often be much stronger than a wife's rights under community property. As a joint owner of separate property, Ella Earl had an immediate right to convey her interest, or to withdraw all available funds from a jointly-owned bank account. By contrast, under community property regimes, only the husband could convey, mortgage, or use the property, although in the Supreme Court's view, he was acting as special agent of the community when he did so.

Had Guy and Ella Earl lived[99] to see the new tax law take shape, what would they have thought? Surely by then their tax advisers would have told them to rescind the 1901 agreement. After the changes in California community property law in 1927, they would have saved income taxes by converting back to the community property regime. Once *Malcolm*, the California test case following *Poe v. Seaborn*, was handed down in 1931, it became clear that California spouses could split all community income. The anomaly is that Ella would have been giving up vested rights under the joint tenancy arrangement for the more tentative rights of a community property wife in order to benefit from income splitting. But by 1948, had they lived that long, they could have benefited from the income-splitting rates of the joint return even though they held property as joint tenants rather than community property.

Conclusion

In the end, the story of Guy and Ella Earl sheds more light on the assignment of income doctrine than Justice Holmes' oft-quoted fruit-and-tree metaphor. An understanding of the factual background of the agreement signed by the Earls at the dawn of the 20th Century, as well as of the social and legal context of the times, should help us apply this doctrine to myriad circumstances in our 21st Century world. Holmes got it right in *Earl*, but not because he imposed the horticultural metaphor. Holmes got it right because he understood the ramifications of the alternative. Congress intended to enact a tax system that was progressive and Holmes believed strongly in carrying out Congressional intent. If gratuitous assignments of income were allowed, the progressive rate structure would be at risk. That principle, protection of progressivity, should guide us today as we determine whether it is appropriate to tax income to the assignor or the assignee. But the tax reverberations of *Earl* continue to be felt outside of the assignment of income area as well.

---

[99] Guy Earl died in 1935 at the age of 75. Coincidentally, Justice Holmes also died in 1935, at the age of 90.

All married couples who file joint tax returns each April 15th are part of Guy and Ella Earl's legacy, as are our modern political and academic debates about the resulting "marriage penalty." Indeed, the nature of the division of property among husbands and wives today can be traced at least in part to *Earl*. As important as Guy and Ella Earls' contributions were to the history of northern California, they played an even bigger role in the development of the tax law.

*

10

Daniel N. Shaviro

The Story of *Knetsch*:
Judicial Doctrines
Combating Tax Avoidance

"I shall not attempt further today to define [it] ... and perhaps I should never succeed in intelligibly doing so. But I know it when I see it." Perhaps inevitably, Justice Stewart's famous statement about pornography[1] has indeed been cited in the context of defining impermissible tax avoidance[2]—and with approval notwithstanding its requiring the exercise of "intuitive judicial judgment"[3] that may be unpredictable in advance.

No case looms larger as a cornerstone of the doctrine defining impermissible tax avoidance than *Knetsch v. United States*.[4] In this case, an individual, with the help (and at the solicitation) of the Sam Houston Life Insurance Company, set up a circle of cash on December 11, 1953, whereby he purported to borrow $4 million from the company at a 3.5% interest rate so that he could invest this money, with the same company, in deferred annuity bonds that offered only a 2.5% return. He thereby arranged to earn about $100,000 per year at a cost of about $140,000 per year. On balance, therefore, he could expect to pay Sam Houston about $40,000 per year while the transaction lasted, along with a $4,000 up-front fee, for the privilege of getting to pay it all that money.

There was also a silver lining, however. If Knetsch, who at the time of the deal was 60 years old, should happen to reach the age of 90, then at that point he would begin receiving a life annuity of $43 per month.

---

[1] Jacobellis v. Ohio, 378 U.S. 184, 197 (1964) (Stewart, J., concurring).

[2] Estate of Baron v. Commissioner, 83 T.C. 542, 559 (1984).

[3] *Id.*

[4] 364 U.S. 361 (1960).

At this rate, so long as he managed to live for a shade more than another 2,325 years, he would get back all the money he had laid out.[5] He would then be able to turn to the more vexing problem of starting to earn an overall positive return on his up-front outlays.

The transaction may initially remind one of the old joke in which someone says he is in the business of making change, in the amount of 5 quarters for every dollar. "How can you stay in business doing that?" he is asked. "That's easy," he replies. "I make it up on volume."

However, Knetsch believed he had a better rationale for engaging in the Sam Houston deal. Under black-letter tax law that applied at the time of the deal, income from deferred annuity bonds was not currently includable in income, but interest expense was generally deductible even if incurred in relation to the purchase of such bonds. Knetsch therefore hoped, like a tax Rumpelstiltskin, to turn pre-tax straw into after-tax spun gold by reporting taxable income from the transaction of negative $140,000 per year.

In 1953, the year in which he entered into the transaction, Knetsch otherwise had taxable income of $202,755, which is the equivalent of $1.4 million in 2002 dollars. The marginal tax rate on his last dollar of this income was 92%,[6] and the average rate on the entire amount he hoped to deduct was nearly 80%.[7] Thus, reporting a $140,000 tax loss would reduce his tax liability by more than $110,000. Accordingly, despite losing $40,000 per year before-tax, he could hope to end up more than $70,000 per year ahead after-tax—at least for the time being, pending the eventual recognition of taxable income on the deferred annuity bonds.

In short, Knetsch was trying to arrange a classic "tax arbitrage." To explain this term, it may be useful to start with the more general meaning of "arbitrage." In financial or other markets, you have a favorable arbitrage opportunity if you can buy a given asset at one price and simultaneously sell it at a higher price without incurring significant transaction costs. For as long as the arbitrage opportunity lasts (which usually is not long), it is effectively a money machine, permitting you to pocket the spread between the prices without taking any net economic

---

[5] Knetsch would be out of pocket about $1.2 million as a result of paying Sam Houston about $40,000 per year for thirty years. At a rate of $43 per month, it would take him 27,907 months, or just over 23,205.5 years, to earn this money back (disregarding the time value of money).

[6] *See* U.S. Dept. of Commerce, Bureau of Statistics, *Historical Statistics of the United States, Colonial Times to 1970*, Part 2 (Chapters N–Z), Table VIII (Kraus International Publications, 1989).

[7] *See* District Court Complaint, Counts 4–6, showing that in 1953 an annuity loan interest deduction of $143,465 reduced Knetsch's reported income tax liability for the year by $113,684.48, or about 79.2% of the amount being deducted.

position. A tax arbitrage is roughly the tax version of this, whereby you profit after-tax from both paying and receiving a dollar because the dollar you pay is treated more favorably than the dollar you receive (e.g., the outlay is deductible while the inflow is not currently or fully includable). The term "tax arbitrage" is commonly used, however, without limitation to literal arbitrages where the same asset is being bought and sold.

Knetsch was cruelly disappointed, however, by the outcome of the case that bears his name. The Supreme Court held (affirming the courts below) that the Sam Houston transaction was a "sham" that did not create genuine indebtedness. Accordingly, not even his out-of-pocket cost of $40,000 per year was deductible, either as interest or—as decided in a subsequent case—on any other ground,[8] notwithstanding that he was out the money and had not gotten any personal consumption benefit from spending it.

By the time of the Supreme Court decision, the specific tax planning ploy that Knetsch tried to exploit had been barred on a prospective basis by the enactment of § 264 in March 1954. One might therefore initially suppose that the case would have only limited precedential significance. Such a supposition would be mistaken, however. The Supreme Court's holding that the Knetsch–Sam Houston transaction was a "sham" has had an immense broader influence, both apparent and real. The merely apparent influence, sagely predicted by Professor Walter Blum in a commentary shortly after *Knetsch* was decided, was its making "the term 'sham' (and its various synonyms) ... more popular than ever in opinion writing ... [where] it will be widely employed, among other uses, to signify that the taxpayer loses."[9]

Knetsch's broader influence is real as well as apparent, however. It decisively established (albeit building on prior case law) that a transaction must meet some minimum standard of economic substance, business purpose, and/or potential for pre-tax profit if it is to be respected for tax purposes. This set of related requirements continues to play a major role in tax planning, in tax audit and litigation controversy, and in tax policy debates. Indeed, if anything, the principle that *Knetsch* articulates is more important today than when the case was decided because the simple tax planning scheme that it struck down is the recognizable ancestor of myriad proposed and actual transactions today. Both the scheme and the administrative or judicial responses that the case exemplifies have co-evolved like parasite and immune system, growing jointly more elaborate without ceasing to resemble closely their ancestral forms.

---

[8] Knetsch v. United States, 348 F.2d 932 (Ct.Cl.1965), *cert. denied*, 383 U.S. 957 (1966).

[9] Walter J. Blum, Knetsch v. United States: *A Pronouncement on Tax Avoidance*, 40 Taxes 296, 311 (1962).

Four decades of familiarity with *Knetsch*'s economic substance requirement have also changed the climate of opinion in tax practice.
When the case was before the Supreme Court, the filers of an amicus
brief supporting the taxpayer felt at liberty to describe the Service
position as "monstrous," not to mention "harsh, incongruous, and
unjust."[10] Today, however, tax lawyers by and large accept *Knetsch*, not
just as an inescapable part of the tax landscape but also as correct and
even necessary. To be sure, when the government moves aggressively
against contemporary tax arbitrages—for example, in broadly attacking
"corporate tax shelter" transactions that gained notoriety beginning in
the late 1990s—some tax lawyers may squeal in terms that would not
have sounded out of place in the *Knetsch* amicus brief.[11] Yet the entire
debate has moved a few steps over to the side. Now the argument is
about how far the *Knetsch* doctrine should reach, not about whether it
should apply at all.

One thing *Knetsch* does not tell us is how much economic substance,
business purpose, or potential for pre-tax profit is needed for a transaction to escape sham status. At what point is the tail of business purpose
(or the claim that there is a tail) large enough to wag the tax dog?
Another thing *Knetsch* does not tell us, but that is well worth thinking
about, is why, as a matter either of statutory interpretation or good tax
policy, there should be an economic substance or business purpose
requirement. Aren't all sorts of permissible deals—even holding tax-
exempt bonds in your portfolio if they offer a lower pre-tax return than
taxable bonds—fundamentally tax-motivated? Can we really draw a line
between holding municipal bonds (which lose money before-tax if you
count the opportunity cost of not holding higher-yielding instruments)
and *Knetsch*? Or between transactions with a shade too little economic
substance and those with just enough?

And why should the Service and the courts care about "economic
substance" anyway? As we will see, Knetsch might have won his case if
only the return on the deferred annuity bonds, while still on average an
expected 2.5%, had been double or nothing (50% chance of earning 5%
and 50% chance of earning zero). If a coin toss to determine the payoff
seemed too frivolous, the parties could have made it depend, say, on
whether oil prices or interest rates went up or down. Knetsch could then
have argued that the deal had economic substance, a 50% chance of
offering a pre-tax profit, and even a business purpose ("I was feeling
lucky").

---

[10] Brief of Amici Curiae Richard H. Appert, Esq., and Converse Murdoch, Esq., at 12.

[11] *See, e.g.*, Kenneth J. Kies, *A Critical Look at "Corporate Tax Shelter" Proposals*, 83
Tax Notes 1463, 1470–71 (1999) ("The overreaching and vague Treasury Department
proposals would have a severely detrimental impact on tax analysis and planning relating
to a large number of legitimate business transactions").

Why, however, should it matter for tax purposes whether or not a given taxpayer "bets" like this while making a tax-favored investment? Why implicitly encourage and reward such risk-taking, by causing it to immunize tax benefits against legal challenge, rather than treating it as irrelevant to whether we should allow the benefits?

The reason, we will see, resembles that for placing the cookie jar in a kindergarten classroom on a high shelf. We don't actually mean to encourage the five-year olds to start stacking up boxes and standing on chairs, or to hand a relative advantage to the taller ones. Rather, we simply figure that this way fewer of them are likely to reach it when the teacher is not looking.

Background

The Legal Context

1. *Substance Over Form or Sham Transaction Doctrine*

   A.   Tax Planning and Tax Arbitrage

The aim of tax planning is to reduce your income tax burden without actually doing much worse economically. Hence the lack of appeal to what Martin Ginsburg jocularly calls the "Herman tax shelter," and describes as follows:

> It is simple, and certainly simplicity is a virtue in the tax field. All you need to do is lend Herman $100,000 in cash. Herman will then default on the loan. Assuming the necessary trade or business context, Herman's default should produce for you a $100,000 deduction, worth whatever your tax bracket makes it worth.[12]

The problem with the "Herman tax shelter" is that, unless your marginal tax rate exceeds 100%, it leaves you worse-off after-tax than if you had done nothing at all. So the key to a potentially appealing tax shelter is that it reduce your taxable income by much more than it reduces your pre-tax economic income.

There are three main tools that you can use to this end. The first is exclusion, or earning a type of income that the income tax does not reach. The second is deferral, or earning a type of income that the tax system will only reach later on. (This may involve accelerating deductions as well as deferring inclusions.) The third is conversion, or earning capital gains that are taxed at a low rate instead of ordinary income that is taxed at a high rate.

Without something to give them extra oomph, however, these tax planning tools may end up offering disappointingly small benefits. In-

---

[12] Martin D. Ginsburg, *The Leaky Tax Shelter*, 53 Taxes 719, 723 (1975).

deed, there are two potential problems with using exclusion, deferral, or conversion to lower your tax burden.

The first potential problem is tax capitalization, or the tendency in some circumstances for market forces to eliminate through price changes any after-tax benefit. One can illustrate this with tax-exempt municipal bonds. If corporate bonds offer a 10% return before-tax and everyone pays tax at a 30% marginal rate, the issuers of municipal bonds may find that they need only offer a 7% return in order to sell their bonds. To the extent this happens, it is true enough that municipal bondholders will avoid paying any (explicit) federal income tax on the bonds. But it is also true that they will only be matching the 7% after-tax return that is available on corporate bonds. So holding municipal bonds does not actually leave them better off.

The second potential problem is that even if assets that offer exclusion, deferral, or conversion leave you better off after-tax, the benefit may be disappointingly limited if you cannot find some way to enhance them. In the movie *The Godfather, Part 2*, one of the characters, asking the young Don Corleone for a kickback, says: "I don't want a lot. Just enough to wet my beak." But not all taxpayers are so modest in their aspirations. Some may want to zero out their tax liabilities altogether (or at least move substantially in that direction), rather than just enjoying an enhanced after-tax return on a given investment. And if, say, a law firm partner with a million-dollar annual draw merely holds all of her investment assets in tax-favored form, that still leaves her with a substantial annual federal income tax liability on her salary if she does not shelter it by incurring tax losses.

Tax arbitrage can address both of these problems. It thus often stands as a vital elixir or enhancer to aggressive tax planning, like the use of grain alcohol to spike the punch at a fraternity mixer. Its relationship to zeroing out is especially straightforward. Consider again the million-dollar law firm partner. If she engages in tax arbitrage on a large enough scale, then, rather than merely deferring the tax on her investment income, she may actually generate tax losses that—if nothing in the tax law stops her—reduce or eliminate the current income tax on her salary.

The relationship between tax arbitrage and tax capitalization is subtler. Tax capitalization results from the tax system's effects on supply and demand. For example, if Congress enacts tax preferences for investing in a given industry, total investment in that industry is likely to increase. This should drive down pre-tax returns in the industry (since the supply of goods it offers is being increased without a matching increase in demand) until the available after-tax return merely equals that available from competing but higher-taxed investments. Where tax arbitrage is done right, however, these effects can be eliminated. Thus, consider again Knetsch and Sam Houston, who both borrowed and lent $4 million to each other. Since this was what Eugene Steuerle calls a "pure tax arbitrage," in which "the taxpayer essentially buys and sells [or borrows and lends] the same asset,"[13] no asset's supply was being affected relative to the demand for it.[14] No new borrowers and no new lenders were showing up in the capital markets to offer or demand funds. Tax gains could therefore be reaped without concern about driving down the pre-tax return on deferred annuity bonds or other saving. They could also in theory be reaped indefinitely. After all, in the absence of tax law impediments, and if Knetsch had enough cash to pay the spread between the rates and was eager to obtain enough deductions, the parties could just as well have exchanged notes for $40 million, or for that matter $400 billion, instead of just $4 million.

Tax arbitrage may also appeal to prospective customers who want to minimize, not just their expected pre-tax loss, but also their worst-case-scenario risk of loss. If they buy and sell the same item, or borrow and lend the same amount, then their lack of a net position in the transaction may help to eliminate downside economic risk. Prospective investors also often want to minimize the amount of cash they must commit to a given transaction. Tax arbitrage can help with this as well since you need not lay out net cash to the extent that you are selling as well as buying, or borrowing as well as lending.

B. Judicial and Other Governmental Responses to Aggressive Tax Planning

Creative and aggressive tax planning, with or without tax arbitrage, sometimes uses black letter rules or their interaction in what may appear to be unintended ways. Even if we doubt that Congressional enacters thought enough about what they were doing to have conscious intentions one way or the other about a given transaction, we may believe that its effects are inconsistent with the hypothetical intent of a reasonable person enacting the rules. Thus, in *Knetsch* itself, suppose we posit that Congress allowed income deferral on annuity bonds because it wanted to encourage retirement saving. In addition, suppose we posit that Congress made interest expense generally deductible as a way of increasing the accuracy of net income measurement. (After all, if you spend $5 to get $6, your profit is only $1, as determined by allowing the $5 expense to be deducted.) Knetsch, however, was not really saving for retirement since he borrowed almost all that he invested and was

---

[13] C. Eugene Steuerle, *Taxes, Loans, and Inflation: How the Nation's Wealth Becomes Misallocated* 60 (1985).

[14] For convenience, I ignore what economists call "income effects," or the possibility that Knetsch's or the owners of Sam Houston's demand for other items would be affected by the money they made after-tax from the transaction.

earning less than he was paying out. Moreover, allowing him the interest deduction, given the current income exclusion, would actually reduce rather than increase the accuracy with which his income from the transaction was being measured.[15] Yet nothing in the Internal Revenue Code, prior to the 1954 enactment of § 264, explicitly barred the transaction.

Sometimes tax planning that is thought to have undesirable results is addressed by amending the Code. An example is § 264, which Congress promptly enacted after the Service had brought Sam Houston's publicly advertised transactions to its attention.[16] Or consider the enactment, many years later, of the § 163(d) investment interest limitation, which denies deductions for investment interest to the extent in excess of net investment income. This provision, had it existed at the time of Knetsch's transaction, would probably have denied him most or all of the tax benefits even if the transaction had not been deemed a sham.[17]

Since at least the 1930s, however, aggressive tax planning has also been addressed through the case law. The often-cited foundational case in this regard is *Helvering v. Gregory*,[18] a case involving conversion of ordinary income into capital gain although not tax arbitrage. In *Gregory*, the taxpayer's wholly owned company, United Mortgage Corporation (UMC), held appreciated shares of the Monitor Securities Corporation. Gregory wanted to sell the Monitor shares and end up with the cash. She knew, however, that if UMC either just gave her the shares or sold them and gave her the cash, she would have ordinary income from the receipt of a dividend. Under the rules prevailing at the time for tax-free corporate reorganizations, however, she could (1) have UMC give the Monitor shares to a new corporation that had no other assets or liabilities, and of which she would be the sole owner, (2) liquidate the new corporation, receiving the Monitor shares as its sole asset, and then

---

[15] Before tax, Knetsch lost $40,000 from the Sam Houston transaction. Given the exclusion, his annual taxable income was measured as minus $140,000 if the interest deduction was allowed, and zero if it was not allowed. The latter measure comes closer than the former to being economically accurate (it is off the mark by only $40,000 rather than $100,000) although a more accurate measure still would have permitted him to deduct the net loss.

[16] *See* H.R. Rep. No. 83–1337, at 31 (1954) ("It has come to your committee's attention that a few insurance companies have promoted [plans resembling that in *Knetsch*].... Your committee's bill will deny an interest deduction in such cases but only as to annuities purchased after March 1, 1954."). Apparently, the transaction that Knetsch decided to engage in after receiving promotional materials from Sam Houston was the very one that the Commissioner brought to the House Ways and Means Committee's attention. *See* Reply Brief for the Petitioners at 9.

[17] Knetsch deducted the interest expense from the Sam Houston loan against ordinary income that otherwise totaled $234,311. The record does not show what amount of this income was net investment income since this term of art did not then exist in the law.

[18] 69 F.2d 809 (2d Cir.1934), *aff'd*, 293 U.S. 465 (1935).

(3) immediately sell these shares for cash. This would yield the same economic end result as a more straightforward distribution from UMC. For tax purposes, however, Gregory hoped to have capital gain (from the liquidating distribution, treated as a sale of the new corporation's stock for the value of the Monitor stock), thus avoiding the higher tax rate on ordinary income.[19]

To this end, Gregory caused a new corporation (Averill) to be formed on September 18, 1928. Three days later, UMC gave Averill the Monitor shares and Averill gave her all of its shares. Three days after that, she liquidated Averill and immediately sold the shares. Or, as the Supreme Court more plaintively put it: "When [Averill's] limited function had been exercised, it was immediately put to death."[20]

Technically speaking, the transaction had been impeccable. All of the explicit statutory requirements pertaining at the time to a specific tax-free reorganization had unambiguously been satisfied, although it is doubtful that Congress had in mind such use of the reorganization rules to convert ordinary income into capital gain. (The rules serve rather to defer tax while assets remain in corporate solution and are merely being re-shuffled a bit.)

To the Board of Tax Appeals (the predecessor to today's Tax Court), Gregory's technical compliance with the rules was good enough to establish that she should win: "A statute so meticulously drafted must be interpreted as a literal expression of the taxing policy and leaves only the small interstices for judicial consideration."[21] In the Second Circuit, however, Judge Learned Hand, writing for a unanimous three-judge panel, reversed and held for the Commissioner in what Joseph Isenbergh has called "an opinion of greater literary power than sharpness of doctrine."[22]

Judge Hand's opinion, along with the Supreme Court's subsequent affirmance, has a curious dual quality, as a result of which, "nearly 70 years after *Helvering v. Gregory* people still debate what its contradictory language means."[23] Much of the opinion reads like plain-vanilla statutory interpretation, using an inference about legislative intent to support going beyond the bare dictionary definition of "reorganization"

---

[19] Under present law, § 336(a) would have made the liquidating distribution taxable at the corporate level, but this provision did not exist at the time.

[20] 293 U.S. at 470.

[21] Gregory v. Commissioner, 27 B.T.A. 223, 225 (1932).

[22] Joseph Isenbergh, *Musings on Form and Substance in Taxation*, 49 U. Chi. L. Rev. 859, 867 (1982).

[23] Charles Kingson, *The Confusion Over Tax Ownership*, 93 Tax Notes 409, 417 (2001).

to involve additional characteristics reflecting common practice in the business world:

> It is quite true, as the Board has very well said, that as the articulation of a statute increases, the room for interpretation must contract; but the meaning of a sentence may be more than that of the separate words, as a melody is more than the notes.... The purpose of the section is plain enough; men engaged in enterprises— industrial, commercial, financial, or any other—might wish to consolidate, or divide, or add to, or subtract from, their holdings. Such transactions were not to be considered as "realizing" any profit [for tax purposes], because the collective interests still remained in [corporate] solution.[24]

Hence, Gregory lost simply because she had not done a "reorganization" of the sort that Congress intended to make tax-free. This point of statutory interpretation aside, however, "it is of no consequence that it was all an elaborate scheme to get rid of income taxes, as it certainly was."[25] Indeed, "[a]ny one may so arrange his affairs that his taxes shall be as low as possible ... there is not even a patriotic duty to increase one's taxes."[26]

So far so good, from the standpoint of taxpayers averse to a broader judicial assault on creative tax planning. However, other language in Judge Hand's opinion suggested that he might be saying somewhat more. Valid reorganizations, he stated, must be "undertaken for reasons germane to the conduct of the venture in hand, not as an ephemeral incident, egregious to its prosecution. To dodge the shareholder's taxes is not one of the transactions contemplated as corporate 'reorganizations.' "[27] Perhaps, then, non-tax purposes and more than "ephemeral" non-tax effects might be necessary, in a wide range of statutory areas, in order for tax planning to be respected.

One also wonders if Judge Hand was really quite so unmoved by the aggressiveness of the tax planning as he insists. The atmospherics do not fully match the ostensible conventionality of the interpretive enterprise. One suspects that, like the first President Bush after the invasion of Kuwait, Hand had first determined: "This will not stand," and only then considered exactly how he would stop it. And whether or not he actually did so, subsequent judges might respond to the atmospherics that suggest this, rather than interpreting *Gregory* as merely a standard exercise in statutory interpretation.

---

[24] 69 F.2d at 810–11.

[25] *Id.* at 810.

[26] *Id.*

[27] *Id.* at 811.

The Supreme Court's legally more authoritative, albeit less eloquent, affirmance of the Hand decision in *Gregory* has a similar dual character. On the one hand, the Court simply found that the reorganization rules happened to require a plan by the taxpayer to reorganize an ongoing corporate business, as opposed to simply a reorganization in the narrow state corporate law sense. So long as this requirement was met, "[t]he legal right of a taxpayer to decrease the amount of what otherwise would be his taxes, or altogether avoid them, cannot be doubted."[28] On the other hand, the Court castigated the transaction as "a mere device which put on the form of a corporate reorganization as a disguise for concealing its real character," not to mention "an elaborate and devious form of conveyance masquerading as a corporate reorganization, and nothing else."[29] To hold for the taxpayer "would be to exalt artifice above reality and to deprive the statutory provision in question of all serious purpose."[30] All this rhetoric seems to suggest that courts should in general search assiduously for underlying statutory purposes when they detect insultingly transparent tax planning "devices," "disguises," "masquerades," and "artifices."

Reflecting its dual character, *Gregory* swiftly came to mean "all things to all men."[31] Courts siding with the taxpayer could easily distinguish it if they were so minded—better still, after noting that the Supreme Court had "repeatedly stated that the taxpayer's desire to reduce her taxes was irrelevant."[32] Indeed, *Gregory* could readily be distinguished, even in evaluating transactions that, to the less discriminating eye, may have seemed every bit as pre-wired and artificial. In *Chamberlin v. Commissioner,*[33] for example, the holders of a company's common stock (the only outstanding shares) succeeded in converting ordinary income into capital gain in the dividend setting—the very same aim as in *Gregory*—by a route that one might have thought comparably "elaborate and devious." First, the corporation issued preferred stock on a pro rata basis to the shareholders. Then, only two days later and in a pre-arranged transaction, the shareholders sold the preferred shares to an insurance company for cash. They ended up, therefore, with cash that effectively came out of the company (since, over a seven-year period, the preferred stock would be mandatorily redeemed) and with no change in their relative ownership interests. The Commissioner duly cited *Gregory*

---

[28] 293 U.S. at 469.

[29] *Id.* at 469–70.

[30] *Id.* at 470.

[31] Randolph Paul, *Studies in Federal Taxation* 125 (1940), *quoted in* Blum, *supra* note 9, at 302 n.40.

[32] Gilbert v. Commissioner, 248 F.2d 399, 404 (2d Cir.1957).

[33] 207 F.2d 462 (6th Cir.1953), *cert. denied*, 347 U.S. 918 (1954).

in challenging the transaction, only to see the Sixth Circuit distinguish it almost offhandedly, on the seemingly irrelevant ground that, in the hands of the insurance companies,—a separate taxpayer—the preferred stock was not a sham asset. Even the prearranged sale did not trouble the Sixth Circuit since it had, after all, occurred a whole two days after the preferred stock issuance.[34]

Many other courts, by contrast, viewed *Gregory* as a kind of "philosophical pronouncement" mandating application of "an overriding principle in dealing with tax-avoidance plans: If the arrangement departs from normal family or business patterns or contains an element of artificiality, it is to be viewed with skepticism, scrutinized carefully and rejected if some weakness in it can be detected."[35] Overall, then, given the importance of a court's judicial philosophy to how it would choose between *Gregory*'s two threads, the case operated somewhat in the fashion of a floating mine in a harbor. It occupied no fixed position that one definitely had to steer around, but instead posed a low-probability threat (given the odds against ending up in court as well as the chance of prevailing) across a broader tax planning area.

Two types of transactions, however, were clearly most likely to face attack under *Gregory*. The first were those where the taxpayer arguably inserted an extra step in an otherwise straightforward transaction, making it more circuitous for tax reasons. The extra step could therefore be attacked as a sham, albeit that something (such as the effective payment of a dividend) had undeniably happened overall. *Gregory* itself is such a case, as is *Chamberlin*. Second, *Gregory* invited attacking tax arbitrages, in which the Service could argue that nothing had happened overall because two offsetting steps, each concededly significant if considered in isolation, had left the taxpayer right back where she started. This second category might even prove to be easier judicial pickings for the Service. It did not as readily encourage the taxpayer retort that, given a real business objective to go from Point A to Point B, there was no legal requirement that she choose the high-tax rather than the low-tax route.

2.   *The Transactions in* Knetsch

Again, the key to tax arbitrage is pairing together distinct provisions in the Internal Revenue Code in order to create a large tax loss while

---

[34] *Id.* at 468 ("the legal effect of the dividend ... is determined at the time of its distribution, not by what the shareholders do with it after its receipt") and 470–71 (distinguishing *Gregory*). Congress promptly barred *Chamberlin*-style "preferred stock bailouts" from occurring in the future through the enactment of what is now § 306.

[35] Blum, *supra* note 9, at 302 n.40. Prominent Supreme Court cases, in the first few year after *Gregory*, that followed it in striking down transactions as shams include *Higgins v. Smith*, 308 U.S. 473 (1940) (disregarding loss sale to a wholly owned corporation), and *Griffiths v. Commissioner*, 308 U.S. 355 (1939) (disregarding installment sale through a wholly owned corporate conduit).

minimizing the expected economic loss, downside economic risk, and required investment of cash out of pocket. Designing and executing a commercially appealing tax arbitrage is apparently hard enough that those who are good at it can make a nice living, even though they may have to stand by, watching helplessly, when others decide to steal their ideas without paying compensation. (You cannot patent or copyright tax planning ideas, nor can you easily promote them widely without risking disclosure to trade competitors.)

Thus, in assessing the cleverness of the idea that underlay *Knetsch*, we should not be too dismissive, even if it seems obvious once pointed out. Many great ideas are obvious *ex post*. Hence, the ubiquity of the expression: "Why didn't I think of that?"

The idea that someone came up with in the 1930s[36] was as follows. Since the unpaid income on annuities was deferrable and interest expense generally deductible, a company in the annuity business could sell net deductions to a paying customer without actually requiring her to do much of anything on balance (beyond paying up-front and annual transaction fees). For example, you could sell someone a million-dollar, single-premium annuity, financed by lending her the million dollars to buy it with. The loan could be secured by the annuity for the company's protection, and made nonrecourse (i.e., payable only out of the annuity's value) for the customer's protection. Each year, the annuity's cash surrender value (i.e., the actuarially fair amount to which the customer would be entitled upon surrendering her constantly appreciating rights to future payment) would rise by the applicable interest rate. The company then could let her borrow a portion of the interest expense she owed on the loan (again, nonrecourse) by simply pledging the newly accrued cash surrender value.

The bottom line was that no money, apart from transaction fees, would ever need to change hands. For tax purposes, however, the customer would deduct the entire gross interest expense portrayed on the transaction documents. To be sure, she would also eventually realize offsetting taxable income when the annuity matured, at which point she would be deemed to pay back the loan by transferring back the rights that she had thus far merely pledged. However, this evil day could be postponed for decades by giving the annuity a distant maturity date.

The transaction apparently did not catch on significantly until the late 1940s, when it became clear that tax rates above those in the 1930s, while introduced initially to pay for World War II, were here to stay.[37] At

---

[36] *See* Oral Argument at 3 (Oct. 17, 1960) (Lee McLane).

[37] *Id.* (In the 1930s, the transaction "never really caught hold, I suppose, because the income tax rates, among other things, were not high enough to make it terribly attractive to people").

this point, however, the fact that one did not need much free cash on hand in order to engage in it may have given it special appeal among high-earners who were not dynastically wealthy or big savers. Its emergence (through public marketing efforts) shortly after World War II probably reflects the contemporaneous transformation of the income tax from a "class tax" on the rich to a "mass tax" on most working Americans.[38] The brave new world not only increased total demand for tax shelters, but extended it to a new audience less likely than the taxpayers of the 1930s to have regular access to personalized expert tax and investment advice.

Some relatively cautious taxpayers sought advance private letter rulings from the Commissioner stating that their transactions would be effective for tax purposes. In general, the Service issues such rulings to taxpayers who seek guidance, under stipulated facts, regarding how it would treat transactions that they are considering. The rulings typically do not receive high-level internal review, which would slow down issuance and reduce the amount of guidance that could be provided. They therefore are expressly directed only to the taxpayers requesting them, and explicitly lack precedential value as applied to other taxpayers. Private rulings are not even supposed to be taken as evidence of Service administrative practice, or to indicate how it is likely to view any given set of facts in the future. Taxpayers nonetheless frequently treat them as evidence in this regard—unsurprisingly, since in truth they plainly can show consistent patterns that one might surmise will probably continue (all else equal), if only out of inertia.

In keeping with the Service effort to minimize any reliance on private letter rulings by taxpayers other than those to whom they were issued, they were not even published, and thus were not generally available, until a Freedom of Information Act lawsuit in the 1970s forced their release prospectively. However, the secrecy that prevailed at the time of *Knetsch* could not prevent taxpayers to whom rulings were issued from sharing them with their tax advisors, transactional counter-parties, or others. Moreover, the Service could not bar anyone who obtained copies of private rulings from disseminating them. Thus, the Service's non-publication policy merely created an informal market in private rulings. Counsel in the know—such as those whose practice frequently involved preparing ruling requests—would brandish the rulings they had in their files as evidence of Service practice, not to mention their own expertise. Counsel also would often limit any broader dissemination that

---

[38] *See, e.g.,* W. Elliot Brownlee, *Federal Taxation in America: A Short History* 96–97 (1996) (noting that the number of individuals paying income tax grew from 3.9 million in 1939 to 42.6 million in 1945 (including 60% of the labor force), while the revenues from this tax grew more than fifteen-fold).

might limit their competitive advantage over less well-informed trade rivals.

On at least eight occasions between November 1947 and November 1952, the Service issued favorable rulings concerning debt-financed, single-premium deferred annuities.[39] This may well have reflected, on the part of the functionaries who examined the ruling requests, a mechanical and unreflective response to the transactions' apparent technical merit, without regard to the broader policy and revenue implications, or the possible legal relevance of *Gregory v. Helvering* and its progeny. Certainly the rulings were quite terse and lacking in legal analysis.[40]

Perhaps the most enterprising of the eight successful ruling applicants was Mr. R. C. Salley of Houston, Texas, who received his on August 1, 1952. Salley, in addition to himself purchasing $1 million of the deferred annuity bonds ($6.8 million in 2002 dollars), was President and Treasurer of the Sam Houston Life Insurance Company, and owned about half of its stock. Sam Houston began actively promoting the deal, and showing Salley's private letter ruling to prospective customers to establish that the deal would work.[41] Indeed, Sam Houston may have been formed simply to do these deals. In each of the years from 1952 through 1954 (and perhaps other years as well), over 99% of its book reserves as an insurance company were for similarly debt-financed, single-premium, 30–year deferred annuity bonds. All of the deals that the Service subsequently challenged in litigation were the work of Sam Houston or one other company, the Standard Life Insurance Company of Indiana, although others may have offered the deal and simply escaped notice.[42]

Sam Houston regularly advertised the transaction in the *Wall Street Journal* and the *Journal of Commerce*. A typical advertisement would bear the headline of "Income Tax Reduction," or else "Tax Sheltered Investment." It then would state, in part: "You can legally convert into a Capital Asset the money you are compelled to pay out in income taxes, through the purchase of this Company's COPYRIGHTED ANNUITIES,

---

[39] *See* Brief of Amici Curiae at 2.

[40] In illustration, the following is the entire analysis section (after stating the facts) of a private letter ruling that was issued in 1947: "Section 23(b) of the Internal Revenue Code provides that in computing net income there shall be allowed as a deduction all interest paid or accrued within the taxable year on indebtedness, with certain exceptions not here material. Based upon the information submitted, it is the opinion of this office that if you purchase a contract ... [identical to the one you submitted], the interest paid or accrued on a loan obtained to pay the premium thereon will be allowable as a deduction under Section 23(b) of the Internal Revenue Code." *See* Petition for Writ of *Certiorari* at 7–8, n.1.

[41] *See* Salley v. Commissioner, 21 T.C.M. (CCH) 412, 412–13 (1962), *aff'd*, 319 F.2d 847 (5th Cir.1963).

[42] *See* Oral Argument at 4 (Oct. 8, 1960) (Grant Wiprud) (confirming that Service was unaware of others doing the deal).

with borrowed money."[43] Sam Houston sent out unsolicited direct mailings. Prospective customers would be referred to one of the company's approximately 75 sales agents. In due course, they typically would be shown Mr. Salley's ruling.

The Factual Context

Taxpayer Karl F. Knetsch now enters our story. In 1953, he was a 60–year-old Los Angeles resident, earning enough highly-taxed income to be interested in tax sheltering. At some point during the year, he received a direct mailing from Sam Houston touting the tax benefits of debt-financed, single premium deferred annuities. By the end of the year, he had decided to act.

On December 11, 1953, Knetsch purchased ten identical annuities from Sam Houston for $400,400 each, making the total purchase price $4,004,000 ($27 million in 2002 dollars). Of this amount, $4 million was the stated value of the bonds, and $4,000 was a fee for Sam Houston's services. He paid the fee by personal check, and borrowed the remaining $4 million from the company. This loan was secured by the annuities and was nonrecourse. Thus, he was not personally liable to repay it; only the annuities (which were worth exactly the same amount) could be used for this purpose.

The annuities had a 30–year term, and thus would start offering Knetsch monthly payments starting when he reached the age of 90, and terminating with his death. He could elect to accelerate the maturity date when payments started, although this would result in a downward adjustment of the monthly payments in order to keep constant their actuarially expected value. In the event that he died before age 90, his heirs would get back his initial $4,000 investment, or the annuities' cash surrender value ($4 million plus annual interest that they earned minus any debt to which they were subject) if greater.

The interest rate on Knetsch's $4 million loan was 3.5%, payable annually in advance. Thus, he immediately owed Sam Houston $140,000 for the first year's interest. He paid this amount by cashier's check on December 11, 1953. His annuities similarly accrued interest at the start of the year, but at a rate of only 2.5% annually, or $100,000.

On December 16, Sam Houston gave Knetsch a check for $99,000, thereby offsetting most of his December 11 payment. This amount was styled a loan, secured by the appreciation of the annuity bonds and again nonrecourse. Since this new loan was also for 3.5% interest, payable in advance, Knetsch on December 16 gave Sam Houston a personal check for $3,465, the amount due on it for the next year.

---

[43] *Quoted in Salley*, 21 T.C.M. (CCH) at 413 (capital letters in original).

In sum, the $99,000 loan on December 16, in combination with the $4 million loan on December 11, left the annuities with a net cash surrender value of $1,000. If, as expected, Knetsch continued each year to borrow just enough to leave the bonds with this net cash surrender value, then he could look forward, once he reached the age of 90, to receiving $43 per month for as long as he lived.

Taxes aside, this would plainly be a rather meager prize to have gotten in exchange for $4,000 up-front followed by more than $40,000 per year for the next thirty years. One could conceivably imagine a scenario in which Knetsch would actually earn a profit before tax—although this might, in the words of *Peter Pan*, require "happy thoughts and faith and trust, and a sprinkling of Tinker Bell's pixie dust." Specifically, suppose interest rates dropped so steeply that Knetsch could now borrow from a third party at 1.5%. Now the pre-tax interest rate arbitrage would favor him. Sam Houston was obligated to keep accruing interest on the annuity bonds at 2.5% until they matured or he turned them in or died, but it could not compel him to keep on borrowing at 3.5%. There is no evidence, however, that he was aware of this possibility, and his lawyers did not subsequently advance it as a rationale for the transaction.[44]

Another thing Knetsch evidently did not realize, as he passed his personal and cashier's checks across the table to the sales representative, was that the government was hot on Sam Houston's trail. At some point in 1953, it had become aware that Salley's private letter ruling was being widely circulated. Taxpayers had been inquiring as to whether they could rely on it. On November 23, 1953—eighteen days before Knetsch's transaction—it sent Salley a letter advising him that it had received these inquiries, was considering revoking his ruling, and that neither he nor anyone else should rely on it. Revocation followed the next year, and Salley ended up separately litigating his liability both for 1952 and 1953 (since the revocation was partly retroactive) and for 1954 through 1956.[45] He lost both cases under the authority of *Knetsch*, which the Supreme Court had by then decided, and which he unsuccessfully tried to distinguish.

The record does not show whether Knetsch was aware either of the Salley ruling or of its revocation. He did not subsequently assert in the litigation that he had been aware of any private rulings allowing the deductions. One precautionary step that he—unlike Salley—did *not* take,

---

[44] This possibility of pre-tax profit appears to have been detected for the first time by Walter Blum in an article discussing the Supreme Court decision. *See* Blum, *supra* note 9.

[45] *See Salley* 21 T.C.M. (CCH) at 412 (1954–56 taxable years); Salley v. United States, 239 F.Supp. 161 (S.D.Tex.1965) (1952–53 taxable years). For the two earlier taxable years, Salley was allowed to deduct his out-of-pocket expenses due to his reliance on the private ruling.

however, was to increase his cash investment in the deal (which might have made it look more legitimate).[46]

The threat to Knetsch's tax position soon went considerably beyond the Salley revocation letter, however. Early in 1954, Treasury representatives went to the Ways and Means Committee, which initiates tax legislation in the House of Representatives, seeking corrective legislation to address Sam Houston-style transactions. On March 9, 1954, the Ways and Means Committee reported out proposed legislation extending the interest disallowance rule to annuities. The Committee explained the proposal as follows:

> It has come to your committee's attention that a few insurance companies have promoted a plan for selling annuity contracts based on the tax advantage derived from omission of annuities from the treatment accorded single-premium life insurance or endowment contracts. The annuity is sold for a nominal cash payment with a loan to cover the balance of the single-premium cost of the annuity. Interest on the loan (which may be a nonrecourse loan) is then taken as a deduction annually by the purchaser with a resulting tax saving that reduces the real interest cost below the increment in value produced by the annuity.[47]

However, the new rule applied only to annuity contracts entered into after March 1, 1954. Knetsch's deal was therefore "grandfathered." The new legislation would not affect it, even with respect to interest deductions incurred after the effective date. The Service had sought a rule that would have caught taxpayers such as Knetsch, by disallowing post-effective date interest deductions even on preexisting contracts.[48]

At this point, Knetsch, if (as seems unlikely) he had been closely following legislative developments, must have felt the same sense of relief as the proverbial silent movie damsel who is rescued from the railroad tracks just before a train thunders by. He had seemingly been fortunate. To be sure, there had never been much chance that the legislation would apply retroactively to the interest deductions that he claimed on his 1953 return (involving the payments denominated interest that he made in December of that year). However, adoption of the transition rule that the Service was seeking would not have been a huge surprise. Such a rule would have made it imperative for him to unwind

---

[46] Salley had increased his cash investment in his own deferred annuity bonds by $3,475 at the end of 1953, perhaps in response to the previous month's letter threatening revocation. 239 F.Supp. at 163.

[47] H.R. Rep. No. 83–1337, pt. 1, at 31 (1954).

[48] See Oral Argument at 13 (Oct. 18, 1960) (Grant Wiprud) (conceding that, so far as he knew, the Commissioner had sought broader relief).

the deal before making the next set of interest payments that were due in December 1954.

Only eight days later, however, on March 17, 1954, Knetsch was back on the railroad tracks, and indeed in worse peril than before. The Service, which—according to Knetsch's attorneys in their subsequent Supreme Court brief[49]—was bitterly disappointed by the effective date provision in the Ways and Means bill, published Revenue Ruling 54–94, taking direct aim at pre-effective date transactions. The ruling begins by stating:

> The attention of the Internal Revenue Service has been called to several situations where taxpayers are attempting to derive sup- posed tax benefits in connection with transactions designed to obtain interest deductions, for Federal income tax purposes. The question is whether the amounts designed as "interest" are deduct- ible under [pre–1954 law].[50]

It then describes two transactions, the first of which is basically identical to that engaged in by Knetsch,[51] before offering the following commentary:

> It is the view of the Internal Revenue that amounts paid by taxpayer and designated as "interest" in the above examples are not interest within the meaning of ... [the pre–1954] Code, and are not deduct- ible for Federal income tax purposes....
>
> As a matter of substance, the taxpayer does not borrow any money, hence there is no "debt" on which he pays "interest." An instrument that is called a "note" will not be treated as an indebt- edness where it does not in fact represent an indebtedness.[52]

Finally, the ruling closes by quoting general dicta from a Second Circuit case, to the effect that, "in construing words of a tax statute which describe commercial or industrial transactions, we are to under- stand them to refer to transactions entered upon for commercial or industrial purposes and not to include transactions entered upon for no other motive but to escape taxation."[53] Exit stage right, breathing

---

[49] *See* Knetsch Brief at 10.

[50] Rev. Rul. 54–94, 1954–1 C.B. 53.

[51] The second transaction described in Revenue Ruling 54–94 involves a purported debt-financed purchase of U.S. Treasury bonds. It appears to resemble a transaction that the government later successfully challenged in Goldstein v. Commissioner, 364 F.2d 734 (2d Cir.1966), *cert. denied*, 385 U.S. 1005 (1967).

[52] Rev. Rul. 54–94, 1954–1 C.B. 53.

[53] *Id.* (quoting Commissioner v. Transport Trading & Terminal Corp., 176 F.2d 570, 572 (2d Cir.1949)).

heavily and (in the pro-taxpayer movie version) twisting the villainous mustachios of a Snidely Whiplash.

In evaluating the legal significance of Revenue Ruling 54–94, one should note that published Service rulings are not legal precedent of the same kind as Treasury regulations that have been promulgated subject to the notice and comment requirements of the Administrative Procedure Act. A Revenue Ruling merely states the Service position on a given matter. In tax litigation, a court may, if it chooses, discount it as merely stating the inevitably self-serving view of one of the litigants (just like the briefs submitted by counsel). Published rulings do, however, show the government's willingness to put its chips publicly on the table in more than just a given pending case, thereby potentially impressing courts that are inclined to defer to its institutional expertise in tax matters.

Revenue Ruling 54–94 was not limited to interest incurred (or annuities executed) after its issuance date. It purported to interpret existing law, and thus to apply retroactively as well as prospectively. Moreover, the Service could be expected to reject any claims of estoppel from taxpayers who had relied on private letter rulings, issued to other taxpayers, that insurance company salesmen had shown them.

The practical issue for Knetsch was therefore clearly posed (whether or not he was aware of Revenue Ruling 54–94). Should he go on making net payments to Sam Houston each December, on the premise that he would thereby generate interest deductions, in the face of this clear indication that the Service did not consider the deductions allowable? Or should he close out the deal, and thus avoid digging himself in any deeper?

For the next two years, Knetsch kept right on digging himself in deeper. In December 1954, he paid Sam Houston "interest" in the amount of $147,105, in exchange for amounts denominated loan receipts in the amount of $104,000. In December 1955, he paid $150,745 and again received $104,000.

On June 29, 1956, the Service issued to Knetsch a statutory notice of deficiency in Federal income tax, stating that he had underpaid by $113,684 for 1953 and $119,613 for 1954. The deficiency notice was based solely on disallowing the interest deductions that he had claimed for those two years by reason of the Sam Houston transaction. The ground for disallowance was that the amounts paid "are not interest within the meaning of . . . the Internal Revenue Code of 1939 and are not deductible for Federal income tax purposes."

The pace of the action then quickened. On July 19, Knetsch paid the deficiencies. On October 8, he filed an administrative claim for refund, relying on a straight black-letter legal argument. The only relevant legal issue, his claim asserted, was whether there had been interest on indebtedness. "Because the claimant, Karl F. Knetsch, executed loan agreements . . . it is clear that indebtedness existed." Moreover, the very definition of interest, as "compensation for money borrowed or the forbearance of money legally owed . . . contemplates that [it] comes into existence in cases other than those where money has changed hands." Here, the loan proceeds and interest had been applied to pay for the bonds and for premiums when due.

By paying the deficiency, Knetsch gave himself the right to contest it in the Court of Claims or Federal district court, where the judges generally are not tax specialists. (Had he contested it without paying up front, his only permissible litigating venue would have been the Tax Court.) On May 3, 1957, having waited for the statutorily prescribed six-month period without favorable Service action, he brought a civil action for refund in the United States District Court for the Southern District of California.

His lawyers, from this stage through the very end, were McLane & McLane, an Arizona law firm that was headed (perhaps unusually for the time) by a husband-and-wife team. Nola McLane, apparently a 1951 graduate of the Yale Law School,[54] was admitted to practice in the Southern District of California. W. Lee McLane, while not admitted there except especially for this case, did all of the oral argumentation, drawing on his background as a former staff member in the IRS Chief Counsel's office.[55]

While Knetsch was evidently willing to invest the McLanes' legal fees in defense of his position, in one other respect he decided not to risk throwing good money after bad. On December 27, 1956, rather than swapping notes with Sam Houston once again, he terminated the transaction by surrendering the ten single premium annuities. This resulted in the discharge of his nonrecourse debt, and he also got a $1,000 check

---

[54] See http://www.law.yale.edu/yls/alum-offexec.htm, listing Nola S. McLane, from the class of 1951, as the Arizona regional representative of the Yale Law School Association. The briefs in *Knetsch* list Nola M. McLane as counsel, but this may be the same individual despite the difference in middle initial. It would seem a bit coincidental for two attorneys named Nola McLane, both at some point from Arizona, to have been around at the same time, especially given the relative paucity of female attorneys in the 1950s. Moreover, the age for the litigating Ms. McLane that would be suggested by a 1951 law school graduation date seems plausible given the existence of a 1998 Arizona state tax proceeding involving the spouses, Nola McLane (no middle initial provided) and William L. McLane. *See William L. and Nola McLane v. Arizona Department of Revenue*, No. 1642–96–I, October 20, 1998, 98 STN 244–8 in Lexis.

[55] See Transcript at 90. *McLane and McLane v. Arizona Dep't of Revenue, supra*, is my evidence that the McLanes were married in 1957, assuming that these were the same individuals as those in the 1998 litigation. It would not appear to be a huge stretch to regard "W. Lee McLane" and "William L. McLane" as the same individual given, for example, their shared Arizona residence and association with Nola McLane.

from Sam Houston since this amount was the annuities' net cash surrender value.

As a postscript, on his 1956 income tax return, Knetsch claimed a deduction in the amount of $137,315. This amount represented his out-of-pocket loss, or the excess of the amounts he had paid to Sam Houston between 1953 and 1955 over the amounts he had received from the company. Presumably, this was a fallback reporting position, meant to ensure that he would get to deduct his out-of-pocket costs before his right to file an amended return lapsed, even if the Service succeeded in requiring adjustments for 1953 through 1955. It was logically inconsistent with the position he had taken on the earlier tax returns since it involved deducting the very same net amounts all over again.

Had Knetsch computed his taxable income for 1956 in a manner that was consistent with his previous three years' reporting positions, he would instead have reported gain in the amount of $304,000. Under his view of the transaction, this was the excess of his amount realized upon surrendering the annuities ($1,000 cash plus $4,307,000 discharge of indebtedness)[56] over his cost basis of $4,004,000 ($4,000 cash plus $4 million in debt). The gain probably would have been ordinary income, rather than capital gain upon the sale or exchange of a capital asset, notwithstanding the claim to the contrary in Sam Houston's advertising,[57] although at the time the advertisements were placed there may have been a decent argument for capital gain.

Prior Proceedings

The District Court

1. *Initial Pre–Trial Maneuvering*

The complaint that Knetsch filed on May 3, 1957 set forth the basic facts of the transaction and his unsuccessful refund claim, along with the boilerplate legal assertion that the Service decision to disallow his interest deductions from the Sam Houston loans was "erroneous, illegal, and without warrant in law." The Service answered the complaint on July 3, admitting all of the asserted facts (a couple of trivial corrections aside) apart from the legal boilerplate.

The case was assigned to William C. Mathes, an experienced judge[58] who would prove quick to draw conclusions but willing to re-think them.

---

[56] Knetsch purported to borrow $4 million and then an additional $99,000 in 1953, $104,000 in 1954, and $104,000 in 1955, for a total of $4,307,000.

[57] See Commissioner v. Phillips, 275 F.2d 33, 34 (4th Cir.1960) and the cases on surrender of annuities that are cited therein, holding that the surrender of an annuity to the issuer is not a "sale or exchange" as required to qualify for capital gains treatment.

[58] Judge Mathes had been appointed by President Truman in 1945 after twenty-one years in practice and continued serving until his death in 1967. *See* http://air.fjc.gov/serv-

This was going to be a bench trial, rather than one decided by a jury. Although the facts were going to be stipulated, the first order of business for each party was to try to tilt the case in its favor by getting in all the evidence that it liked, while challenging some of the items that the other party wanted to place in the record.

The six main disputes concerning what evidence was admissible, and what facts legally relevant, were as follows:

1) The government wanted to introduce into evidence a sample Sam Houston advertisement for the transaction, along with the mailing that the company had sent to Knetsch. When the latter item proved to be unavailable, Robert Wyshak, the government attorney who was arguing the case before Judge Mathes, sent his own customer letter to Sam Houston requesting information about the deal. It duly responded by sending him literature that Knetsch, through Lee McLane, was kind enough to admit was the same in substance as that which the company had sent him in 1953.

Both the advertisement and the literature were quite clear about the deal's character as a tax planning tool. The government argued that they were therefore relevant to Knetsch's tax avoidance intent. Knetsch responded that documents from Sam Houston only showed its intent, not his, and that "there is no rational connection between this fact and the issue of whether Knetsch subsequently became indebted to the company."[59]

2) The government wanted to submit year-end financial statements from Sam Houston, along with a summary that the company had issued (presumably for state regulatory purposes) concerning its outstanding instruments. The purpose was to show that nearly all Sam Houston did was engage in a series of highly similar "fictitious" transactions that had "no economic substance."[60] Knetsch, however, objected that its balance sheets and the character of its other annuities were wholly irrelevant to the straightforward legal question of whether he had paid interest on indebtedness.[61]

3) Knetsch wanted to enter into evidence the private letter ruling that had been issued in 1952 to R. C. Salley. While he did not claim to have seen or relied on the ruling at the time of his deal, it ostensibly would help to rebut the government's argument that he had engaged in a tax avoidance transaction that lacked economic substance. The govern-

---

let/uGetInfo?jid=1501. His father had also been a judge. *See* http://www.tsha.utex-as.edu/handbook/online/articles/view/MM/fmafh.html.

[59] Transcript at 32.

[60] *Id.* at 72.

[61] *Id.* at 30–31.

ment, however, objected that the views expressed in a private letter ruling that had been issued to some other taxpayer were irrelevant and immaterial.

4) Knetsch wanted to submit evidence showing that Sam Houston had reported the amounts received from him as interest both on its books and in its federal income tax returns. The government objected that this was irrelevant to the issue of deductibility by Knetsch, and included legally inadmissible opinion evidence as to the merits.

5) Knetsch wanted to enter into evidence a letter issued by the Texas Board of Insurance Commissioners, stating that Knetsch and Sam Houston had entered into a legally valid annuity contract under Texas law. The government objected that this was irrelevant and immaterial.

6) Knetsch offered into evidence his Federal income tax returns for 1955 and 1956, notwithstanding that only his 1953 and 1954 tax liabilities were at issue in the case, arguing that they shed light on his (lack of) tax motivation. The government objected that the returns could not illuminate his earlier intent in 1953 and 1954, and that the court should not be drawn into adjudicating separate taxable years that were in the process of being audited.[62]

Given that this was a bench trial, one might ask: Why go to the trouble of arguing that Judge Mathes should formally exclude items that, by reason of having to rule on them, he nonetheless would have seen? Surely one reason was to influence what Mathes could look at officially, while also setting the stage for any challenges on appeal. In addition, however, the arguments about admissibility were shadow arguments about the merits of the case itself. Mathes' decision might not be likely to depend, say, on whether or not he officially admitted into evidence the Wall Street Journal advertisement that the government was brandishing. But if you could persuade him to accept your characterization of the legal issues, in the course of ruling on admissibility, the case might be considerably more than half won at a point when it seemingly had just begun.

2. *August 4, 1958: Round One to the Taxpayer?*

At 2 p.m. in the afternoon on August 4, 1958, the McLanes and Wyshak rose in Judge Mathes' courtroom to discuss the pretrial conference order in the case. The discussion quickly turned to the disputed items, and Judge Mathes stated that he was "inclined to sustain" Knetsch's objection to admitting the Sam Houston literature mailing, "but will be glad to hear from the defendant before ruling." Wyshak stated without elaboration that it was relevant to Knetsch's intent, and then turned to what he evidently considered the harder sell: the compar-

---

[62] *Id.* at 95.

ability of the exhibit he was offering to the literature that Knetsch had actually received. Before he could get very far, however, Judge Mathes pounced on the issue of intent:

The Court: Would his intent control the situation?

Mr. Wyshak: It wouldn't control, but it would have some bearing on whether there was any indebtedness.

The Court: His subjective intent? I don't see how it could.

Wyshak started to stumble a bit, and retreated to the suggestion that this challenge to the relevance of Knetsch's intent went "more to the weight, your Honor, than to the admissibility of it."[63]

Judge Mathes brushed aside this olive branch:

The Court: I am just wondering how his subjective intent is relevant at all—his intent as objectively manifested.

Mr. Wyshak: Well, this was literature sent him by the company.

The Court: But is there any showing he acted upon it?

Mr. Wyshak: Well, his action was in purchasing these annuities, your Honor.

The Court: Well, he might have non constat purchased without the literature, might he not?

Mr. Wyshak: I beg your pardon?

The Court: He might have purchased without the literature, might he not?

Mr. Wyshak: He might have.

The Court: I will sustain that objection.[64]

Lee McLane, now found himself on the hot seat, trying to justify admission of the evidence showing that Sam Houston had reported Knetsch's payments as interest expense for accounting and federal income tax purposes. If Sam Houston's subjective intent was relevant, Judge Mathes suggested, then "I should reverse my ruling and adopt Mr. Wyshak's view of [the mailing], should I not?" McLane agreed that this evidence should not go in unless the mailing was admitted, and averred that really both should stay out because the parties' subjective intent was irrelevant.[65]

Without definitely resolving this issue, Judge Mathes now turned to the Sam Houston financial statements that the government wanted to

---

[63] *Id.* at 67.

[64] *Id.* at 68.

[65] *Id.*

introduce. Why were they relevant? Was the point to show that Sam Houston lacked the net assets to be financially capable of engaging in the transaction?

> Mr. Wyshak: That is in part it, yes, your Honor. And in addition that . . . over 99% of the so-called reserves for those policies were loans. To show the fictitious nature of the—

> The Court: Well, that wouldn't be any objection to it, would it? The fact that a man is operating on a shoestring or carrying his insurance on a shoestring wouldn't matter, would it?

> Mr. Wyshak: Well, I think it would have a bearing, your Honor, to show the substance of the transaction. In other words, they could have added another zero to it and increased the interest tenfold.[66]

Judge Mathes continued to view the issue as one of borderline insolvency. So what, he asked, if the company had been financially irresponsible in issuing the annuities with so little backing apart from the loans? "How would this tend to show that [the transactions were shams]? How would these exhibits tend to show that? . . . Well, how does this help us materially, assuming it to be relevant? I don't see how it is relevant, in the first place, and even if it were relevant, I don't see how it could be material."[67]

Perhaps the hour was getting late because Judge Mathes, without embodying this view in a ruling, now checked with the parties regarding the number of disputed evidentiary exhibits that remained for him to consider. Would everyone be able to come in tomorrow morning to finish things? They would.

McLane now moved to strike the final blow in what had clearly been a bad day for the government. "If you are going to consider this overnight, I would like to add—before you exhibit any further thought— that these exhibits, it seems to me, do not bear upon the issue of whether or not this plaintiff became indebted."

Moreover, he added, there was now a newly decided Fifth Circuit case (*Knetsch* was in the Ninth Circuit) upholding an identical Sam Houston transaction. In *United States v. Bond*,[68] decided less than three weeks earlier, the Fifth Circuit had allowed the taxpayer's interest deductions. "And I would ask your Honor leave to consider this opinion before you rule on these exhibits."

---

[66] *Id.* at 72–73.

[67] *Id.* at 74.

[68] 258 F.2d 577 (5th Cir.1958).

Judge Mathes promised to do so, and told the parties to return the next morning at 10 a.m.[69] If not for the anachronism (this was 1958, after all), one could imagine the McLanes exchanging high fives as they left the courtroom. Meanwhile, Wyshak and his government colleagues must have looked glum. A judge who had already been voicing at every turn his skepticism about the significance of taxpayer intent now had some new bedtime reading to strengthen this incipient conviction.

In *Bond*, the Fifth Circuit, albeit over Judge Wisdom's dissent, had found the identical transaction that was before it completely unproblematic. If (as the government had conceded) going to a bank to borrow the money to invest in deferred annuity bonds was permissible, the Fifth Circuit failed to see how there could be anything wrong with simplifying things a bit by borrowing directly from the issuer:

> [The government] is not at all articulate in pointing out what are the distinguishing comparative factors. We could hardly believe that they are the fact that no money actually passed, that a check from the lender is not issued, deposited by the borrower, and then a new check in payment of the single premium drawn by lender and delivered to the company issuing the Annuity Bond. Nor can the mere fact that the Maker of the Note has no personal liability deprive the annual payment of its interest status.
>
> But this Bond is not the mere sham supposed. It was, and is, a legitimate Annuity Contract, the issuance of which in Texas subjects the Company to the status of a regulated life insurance company.[70]

3. *August 5, 1958: The Tone Changes*

The *Knetsch* trial resumed promptly at 10:09 the next morning. Judge Mathes affirmed that there were no preliminary matters, and then addressed his first substantive words of the morning directly to Lee McLane:

> The Court: Is it agreed by the plaintiff that the real test here is the substance of the transaction and not the form?
>
> Mr. McLane: Well, that is certainly the Government's argument in these cases, your Honor.
>
> The Court: That is what the Supreme Court says, isn't it?[71]

So much, apparently, for the previous day's cozy two-part harmony in affirming the irrelevance of anything beyond the narrow question: Was there debt? You are arguing against the Supreme Court, Judge

---

[69] Transcript at 75–77.

[70] 258 F.2d at 580 (footnotes omitted).

[71] Transcript at 77–78.

Mathes seemed to be saying—not just, as you may have imagined yesterday, against a beleaguered Mr. Wyshak.

From the distance of more than forty years, this abrupt transformation brings to mind the moment in the movie *Ghostbusters*, when Dr. Venkman (Bill Murray) knocks on Dana's (Sigourney Weaver's) door, and finds her looking strangely transformed. She tells him, in a harshly sepulchral voice: "There is no Dana. I am Zuul."

Just as Venkman, in this scene, cannot reach Dana but only the demon who is Gatekeeper and Minion of Gozer, so McLane could not restore the accommodating Judge Mathes of the previous afternoon. He argued at considerable length that, while substance usually prevails over form, this case was different because it concerned interest expense. "And I would submit to your Honor that the language of the section which provides, 'all interest paid or accrued on indebtedness' [is deductible] may not be modified by reading into the statute that the transaction must have some sort of economic substance. That's the view of the plaintiff as to this particular deduction claim."[72]

Judge Mathes let McLane continue with little interruption, in a noticeable departure from his vigorous colloquies with both sides on the previous day. McLane brought up the 1954 statute, arguing (as *Bond* had explicitly stated) that it foreclosed disallowing interest deductions on pre-effective date contracts. If the deductions had not previously been allowable, the amendment would not have been necessary. "[I]n view of that committee language [concerning the effective date], it seems to me that the matter has been presented to the Congress and resolved."

"Very well, gentlemen," was Judge Mathes' only answer. "Let's take up these exhibits in the pretrial conference order." And he quickly turned to the Sam Houston mailing he had excluded on the previous day, checking with Wyshak on why the letter sent to Knetsch was not being used.

> The Court: Don't we have the papers in the real transaction here?
>
> Mr. Wyshak: Apparently not, your Honor. But . . . the stipulation of facts in the pretrial order sets forth the comparable literature that was sent to Knetsch. We were unable to locate the comparable literature.
>
> The Court: Then this would be admissible as being, in effect, in substance of what was sent to the plaintiff.
>
> Mr. Wyshak: That is correct.

---

[72] *Id.* at 78.

The Court: Very well. The objection will be overruled and [the exhibit] will be received in evidence.[73]

Judge Mathes turned briskly to the items to which the government had objected:

The Court: Some of these matters while logically relevant are material in a rather remote degree. But as Mr. Wyshak suggested yesterday, the objection it seems to me goes to the weight rather than the admissibility of them. But I am receiving this material as bearing on the issue of whether the transaction had substance as well as form.[74]

No one mentioned that, when Wyshak had actually mentioned weight and admissibility on the previous day, Judge Mathes had brushed him off by "wondering how ... subjective intent is relevant at all."

Perhaps after pinching himself, Wyshak reminded the judge about the government's objection to admitting the R. C. Salley private letter ruling.

Mr. Wyshak: ... [W]e submit that it's merely one man's opinion in Washington with respect to another taxpayer and in no way binding on this court and in no way binding on the United States.

Mr. McLane: We do not, of course, offer it with any thought that it is binding, your Honor, but merely as rebuttal to the arguments which will be made ... with respect to the substance of the transactions and whether or not there a tax avoidance was the motive of the participants.

Mr. Wyshak: Your Honor, that correspondence merely relates to whether one man in Washington thinks that [someone else] would be entitled to a deduction in certain circumstances. And I submit that it is completely irrelevant and immaterial to the issues before the court here.

Mr. McLane: Except that that man is a real defendant here, your Honor.

The Court: How do you mean "a real defendant"?

Mr. McLane: The Commissioner of Internal Revenue issued the letter.

The Court: Well, of course, the Commissioner, if he is wrong on the law, he is hopeless too, isn't he?

Judge Mathes then began to bridge the gap a bit between his views on the succeeding days. Tax avoidance motives were immaterial "if the

----

[73] *Id.* at 82.

[74] *Id.* at 83.

transaction is a bona fide transaction having substance. The fact that one of the motivations was to save taxes, if that were a ground, why, the Internal Revenue would own the country today, wouldn't it, if that were a ground for disallowance of transactions?"[75]

McLane hastened to agree with the friendliest words he had heard since returning to the courtroom. But there is an old saying: Disregard any words in a sentence that come after "but." As in, "I would like to, but ... " or "I love you, but ... " Here, perhaps the word "if" was playing a similar role. Tax avoidance motive was immaterial *"if* the transaction is a bona fide transaction having substance" (emphasis added).

Judge Mathes then sustained the government's objection to admitting the private letter ruling into evidence. And he asked Wyshak: "Isn't [the letter from the Texas Board of Insurance Commissioners in the same category?"

Mr. Wyshak: Yes, your Honor.

The Court: I will sustain the objection to those as self-serving and incompetent, irrelevant and immaterial.[76]

McLane rose to defend the Texas commissioners' letter, noting that the court in *Bond* had emphasized a similar letter. Judge Mathes reversed himself, agreeing that it could come in after all but implying that it might have little weight.[77] He then admitted as well Knetsch's evidence of how Sam Houston had reported the interest payments for financial tax purposes although "I think a ruling could be made either way in the matter ... without any great prejudice to either side and without being reversible error."[78]

All other contested items were then admitted, leaving only the private letter rulings as beyond the pale. One passing and apparently sardonic comment from the bench may have been of interest, however. Judge Mathes noted that, "in all of these situations where substance governs over form, why, the form is usually always impeccable in these situations."[79] So much, perhaps, for the transaction's validity under Texas law.

While Judge Mathes admitted Knetsch's 1955 and 1956 income tax returns, he did so only with "misgivings."[80] The purpose for which they

---

[75] *Id.* at 84.

[76] *Id.* at 84–85.

[77] *Id.* at 87.

[78] *Id.* at 88.

[79] *Id.*

[80] *Id.* at 96.

were being offered was perhaps rather strained. Again, Knetsch had reported a loss of $137,315 on his 1956 return, but would have instead reported a $304,000 gain if computed consistently with his reporting position over the prior three taxable years. McLane proposed to show, using the actual 1956 return as a starting point from which to make this adjustment, that (consistently reported) the transaction actually increased Knetsch's income tax liability for the years 1953 through 1956. This supposedly would rebut the government's claim that it involved tax avoidance, notwithstanding that Knetsch could not possibly show that he had anticipated any such premature windup back in 1953.

Judge Mathes then set the schedule for the rest of the trial, involving briefs by both sides and a return to his courtroom for oral argument on October 20, 1958. "It's an interesting case," he commented, before bringing the day's proceedings to a close.

What had happened between the afternoon of August 4 and the morning of August 5 to change Judge Mathes' view of the case? The most likely surmise is perhaps the dullest: that he spent the evening between those two sessions catching up on things.

August 4, 1958 was a Monday. It is conceivable, given the time of year, that the Judge had just returned from a vacation. Even if not, at the start of that day's proceedings he was evidently still getting his bearings.[81] His initial idea, that an intent to save taxes would be legally harmless to the taxpayer, is one that he continued to hold on August 5.[82] In the interim, however, he seems to have become newly aware of substance over form doctrine, which he had not even mentioned on August 4. Presumably, the government's initial written filings had mentioned it (*Bond* does not).[83] And evidently it resonated with him, as the majority opinion and even the dissent in *Bond* did not.[84]

4.   *October 20, 1958: The Axe Falls*

The final day of the *Knetsch* trial was the shortest. Judge Mathes had decided that he did not need to hear the parties' oral arguments after all:

---

[81] Thus, near the start of the August 4 hearing, Judge Mathes expressed uncertainty about the underlying factual issues and how he had previously ruled. *See* Transcript at 71.

[82] *Id.* at 84.

[83] The majority opinion in *Bond* discusses (and dismisses) the government's assertion that the transaction was a sham, but without mentioning substance over form doctrine as such or citing Supreme Court authorities on this point.

[84] The dissent in *Bond* concludes that the transaction did not give rise to interest expense, within the term's ordinary meaning, because "no money or other economic benefits were advanced to the taxpayer by the company." 258 F.2d at 584. Thus, it does not seem to have directly inspired Judge Mathes' reliance on substance over form doctrine although (as discussed below) he took note of its dismissal of the legal relevance of the 1954 legislative history.

The Court: Well, gentlemen, I could take this under submission and write an opinion after some time, but I feel prepared to decide it and I shall decide it now. . . .

It would serve no useful purpose here to go through another analysis of this transaction. We have discussed the non-recourse feature of the transaction and the other features of it. I am of the opinion that, while in form the payments were compensation for the use or forbearance of money, they were not in substance, and that as a payment of interest the transaction was a sham.

As to the effect of the 1954 amendment, with all deference to [the signers of the majority opinion in *Bond*], whom I respect highly, I could adopt most readily here the first two paragraphs of Judge Wisdom's dissent.[85]

Finding that the payments in controversy do not constitute interest paid on indebtedness, the Court must necessarily find in favor of the defendant. . . .

It will be interesting to follow the course of this problem. I suspect you will hear some more of it in the future.[86]

The Ninth Circuit

Knetsch promptly appealed Judge Mathes' decision to the United States Court of Appeals for the Ninth Circuit. He contested not only its legal conclusions but various underlying findings of fact, such as that his only motive in the deal was to secure interest deductions.

While the Ninth Circuit was considering the case, a circuit split emerged concerning debt-financed deferred annuity bond transactions. Whereas the taxpayer had won in the Fifth Circuit in *Bond* in July 1958, the government won in the Third Circuit in *Weller v. Commissioner*,[87] decided on September 9, 1959. This was a consolidated appeal of two Tax Court decisions that had treated as shams a pair of Sam Houston-style transactions engineered by the Standard Life Insurance Company of Indiana.[88]

---

[85] Judge Wisdom had observed that the amendment merely listed certain items that henceforth were not deductible, and "does not purport to say what items *are* deductible." *Bond*, 258 F.2d at 584 (Wisdom, J., dissenting) (emphasis added).

[86] Transcript at 103–04.

[87] 270 F.2d 294 (3d Cir.1959), *cert. denied*, 364 U.S. 908 (1960).

[88] The case on appeal besides *Weller* was *Emmons v. Commissioner*, 31 T.C. 26 (1958). The Tax Court decisions in favor of the government were dated October 10, 1958, or ten days before Judge Mathes' decision in *Knetsch*, but nothing in the record indicates that he was aware of it.

The Third Circuit in *Weller* began its consideration of the legal issues by quoting extensively from *Gregory v. Helvering* and similar Supreme Court precedents. It then continued:

> Any case of this nature is beset with difficulties, for in viewing the substance of the entire transaction one is faced with the rule ... that enjoins us to disregard the motive of tax avoidance. That is not to say that we are confronted with a dilemma. Far from it.[89]

The court then quoted Judge Learned Hand, from a post-*Gregory* opinion, to the effect that, if "the taxpayer enters into a transaction that does not appreciably affect his beneficial interest except to reduce his tax, the law will disregard it."[90] The Tax Court had reasonably found that these were two such cases. Finally, the court dismissed the taxpayers' arguments that the transactions had not been shams under state law (irrelevant to the tax issue) and that the 1954 legislative history foreclosed a pro-government verdict under prior law. And as for the *Bond* case, "[w]e agree ... with the dissenting opinion of Judge Wisdom."[91]

The Ninth Circuit therefore had ample room to decide Knetsch's appeal either way. Its unpublished decision, issued on November 16, 1959, was short and to the point. The District Court's factual findings concerning the transaction's lack of any non-tax substance or purpose had "ample support in the record." Both *Bond* and *Weller* had "carefully considered [the issue].... We find ourselves in agreement with [the latter]."[92] Hence, the district court's judgment in favor of the government was affirmed.

The Ninth Circuit decision left Knetsch with only one remaining recourse: to petition the United States Supreme Court for a writ of *certiorari*. Ordinarily, this is an extreme long shot since the Supreme Court accepts so few cases for discretionary review (and is often candidly unenthusiastic about tax cases).[93] However, given Knetsch's large financial stake in the outcome, not to mention his attorneys' chance of a lifetime to argue before the Supreme Court, an appeal would clearly be

---

[89] *Weller*, 270 F.2d at 297.

[90] *Id.* (quoting Gilbert v. Commissioner, 248 F.2d 399, 411–12 (2d Cir.1957) (Hand, J., dissenting on an unrelated procedural matter)).

[91] 270 F.2d at 297–99.

[92] Transcript at 112.

[93] *See, e.g., Dobson v. Commissioner*, 320 U.S. 489 (1943), and *Commissioner v. Duberstein*, 363 U.S. 278 (1960), both of which attempt (though in different ways) to limit appellate judicial review in tax cases. It is not clear whether the Supreme Court's frequent aversion to reviewing tax cases reflects the personal preferences and interests of various Justices or a sense of lesser institutional competence in the tax area.

worth trying even if its odds of being accepted were no better than that of the average appellate tax case.

The Supreme Court Decision

The Briefs

1. *Knetsch's Petition for a Writ of* Certiorari *and Opening Brief*

    A.   The Taxpayer's Tactical Choice

As it happened, *Knetsch* did not figure to be as hard a case as most to get the Supreme Court to review. This is clear not just in retrospect, when we can observe that it was in fact accepted for review, but based on what was known at that time. The taxpayer could point to a clear split between the circuits since the Fifth Circuit had upheld a similar transaction in *Bond* while the Third Circuit (in *Weller*) as well as the Ninth Circuit had decided in favor of the government. More appellate decisions were on the way.[94] Clearly, then, this was a "hot" issue, albeit one with no direct application to transactions after the March 1, 1954 effective date. Moreover, in response to taxpayer petitions seeking a writ of *certiorari* in *Weller* (and the consolidated case of *Emmons v. Commissioner*), the government had already stated that it did not oppose Supreme Court review.[95] Thus, there may have been more suspense for Knetsch's attorneys, the McLanes—would theirs be the case to be accepted?—than for Knetsch himself regarding whether Supreme Court review would be available.

For whatever reason, *Knetsch* was the case that the Supreme Court decided to hear. However, even if this outcome had been completely predictable in advance (which it clearly was not, especially from the McLanes' standpoint given *Weller*), the McLanes had every reason to make their petition for a writ of *certiorari* as persuasive, and successful in framing the issues advantageously, as they possibly could. As the saying goes, you don't get a second chance to make a good first impression.

In deciding how to argue the case, the McLanes no doubt consulted *United States v. Bond*, since this was the appellate case that the

---

[94] On July 5, 1960, or after the petition for *certiorari* was granted but before Knetsch's opening brief, the Second Circuit joined the Third and Ninth Circuits in siding with the Commissioner with regard to a similar transaction. *See* Diggs v. Commissioner, 281 F.2d 326 (2d Cir.), *cert. denied*, 364 U.S. 908 (1960). And note other subsequent decisions such as *Salley*.

[95] *See* Memorandum for the United States (January 6, 1960) (noting that the government had not opposed taxpayer motions for a writ of *certiorari* in *Weller* and the jointly decided *Emmons* case). The government had not appealed the adverse Fifth Circuit decision in *Bond*, perhaps because it had more to gain from building support for its position through decisions in other circuits.

taxpayers had won. In *Bond*, the Fifth Circuit had begun by finding that the transaction involved "indebtedness" and was not a sham.[96] It had then gone on to argue that the legislative history of interest deductions for debt-financed annuities, extending from the 1930s through 1954, showed that Congress had consistently intended to allow an interest deduction with respect to pre-March 1954 annuities.

These are indeed the arguments that the McLanes made on Knetsch's behalf, both in his petition for a writ of *certiorari* and in his opening brief once *certiorari* was granted. However, they made critical changes in both the order and the content of the arguments.

The "Question Presented," in both briefs, was "[w]hether the courts below have the power to disallow" interest expense on a pre-effective date contract "in view of the clear intent of Congress ... in 1954."[97] Not only did the legislative history argument go first and receive by far the greater emphasis, but it was now drawn more narrowly, to focus exclusively on what had happened in 1954. Only after this argument had been thoroughly made did the briefs go on to argue that Knetsch's transaction involved true indebtedness and was not a sham.

B. Knetsch's Legislative History Argument

As Knetsch's briefs told the story, the Supreme Court faced a separation of powers morality play. The Treasury had alerted the Ways and Means Committee to the Sam Houston transactions. It had sought a rule denying subsequent interest deductions even on preexisting contracts. "But what did Congress give to the Treasury as opposed to what it was asked to do?"[98] As the committee report showed, it had acceded only as to post-effective date contracts. "In other words, "Congress gave the Commissioner only half of the apple,"[99] while deliberately and affirmatively protecting, without regard to the prior state of the law, taxpayers who had entered into pre-effective date contracts.

Knetsch urged this conclusion despite the fact that all Congress actually enacted in 1954 was a deduction disallowance rule. His reliance on the legislative history brings to mind the joke among tax lawyers that, if the legislative history is ambiguous, you might consider consulting the statute. It also begs the question of how the quoted language could have meant what he insisted, when all it said was that *this bill*

---

[96] The Fifth Circuit's main ground for finding actual indebtedness was that money need not actually change hands in a debt transaction. Its main ground for finding no sham was the legitimacy of the annuity as a bona fide issuance under state insurance law. *Bond*, 258 F.2d at 580.

[97] Petition for Writ of *Certiorari* at 2; Knetsch Brief at 2.

[98] Petition for Writ of *Certiorari* at 9.

[99] *Id.*

would deny deductions only if they pertained to post-effective date contracts.

Knetsch's briefs then turned to the snake in the garden. The Commissioner, "discovering . . . that his request for remedial legislation had been granted only in part, refused to abide by the decision of the Ways and Means Committee and determined to seize the other half of the apple by creating a legal issue to submit to the courts." Hence the issuance of Revenue Ruling 54–94, "which was the Commissioner's open move to avoid the effect of Congress' refusal to retroactively legislate." The Commissioner had evidently been unmoved by the fact that this required him to "reverse[] his field," by stating that the interest deductions had never been allowable after telling the Congress that they were (and thus necessitated corrective legislation).[100]

Against this background, Knetsch asserted, the courts could not decide in favor of the Commissioner without overstepping "the proper role to be played by the judiciary under our system of government." Congress had "already legislated on the specific problem" at issue in the case. Thus, to sustain the lower courts, "it would be necessary for the Court to contravene, both in spirit and in substance, the decision which has already been made by the Congress regarding the particular deduction involved here."[101]

C. Knetsch's Argument That the Transaction Involved "Indebtedness" and Was Not a Sham

A second line of argument rejected the government's claims that Knetsch had not owed "indebtedness" and had been solely motivated by tax avoidance. To support for the former, he discerned and rejected a government argument that there could not be a bona fide debt absence "payments for the use of borrowed money."[102] The Commissioner ostensibly failed to recognize that indebtedness could be supported by the "forbearance" as well as the "use" of money—in particular, by not making him pay cash for his $4 million worth of annuity bonds. Requiring cash owed actually to be advanced, rather than foregone for the period of the loan, would have grave consequences in a credit economy, where consumers frequently bought items such as houses or cars without immediately paying for them in cash.[103]

As for the government's claim that the transaction had been purely tax-motivated, Knetsch noted that, even if the interest deductions were allowed, he would end up losing more than $50,000 after-tax. (This

---

[100] *Id.* at 10.

[101] Petitioner's Brief at 10.

[102] Petition for Writ of *Certiorari* at 16 (quoting Rev. Rul. 54–94, 1954–1 C.B. 53).

[103] *Id.* at 17–19.

reflected the 1956 termination of the deal, presumably unexpected up front, which resulted in his realizing more than $300,000 of taxable gain.) "Therefore, how it can be said that Knetsch's sole or primary motive was tax avoidance which [sic] his actual cash loss is $50,650.36, even if all claimed interest deductions are allowed, is beyond petitioners' understanding."[104] Knetsch did not, however, offer much explanation of what possibly could have been his motivation for the deal if it was not tax savings, given the deal's built-in adverse pre-tax economics.[105]

2. Amicus Briefs Filed in Support of Knetsch's Position

With the consent of both parties, two amicus briefs were filed in support of Knetsch's position. Each was filed by attorneys for taxpayers in other pending cases concerning the same basic transaction. Whether by chance or conscious coordination, the three allied briefs carved up the waterfront by making entirely distinct arguments against disallowance of the interest deductions.

A. The McGregor Brief

Douglas W. McGregor, the attorney for the taxpayer in *Salley*, filed a brief arguing that the validity of an annuity contract under Texas law foreclosed treating it as a sham for federal income tax purposes. While Congress admittedly had the power to disregard state law in determining what was valid indebtedness for federal income tax purposes, there was no indication in the pre–1954 statutes or legislative histories that it had meant to do so.[106] This was among the main arguments that had persuaded the Fifth Circuit in *Bond* to decide in favor of the taxpayer.[107]

B. The Appert–Murdoch Brief

Richard H. Appert and Converse Murdoch, counsel for the taxpayers in *Weller* and *Emmons*, filed the second amicus brief. They argued that, by denying deductions that the widely circulated pre–1954 private letter rulings had suggested were permissible, the Commissioner was "abusing his discretionary authority to limit the retroactive effects of rulings.... Also, the Commissioner is discriminating between persons who did not happen to receive letter rulings addressed to them and those who did."[108]

---

[104] Petitioner's Brief at 26.

[105] The closest Knetsch came to offering such an argument was in noting that in thirty years he would have been entitled to receive $43 per month, and that he had retained $1,000 of net value in the annuity contracts. *See* Petition for Writ of *Certiorari* at 22–23. No argument was offered, however, that these benefits were commensurate with the deal's out-of-pocket costs.

[106] *See* McGregor Brief at 9–13.

[107] United States v. Bond, 258 F.2d 577, 580 (5th Cir.1958).

[108] Appert-Murdoch Brief at 2.

On the first of these two points, Appert and Murdoch noted that the Commissioner's eight favorable private rulings—clearly evincing a consistent position over a five year period—had been widely circulated, and relied upon by taxpayers other than those to whom the rulings were addressed. "[T]he number of rulings clearly evidenced an established administrative position upon which the taxpayers were justified in relying."[109] Existing case law showed that, under certain circumstances, the Service may not revoke its administrative constructions of prior law without grandfathering prior transactions.[110]

Appert and Murdoch conceded that their key precedent involved an official Treasury Regulation, rather than unpublished private letter rulings. This difference was "not significant for present purposes," however, given the large number of the private rulings, the publicity they had received, and the fact that many taxpayers were shown copies of the rulings (albeit by promoters, not the Service!) and had relied on them.[111] Surely it was "unrealistic to suppose that a taxpayer who was not a lawyer specializing in tax law would have greater respect for (or even access to) a Treasury Regulation than he would for a letter signed by or for the nation's chief tax officer and covering explicitly the exact problem involved in the plan he was about to adopt."[112]

Worse still, however, the Service was guilty of bias in how it had chosen to apply its new position retroactively. Taxpayers who had actually received private rulings—or, as the brief put it, happened to "have letters with their names at the top"[113]—were being protected against detrimental reliance by being allowed, at the least, to deduct their cash out of pocket prior to the time of revocation. No such relief was being offered to non-recipients, however:

> Such a result is monstrous. It should not be countenanced by this Court. The presence or absence of a particular person's name on what is concededly a written statement of the position of the Commissioner ... is not of sufficient significance to warrant such a harsh, incongruous, and unjust result as that for which the Commissioner contends.

> There is no consideration of administrative expediency which can sacrifice such a sacrifice of basic principles of even handed justice....[114]

---

[109] *Id.* at 5.

[110] *Id.* (citing Helvering v. R.J. Reynolds Tobacco Co., 306 U.S. 110 (1939); Provost v. United States, 269 U.S. 443 458 (1926)).

[111] Appert-Murdoch Brief at 8.

[112] *Id.* at 8–9.

[113] *Id.* at 11.

[114] *Id.* at 13.

To be sure, the government might offer an answer to this equal protection claim, echoing that of certain courts below, but it would not wash:

> The Third Circuit, in the *Weller* case and *Emmons* case approved the government's actions in this area on the ground that there was no discrimination since all taxpayers *without rulings* are being treated equally. This seems the equivalent of saying that there is no discrimination against negroes [sic] if all negroes are treated in the same way—unfair as the treatment may be.[115]

One is almost inclined to wonder whether the author of these extraordinary words laughed after writing them. Race is a status; not filing for a private ruling a deliberate choice. And to compare limiting reliance claims to taxpayers who had something they were meant to rely on to America's long and sad history of invidious racial discrimination gives fresh meaning to the idea of impassioned advocacy.

Appert and Murdoch could perhaps have ended on this high note. Instead, however, they added a further, perhaps more interesting, argument. How could the government complain of impermissible tax avoidance, Appert and Murdoch asked, simply because Knetsch had "arranged his transaction in such a manner that he would be certain" of his yearly economic accretion as well as his interest expense? Had he borrowed at 6%, rather than merely 3-1/2%, in order to hold a speculative stock, he would have been permitted the interest deductions even if he ended up with a loss. He therefore was being denied the deductions here, "not really because of any lack of economic reality, but because of the certainty of his [annual 2-1/2%] economic benefit" on the annuity bonds.[116]

3. *The Government's Brief*

The government's brief, while more than twice as long as any of those to which it was responding, emphasized one central point. Under the pre–1954 law that controlled, Knetsch was not entitled to interest deductions unless "money [was] actually paid for the use or forbearance of money actually borrowed, or equivalent economic benefits advanced."[117] Knetsch, however, had "employ[ed] only a ritual of forms,

---

[115] *Id.* at 14. The brief then went on to cite the foundational equal protection case of *Yick Wo v. Hopkins*, 118 U.S. 356 (1886), although it left out *Brown v. Board of Education*, 347 U.S. 483 (1954)—perhaps because no one would even dare argue here that the treatment of taxpayers without rulings, though nominally separate, was in fact equal.

[116] *Id.* at 17.

[117] Government Brief at 18–19.

without commercial meaning or substance."[118] Reciprocal and offsetting obligations, such as those involved here, lacked the reality that would have existed had Knetsch borrowed against his annuities only after an "appreciable period of time,"[119] or actually received property for his own use, as in the case of a conventional purchase money mortgage.[120] The "interest" in this case—the word, along with others such as "loan" and "annuity savings bonds" always had quotation marks around it when referring to Knetsch's "scheme"—could not be deducted given that the income tax law had never been "so framed that taxpayers need only employ certain labels to avail themselves of its benefits."[121]

The government then went on to rebut the other side's main arguments. In so doing, however, it misinterpreted Knetsch's legislative history argument—albeit to make it more legally credible—as one about the 1939 Code rather than the 1954 Code, with the latter being treated merely as evidentiary of the prior state of the law.[122] So construed, Knetsch had misinterpreted Congress's intent in 1954, which had been to adopt an "omnibus rule" that "deal[t] broadly with all situations . . . whether or not in a particular case the claimed deduction qualified" under prior law.[123] Since the example in the legislative history was "not necessarily devoid of all economic substance,"[124] it did not even show that Congress in 1954 had believed that Knetsch's transaction worked under prior law. Even if it had shown this, however, it would have little weight since "Congress is as likely to be wrong as anyone else, in its interpretation of prior law."[125]

The government spent little time on the other main arguments in the taxpayer briefs. Knetsch's "curious" argument that he could not have had a tax avoidance motive since he was "doomed to sustain a large out-of-pocket loss" even if allowed the deductions was "incredible."[126] Why would he have done the deal, in that case? But in any event the

---

[118] *Id.* at 21.

[119] *Id.* at 23.

[120] *Id.* at 24.

[121] *Id.* at 36.

[122] Again, Knetsch's argument, that Congress in 1954 had affirmatively provided an interest deduction for pre-effective date transactions, suffered from the objections that Congress had only enacted a deduction disallowance statute and in the legislative history had said that "[y]our committee's bill" was limited in its reach to post-effective date contracts.

[123] Government Brief at 39.

[124] *Id.* at 38.

[125] *Id.* at 40.

[126] *Id.* at 28–29.

after-tax loss had resulted from Knetsch's surrendering the bonds in 1956, contrary to his initial expectation, an act that had occurred only because his deductions had been disallowed on audit.[127]

Turning to the amicus briefs, the government dismissed McGregor's argument about the enforceability of the annuity bonds under Texas law. This was irrelevant because, "for the purposes of the federal tax laws, local laws are not controlling unless Congress has made them so."[128] As for Appert and Murdoch, "private rulings are always expressly confined to the particular transaction disclosed by the applicant for the ruling." This was deliberately done to prevent their being relied on more broadly. Their lack of precedential value was settled law.[129] Knetsch, in any event, had not even claimed reliance. As for the equal protection argument, taxpayers who had not received rulings were different from those who had, so no abuse of discretion could be claimed.[130]

4. Knetsch's Reply Brief

Knetsch's reply brief emphasized one main point.[131] The government, "[i]n its attempt to avoid the force of" Knetsch's argument about the 1954 legislative history, had "utilized a variety of techniques," in particular "answer[ing] contentions which were not made."[132] Congress in 1954 had not merely expressed an opinion about the deductibility of Knetsch's (and other similar) payments under the 1939 Code. Rather, it had "affirmatively legislated that such payments were interest," by describing the basic transaction and then (in the legislative history) stating that " 'in such cases' the amounts would be disallowed only" for post-effective date annuity contracts.[133]

Oral Argument

With the filing of Knetsch's reply brief, only the oral argument remained. On October 17, 1960, Lee McLane gave his opening statement on behalf of Knetsch. He found the Court no less baffled than the government by his argument that the 1954 enactment did not merely elucidate the prior state of the law, but actually controlled. As he read the text of the 1954 law, one of the Justices asked:

---

[127] Id. at 29.

[128] Id. at 42 (emphasis removed).

[129] Id. at 45.

[130] Id. at 49.

[131] The reply brief also restated various arguments from Knetsch's initial brief and the amicus briefs that need not be recounted here.

[132] Reply Brief at 2.

[133] Id. at 8.

The Court: That was not in effect at the time of these transactions?

Mr. McLane: No, it was not, Mr. Justice.

The Court: It came into effect after them?

Mr. McLane: It came into effect in 1954. The annuities involved in this matter were purchased in 1953. But we have two taxable years involved, '53 and '54.

The Court: What statute was in force at the time of these transactions? . . .

Mr. McLane: 1939 Code, Section 23(b) and Section 24(a)(6) were in effect for the year 1953.[134]

He then proceeded with more background information about the litigation without noting that, on its face, the 1954 statute did not apply to this pre-effective date transaction even in 1954. When he returned to the statute, however, quoting the relevant language from the 1954 committee report, Justice Harlan was ready for him, stating "I don't know whether this is of any significance" and adding that "[m]aybe it's not material."[135]

McLane gamely stuck to his argument that Congress's ostensibly clear 1954 intent should control. The Court mainly let him proceed with interruption. He closed early to leave himself with rebuttal time, and the Court then adjourned for the day.

The proceedings on October 18 began with Grant Wiprud's oral argument on behalf of the government. Wiprud, by now, realized that McLane was arguing that the 1954 enactment directly controlled, as opposed to merely shedding light on the prior state of the law. However, when he so described the taxpayer's argument, a Justice asked him "whether your characterization of the petitioner's argument [is] really entirely fair. It seems to me he does rely on [1939 law]."[136] Wiprud responded that, indeed, he didn't.

This was not the only point confusing the Court. McLane's argument that Knetsch could not possibly have been engaged in a tax avoidance deal, since he had been certain of losing money after-tax even with the deductions, had left a greater impression. Well before Wiprud reached this argument, one of the Justices asked him: "You're going to

---

[134] Oral Argument at 2 (Oct. 17, 1960).

[135] *Id.* at 3. McLane names Justice Harlan as the other party to the colloquy. Justice Harlan may not have been saying that the 1954 statute was irrelevant since he also mentions "the additional borrowings made by the taxpayer." *Id.* This raises the possibility that he misunderstood the effective date rule as based on when one borrowed rather than when one had purchased a given annuity.

[136] Oral Argument at 3 (Oct. 18, 1960).

deal with his argument that, even under the way this was dealt with, he stood to gain no tax advantage?"[137] The Court then brought the issue up again as he continued to run through the government's affirmative arguments.

The Court: He says he doesn't get a tax benefit.

Mr. Wiprud: And we say he does not get it, yes, Your Honor.

The Court: Do you disagree with his argument on that? I don't want to go through all the rigmarole, because frankly, I'd get lost, I'm afraid. But do you claim that he inevitably does get a tax benefit from this?

Mr. Wiprud: He would if his deductions were allowed, Your Honor. But we say that they should not be allowed.

The Court: No, no, even if these deductions are allowed.

Mr. Wiprud: He would be money in pocket, yes, Your Honor.

The Court: He says he doesn't. He gave some illustrations that puzzle me as to what the answer to them is.

Mr. Wiprud: Yes.

The Court: I wish you'd deal with them.

Mr. Wiprud: He makes a curious argument that when he entered this transaction he was doomed to an out-of-pocket loss whether or not the interest deductions are allowed, and therefore he had no tax motive.

The Court: Well, can you answer that?[138]

Wiprud called the argument "incredible," and then more cogently noted that Knetsch would have been way ahead after-tax for thirty years if the deal had not been prematurely terminated.

They turned to the *Gregory* case (mistakenly called *Helvering* by one of the Justices),[139] in connection with the question of why anything was wrong with this deal when taxpayers in high brackets routinely and permissibly seek tax losses. A Justice noted that "*Helvering* certainly no longer stands for the proposition—it never did—that you can't be very contriving in getting a benefit out of the taxing structure."[140] He then

---

[137] *Id.* at 6.

[138] *Id.* at 10–11.

[139] *See id.* at 11. As students in introductory tax courses typically learn early on, Helvering was for many years the named litigant for the government in all tax cases that rose through the Board of Tax Appeals, thus making the name quite useless as a reference to any particular case.

[140] *Id.*

shrewdly observed that the opinion "first rejects [this proposition] and then relies on it."[141]

So the government would have to show that this was a sham transaction, not merely that it was contrived:

The Court: [I]f this is a fiction, if this is an artifact—whatever word you use—then you don't have to say he can't get a benefit by monkeying around with the tax structure.

Mr. Wiprud: Right.

The Court: It's done every day, all over the United States, by perfectly honest people; and if you can do it without sham, you can do it; isn't that right?

Mr. Wiprud: That's correct, Your Honor.

The Court: All right.

Mr. Wiprud: We say that it is merely cumulative in this case, and that—

The Court: But something that isn't so can't be cumulative. Something that is nothing can't be cumulative.

Mr. Wiprud: We submit it is so in this case, Your Honor.[142]

Wiprud then turned to the 1954 legislation, only to encounter more flak. Conceding that the government had sought legislation that would apply to pre-effective date contracts, Wiprud insisted that it was merely trying to clarify the state of the law, and ensure that it would win in all cases even absent a sham. One of the Justices brought up the committee report language that McLane had been emphasizing:

The Court: Well, how do you get away from that? ... Well, was the report talking about some other type of transaction or about this very type of transaction ...?

Mr. Wiprud: ... [W]e don't think they were meaning to pass judgment on it, to say that this kind of scheme represents genuine interest payments. But they were just simply saying: This area is fraught with tax avoidance possibilities. Therefore, for the future, we're going to bar genuine interest payments and, *a fortiori*, sham interest payments, simply to preclude any controversy in the area. And, of course, what a later Congress thinks an earlier Congress intended, as this Court has said ... is a hazardous speculation.[143]

---

[141] *Id.* at 12.

[142] *Id.* at 13.

[143] *Id.* at 15.

His time was soon up, and McLane rose for rebuttal. The Court once again let him speak with fewer interruptions than Wiprud. Near the end, however, Justice Stewart noted that his economic loss argument relied on Knetsch's having surrendered the annuities in 1956 after his deductions had been disallowed.[144] Another question then forced McLane to close by acknowledging that the annuity would have yielded Knetsch only $43 a month at age 90, after making huge payments for thirty years.[145]

Which way was the Court leaning? Perhaps this depended on whether being argued with extensively (more Wiprud's experience than McLane's) was a good sign or a bad one. Had the Justices been quieter for McLane because they agreed with him, or thought him not worth arguing with? Had they challenged Wiprud more extensively to address their remaining doubts and help them craft the opinion, or because they thought he was wrong?

The Opinion

Less than a month later, on November 14, 1960, the Supreme Court announced its decision. The government had prevailed by a vote of 6 to 3, in an opinion by Justice Brennan. After reciting the facts, the opinion quoted the statement in *Gregory* (the Supreme Court affirmance) that, a taxpayer's "legal right ... to decrease" his taxes "cannot be doubted." Here as in *Gregory*, however, one still needed to ask whether "what was done, apart from the tax motive, was the thing which the statute intended."[146] Here, there had been only a "fiction ... For it is patent that there was nothing of substance to be realized by Knetsch from this transaction beyond a tax deduction."[147]

The opinion turned to Knetsch's argument—which the Court now understood—that Congress had actually meant in 1954 "to authorize the deduction of payments made under sham transactions entered into before 1954." But, in the search for any evidence of this intent, "[w]e look in vain."[148] Congress had been concerned about bona fide transactions that it thought ought not to work. There was nothing in the committee reports "to suggest that, in exempting pre–1954 annuities Congress intended to protect sham transactions."[149]

---

[144] *Id.* at 18.

[145] *Id.* at 19.

[146] *Knetsch*, 364 U.S. at 365 (quoting Gregory v. Helvering, 293 U.S. 465, 469 (1935)).

[147] *Id.* at 366.

[148] *Id.* at 367.

[149] *Id.* at 369 (footnote omitted).

The opinion closed by mentioning the Appert–Murdoch argument about reliance on private ruling letters that had been issued to other taxpayers. However, since Knetsch had never advanced this argument, "we have no reason to pass upon it." The judgment of the Ninth Circuit was affirmed.[150]

Justice Douglas offered a brief dissent, with which Justices Whittaker and Stewart concurred. The dissent accepted that Knetsch had anticipated a pre-tax loss, but saw nothing wrong with this. "[T]he same may be true where a taxpayer borrows money at 5% or 6% interest to purchase securities that pay only nominal interest; or where, with money in the bank earning 3%, he borrows from the self-same bank at a higher rate."[151]

Notwithstanding any intent to benefit from tax deductions, the dissent thought this allowable "as long as the transaction itself is not hocus-pocus." Here, "[t]he insurance company existed; it operated under Texas law; it was authorized to issue these policies and to make these annuity loans."[152]

The dissent warned that, "[t]o disallow the 'interest deduction because the annuity device was devoid of commercial substance is to draw a line which will affect a host of situations not now before us and which, with all deference, I do not think we can maintain when other cases reach here. The remedy is legislative. Evils or abuses can be particularized by Congress.... Since these transactions were real and legitimate in the insurance world and were consummated within the limits allowed by insurance policies, I would recognize them tax-wise."[153]

This viewpoint is still frequently expressed. However, just as the outcome of the Civil War foreclosed certain arguments about states' rights, so that in *Knetsch* decisively put to rest Justice Douglas' first proposition, that commercial substance is unnecessary if a transaction is valid under state law. The issue ever since has been whether a given transaction has sufficient economic substance to be respected for tax purposes, and of what the requisite substance might consist.

Postscript

The Supreme Court decision doomed Knetsch's hope of claiming interest deductions, not only for 1953 and 1954, which were the years at issue in the case, but also for 1955, which had been under audit but awaiting a resolution for the earlier years. For 1956, however, the loss

---

[150] *Id.* at 370.

[151] *Id.* (Douglas, J., dissenting).

[152] *Id.*

[153] *Id.* at 371.

deduction of $137,315 that he had claimed was not necessarily foreclosed, since it reflected his out-of-pocket loss from abandoning the transaction, as computed under the assumption that it had been a sham. He could argue, without (at least directly and unmistakably) contradicting the Supreme Court decision, that this deduction was allowable under § 165(c)(2), pertaining to losses incurred in transactions entered into for profit.

The Service, however, denied this deduction. Knetsch paid the resulting deficiency on January 4, 1961 and once again filed suit for a refund. The McLanes remained his attorneys. This time, however, he decided to try his luck in the Court of Claims, rather than federal district court.

On July 16, 1965, Knetsch got the bad news that he had lost once again.[154] The Court of Claims held that he had not had the requisite profit motive, given the finding in the earlier case that the transaction had been tax-motivated. Two main considerations supported rejecting his argument that his undeniable pursuit of *after-tax* profit should support allowing the deduction. First, since tax savings are not themselves taxable, the expenses incurred in seeking them should not be deductible.[155] Thus, the requisite profit motive had to relate to pre-tax income. Second, under the doctrine of *Gregory v. Helvering,* income tax rules should generally be construed to "refer to transactions entered upon for commercial and industrial purposes and not to include transactions entered upon for no other motive but to escape taxation."[156]

The Immediate Impact of *Knetsch*

A *Step Beyond* Gregory

Knetsch truly is a "landmark decision"[157] that has significantly influenced the income tax common law and, consequently, tax practice.

---

[154] Knetsch v. United States, 348 F.2d 932 (Ct.Cl.1965), *cert. denied,* 383 U.S. 957 (1966).

[155] 348 F.2d at 937. Compare § 265, denying deductions for certain expenses incurred to earn tax-exempt income (such as interest expense on indebtedness incurred or continued to purchase or carry tax-exempt bonds).

[156] *Id.* (quoting Judge Learned Hand in *Commissioner v. Transport Trading & Terminal Corp.,* 176 F.2d 570, 572 (2d Cir.1949)). Knetsch also argued for a deduction under § 212, which allows deductions incurred to earn income (though not in a business), but lost on the same ground that a pre-tax profit motive was required. In addition, the Court of Claims rejected estoppel and equal treatment arguments that were essentially variations of arguments made unsuccessfully to the Supreme Court in *Knetsch. See* 348 F.2d at 935, 939–41.

[157] *See, e.g.,* Boris I. Bittker & Martin J. McMahon, *Federal Taxation of Individuals* 18–21 (2d ed. 1988).

While courts cite it less frequently than *Gregory v. Helvering*,[158] its direct influence on subsequent case law—even if not its broader penumbral influence—has probably been greater, for two reasons.

First, *Knetsch* avoids what I earlier called *Gregory*'s "curious dual quality," by decisively embracing the broad interpretation, that economic substance is generally required in tax deals. *Knetsch* cannot plausibly be interpreted as merely elucidating the meaning of "indebtedness" in the 1939 interest deduction statute. And, unlike *Gregory*, it could never be described as meaning "all things to all men."[159] It plainly requires some quantum of business or other non-tax purpose and effect, as well as (for business or investment transactions) some prospect of pre-tax profit, across a broad range of substantive areas.

Second, the fact that *Knetsch* deals with an arbitrage, rather than the attempted conversion of ordinary income into capital gain like *Gregory*, gives it both a clearer import and a more vital role in the federal income tax system. We can start with the clearer import. In *Gregory*, the taxpayer actually did something on balance, by selling Monitor shares for cash and extracting wealth from corporate solution. Her sin was simply inserting a needless extra step in the transaction, and pursuing the "true" end only indirectly. Yet counting the number of separate steps, and determining whether the taxpayer has impermissibly inserted an extra one, or instead merely chosen an allowable low-tax rather than a high-tax route to the same end, can be arbitrary and semantic.[160] In the *Knetsch* setting, while there may be serious line-drawing problems (how much substance is enough?), at least the nature of the inquiry is a bit clearer. It concerns whether the taxpayer actually did anything, on balance, that could be sufficiently rationalized as offering a potentially positive pre-tax payoff.

The fact that *Knetsch* concerned a loss-generating arbitrage, rather than attempted conversion, also raised the stakes for the income tax system. By realizing her corporate-level gain at all, Gregory was already departing from the optimal tax planning approach, which would have been to hold the appreciated Monitor securities in corporate solution indefinitely. The device that she attempted, which aimed to mitigate the tax damage, would not otherwise have been worthwhile. By contrast, *any* taxpayer would be potentially interested in a *Knetsch*-style transaction if

---

[158] Note that, in a Lexis search, I found 673 *Knetsch* cites vs. 1059 for *Gregory* for 1961 through early 2002.

[159] Paul, *supra* note 31, at 125.

[160] Thus, in *Chamberlin v. Commissioner*, 207 F.2d 462 (6th Cir.1953), *cert. denied*, 347 U.S. 918 (1954), the determination of whether "the transaction" had needless extra steps would depend on whether one included in its scope the insurance company's short-term financing.

the tax losses that it generated could be used to offset other taxable income.[161]

The big question, of course, is how much economic substance is required (and of what it consists).[162] While gauging how the courts are likely to evaluate a given borderline transaction is at best an art rather than a science, one could easily exaggerate the indeterminacy by focusing solely on litigated cases that elicit differing expert predictions *ex ante* or inconsistent judicial results *ex post*. There also is an important "dog that didn't bark" phenomenon (in Sherlock Holmes' famous phrase).[163] Loss-generating deals that would plainly run afoul of *Knetsch* because they have so little non-tax content (and thus would appeal to taxpayers who really don't want to do anything other than save taxes) are not even considered given the shadow that the case casts. Or, at least, they are not considered by reputable practitioners who are counting on more than the "audit lottery" (the probability that a given transaction will escape detection by the Service given its low audit rates).

In a quick tour of how the *Knetsch* doctrine has played out over time, two particular stops are worth making. The first is *Goldstein v. Commissioner*,[164] an influential (albeit merely appellate) case that interprets the doctrine's reach relatively expansively. The second is *Frank Lyon Co. v. United States*,[165] the most significant Supreme Court case since *Knetsch* on the subject of tax avoidance, and one that (albeit without citing *Knetsch*) seems to take a narrow view of the limits on permissible tax planning.

Goldstein *and the Requirement of Purposive Activity in Non–Sham Transactions*

Revenue Ruling 54–94 had targeted two distinct transactions: that in *Knetsch*, and another that lost repeatedly in court both before and

---

[161] However, even if a *Knetsch*-style transaction otherwise worked, its appeal would depend on such factors as (1) the ratio between out-of-pocket losses and tax losses, (2) the marginal rate at which the deductions were being taken, (3) the length of the deferral before phantom taxable income (from deemed recovery of the phantom losses) would have to be reported, and (4) the value of deferral given the applicable interest or discount rate.

[162] One recent example of a case in which the meaning of economic substance and pre-tax profit were disputed is Compaq v. Commissioner, 277 F.3d 778 (5th Cir.2001), *rev'g* 113 T.C. 214 (1999). Among the issues in *Compaq* were how to treat foreign taxes in computing pre-tax profit, and whether eliminating economic risk, just like accepting it, is evidence of economic substance. For a strongly critical view of this decision, see Daniel N. Shaviro & David A. Weisbach, *The Fifth Circuit Gets It Wrong in* Compaq v. Commissioner, 94 Tax Notes 511 (2002).

[163] *See* Sir Arthur Conan Doyle, *Silver Blaze*, in *The Complete Sherlock Holmes* (1938).

[164] 364 F.2d 734 (2d Cir.1966), *cert. denied*, 385 U.S. 1005 (1967).

[165] 435 U.S. 561 (1978).

after *Knetsch* was decided in 1960.[166] Here, the basic idea was to engage in a debt-financed acquisition of Treasury bonds that did not pay interest (and yielded no taxable income) until maturity. The counterparty (a bank or broker) would retain the bonds as security for the loan, and eventually settle the loan by selling the bonds. Thus, the transaction's main economic consequence to the taxpayer was that she had to pay the spread between the return on the Treasury bonds and the higher rate of interest on the loan, giving her a pre-tax loss. For tax purposes, however, she could immediately deduct all the interest she paid, while deferring her interest income until maturity.

The transaction therefore worked a lot like that in *Knetsch*. The taxpayer was deliberately accepting a pre-tax economic loss in the hope that the larger reported loss for tax purposes (until maturity) would leave her ahead after-tax. There were a couple of differences, however. For one, here someone actually was doing something—buying Treasury bonds—although arguably it really was the bank or broker, not the taxpayer. For another, the taxpayer might actually bear some economic risk under the deal, relating to changes in the Treasury bonds' value. Thus, a pre-tax profit was perhaps not literally impossible—although, under the numbers in an actual deal, it might be unlikely.

Many of these deals were promoted by a Boston broker named M. Eli Livingstone, who did not always carry them out as promised. His prominence appears to have contributed to their hostile reception in the courts, as "Livingstone plans"[167] became infamous and clearly were shams in cases where he did not actually buy and hold Treasury bonds for the entire period of ostensible client ownership. Most of the cases, therefore, added relatively little to *Knetsch*'s sham transaction doctrine.

Goldstein v. Commissioner, however, was in some respects quite different. It not only lacked the notorious Mr. Livingstone,[168] but was meticulously executed using arm's length parties, none of them predominantly in the tax shelter business. What is more, the underlying tax-

---

[166] *See, e.g.*, Jockmus v. United States, 335 F.2d 23 (2d Cir.1964); Bornstein v. Commissioner, 334 F.2d 779 (1st Cir.1964); Dooley v. Commissioner, 332 F.2d 463 (7th Cir.1964); Gheen v. Commissioner, 331 F.2d 470 (6th Cir.1964); Bridges v. Commissioner, 325 F.2d 180 (4th Cir.1963); Rubin v. United States, 304 F.2d 766 (7th Cir.1962); MacRae v. Commissioner, 294 F.2d 56 (9th Cir.1961); Becker v. Commissioner, 277 F.2d 146 (2d Cir.1960); Lynch v. Commissioner, 273 F.2d 867 (2d Cir.1959); Goodstein v. Commissioner, 267 F.2d 127 (1st Cir.1959); and Nichols v. Commissioner, 43 T.C. 842 (1965).

[167] *See, e.g., Bornstein*, 334 F.2d at 779 ("This is another of the Eli Livingston enterprises that have been translated by the courts into deduct now and pay later."); *Dooley*, 332 F.2d at 463 ("This is another of the so-called Livingston cases").

[168] On Livingstone's notoriety, see *Jockmus*, 335 F.2d at 25 (noting that Livingstone's "schemes for tax avoidance have had an extensive history of failure"); *Nichols*, 43 T.C. at 882–86 (finding that he had defrauded the taxpayer by making false claims not only about the transaction's prospects of success but about the trades that he was actually executing).

planning motivation in *Goldstein* merited considerable sympathy, albeit for reasons that one might argue were legally irrelevant.

Tillie Goldstein, in 1958, was a housewife with a retired husband. Their taxable income for the year would therefore have been under $1,000, except for one thing. She acquired a winning Irish Sweepstakes ticket that paid her $140,000.

While this was good news for Goldstein economically, it posed a tax problem for her. The Sweepstakes winnings pushed her, as a one-time proposition, into a high tax bracket. (She otherwise would not even have had to file a return.)[169] If nothing were done, she would end up paying a lot more tax than if winnings with the same present value had been spread out for tax purposes over several years. Such spreading, or "income averaging" as it is sometimes called, would arguably have been appropriate in terms of the underlying distributional aims of the federal income tax. After all, the bunching of a given amount of income into a single year does not really make one better off from a lifetime perspective. The higher tax burden that may result from bunching is merely an artifact of the annual accounting approach that the income tax follows for administrative convenience.[170]

Before the year was out, Goldstein's son, a certified public accountant with the *Death of a Salesman*-ish name of Bernard, had "either volunteered or [been] enlisted"[171] to ride to the rescue. Bernard carried out a Livingstone-style transaction on behalf of his mother, but without the dubious accoutrements of the real (i.e., sham) thing. Legitimate banks actually purchased and held nearly $1 million worth of Treasury bonds on Goldstein's behalf, earning interest at 1-1/2% while she was borrowing at 4%, with a considerable pre-payment to increase her 1958 deductions. Overall for 1958, the transaction induced her to claim $81,397 of deductions, thereby reducing her reported income tax liability by $55,193 (indicating an average tax rate of 67.8% across this income range).

The Tax Court held that the transaction was a sham. Upon appeal, however, the Second Circuit found this holding to be in error. It concluded, "in the interest of candor," that the term "sham" should be reserved for Livingstone-style transactions that had not involved such features as recourse indebtedness and arm's length transactions with

---

[169] *See* Historical Statistics of the United States, Colonial Times to 1970, Part 2 (Chapters N–Z), Table VII (no obligation for married couples to file tax return in 1958 if their combined gross income was less than $1,200, or $2,400 for those over the age of 65).

[170] On the administrative reasons for annual accounting, see, *Burnet v. Sanford & Brooks Co.*, 282 U.S. 359 (1931).

[171] *Goldstein*, 364 F.2d at 736.

parties that were not tax shelter promoters.[172] Accordingly, here, unlike
in cases such as *Knetsch*, there had been bona fide indebtedness.

The Second Circuit nonetheless affirmed. Although the Tax Court
had erred in finding a sham, one of its findings "seems capable of
reasoned development to support the result reached in this case by that
court."[173] It had found that Goldstein's purpose in entering into the
transactions "was not to derive any economic gain ... but was solely an
attempt to obtain an interest deduction as an offset to her sweepstake
winnings." This finding was supported by a smoking gun memo that
Bernard had prepared in 1958 (and guilelessly kept on hand), belying the
belated claim of speculation in Treasury bonds.[174]

This absence of a pre-tax profit motive, the Second Circuit held,
meant that Goldstein's claimed interest deductions, while actually representing interest paid, were not deductible under the statute that made
interest expense generally deductible. The tax code "does not permit a
deduction for interest paid or accrued in loan arrangements ... that can
not with reason be said to have purpose, substance, or utility apart from
their anticipated tax consequences [citing *Knetsch*]."[175] "Purposive activity" was required even if it involved "mixed motives"; there had to be
"some substance to the loan arrangement beyond the taxpayer's desire
to secure the deduction."[176]

At least as a matter of formal doctrine, the Second Circuit decision
in *Goldstein* went beyond *Knetsch*, by not restricting its reach to
"shams." Was this merely an aesthetic or labeling change, reflecting no
more than the court's admitted concern about "candor"? Perhaps it was
to some extent, but not entirely. *Goldstein* not only authorized deduction
disallowance where a court was not comfortable calling something a
"sham," but made a couple of (at least atmospherically) important
points about how broadly the Service could challenge aggressive tax
planning. The usual trappings of sham, such as the use of tax shelter
promoters, were apparently unnecessary for the taxpayer to lose. Genuine economic risks, such as that of a change in the market value of
Treasury bonds, might be disregarded if they were not great enough
(whether objectively or subjectively). And *Knetsch* could be invoked even
in the absence of a literal arbitrage where exactly the same asset was
bought and sold between the parties. Here, Treasury bonds were actually
being purchased in the market, offset only imperfectly by the creation of
a debt arrangement between the literal and nominal purchaser. This

---

[172] *Id*. at 738.

[173] *Id*.

[174] *See id*. at 739.

[175] *Id*. at 741.

[176] *Id*. at 742.

broadening or clarification (whichever one considered it) could potentially have important implications for future tax planning schemes that might involve using actual third-party financial assets.

Frank Lyon Co.: *Better Three Than Two (Parties to a Sale–Leaseback) and Better Two Than One (Regulatory Systems Being Avoided)*

As of 2002, the Supreme Court has revisited anti-tax avoidance doctrine only once since *Knetsch*.[177] In *Frank Lyon Co. v. United States*,[178] it evened up the score a bit by deciding an anti-tax avoidance case in favor of the taxpayer.

Lyon involved the financing of an office building constructed by Worthen, an Arkansas bank. Rather than itself retaining title to the office building, Worthen arranged a sale-leaseback with Frank Lyon (or rather his eponymous company). Lyon was a Worthen customer who sat on its Board of Directors and employed the same attorney.[179] Under the arrangement, his company (henceforth, "Lyon") acquired title to the building piece by piece as it was constructed, and took over responsibility for payments under a construction mortgage with the New York Life Insurance Company that Worthen, being in a hurry to complete the job, had already arranged. Lyon also supplied $500,000 cash towards financing the construction.

Lyon leased the building back to Worthen for a twenty-five year term, which Worthen could extend under favorable terms for another forty years. Worthen also had the option to repurchase legal title to the building after eleven years, by paying Lyon the outstanding balance on the New York Life mortgage, plus its $500,000 with interest. The payments from Worthen to Lyon under the lease precisely equaled those from Lyon to New York Life under the mortgage. Accordingly, the deal had no cash flow consequences for Lyon for twenty-five years, except that it had advanced $500,000 cash that it hoped to get back (perhaps in as little as eleven years) with interest.

If respected for tax purposes, the deal's chief tax consequence was that it would entitle Lyon, rather than Worthen, to claim depreciation deductions with respect to the building.[180] However, the parties also had

---

[177] If one counted *Cottage Savings Ass'n v. Commissioner*, 499 U.S. 554 (1991) (discussed in Chapter 2 of *Tax Stories*), the number of such Supreme Court cases would double. Arguably, however, *Cottage Savings* is better viewed as a case on the particularities of realization doctrine.

[178] 435 U.S. 561 (1978).

[179] *See* Bernard Wolfman, *The Supreme Court in the* Lyon's *Den: A Failure of Judicial Process*, 66 Cornell L. Rev. 1075, 1077 (1981).

[180] In addition, by investing $500,000 of loose cash in the deal, Lyon apparently avoided imposition of a penalty tax, the accumulated earnings tax of § 531. *Id.* at 1077–78.

a non-tax reason for doing the deal, which in fact had actually induced Worthen to start looking for a sale-leaseback partner. Usury restrictions under Arkansas banking law would prevent Worthen from paying more than a 6% rate on its indebtedness, and a rate so low was commercially unfeasible. In addition, both federal and state banking rules limited Worthen's ability to carry so high a long-term construction mortgage (relative to its capital stock) as a balance sheet liability.

Fortunately for Worthen, however, both the federal and the state banking regulators were quite happy to approve an end-run around the inconvenient banking rules. They approved the sale-leaseback, even though it did little to change the economics of the deal, and thus might have been thought to subvert the rules' underlying policy objectives. Two possible explanations of this regulatory pliability were (1) a belief (possibly justified) that the rules being avoided were archaic and silly, or (2) the phenomenon of "regulatory capture," whereby administrative agencies end up collaborating closely with the interest groups that they are supposed to be regulating.

The Service challenged Lyon's depreciation deductions, on the ground that it was not the tax owner of the Worthen Building. The sale-leaseback transaction was a sham, and in substance Lyon had merely lent Worthen $500,000 while acting as a conduit for the New York Life mortgage. The Service lost in Arkansas district court, but won on appeal to the Eighth Circuit. The Supreme Court, however, reversed the Eighth Circuit's reversal by a 7–2 vote, holding that the sale-leaseback was effective for tax purposes.

The decision's exact meaning is muddied by a mammoth, indeed James Joycean, 390–word sentence listing the twenty-six main factual circumstances that "convince us that Lyon has far the better of the case."[181] These included an asserted "absence of any differential in tax rates"[182] between the parties, as a result of which the Court found it "not inappropriate to note that the Government is likely to lose little revenue, if any, as a result of the shape given the transaction by the parties."[183] The factors most emphasized throughout the opinion, however, were (1) the regulatory impediments to Worthen's borrowing directly, (2) the fact that the transaction involved three parties rather than just two, and (3) Lyon's supposedly substantial economic risks.

The first of these factors is probably *Lyon*'s least controversial and most broadly applicable legacy. It fits well with the notion (found in

---

[181] 435 U.S. at 582–83.

[182] *Id.* at 583.

[183] *Id.* at 580. This belief was apparently mistaken. *See* Wolfman, *supra* note 179, at 1095–98.

Gregory and *Knetsch* as well) that an admixture of non-tax motivations may save a significantly tax-driven deal from being considered a sham. It has, however, a perverse "two for the price of one" effect on planning to avoid adverse tax and regulatory rules. Avoid tax rules alone and you may lose, but throw in some avoidance of regulatory rules to boot, and apparently you win.

The second factor, *Lyon*'s being a three-party deal, remains a mystery since it seemingly would have made little difference if either Lyon alone or New York Life alone had provided all the financing and held legal title.[184] This requirement "bec[a]me the basis for tax lawyers to make a laughingstock of the Court, as they now do when quite routinely they add unnecessary third parties to financing transactions in order to qualify for the shelter of *Frank Lyon*."[185]

The third factor, Lyon's supposed economic risk, has been questioned in the literature as well since the present value of Lyon's economic stake, other than that of a default by Worthen that a lender would also bear, was trivial.[186] Its impact on the broader case law has been muted by the sheer multitude of tax cases that find a given taxpayer's risk in a given deal either sufficient or inadequate to dispel a Service claim of sham. *Lyon* is certainly worth citing if you are counsel for the taxpayer in such a case, but the government has plenty of cases to cite as well. The one area in which it has proven decisive is that of sale-leasebacks, which ever since have had a distinctively lower economic substance standard than most other transactions.[187] Practitioner David Hariton calls the existing regime for sale-leasebacks "silly leasing,"[188] which he explains as follows:

> In "silly leasing," a taxpayer purports, by means of certain formal documentary incantations, to pass the burdens and benefits of ownership of depreciable property to the taxpayer who is in the best position to use the relevant tax benefits. But everyone involved in the process, including the Service, recognizes that these benefits and burdens are not very significant as an economic matter. The Service merely requires that the lease have a *de minimis* amount of econom-

---

[184] *Id.* at 1087–88.

[185] *Id.* at 1099–1100.

[186] *See id.* at 1090, noting that Lyon bore no economic risk apart from that of default by Worthen for at least twenty-five years.

[187] *See, e.g.*, Rev. Proc. 75–21, 1975–1 C.B. 715 (establishing fairly lenient standards under which the Service will issue an advance ruling stating that the form of a given sale-leaseback will be respected).

[188] David P. Hariton, *Tax Benefits, Tax Administration, and Legislative Intent*, Tax Forum Paper No. 540 at 7 (March 6, 2000).

ic substance, by reference to certain technical rulings and procedures.[189]

The Continuing Importance of *Knetsch* Today

Knetsch is the principal Supreme Court case standing for the proposition that aggressive tax planning may not be respected for tax purposes
unless it meets some minimum standard of economic substance. More
specifically, while "[a]ny one may so arrange his affairs that his taxes
shall be as low as possible,"[190] such arrangements may be ineffective
unless they additionally serve non-tax purposes, have non-tax effects
(pertaining, for example, to the risks that the taxpayer bears), and, in
the business or investment setting, present some prospect of pre-tax
profit. The result is to deter some tax planning deals, while inducing
others to be carefully shaped to meet these requirements.

Why does an economic substance rule give taxpayers pause? If it
merely meant jumping through a couple of extra hoops at no real
inconvenience, then only the sloppy or poorly advised would ever find it
a problem. To see why it matters, however, recall the comment in the
Appert–Murdoch amicus brief that Knetsch's deductions were being
challenged merely "because of the certainty of his economic benefit" on
the annuity bonds. The brief noted that the deductions clearly would
have been allowable had his investment, while offering (on average) the
same expected return of 2–1/2%, had presented sufficient prospect of
doing either better or worse.

To make the point more concrete, suppose that Knetsch in 1953 had
been offered the same deal, but with one significant change that was
guaranteed to make it work for tax purposes: the return on the bonds
would be double or nothing. Thus, if an honest coin toss came up heads,
he would get a 5% return on his $4 million of deferred annuity bonds,
leaving him $60,000 ahead before tax each year. If it came up tails, he
would earn zero on the bonds and therefore be $140,000 behind. (Sup-
pose further that he had to commit to a thirty-year term for the
investment before the coin toss.) Or, if a coin toss appears too silly,[191]
then suppose the double-or-nothing outcome depended, say, on whether
interest rates or oil prices went up or down over the next six months.

Would Knetsch have been willing to do this deal? While we cannot
know for sure, it is very plausible that he would not. People are often
risk-averse—they would rather not risk a huge loss even given an

---

[189] *Id.*

[190] Helvering v. Gregory, 69 F.2d 809, 810 (2d Cir.1934), *aff'd*, 293 U.S. 465 (1935).

[191] A bet on the toss of a coin might also run afoul of § 165(d), limiting gambling loss
deductions to the amount of gambling gains.

offsetting chance of a huge gain. (Would you, for example, be willing to make a million-dollar bet on a coin toss?) This is why we have an insurance industry, which makes money by charging people more than their expected loss, so that they can have some protection against a really big loss.

The prospect of deterring aggressive tax planning provides the best rationale for imposing a risk requirement. Why should we otherwise care whether Knetsch chooses to bear a given set of risks or not? Surely that is his business, and does not meaningfully inform the question of whether we should want to tax him or not. (We might want to tax better-off people more than worse-off people, but why tax risk-accepters either more or less than risk-avoiders, if they differ merely in personal taste?)

Similarly, there is something "surreal" about looking at pre-tax profit when "[t]he only meaningful number [to an economically rational taxpayer] is after-tax profits."[192] We do not object when taxpayers accept a reduced (though positive) pre-tax profit for tax reasons—for example, by purchasing tax-exempt municipal bonds that offer a lower return than otherwise equivalent (but taxable) bonds. In a purely tax-motivated deal such as Knetsch's, however, building in a pre-tax profit may prove awkward given the need to compensate the promoters. So the requirement may sometimes work as a filter, discouraging such deals relative to those where the taxpayer has non-tax motivations.

Knetsch's economic substance approach is more significant than ever in an era when, against a background of globalization and financial innovation, "hordes of 'investment bankers' spend many hours scouring the Code and regulations for fault lines from which 'structured products' can be developed."[193] For example, the approach has played a central role in the spate of high-profile "corporate tax shelter" cases that emerged in the late 1990s and have continued unabated in the early 2000s. While the government has won some of these cases and taxpayers have won others, the common ground in all has been that formal compliance with the specific black-letter rules that apply to a given transaction is not automatically enough.

To be sure, even if *Knetsch* (and *Gregory*) had gone the other way, aggressive tax planning transactions would not be entirely uncontrollable. Congress can respond with statutory changes that prospectively eliminate a given tax planning opportunity. By the time this happens, however, a lot of revenue may be lost, and numerous economically wasteful deals consummated. Moreover, a policy of responding only

---

[192] Shaviro & Weisbach, *supra* note 162, at 515.

[193] H. David Rosenbloom, *The David R. Tillinghast Lecture: International Tax Arbitrage and the 'International Tax System'*, 53 Tax L. Rev. 137, 141 (2000).

prospectively through new legislation gives the above-mentioned hordes of investment bankers a big incentive to search intensively for as many new fault lines as they can find, and then to mass-market the deals until Congress's inevitable response takes effect.

There are also contrary arguments. Given that one cannot specify the exact amount of substance that is required (or even exactly what it involves), the approach naturally promotes uncertainty about which transactions are permissible. Moreover, some critics view it as encouraging judges to apply an overly subjective "smell test," unduly driven by a "visceral" rather than "cerebral" reluctance to let taxpayers "put one over" on them.

Conclusion

While the United States income tax law has developed well past the point where one could imagine that *Knetsch* would ever be expressly renounced, we are poised, as I write these words, at a significant crossroads concerning its breadth of application. The pro-government and pro-taxpayer corporate tax shelter cases, while generally purporting to apply the same doctrine, do so in such a markedly different spirit that the Supreme Court may at some point once again feel called on to supply further guidance. So we do not yet know, in the words of the eponymous short story, which will come out of the opened door—"the lady or the tiger?"

Biographies of *Tax Stories* Contributors

Joseph Bankman is Ralph M. Parsons Professor of Law and Business at Stanford Law School. He is the author of numerous books and articles on tax law, including a leading income tax casebook (*Federal Income Taxation* (Aspen, 12th ed. 2000) (with William A. Klein & Daniel N. Shaviro)) and student guide (*Federal Income Tax: Examples and Explanations* (Aspen, 2d ed., 1998) (with Thomas D. Griffith & Katherine Platt)), as well as articles such as *Modeling the Tax Shelter World*, 55 Tax L. Rev. 455 (2002); *The Economic Substance Doctrine*, 64 S. Cal. L. Rev. 5 (2000); *Why Start–Ups?*, 51 Stan. L. Rev. 289 (1999) (with Ronald J. Gilson); and *Winners and Losers in the Shift to a Consumption Tax*, 86 Geo. L.J. 539 (1998) (with Barbara H. Fried). Professor Bankman is a member of the Executive Board of the AALS Tax Section and is co-editor of two electronic journals of *Tax Law Abstracts*: *Tax Law & Policy* and *Practitioner Series* (with Paul L. Caron) (www.ssrn.com).

Karen B. Brown is Donald Phillip Rothschild Research Professor of Law at The George Washington University Law School. She is the author and editor of numerous books and articles on tax law, including *Taxing America* (New York University Press, 1996) (with Mary Louise Fellows); *Missing Africa: Should U.S. International Tax Rules Accommodate Investment in Developing Countries?*, 23 U. Pa. J. Int'l Econ. L. 45 (2002); *Harmful Tax Competition: The OECD View*, 32 Geo. Wash. J. Int'l L. & Econ. 311 (1999); *Not Color-or Gender–Neutral: New Tax Treatment of Employment Discrimination Damages*, 7 S. Cal. Rev. L. & Women's Stud. 223 (1998); *Neutral International Tax Rules Allocating Costs: Successful Formula for U.S. Research and Development*, 1 Fla. Tax Rev. 333 (1993); and *Applying Circular Reasoning to Linear Transactions: Substance over Form Theory in U.S. and U.K. Tax Law*, 15 Hastings Int'l & Comp. L. Rev. 169 (1992). Professor Brown is a member of the American Law Institute and the International Fiscal Association. She would like to thank her research assistants, Jill Lyon, Kirsty McGuire, Tanva Mahitivanichcha and Tree Martschink, for their excellent work, and Professor Robert J. Peroni for his review and support.

Additional hearty thanks go to the following members of the George Washington University Law School community for assistance above and beyond the call of duty: Larry Ross, reference librarian; Ethel Leslie, interlibrary loan coordinator; and Ms. Leslie's extraordinary staff.

Patricia A. Cain is Aliber Family Professor of Law at the University of Iowa College of Law. She is the author of numerous books and articles on tax law, feminist legal theory, and law and sexuality issues, including a book on the struggle for lesbian and gay equality, *Rainbow Rights: The Role of Lawyers and Courts in the Lesbian and Gay Civil Rights Movement* (Westview Press, 2000), as well as articles such as *Dependency, Taxes, and Alternative Families*, 5 J. Gender, Race & Justice 267 (2002); *Heterosexual Privilege and the Internal Revenue Code*, 34 U.S.F. L. Rev. 465 (2000); *Litigating for Lesbian and Gay Rights: A Legal History*, 79 Va. L. Rev. 1551 (1993); *Same-Sex Couples and the Federal Tax Laws*, 1 Law & Sexuality 97 (1991); and *Feminist Legal Scholarship*, 77 Iowa L. Rev. 19 (1991). Professor Cain is a member of the American Law Institute and a Past–President of the Society of American Law Teachers. Professor Cain thanks her research assistant, Melissa Goodman, J.D. Iowa 2003, and the research librarians of the University of Iowa Law Library, especially Val Russell, for their help in researching the Earl story. She also thanks her partner, Jean Love, and tax friend and colleague, Joseph Dodge, for their comments on early drafts. She is indebted to Paul Caron for conceiving of this project and giving her the chance to dig through early California history and uncover the story of Guy Earl's life.

Paul L. Caron is Charles Hartsock Professor of Law at the University of Cincinnati College of Law. He is the author of numerous books and articles on tax law, including a leading estate and gift tax casebook (*Federal Wealth Transfer Taxation: Cases and Materials* (Foundation Press, 5th ed. 2002) (with Paul R. McDaniel & James R. Repetti)) and student problem book (*Federal Wealth Transfer Taxation: Study Problems* (Foundation Press, 2d ed. 2002) (with Paul R. McDaniel & James R. Repetti)), as well as *Federal Income Tax Anthology* (Anderson, 1997) (with Karen C. Burke & Grayson M.P. McCouch); *The Federal Tax Implications of* Bush v. Gore, 79 Wash. U. L.Q. 749 (2001); *The Associate Dean for Research Position: Encouraging and Promoting Scholarship*, 33 U. Tol. L. Rev. 233 (2001) (with Joseph P. Tomain) (Leadership in Legal Education Symposium); and *Tax Myopia Meets Tax Hyperopia: The Unproven Case of Increased Judicial Deference to Revenue Rulings*, 57 Ohio St. L.J. 637 (1996). Professor Caron is the co-editor of three electronic journals of *Tax Law Abstracts*: *Tax Law & Policy* and *Practitioner Series* (with Joseph Bankman) and *International and Comparative Tax* (with Robert A. Green). He also is the editor of the *Tax Law Subject Guide* on JURIST: The Legal Education Network (http://jurist.law.pitt.edu), and the owner and moderator of TaxProf, the AALS Tax Section e-mail discussion list of over 250 tax law professors. Professor Caron wants to thank three people who made enormous contributions to *Tax Stories*: Meribethe Richards, University of Cincinnati College of Law Class of 2004 and research assistant extraordinaire, who performed a myriad of editing and production tasks in putting ten chapters by ten different authors into the format you see in this book; Joe Hodnicki, Web Services Coordinator at the University of Cincinnati College of Law, who designed and stocked the *Tax Stories* web site with the judicial opinions, briefs, and oral arguments for the ten cases (www.law.uc.edu/TaxStories); and Steve Errick, Publisher of Foundation Press, who shared the vision for a *Law Stories* series of books and provided enormous help and encouragement in assembling teams of editors and contributors to produce books in other subject areas.

Joseph M. Dodge is Stearns, Weaver, Miller, Weissler, Alhadeff & Sitterson Professor of Law at Florida State University College of Law. He is the author of numerous books and articles on tax law, including a leading income tax casebook (*Federal Income Tax: Doctrine, Structure, and Policy* (Lexis, 2d ed. 1999) (with J. Clifford Fleming, Jr. & Deborah A. Geier)) and student guide (*The Logic of Tax: Federal Income Tax Theory and Policy* (West, 1989)), as well as articles such as *A Deemed Realization Approach is Superior to Carryover Basis (and Avoids Most of the Problems of the Estate and Gift Tax)*, 54 Tax L. Rev. 421 (2001); *Accessions to Wealth, Realizations of Gross Income, and Dominion and Control: Applying the "Claim of Right Doctrine" to Found Objects, Including Record–Setting Baseballs*, 4 Fla. Tax Rev. 685 (2000); *Taxes and Torts*, 77 Cornell L. Rev. 601 (1992); and Zarin v. Commissioner: *Musings on Cancellation of Indebtedness Income and Consumption in an Income Tax Base*, 45 Tax L. Rev. 677 (1990). Professor Dodge is a member of the American College of Trust and Estate Counsel and a past chair of the AALS Tax Section and the AALS Donative Transfers Section. He wants to thank his colleague Steven A. Bank for reading an earlier draft of his chapter.

Marjorie E. Kornhauser is Professor of Law at Tulane Law School. She is the author of numerous articles on tax law, including *A Legislator Named Sue: Re–Imagining the Income Tax*, 5 J. Gender, Race & Justice 289 (2002); *For God and Country: Taxing Conscience*, 1999 Wis. L. Rev. 939; *Through the Looking Glass with Alice and Larry: The Nature of Scholarship*, 76 N.C. L. Rev. 1609 (1998); *The Morality of Money: U.S. Attitudes Toward Wealth and the Income Tax*, 70 Ind. L. J. 119 (1994); *Love, Money, and the IRS: Family, Income Sharing, and the Joint Income Tax Return*, 45 Hastings L.J. (1993); and *The Rhetoric of the Anti–Progressive Income Tax Movement: A Typical Male Reaction*, 86

Mich. L. Rev. 465 (1987). Professor Kornhauser wants to thank her research assistant, Tara Conklin, for her help.

Joel S. Newman is Professor of Law at Wake Forest University School of Law. He is the author of numerous books and articles on tax law, including a leading income tax casebook (*Federal Income Tax: Cases, Problems and Materials* (West, 2d ed. 2002)), as well as articles such as *Islamic and Jewish Perspectives on Interest*, 89 Tax Notes 1311 (2000); *The Audit Lottery: Don't Ask, Don't Tell*, 86 Tax Notes 1438 (2000); *Circular 230 Revisions "Faned" Indifference to Solicitation*, 84 Tax Notes 1531 (1999) (with Michael B. Lang); *Pay Now, Die Later: Taxes, Politics, and Preneed Funeral Trusts*, 80 Tax Notes 711 (1998); *A Comparative Look at Three British Tax Cases*, 67 Tax Notes 1509 (1995). Professor Newman is a member of the American Law Institute and a commentator on the ABA's Central and East European Law Initiative.

Russell K. Osgood is President of Grinnell College and the former Dean of Cornell Law School (1988–98). He is the author of numerous books and articles on tax law, legal history, and constitutional law, including a leading employee benefits casebook (*Cases and Materials on Employee Benefits* (West, 1996) (with Peter J. Wiedenbeck)) and pension treatise (*The Law of Pensions and Profit–Sharing* (Little Brown, 1984)), as well as articles such as *The Enterprise of Judging*, 17 Harv. J. Law & Public Pol'y 13 (1994); *The Law in Massachusetts: The Supreme Judicial Court 1692–1992* (1992); *Early Versions and Practices of Separation of Powers: A Comment*, 30 Wm. & Mary L. Rev. 279 (1989); and *The Ages and Themes of Income Taxation: Savings and Investment*, 68 Cornell L. Rev. 521 (1983). President Osgood is a member of the Massachusetts Historical Society, Selden Society, Stair Society, and Essex Institute.

Deborah H. Schenk is Ronald and Marilyn Grossman Professor of Tax Law at New York University School of Law. She is the author of numerous books and articles on tax law, including a leading income tax casebook (*Federal Income Taxation: Principles and Policy* (Foundation Press, 4th ed. 2001) (with Michael J. Graetz)), as well as *Ethical Problems in Federal Tax Practice* (Aspen, 3d ed. 1995) (with Bernard Wolfman & James P. Holden); *Old Wine in Old Bottles: Simplification of Family Status Tax Issues*, 91 Tax Notes 1437 (2001); *Saving the Income Tax with a Wealth Tax*, 53 Tax L. Rev. 423 (2000); *Taxation of Equity Derivatives: A Partial Integration Proposal*, 50 Tax L. Rev. 571 (1995); and *The Case for a Capital Gains Preference*, 48 Tax L. Rev. 319 (1993) (with Noë B. Cunningham). Professor Schenk is the Editor-in-Chief of the *Tax Law Review*; the vice president of the American Tax Policy Institute; and a member of the American Law Institute.

Daniel N. Shaviro is Professor of Law at New York University School of Law. He is the author of numerous books and articles on tax law, including a leading income tax casebook (*Federal Income Taxation* (Aspen, 12th ed. 2000) (with Joseph Bankman & William A. Klein)), as well as *When Rules Change: An Economic and Political Analysis of Transition Relief and Retroactivity* (University of Chicago Press, 2000); *Making Sense of Social Security Reform* (University of Chicago Press, 2000); *Does More Sophisticated Mean Better? A Critique of Alternative Approaches to Sourcing the Interest Expense of U.S. Multinationals*, 54 Tax L. Rev. 353 (2001); *Economic Substance, Corporate Tax Shelters, and the* Compaq *Case*, 88 Tax Notes 221 (2000); and *The Minimum Wage, the Earned Income Credit and Optimal Subsidy Policy*, 64 U. Chi. L. Rev. 405 (1997).

George K. Yin is Howard W. Smith Professor of Law and Barron F. Black Research Professor at the University of Virginia. He is a former Tax Counsel to the U.S. Senate Finance Committee (1983–85) and later served as Reporter to the American Law Institute's project on private businesses (1994–99), in which capacity he published (with co-reporter David J. Shakow) *Federal Income Tax Project: Taxation of Private Business Enterprises: Reporters' Study* (ALI, 1999). Among his other publications are *The Problem of Corporate Tax Shelters: Uncertain Dimensions, Unwise Approaches*, 55 Tax L. Rev. 405 (2002); *Getting Serious About Corporate Tax Shelters: Taking a Lesson from History*, 54 S.M.U. L. Rev. 209 (2001); *The Future Taxation of Private Business Firms*, 4 Fla. Tax Rev. 141 (1999); *Improving the Delivery of Benefits to the Working Poor: Proposals to Reform the Earned Income Tax Credit Program*, 11 Amer. J. Tax Policy 225 (1994) [with J.K. Scholz, J.B. Forman and M.J. Mazur]; and *Corporate Tax Integration and the Search for the Pragmatic Ideal*, 47 Tax L. Rev. 431 (1992). Professor Yin thanks Paul Caron for conceiving of this project and inviting him to join it; Deborah Geier, George Mundstock, David Shakow, Tom White, and the participants of a University of Virginia law school workshop for their review of a prior draft; and Anne Lozier, Manuscripts Assistant, Special Collections, Harvard Law School library, Kent Olson, Director of Reference, Research and Instruction, University of Virginia law library, and Professor Kirk Stark, UCLA School of Law, for their assistance in identifying and securing valuable research material for him.

†